THE
FIFTH
GOSPEL

Joseph Smith Translation

THE
FIFTH
GOSPEL

Joseph Smith Translation

LARRY WARD

First Edition 2011
Editors: Lyman De Platt
         Tammy J. Graf

Second Edition 2013
Editor: Kelley Ward

Third Edition 2013
Editor: Kelley Ward

Library Of Congress Control Number 2011941697

ISBN 978-0-9846670-4-8 (English Edition)
ISBN 978-0-9846670-1-7 (Spanish Edition)
ISBN 978-0-9846670-3-1 (Epub)
ISBN 978-0-9846670-2-4 (Mobi)

Cover Picture:
One of the main roads from 2,000 years ago in old city Jerusalem in Israel.
Archeological excavations had exposed this road and the pillars. It is located in the
Jewish quarter, and is a main tourist attraction.

Printed and bound in the United States of America

"One of the grand fundamental principles of Mormonism
is to receive truth, let it come from whence it may"

Joseph Smith – HC 5:499

CONTENTS

PREFACE

The Fifth Gospel is a single narrative of all four gospels, based on the 1867 edition of *The Holy Scriptures* as translated by the prophet Joseph Smith Jr. Today, it is commonly referred to as the *Joseph Smith Translation*. Taking the gospels and making a single narrative of them is not a new idea. The first recorded work is by Tatian (abt. 160-175 A.D.) and is called the *Diatessaron*. It included about 72 percent of the four gospels. Missing were Joseph Smith's corrections, the genealogies of Joseph, and the story of the woman taken in adultery. With these additions, *The Fifth Gospel* contains 108 percent by word count. I did not learn about the *Diatessaron* until after *The Fifth Gospel* was written. While the first part of the chronology is similar, *The Fifth Gospel* has a remarkably different sequence of events, including a second ascension.

In 1830, when Joseph was told to translate the *Bible*, the *Book of Mormon,* which contains a fullness of the gospel, had already been published. What truths were so momentous that they needed to be restored and that we did not already have? The answer is found, in part, in section 93 of the *Doctrine and Covenants*: our Lord revealed part of John the Apostle's testimony in verses [a]6-17, and in verse 19, He tells us why - "that you may understand and know how to worship, and know what you worship". The one thing our Lord could not do over in a subsequent revelation in the *Doctrine and Covenants* was His life in mortality so richly preserved in the four gospels and made clearer with the JST. I believe this was our Lord's primary reason for directing Joseph to translate the *Bible*.

The 'key of knowledge' is the fullness of the scriptures (*Luke 11:53*, JST). The irony is, we only have about 20 percent of the JST included in our LDS scriptures. In another verse Luke writes, "he that hath ears to hear, let him hear". Joseph added, "These things he said, signifying that which was written, verily must all be fulfilled" (*Luke 14:38*). Or in other words, scripture was being fulfilled. This correction is not found in our scriptures. As I contemplated this last scripture, it does not appear to be a parable, simile,

---

[a] Easy Reference p. 184

metaphor, or any of the usual figures of speech associated with the generally known teaching methods that Jesus used. After some research, I decided that they are [a]conundrums and have pointed out many of them in *The Fifth Gospel*. A careful study of them will give new insight into Jesus' teachings. It was while I was contemplating one of them, [b]*Luke 10:23* JST, that I came to understand who Jesus Christ is. It is in the Joseph Smith Translation that we find the fullness of knowing who He is.

Jesus Christ taught us His gospel, atoned for our sins, gave us the gift of the resurrection and the opportunity to attain eternal life. Only He has redeeming power, so it makes sense that whatever book is written be His words, with as few comments from others as possible. *The Fifth Gospel* is arranged to permit the reader freedom from commentary, unless needed. [c]Footnotes will direct you where to obtain additional information. This spares the reader of having to read things you already know.

Although many of the events may be impossible to put in chronological order, it is the events and principles being taught that are essential. Some events - such as the time Jesus entered into a ship and taught the multitude the Parable of the Sower - were immediately followed by Jesus giving the interpretation to His apostles. Since the Lord, Himself, said [d]that unto them only it was given to know the mysteries of the kingdom, it seems unlikely that He would have taught the multitude a single parable, consisting of eight verses, and then left, in order to teach the apostles. It is also evident that our Lord taught the same parables and doctrines more than once. Most of His teachings were taught in the Sermon on the Mount; however, many of the subsequent parables take on more meaning if the doctrinal teaching precedes it. For this reason, there is some duplication. An example is the Parable of the Good Samaritan. Loving our neighbor had been taught in the Sermon on the Mount, but it was not until the lawyer asked; "who is my neighbor?" that we received the [e]Parable of the Good Samaritan.

In parts of the narration, where there was more than one gospel writ-

---

[a] Dictionary - Conundrum
[b] p. 115
[c] Example
[d] Luke 8:10
[e] p. 125

er, [a][part of another writer was inserted] to provide further insight not found in that gospel, and in other cases, whole verses were substituted with footnotes, indicating the substitution. Having a copy of the JST is necessary to look up references. While there may be a few discrepancies with the newer editions of the JST from the 1867 edition, (which this book is based upon), it became apparent that the 1867 edition had numerous editing errors. *Joseph Smith's New Translation of the Bible – Original Manuscripts* were consulted to edit *The Fifth Gospel.*

At the time Joseph commenced work he was told another reason why the translation was necessary - so that we "may be prepared for things to come" (*D&C 45:61*). As our Lord's second coming draws nearer, what benefit is there for us to be here if we do not fully understand who He is, for neither the giver of the gift nor the receiver would be edified. May we all come to more fully appreciate these wonderful gospels from the JST about our Lord and Savior, Jesus Christ, and to prepare to meet Him whether in this life or the next.

Author - Larry Ward

---

[a]   Example

ABBREVIATIONS

D&C . . . . Doctrine and Covenants

Dictionary . . . . Dictionary at the end of this book

Dummelow . . . Dummelow's Bible Commentary

HC . . . . History of The Church

JST . . . . Joseph Smith New Translation of The Bible - Original Manuscripts

NT . . . . New Testament

OT . . . . Old Testament

Smith's . . . . Smith's Bible Dictionary

T to the F . . . . . True to the Faith

HOW TO USE FOOTNOTES

Footnotes outside of the verse indicate the gospel verse quoted.

Footnotes within a verse refer to a definition, footnote, or easy reference starting on page 179, or the dictionary.

↗ª1 And Jesus, seeing the multitude, went up into a mountain; and when he was set down, his disciples came unto him;

2 And he opened his mouth, and taught them, saying,

↗ᵇBlessed are they who shall believe on me; and again, more blessed are they who shall believe on your words, when ye . . .

ª Matthew 5:1-33
ᵇ Dictionary - Beatitudes

CHRONOLOGY

*Parable of the Unclean Spirit is not in chronological order to help in understanding.

THE FIFTH GOSPEL

Prologue

[a]1 As I am a messenger of [b]Jesus Christ, and knowing that many have taken in hand to set forth in order a declaration of those things which are most surely believed among us;

2 Even as they delivered them unto us, who from the beginning were eyewitnesses and ministers of the word;

[c]1 In the beginning was the [d]gospel preached through the [e]Son. And the gospel was the word, and the word was with the Son, and the Son was with [f]God, and the Son was of God.

2 The same was in the beginning with God.

3 [g]All things were made by him; and without him was not anything made which was made.

4 In him was the gospel, and the gospel was the life, and the life was the light of men;

5 And the light shineth in the world, and the world perceiveth it not.[h]

[i]11 He came unto his own, and his own received him not.

12 But as many as received him, to them gave he power to become the sons of God; only to them who believe on his name.

13 He was born, not of blood, nor of the will of the flesh, nor of the will of man, but of God.

14 And the same word was made flesh, and dwelt among us, and we beheld his glory, the glory as of the [j]Only Begotten of *the* Father, full of grace and truth,

Angel announces John's birth

[k]5 There was in the days of [l]Herod, the king of Judea, a certain priest named [m]Zacharias, of the course of Abia; and his wife being of the daughters of Aaron, and her name [n]Elizabeth,

6 Were both righteous before God, walking in all the commandments and ordinances of the [o]Lord blameless;

7 And they had no child. Elizabeth was barren, and they were both well stricken in years.

8 And while he executed the priest's office before God, in the order of his [p]priesthood,

---

a   Luke 1:1-2
b   Dictionary - Jesus Christ
c   John 1:1-5
d   Dictionary - Gospel
e   Dictionary - Son of God
f   Dictionary - God
g   Easy Ref. Hebrews 1:2
h   Compare D&C 93:6-17 in E.R.
i   John 1:11-14

j   Dictionary - Only Begotten
k   Luke 1:5-25
l   Dictionary - Herod
m   Dictionary - Zacharias
n   Dictionary - Elizabeth
o   Dictionary - Lord
p   Dictionary - Priesthood

9 According to the law, (his lot was to burn ªincense when he went into the ᵇtemple of the Lord,)

10 The whole multitude of the people were praying without at the time of incense.

11 And there appeared unto him an ᶜangel of the Lord, standing on the right side of the altar of incense.

12 And when Zacharias saw the angel, he was troubled and ᵈfear fell upon him.

13 But the angel said unto him, Fear not, Zacharias, for thy prayer is heard, and thy wife Elizabeth shall bear thee a son, and thou shalt call his name ᵉJohn.

14 Thou shalt have joy and gladness, and many shall rejoice at his birth;

15 For he shall be great in the sight of the Lord, and shall ᶠdrink neither wine nor strong drink; and he shall be filled with the ᵍHoly Ghost, even from his mother's womb.

16 And many of the children of ʰIsrael shall he turn to the Lord their God;

17 And he shall go before the Lord in the spirit and power of ⁱElias, to turn the hearts of the fathers to the children, and the disobedient to the wisdom of the just, to make ready a people prepared for the Lord.

18 And Zacharias said unto the angel, Whereby shall I know this? for I am an old man, and my wife is well stricken in years.

19 And the angel answering, said unto him, I am ʲGabriel, who stand in the presence of God, and am sent to speak unto thee, and to show you these glad tidings.

20 And behold, thou shalt be dumb, and not able to speak until the day that these things shall be performed, because thou believest not my words, which shall be fulfilled in their season.

21 And the people waited for Zacharias, and marveled that he tarried so long in the temple.

22 And when he came out, he could not speak unto them; and they perceived that he had seen a vision in the temple; for he beckoned unto them, and remained speechless.

23 And as soon as the ᵏdays of his ministration were accomplished, he departed to his own house.

24 And after those days, his wife Elizabeth conceived, and hid herself five months, saying,

---

ª Dictionary - Incense
ᵇ Dictionary - Temple
ᶜ Angel Gabriel - verse 19
ᵈ Dictionary - Fear
ᵉ Dictionary - John the Baptist
ᶠ Dictionary - Nazarite
ᵍ Dictionary - Holy Ghost
ʰ Dictionary - Israel

ⁱ Dictionary - Elias
ʲ Dictionary - Gabriel
ᵏ Easy Ref. Leviticus 8:33

25 Thus hath the Lord dealt with me in the days wherein he looked on me, to take away my reproach from among men.

Angel announces Jesus' birth

[a]26 And in the sixth month the angel Gabriel was sent from God, unto a city of [b]Galilee, named [c]Nazareth,

27 To a virgin, [d]espoused to a man whose name was [e]Joseph, of the house of David; and the virgin's name was [f]Mary.

28 And the angel came in unto her, and said, Hail, thou virgin, who art highly favored of the Lord. The Lord is with thee, for thou art chosen and blessed among women.

29 And when she saw the angel, she was troubled at his saying, and pondered in her mind what manner of salutation this should be.

30 And the angel said unto her, Fear not, Mary, for thou hast found favor with God.

31 And behold, thou shalt conceive, and bring forth a son, and shall call his name Jesus.

32 He shall be great, and shall be called the Son of the Highest; and the Lord God shall give unto him the throne of his father [g]David;

33 And he shall [h]reign over the house of Jacob forever, and of his kingdom there shall be no end.

34 Then said Mary unto the angel; How can this be?

35 And the angel answered and said unto her, Of the Holy Ghost and the power of the Highest. Therefore also, that holy child that shall be born of thee shall be called the Son of God.

36 And behold, thy cousin Elizabeth, she hath also conceived a son, in her old age; and this is the sixth month with her who is called barren.

37 For with God nothing can be impossible.

38 And Mary said, Behold the handmaid of the Lord; be it unto me according to thy word. And the angel departed from her.

Mary visits Elizabeth

[i]39 And in those days, Mary went into the [j]hill country with haste, into a city of Judea,

40 And entered into the house of Zacharias, and saluted Elizabeth.

41 And it came to pass, that when Elizabeth heard the salutation of Mary, the babe leaped in her womb.

---

a   Luke 1:26-38
b   see Map 1. Also see Dictionary Galilee
c   see Map 1
d   Dictionary - Espouse
e   Dictionary - Joseph (1)
f   Dictionary - Mary (1)
g   Dictionary - David
h   Easy Ref. Micah 4:7
i   Luke 1:39-55
j   see Map 1 - wilderness Judea

42 And Elizabeth was filled with the Holy Ghost, and she spake out with a loud voice and said, Blessed art thou among women, and blessed is the fruit of thy womb.

43 And why is it, that this blessing is upon me, that the mother of my Lord should come to me? For lo, as soon as the voice of thy salutation sounded in mine ears, the babe leaped in my womb for joy.

44 And blessed art thou who believed, for those things which were told thee by the angel of the Lord, shall be fulfilled.

45 And Mary said, My soul doth magnify the Lord,

46 And my spirit rejoiceth in God my Savior.

47 For he hath regarded the low estate of his handmaiden; for behold, from henceforth all generations shall call me blessed.

48 For he who is mighty hath done to me great things; and I will magnify his holy name,

49 For his ᵃmercy on those who fear him from generation to generation.

50 He hath showed strength with his arm; he hath scattered the proud in the imagination of their hearts.

51 He hath put down the mighty from their high seats; and exalted them of low degree.

52 He hath filled the hungry with good things; but the rich he hath sent empty away.

53 He hath helped his servant ᵇIsrael in remembrance of mercy,

54 As he spake to our fathers, to ᶜAbraham, and to his seed for ever.

55 And Mary abode with Elizabeth about three months, and returned to her own house.

Birth of John the Baptist

ᵈ56 And now Elizabeth's full time came that she should be delivered; and she brought forth a son.

57 And her neighbors, and her cousins heard how the Lord had showed great mercy unto her; and they rejoiced with her.

58 And it came to pass, that on the eighth day they came to ᵉcircumcise the child; and they called him Zacharias, after the name of his father.

59 And his mother answered and said, Not so; but he shall be called John.

60 And they said unto her, There is none of thy kindred that is called by this name.

61 And they made signs to his father, and asked him how he would have him called.

ᵃ   Dictionary - Mercy

ᵇ   Dictionary - El
ᶜ   Dictionary - Abraham
ᵈ   Luke 1:56-65
ᵉ   Dictionary - Circumcision

62 And he asked for a writing table, and wrote, saying, His name is John, and they all marveled.

63 And his mouth was opened immediately, and he spake with his tongue, and praised God.

64 And fear came on all who dwelt round about them. And all these sayings were noised abroad throughout all the hill country of Judea.

65 And all they that heard them laid them up in their hearts, saying, what manner of child shall this be? And the hand of the Lord was with it.

Zacharias prophesies of John's mission

[a]66 And its father Zacharias was filled with the Holy Ghost, and prophesied, saying,

67 Blessed be the Lord God of Israel; for he hath visited and redeemed his people,

68 And hath raised up an horn of salvation for us, in the house of his servant David,

69 As he spake by the mouth of his holy prophets, ever since the world began,

70 That we should be saved from our enemies, and from the hand of all those who hate us;

71 To perform the mercy promised to our fathers, and to remember his holy covenant;

72 The oath which he swear to our father Abraham,

73 That he would grant unto us, that we being delivered out of the hand of our enemies, might serve him without fear,

74 In holiness and righteousness before him, all the days of our lives.

75 And thou, child, shalt be called the [b]prophet of the Highest, for thou shalt go before the face of the Lord to prepare his ways;

76 To give [c]knowledge of [d]salvation unto his people, by baptism for the [e]remission of their sins,

77 Through the tender mercy of our God; whereby the day spring from on high hath visited us,

78 To give light to them who sit in [f]darkness and the shadow of death; to guide our feet into the way of peace.

79 And the child grew, and waxed strong in spirit, and was in the deserts till the day of his showing unto Israel.

Joseph sees a vision

[g]1 Now, as it is written, the birth of Jesus Christ was on this wise. After his mother, Mary, was espoused to Joseph, before they

---

[a] Luke 1:66-79
[b] Dictionary - Prophet
[c] Dictionary - Knowledge
[d] Dictionary - Salvation
[e] Dictionary - Remission of Sins
[f] Dictionary - Darkness
[g] Matthew 2:1-8

came together, she was found with child of the Holy Ghost.

2 Then Joseph, her husband, being a just man, and not willing to make her a public example, was minded to put her away [a]privaly.

3 But while he thought on these things, behold, the angel of the Lord appeared unto him in a vision, saying, Joseph, thou son of David, fear not to take unto thee Mary thy wife; for that which is conceived in her, is of the Holy Ghost.

4 And she shall bring forth a son, and thou shalt call his name [b]Jesus; for he shall save his people from their sins.

5 Now this took place, that all things might be fulfilled, which were spoken of the Lord, by the prophets, saying,

6 [c]Behold, a virgin shall be with child, and shall bring forth a son, and they shall call his name Emmanuel, (which, being interpreted, is, God with us.)

7 Then Joseph, awaking out of his vision, did as the angel of the Lord had bidden him, and took unto him his wife;

8 And knew her not until she had brought forth her [d]first born son; and they called his name Jesus.

Joseph and Mary go to Bethlehem to be taxed

[e]1 And it came to pass in those days, that there went out a decree from [f]Caesar Augustus, that all his [g]empire should be taxed.

2 This same taxing was when Cyrenius was governor of Syria.

3 And all went to be taxed, every one in his [h]own city.

4 And Joseph also went up from Galilee, out of the city of Nazareth, into Judea, unto the city of David, which is called Bethlehem; (because he was of the house and lineage of David,)

5 To be taxed, with Mary his espoused wife, she being great with child.

Birth of Jesus

[i]6 And so it was, that while they were there, the days were accomplished that she should be delivered.

7 And she brought forth her first born son, and wrapped him in swaddling clothes, and laid him in a manger, because there was none to give room for them in the inns.

8 And there were in the same country, shepherds abiding in the field, keeping watch over their

---

[a]   privately
[b]   Dictionary - Jesus
[c]   Easy Ref. Isaiah 7:14
[d]   Dictionary - First born

[e]   Luke 2:1-5
[f]   Dictionary - Caesar
[g]   Dictionary - Roman Empire
[h]   where they were born
[i]   Luke 2:6-20

flocks by night.

9 And lo, an angel of the Lord appeared unto them, and the glory of the Lord shone round about them; and they were sore afraid.

10 But the angel said unto them, Fear not, for behold, I bring you good tidings of great joy, which shall be to all people.

11 For unto you is born this day, in the [a]city of David, a Savior, who is [b]Christ the Lord.

12 And this is the way you shall find the babe, he is wrapped in swaddling clothes, and is lying in a manger.

13 And suddenly there was with the angel, a multitude of the heavenly host, praising God, and saying,

14 Glory to God in the highest; and on earth, peace; good will to men.

15 And it came to pass, when the angels were gone away from them into [c]heaven, the shepherds said one to another, Let us now go, even unto Bethlehem, and see this thing which is come to pass, which the Lord has made known unto us.

16 And they came with haste, and found Mary and Joseph, and the babe lying in a manger.

17 And when they had seen, they made known abroad the saying which was told them concerning this child.

18 All they who heard it, wondered at those things which were told them by the shepherds;

19 But Mary kept all these things and pondered them in her heart.

20 And the shepherds returned, glorifying and praising God for all the things which they had heard and seen, as they were manifested unto them.

Jesus presented at the Temple

[d]21 And when eight days were accomplished for the circumcising of the child, his name was called Jesus; which was so named of the angel, before he was conceived.

22 And when the days of her [e]purification, according to the [f]law of Moses, were accomplished; they brought him to [g]Jerusalem, to present him to the Lord;

23 As it is written in the law of the Lord, Every male which [h]openeth the womb shall be called holy to the Lord;

24 And to offer a [i]sacrifice according to that which is [j]written in the law of the Lord, A pair of turtledoves, or two young

---

a   Bethlehem
b   Dictionary - Christ
c   Dictionary - Heaven

d   Luke 2:21-24
e   Dictionary - Purification
f   Dictionary - Law of Moses
g   Map 1 - also Dictionary
h   Easy Ref. Exodus 13:2
i   Dictionary - Sacrifice
j   Easy Ref. Leviticus 1:14

pigeons.

Simeon prophesies

[a]25 And behold, there was a man at Jerusalem, whose name was Simeon; and the same man was just and devout, waiting for the consolation of Israel; and the Holy Ghost was upon him.

26 And it was revealed unto him by the Holy Ghost, that he should not see death before he had seen the Lord's Christ.

27 And he came by the spirit into the temple; and when the parents brought in the child, even Jesus, to do for him after the [b]custom of the law,

28 Then took he him up in his arms, and blessed God, and said,

29 Lord, now lettest thy servant depart in peace, according to thy word;

30 For mine eyes have seen thy salvation,

31 Which thou hast prepared before the face of all people;

32 A light to lighten the [c]Gentiles, and the glory of thy people Israel.

33 And Joseph, and Mary, marveled at those things which were spoken of the child.

34 And Simeon blessed them, and said unto Mary, Behold, this child is set for the fall and rising again of many in Israel; and for a sign which shall be spoken against;

35 Yea, a spear shall pierce through him to the wounding of thine own soul also; that the thoughts of many hearts may be revealed.

Anna gives thanks

[d]36 And there was one Anna, a prophetess, the daughter of Phanuel, of the [e]tribe of Asher. She was of great age, and had lived with a husband only seven years, whom she married in her youth,

37 And she lived a widow about fourscore and four years, who departed not from the temple, but served God with fastings and prayers, night and day.

38 And she, coming in that instant, gave thanks likewise unto the Lord, and spake of him, to all those who looked for redemption in Jerusalem.

Wise Men give gifts to Jesus

[f]1 Now when Jesus was born in Bethlehem of Judea, in the days of Herod the king, behold, there came [g]wise men from the east to Jerusalem,

2 Saying, Where is the child that is born, the [h]Messiah of the

---

a   Luke 2:25-35
b   Circumcision
c   Dictionary - Gentile
d   Luke 2:36-38
e   tribe of Israel
f   Matthew 3:1-12
g   Dictionary - Magi
h   Dictionary - Messiah

ᵃJews? for we have seen his star in the east, and have come to ᵇworship him,

3 When Herod the king had heard of the child, he was troubled, and all Jerusalem with him.

4 And when he had gathered all the chief priests, and ᶜscribes of the people together, he demanded of them, saying, Where is the place that is written of by the prophets, in which Christ should be born? For he greatly feared, yet he believed not the prophets.

5 And they said unto him, It is written by the prophets, that he should be born in Bethlehem of Judea, for thus have they said,

6 The word of the Lord came unto us, saying, And thou, ᵈBethlehem, which lieth in the land of Judea, in thee shall be born a prince, which art not the least among the princes of Judea; for out of thee shall come the Messiah, who shall save my people Israel.

7 Then Herod, when he had called the wise men privately, inquired of them diligently at what time the star appeared.

8 And he sent them to Bethlehem, and said, Go and search diligently for the young child; and when ye have found the child, bring me word again, that I may come and worship him also.

9 When they heard the king, they departed; and lo, the star which they saw in the east, went before them, until it came and stood over where the young child was.

10 When they saw the star, they rejoiced with exceeding great joy.

11 And when they were come into the house, they saw the young child, with Mary his mother, and fell down and worshipped him. And when they had opened their treasures, they presented him gifts; gold, and ᵉfrankincense, and ᶠmyrrh.

12 And being warned of God in a dream that they should not return to Herod, they departed into their own country another way.

Joseph flees to Egypt

ᵍ13 And when they were departed, behold, the angel of the Lord, appeared to Joseph in a vision, saying, Arise and take the young child and his mother, and flee into Egypt, and tarry thou there until I bring thee word; for Herod will seek the young child to destroy him.

14 And then he arose, and took the young child, and the child's mother, by night, and departed into Egypt;

ᵃ   Dictionary - Jew
ᵇ   Dictionary - Worship
ᶜ   Dictionary - Scribe
ᵈ   Easy Ref. Micah 5:2

ᵉ   Dictionary - Frankincense
ᶠ   Dictionary - Myrrh
ᵍ   Matthew 3:13-18

15 And was there until the death of Herod, that it might be fulfilled which was spoken of the Lord, by the prophet, saying, [a]Out of Egypt have I called my son.

16 Then Herod, when he saw that he was mocked of the wise men, was exceeding [b]wroth; and sent forth and slew all the children which were in Bethlehem, and all the coasts thereof, from two years old and under, according to the time which he had diligently inquired of the wise men.

17 Then was fulfilled that which was spoken of by Jeremiah the prophet, saying,

18 [c]In Ramah there was a voice heard, lamentation, and weeping, and great mourning; Rachael weeping for the loss of her children, and would not be comforted because they were not.

Joseph told to go back to the land of Israel

[d]19 But when Herod was [e]dead, behold, an angel of the Lord appeared in a vision to Joseph in Egypt,

20 Saying, Arise, and take the young child and his mother, and go into the land of Israel; for they are dead who sought the young child's life.

21 And he arose, and took the young child and his mother, and came into the land of Israel.

22 But when he heard that [f]Archelaus did reign in Judea, in the stead of his father Herod, he was afraid to go thither; but, notwithstanding, being warned of God in a vision, he went into the eastern part of Galilee;

23 And he came and dwelt in a city called [g]Nazareth, that it might be fulfilled which was spoken by the prophets, [h]He shall be called a [i]Nazarene.

24 And it came to pass that Jesus grew up with his brethren, and waxed strong, and waited upon the Lord for the time of his ministry to come.

25 And he served under his father, and he spake not as other men, neither could he be taught; for he needed not that any man should teach him.

Jesus teaches in the Temple

[j]41 Now his parents went to Jerusalem every year, at the feast of the [k]passover.

42 And when he was twelve years

---

[a] Easy Ref. Hosea 11:1
[b] highly incensed
[c] Easy Ref. Jeremiah 31:15
[d] Matthew 3:19-25
[e] a few months after slaying the infants
[f] Dictionary - Archelaus
[g] Dictionary - Nazareth
[h] lost scripture
[i] Dictionary - Nazarene
[j] Luke 2:41-52
[k] Dictionary - Feasts

old, they went up to Jerusalem, after the custom, to the feast.

43 And when they had fulfilled the days, as they returned, the child Jesus tarried behind, in Jerusalem; and Joseph and his mother knew not that he tarried;

44 But they, supposing him to have been in the company, went a day's journey; and they sought him among his kindred and acquaintance.

45 And when they found him not, they turned back again to Jerusalem, seeking him.

46 And it came to pass, after three days they found him in the temple, sitting in the midst of the doctors, and they were hearing him, and asking him questions.

47 And all who heard him were astonished at his understanding, . and answers.

48 And when his parents saw him, they were amazed; and his mother said unto him, Son, why hast thou thus dealt with us? Behold, thy father and I have sought thee sorrowing.

49 And he said unto them, Why is it that ye sought me? Know ye not that I must be about *my* Father's business?

50 And they understood not the saying which he spoke unto them.

51 And he went down with them, and came to Nazareth, and was subject unto them. And his mother kept all these sayings in her heart.

52 And Jesus increased in wisdom and stature, and in favor with God and man.

[a]26 And after many years, the hour of his ministry drew nigh.

John the Baptist begins his ministry

[b]1 Now in the fifteenth year of the reign of [c]Tiberius Caesar, [d]Pontius Pilate being governor of [e]Judea, and Herod being [f]tetrarch of Galilee, and his brother [g]Philip tetrarch of [h]Iturea and of the region of Trachonitis, and Lysanias the tetrarch of Abilene; [i]Annas and [j]Caiaphas being the [k]high priests.

2 Now in this same year, the word of God came unto John, the son of Zacharias, in the wilderness.

[l]27 And in those days came John the Baptist, preaching in the wilderness of Judea,

28 And saying, [m]Repent ye; for the kingdom of heaven is at hand.

29 For I am he who was spoken

---

[a] Matthew 3:26
[b] Luke 3:1-2
[c] Dictionary - Tiberius
[d] Dictionary - Pontius Pilate
[e] see Map 1
[f] Dictionary - Tetrarch
[g] Herod the Great's son
[h] see Map 1
[i] Dictionary - Annas
[j] Dictionary - Caiaphas
[k] Dictionary - High Priest
[l] Matthew 3:27-32
[m] Dictionary - Repentance

of by the prophet [a]Esaias, saying, [b]The voice of one crying in the wilderness, Prepare ye the way of the Lord and make his paths straight.

30 And the same John had his [c]raiment of [d]camels hair, and a leathern girdle about his loins; and his food was [e]locusts and wild honey.

31 Then went out to him Jerusalem, and all Judea, and all the region round about Jordan,

32 And many were baptized of him in [f][the river] [g]Jordan, confessing their sins.

Jews send Priests and Levites to inquire about John

[h]20 This is the record of John, when the Jews sent priests and [i]Levites from Jerusalem, to ask him; Who art thou?

21 And he confessed, and denied not that he was Elias; but confessed, saying; I am not the [j]Christ.

22 And they asked him, saying; How art thou then Elias? And he said; I am not that Elias who was to restore all things. And they asked him, saying, Art thou that prophet? And he answered, No.

23 Then said they unto him, Who art thou? that we may give an answer to them that sent us. What sayest thou of thyself?

24 He said, I am the voice of one crying in the wilderness, Make straight the way of the Lord, as said the prophet Esaias.

25 And they who were sent were of the [k]Pharisees.

26 And they asked him, and said unto him; Why baptizest thou then, if thou be not the Christ, nor Elias who was to restore all things, neither that prophet?

27 John answered them, saying; I baptize with water, but there standeth one among you, whom ye know not;

28 He it is of whom I bear record. He is the prophet, even Elias, who, coming after me, is preferred before me, whose shoe's latchet I am not worthy to unloose, or whose place I am not able to fill; for he shall baptize, not only with water, but with fire, and with the Holy Ghost.

John calls Pharisees and Sadducees to repentance

[l]33 But when he saw many of the Pharisees and [m]Sadducees come to his baptism, he said unto them,

---

[a] Dictionary - Esaias
[b] Easy Ref. Isaiah 40:3
[c] clothing
[d] Dictionary - Camels' hair
[e] Dictionary - Locust
[f] Mark 1:5
[g] Dictionary - Jordan River
[h] John 1:20-28
[i] Dictionary - Levites
[j] Greek for Messiah

---

[k] Dictionary - Pharisee
[l] Matthew 3:33-37
[m] Dictionary - Sadducee

O, generation of ᵃvipers! who hath warned you to flee from the wrath to come?

34 Why is it that ye receive not the preaching of him whom God hath sent? If ye receive not this in your hearts, ye receive not me; and if ye receive not me, ye receive not him of whom I am sent to bear record; and for your sins ye have no cloak.

35 Repent, therefore, and bring forth fruits meet for repentance;

36 And think not to say within yourselves, We are the children of Abraham, and we only have power to bring ᵇseed unto our father Abraham; for I say unto you that God is able of these stones to raise up children unto Abraham.

37 And now, also, the axe is laid unto the root of the trees; therefore every tree which bringeth not forth good fruit, shall be hewn down, and cast into the fire.

ᶜ15 And the people asked him, saying, What shall we do then?

16 He answered and said unto them, He that hath two coats, let him impart to him that hath none; and he that hath meat, let him do likewise.

17 Then came also ᵈpublicans to be baptized, and said unto him, Master, what shall we do?

18 And he said unto them, Exact no more than that which is appointed unto you.

19 For it is well known unto you, . . . that after the manner of the Jews, and according to the custom of their law in receiving money into the treasury, that out of the abundance which was received, was appointed unto the poor, every man his portion;

20 And after this manner did the publicans also, wherefore John said unto them, Exact no more than that which is appointed you.

21 And the soldiers likewise demanded of him, saying, And what shall we do? And he said unto them, Do violence to no man, neither accuse any falsely; and be content with your wages.

John teaches about the Messiah

ᵉ5 For behold, and lo, he shall come, as it is written in the book of the prophets, to take away the sins of the world, and to bring salvation unto the heathen nations, to gather together ᶠthose who are lost, who are of the sheepfold of Israel;

6 Yea, even the dispersed and afflicted; and also to prepare the way, and make possible the preaching of the gospel unto the Gentiles;

7 And to be a light unto all who

ᵃ   venomous snake
ᵇ   Dictionary - Seed of Abraham
ᶜ   Luke 3:15-21
ᵈ   Dictionary - Publican

ᵉ   Luke 3:5-11
ᶠ   lost tribes of Israel

sit in darkness, unto the uttermost parts of the earth; to bring to pass the resurrection from the dead, and to ascend up on high, to dwell on the right hand of *the* Father,

8 Until the fullness of time, and the law and the testimony shall be sealed, and the [a]keys of the kingdom shall be delivered up again unto *the* Father;

9 To administer justice unto all; to come down in judgment upon all, and to convince all the ungodly of their ungodly deeds, which they have committed; and all this in the day that he shall come;

10 For it is a day of power; yea, every valley shall be filled, and every mountain and hill shall be brought low; the crooked shall be made straight, and the rough ways made smooth;

11 [b]And all flesh shall see the salvation of God.

[c]22 And as the people were in expectation, and all men mused in their hearts of John, whether he were the Christ, or not;

23 John answered, saying unto all, I indeed baptize you with water, but there cometh one mightier than I, the latchet of whose shoes I am not worthy to unloose, he shall baptize you with the Holy Ghost, and with fire,

24 Whose fan is in his hand, and he will thoroughly purge his floor, and will gather the wheat into his garner; but the chaff he will burn with fire unquenchable.

25 And many other things, in his exhortation, preached he unto the people.

[d]Genealogy of Joseph

[e]30 And Jesus himself began to be about thirty years of age, having lived with his father, being, as was supposed of the world, the son of Joseph, who was from the loins of Heli,

31 Who was from the loins of Matthat, who was the son of Levi, who was a descendant of Melchi, and of Janna, and of Joseph,

32 And of Mattathias, and of Amos, and of Naum, and of Esli, and of Nagge,

33 And of Maath and of Mattathias, and of Semei, and of Joseph, and of Judah,

34 And of Joanna, and of Resa, and of Zorobabel, and of Salathiel, who was the son of Neri,

35 Who was a descendant of Melchi, and of Addi, and of Cosam, and of Elmodam, and of Er,

36 And of Jose, and of Eliezer, and of Joram, and of Matthat, and of Levi,

37 And of Simeon, and of

---

[a]   Dictionary - Keys of Priesthood
[b]   second coming of Jesus Christ
[c]   Luke 3:22-25

[d]   Dictionary - Genealogy
[e]   Luke 3:30-45

Judah, and of Joseph, and of Jonan, and of Eliakim,

38 And of Melea, and of Menan, and of Mattatha, and of Nathan, and of David,

39 And of Jesse, and of Obed, and of Booz, and of Salmon, and of Naasson,

40 And of Aminadab, and of Aram, and of Esrom, and of ᵃPhares, and of Judah,

41 And of Jacob, and of Isaac, and of ᵇAbraham, and of Terah, and of Nachor,

42 And of Saruch, and of Ragau, and of Phalec, and of Heber, and of Sala,

43 And of Cainan, and of Arphaxad, and of ᶜShem, and of Noah, and of Lamech,

44 And of Methuselah, and of Enoch, and of Jared, and of Maleleel, and of Cainan,

45 And of Enos, and of Seth, and of Adam, who was formed of God, and the first man upon the earth.

Jesus fasts forty days, and Is tempted of the devil

ᵈ1 Then Jesus was led up of the Spirit, into the wilderness, to be with God.

2 And when he had ᵉfasted forty days and forty nights, and had

communed with God, he was afterwards an hungered, and was left to be ᶠtempted of the devil.

3 And when the tempter came to him, he said, If thou be the Son of God, command that these stones be made bread.

4 But Jesus answered and said, It is written, Man shall not live by bread alone, but by every word that proceedeth out of the mouth of God.

5 Then Jesus was taken up into the holy city, and the Spirit setteth him on the ᵍpinnacle of the temple.

6 Then the devil came unto him and said, If thou be the Son of God, cast thyself down, for it is written, He shall give his angels charge concerning thee, and in their hands they shall bear thee up, lest at any time thou dash thy foot against a stone.

7 Jesus said unto him, it is written again, Thou shalt not tempt the Lord thy God.

8 And again, Jesus was in the Spirit, and it taketh him up into an exceeding high mountain, and showed him all the kingdoms of the world and the glory of them.

9 And the devil came unto him again, and said, All these things will I give unto thee, if thou wilt fall down and worship me.

10 Then Jesus said unto him,

ᵃ Easy Ref. Genesis 38:29
ᵇ Easy Ref. Genesis 11:26
ᶜ Easy Ref. Genesis 5:32
ᵈ Matthew 4:1-10
ᵉ Dictionary - Fast

ᶠ Dictionary - Temptation
ᵍ Dictionary - Pinnacle of Temple

Get thee hence, [a]Satan; for it is written, Thou shalt worship the Lord thy God, and him only shalt thou serve . . .

[b]12 And when the devil had ended all the temptation, he departed from him for a season.

Jesus comes to John to be baptized

[c]41 And then cometh Jesus from Galilee to Jordan, unto John, to be baptized of him;

42 But John refused him, saying, I have need to be baptized of thee, and why comest thou to me?

43 And Jesus, answering, said unto him, [d]Suffer me to be baptized of thee, for thus it becometh us to fulfill all righteousness. Then he suffered him.

44 And John went down into the water and baptized him.

45 And Jesus when he was baptized, went up straightway out of the water; and John saw, and lo, the heavens were opened unto him, and he saw the spirit of God descending like a [e]dove and lighting upon Jesus.[f]

46 And lo, he heard a voice from heaven, saying, This is my beloved Son, in whom I am well pleased.

Hear ye him.

John bears testimony of Jesus

[g]29 The next day John seeth Jesus coming unto him, and said; Behold the [h]Lamb of God, who taketh away the [i]sin of the world!

30 And John bear record of him unto the people, saying, This is he of whom I said; After me cometh a man who is preferred before me; for he was before me, and I knew him, and that he should be made manifest to Israel; therefore am I come baptizing with water.

31 And John bear record, saying; When he was baptized of me, I saw the spirit descending from heaven like a dove, and it abode upon him.

32 And I knew him; for he who sent me to baptize with water, the same said unto me; Upon whom thou shalt see the Spirit descending, and remaining on him, the same is he who baptizeth with the Holy Ghost.

33 And I saw, and bear record that this is the Son of God.

34 These things were done in [j]Bethabara, beyond Jordan, where John was baptizing.

35 Again, the next day after, John stood, and two of his

---

[a]   Dictionary - Satan
[b]   Luke 4:12
[c]   Matthew 3:41-46
[d]   permit
[e]   Dictionary - Dove, sign of
[f]   Compare D&C 93:15 in E.R.

[g]   John 1:29-39
[h]   Dictionary - Lamb of God
[i]   Dictionary - Sin
[j]   see Map 1

[a]disciples,

36 And looking upon Jesus as he walked, he said; Behold the Lamb of God!

37 And the two disciples heard him speak, and they followed Jesus.

38 Then Jesus turned, and saw them following him, and said unto them, What seek ye? They say unto him, Rabbi, (which is to say, being interpreted, Master;) Where dwellest thou?

39 And he said unto them; Come and see. And they came and saw where he dwelt, and abode with him that day; for it was about the tenth hour.

Jesus turns water into wine

[b]1 And on the third day of the week, there was a marriage in Cana of Galilee; and the mother of Jesus was there.

2 And Jesus was called, and his disciples, to the marriage.

3 And when they wanted wine, his mother said unto him, they have no wine.

4 Jesus said unto her, Woman what wilt thou have me do for thee? That will I do; for mine hour is not yet come.

5 His mother said unto the servants, Whatsoever he saith unto you, see that you do it.

6 There were set there six water pots of stone, after the manner of the purifying of the Jews, containing two or three [c]firkins apiece.

7 Jesus saith unto them, Fill the water pots with water. And they filled them up to the brim.

8 And he said, Draw out now, and bear unto the governor of the feast. And they bear unto him.

9 When the governor of the feast had tasted the water which was made wine, (and he knew not whence it was, but the servants who drew the water knew,) the governor of the feast called the bridegroom,

10 And said unto him, Every man at the beginning doth set forth good wine; and when men have well drunk, then that which is worse; but thou hast kept the good wine until now.

11 This beginning of miracles did Jesus in Cana of Galilee, and manifested forth his glory; and the [d]faith of his disciples was strengthened in him.

12 After this he went down to Capernaum, he, and his mother, and his brethren, and his disciples; and they continued there not many days.

Jesus bids His disciples 'come follow Me'

[e]13 And Jesus returned in the

---

[a]   Dictionary - Disciple
[b]   John 2:1-12
[c]   Smith's - Greek; metretes, about 9 gallons each
[d]   Dictionary - Faith
[e]   Luke 4:13-15

power of the Spirit, into Galilee:

14 And there went out a fame of him through all the region round about;

15 And he taught in their ^asynagogues, being glorified of all who believed on his name.

^b40 One of the two who heard John, and followed Jesus, was ^cAndrew, ^dSimon Peter's brother.

41 He first findeth his own brother Simon, and said unto him, We have found the ^eMessias, which is, being interpreted, the Christ.

^f1 And it came to pass, as the people pressed upon him, to hear the word of God, he stood by the lake of ^gGennesaret,

2 And saw two ships standing on the lake; but the fishermen were gone out of them, and were wetting their nets.

3 And he entered into one of the ships, which was Simon's, and ^hprayed him that he would thrust out a little from the land. And he sat down, and taught the people out of the ship.

4 Now, when he had done speaking, he said unto Simon, Launch out into the deep, and let down your net for a ⁱdraught.

5 And Simon answering, said unto him, Master, we have toiled all the night, and have taken nothing; nevertheless, at thy word I will let down the net.

6 And when they had done this, they enclosed a great multitude of fishes; and their net brake.

7 And they beckoned unto their partners, who were in the other ship, that they would come and help them. And they came and filled both the ships, so that they began to sink.

8 When Simon Peter saw the multitude of fishes, he fell down at Jesus' knees, saying, Depart from me; for I am a sinful man, O Lord.

9 For he was astonished, and all who were with him, at the draught of the fishes which they had taken.

10 And so were also ^jJames, and ^kJohn, the sons of Zebedee, who were partners with Simon. And Jesus said unto Simon, Fear not from henceforth, for thou shalt catch men.

^l18 And he said unto them, I am he of whom it is written by the prophets; follow me, and I will make you fishers of men.

19 And they, believing on his words, left their net, and straight-

---

^a   Dictionary - Synagogue
^b   John 1:40-41
^c   Dictionary - Andrew the Apostle
^d   Dictionary - Peter the Apostle
^e   Aramaic for Messiah
^f   Luke 5:1-10
^g   Sea of Galilee
^h   asked

ⁱ   quantity of fish taken at one catch
^j   Dictionary - James the Apostle
^k   Dictionary - John the Apostle
^l   Matthew 4:18-19

THE FIFTH GOSPEL 19

way followed him.

[a]43 The day following, Jesus would go forth into Galilee, and findeth [b]Philip, and said unto him, Follow me.

44 Now Philip was at [c]Bethsaida, the city of Andrew and Peter.

45 Philip findeth [d]Nathanael, and said unto him, We have found him, of whom Moses in the law, and the prophets, did write, Jesus of Nazareth, the son of Joseph.

46 And Nathanael said unto him, Can there any good thing come out of Nazareth? Philip said unto him, Come and see.

47 Jesus saw Nathanael coming unto him, and said of him, Behold an Israelite indeed, in whom is no guile!

48 Nathanael said unto him, Whence knowest thou me? Jesus answered and said unto him, Before Philip called thee, when thou wast under the fig tree, I saw thee.

49 Nathanael answered and saith unto him, Rabbi, thou art the Son of God; thou art the King of Israel.

50 Jesus answered and said unto him, Because I said unto thee, I saw thee under the fig tree, believest thou? thou shalt see greater things than these.

51 And he said unto him, Verily, verily, I say unto you, Hereafter ye shall see heaven open, and the angels of God ascending and descending upon the [e]Son of Man.

Jesus eats at Matthew's house

[f]1 And when Jesus was come down from the mountain, great multitudes followed him.

[g]10 And as Jesus passed forth from thence, he saw a man named [h]Matthew, sitting at the place where they received [i]tribute, as was customary in those days, and he said unto him, Follow me. And he arose and followed him.

11 And it came to pass, as Jesus sat at meat in the house, behold, many publicans and sinners came and sat down with him, and with his disciples.

12 And when the Pharisees saw them, they said unto his disciples, Why eateth your master with publicans and sinners?

13 But when Jesus heard them, he said unto them, They that be whole need not a physician, but they that are sick.

14 But go ye and learn what this

---

[a] John 1:43-51
[b] Dictionary - Philip the Apostle
[c] see Map 1 - means house of fish
[d] Dictionary - Nathanael the
      Apostle
[e] Dictionary - Son of Man
[f] Matthew 8:1
[g] Matthew 9:10-23
[h] Dictionary - Matthew the Apostle
[i] Dictionary - Tribute

meaneth, [a]I will have mercy and not sacrifice; for I am not come to call the righteous, but sinners to repentance.

15 And while he was thus teaching, there came to him the disciples of John, saying, Why do we and the Pharisees fast oft, but thy disciples fast not?

16 And Jesus said unto them, Can the children of the bride chamber mourn, as long as the bridegroom is with them?

17 But the days will come, when the bridegroom shall be taken from them, and then shall they fast.

18 Then said the Pharisees unto him, Why will ye not receive us with our baptism, seeing we keep the whole law?

19 But Jesus said unto them, Ye keep not the law. If ye had kept the law, ye would have received me, for [b]I am he who gave the law.

20 I receive not you with your baptism, because it profiteth you nothing.

21 For when that which is new is come, the old is ready to be put away.

22 For no man putteth a piece of new cloth on an old garment; for that which is put in to fill it up, taketh from the garment, and the rent is made worse.

23 Neither do men put new [c]wine into old [d]bottles; else the bottles break, and the wine runneth out, and the bottles perish; but they put new wine into new bottles, and both are preserved.

Jesus casts out an unclean spirit

[e]19 And they went into Capernaum; and straightway on the [f]Sabbath day he entered into the synagogue, and taught.

20 And they were astonished at his doctrine; for he taught them as one that had authority, and not as the scribes.

21 And there was in their synagogue a man with an [g]unclean spirit; and he cried out, saying, Let us alone; what have we to do with thee, thou Jesus of Nazareth? Art thou come to destroy us? I know thee, whom thou art, the Holy One of God.

22 And Jesus rebuked him, saying, Hold thy peace, and come out of him.

23 And when the unclean spirit had [h]torn him, and cried with a loud voice, he came out of him.

24 And they were all amazed, insomuch that they questioned among themselves, saying, What

---

a   Dictionary - Conundrum
b   Dictionary - Jehovah
c   Dictionary - Wine
d   skins of goats or oxen
e   Mark 1:19-29
f   Dictionary - Sabbath
g   Dictionary - Unclean Spirit
h   Dummelow - convulsed

thing is this? What new doctrine is this? For with authority commandeth he even the unclean spirits, and they do obey him.

25 And immediately his fame spread abroad throughout all the region round about Galilee.

26 And forthwith when they were come out of the synagogue, they entered into the house of Simon and Andrew, with James and John.

27 But Simon's wife's mother lay sick of a fever; and they besought him for her, ᵃ[to heal her.]

28 And he came and took her by the hand, and lifted her up; and immediately the fever left her, and she came and ministered unto them.

29 And at evening after sunset, they brought unto him all that were diseased, and them that were possessed with ᵇdevils; and all the city was gathered together at the door.

ᶜ17 That it might be fulfilled which was spoken by Esaias the prophet, saying, Himself took our infirmities and bear our sicknesses.

ᵈ30 And he healed many that were sick of diverse diseases, and cast out many devils; and suffered not the devils to speak, because they knew him.

ᵃ   Luke 4:38
ᵇ   Dictionary - Devil
ᶜ   Matthew 8:17
ᵈ   Mark 1:30

Jesus is accused of casting out devils by the power of the devil

ᵉ20 But when the Pharisees heard that he had cast out the devil, they said, This man doth cast out devils, but by ᶠBeelzebub the prince of devils.

21 And Jesus knew their thoughts, and said unto them, Every kingdom divided against itself is brought to desolation; and every city or house divided against itself, shall not stand. And if Satan cast out Satan, he is divided against himself: how then shall his kingdom stand?

22 And if I by Beelzebub cast out devils, by whom do your children cast out devils? Therefore they shall be your judges.

23 But if I cast out devils by the Spirit of God, then the kingdom of God is come unto you. For they also cast out devils by the Spirit of God, for unto them is given power over devils, that they may cast them out.

24 Or else, how can one enter into a strong man's house, and spoil his goods, except he first bind the strong man, and then he will spoil his house?

25 He that is not with me is against me, and he that gathereth not with me scattereth abroad.

ᵉ   Matthew 12:20-25
ᶠ   Dictionary - Beelzebub

[a]28 Either make the tree good and his fruit good; or else make the tree corrupt, and his fruit corrupt; for the tree is known by the fruit.

29 And Jesus said, O ye generation of vipers! how can ye, being evil, speak good things? For out of the abundance of the heart the mouth speaketh.

30 A good man, out of the good treasure of the heart, bringeth forth good things; and an evil man out of the evil treasure, bringeth forth evil things.

31 And again I say unto you, That every idle word that men shall speak, they shall give an account thereof in the day of judgment.

32 For by thy words thou shalt be justified, and by thy words thou shalt be condemned.

The sign of Jonas

[b]33 Then certain of the scribes and of the Pharisees answered, saying, Master, we would see a sign from thee. But he answered and said unto them,

34 An evil and adulterous generation seeketh after a sign; and there shall no sign be given to it, but the sign of the prophet [c]Jonas; for as Jonas was three days and three nights in the whale's belly, so shall the Son of Man be three days and three nights in the heart of the earth.

35 The men of [d]Ninevah shall rise up in judgment with this generation, and shall condemn it, because they repented at the preaching of Jonas; and ye, behold, a greater than Jonas is here.

36 The [e]queen of the south shall rise up in the day of judgment with this generation, and shall condemn it; for she came from the uttermost parts of the earth to hear the wisdom of [f]Solomon; and ye, behold, a greater than Solomon is here.

His mother and brethren ask to speak with Jesus

[g]40 And while he yet talked to the people, behold, his mother and his brethren stood without, desiring to speak with him.

41 Then one said unto him, Behold, thy mother and thy brethren stand without, desiring to speak with thee.

42 But he answered and said unto the man that told him, Who is my mother? and who are my brethren?

43 And he stretched forth his hand towards his disciples, and said, Behold my mother and my brethren!

44 And he gave them charge concerning her, saying, I go my

---

a   Matthew 12:28-32
b   Matthew 12:33-36
c   Easy Ref. Jonah 2:10
d   O.T. city, Jonah 1:2
e   Queen of Sheeba
f   Dictionary - Solomon
g   Matthew 12:40-44

way, for *my* Father hath sent me. And whosoever shall do the will of *my* Father which is in heaven, the same is my brother, and sister, and mother.

Jesus ordains His twelve Apostles

[a]31 And in the morning, rising up a great while before day, he went out and departed into a solitary place, and there prayed.

32 And Simon and they that were with him, followed after him.

33 And when they had found him, they said unto him, All men seek for thee.

[b]12 And he goeth up into a mountain, and calleth whom he would: and they came unto him.

13 And he ordained twelve, [c][whom also he named [d]apostles,] that they should be with him, and that he might send them forth to preach, and to have power to heal sicknesses, and to cast out devils.

14 And Simon he surnamed Peter; and James the son of Zebedee, and John the brother of James; and he surnamed them Boanerges, which is, The sons of thunder; and Andrew, and Philip, and [e]Bartholomew and Matthew, and [f]Thomas, and [g]James the son of Alpheus, and Thaddeus, and Simon the Canaanite, and [h]Judas Iscariot, which also betrayed him; and they went into a house.

15 And the multitude cometh together again, so that they could not so much as eat bread.

16 And when his friends heard him speak, they went out to lay hold on him; for they said, He is beside himself.

Jesus instructs the Apostles

[i]36 This he spake unto his disciples, saying, Sell that ye have and give alms; provide not for yourselves bags which wax old, but rather provide a treasure in the heavens, that faileth not; where no thief approacheth, neither moth corrupteth.

37 For where your treasure is, there will your heart be also.

[j]7 But who of you, having a servant plowing, or feeding cattle, will say unto him when he is come from the field, Go and sit down to meat?

8 Will he not rather say unto him, Make ready wherewith I may sup, and gird yourself and serve me till I have eaten and drunken; and afterward, by and by, you shall eat

---

[a] Mark 1:31-33
[b] Mark 3:12-16
[c] Luke 6:13
[d] Dictionary - Apostle
[e] Dictionary - Bartholomew the Apostle

[f] Dictionary - Thomas the Apostle
[g] Dictionary - 2nd James, Apostle
[h] Dictionary - Judas the Apostle
[i] Luke 12:36-37
[j] Luke 17:7-10

and drink?

9 Doth he thank that servant because he doeth the things which were commanded him? I say unto you, Nay.

10 So likewise ye, when ye shall have done all those things which are commanded you, say, We are unprofitable servants. We have done that which was no more than our duty to do.

[a]38 Let your loins be girded about, and have your lights burning;

39 That ye yourselves may be like unto men who wait for their Lord, when he will return from the wedding; that, when he cometh and knocketh, they may open unto him immediately.

40 Verily I say unto you, Blessed are those servants, whom the Lord when he cometh shall find watching; for he shall gird himself, and make them sit down to meat, and will come forth and serve them.

41 For, behold, he cometh in the first watch of the night, and he shall also come in the second watch, and again he shall come in the third watch.

42 And verily I say unto you, He hath already come, as it is written of him; and again when he shall come in the second watch, or come in the third watch, blessed are those servants when he cometh, that he shall find so doing:

43 For the Lord of those servants shall gird himself, and make them to sit down to meat, and will come forth and serve them.

44 And now, verily I say these things unto you, that ye may know this, that the coming of the Lord is as a thief in the night.

45 And it is like unto a man who is an householder, who, if he watcheth not his goods, the thief cometh in an hour of which he is not aware, and taketh his goods, and divideth them among his fellows.

46 And they said among themselves, if the good man of the house had known what hour the thief would come, he would have watched, and not have suffered his house to be broken through, and the loss of his goods.

47 And he said unto them, Verily I say unto you, be ye therefore ready also; for the Son of Man cometh at an hour when ye think not.

48 Then Peter said unto him, Lord, speakest thou this [b]parable unto us, or unto all?

49 And the Lord said, I speak unto those whom the Lord shall make rulers over his household, to give his children their portion of meat in due season.

50 And they said, Who then is that faithful and wise servant?

51 And the Lord said unto

---

[a]   Luke 12:38-59

[b]   Dictionary - Parable

them, It is that servant who watch-eth, to impart his portion of meat in due season.

52 Blessed be that servant whom his Lord shall find, when he cometh, so doing.

53 Of a truth I say unto you, that he will make him ruler over all that he hath.

54 But the evil servant is he who is not found watching. And if that servant is not found watching, he will say in his heart, My Lord delayeth his coming; and shall be-gin to beat the man servants and the maidens, and to eat, and drink, and to be drunken.

55 The Lord of that servant will come in a day he looketh not for, and at an hour when he is not aware, and will cut him down, and will appoint him his portion with the unbelievers.

56 And the servant who knew his Lord's will, and prepared not for his Lord's coming, neither did according to his will, shall be beat-en with many stripes.

57 But he that knew not his Lord's will, and did commit things worthy of stripes, shall be beaten with few. For unto whomsoever much is given, of him shall much be required; and to whom the Lord has committed much, of him will men ask the more;

58 For they are not well pleased with the Lord's doings; therefore I am come to send fire on the earth; and what is it to you, if I will that it be already kindled?

59 But I have a baptism to be baptized with; and how am I straightened until it be accomplished!

First cleansing of the Temple

[a]13 And the Jews' Passover was at hand, and Jesus went up to Jerusalem,

14 And found in the temple those who sold oxen, and sheep, and doves, and the changers of money sitting.

15 And when he had made a scourge of small cords, he drove them all out of the temple, and the sheep, and the oxen; and poured out the changers' money, and over-threw the tables;

16 And said unto them who sold doves, Take these things hence; make not *my* Father's house a house of merchandise.

17 And his disciples remem-bered that it was written, [b]The zeal of thy house hath eaten me up.

18 Then spake the Jews and said unto him, What sign showest thou unto us, seeing thou doest these things?

19 Jesus answered and said unto them, [c]Destroy this temple, and in three days I will raise it up.

---

[a] John 2:13-25
[b] Easy Ref. Psalms 69:9
[c] Dictionary - Conundrum

20 Then said the Jews, Forty and six years was this temple in building, and wilt thou rear it up, in three days?

21 But he spake of the temple of his body.

22 When therefore he was risen from the dead, his disciples remembered that he had said this unto them, and they remembered the [a]scriptures, and the word which Jesus had said unto them.

23 Now when he was in Jerusalem, at the passover, on the feast day, many believed on his name, when they saw the miracles which he did.

24 But Jesus did not commit himself unto them, because he knew all things,

25 And needed not that any should testify of man; for he knew what was in man.

Jesus calls the Pharisees, Scribes, and Lawyers to repentance

[b]38 As he spake, a certain Pharisee besought him to dine with him; and he went in, and sat down to meat.

39 And when the Pharisee saw him, he marveled that he had not first washed before dinner.

40 And the Lord said unto him; Now do you Pharisees make clean the outside of the cup and the plat-

ter; but your inward parts are full of ravening and wickedness.

41 O [c]fools, did not he who made that which is without, make that which is within also?

42 But if ye would rather give alms of such things as ye have; and observe to do all things which I have commanded you, then would your inward parts be clean also.

43 But I say unto you, Woe be unto you Pharisees! For ye [d]tithe mint, and rue, and all manner of herbs, and pass over judgment, and the [e]love of God; these ought ye to have done, and not to leave the other undone.

44 Woe unto you, Pharisees! for you love the uppermost seats in the synagogue, and greetings in the markets.

45 Woe unto you, scribes and Pharisees, [f]hypocrites! For ye are as graves which appear not, and the men who walk over are not aware of them.

46 Then answered one of the lawyers, and said unto him, Master, thus saying, thou reproachest us also.

47 And he said, Woe unto you lawyers, also! For ye lade men with burdens grievous to be borne, and ye yourselves touch not the burdens with one of your fingers.

---

[a]   Dictionary - Scriptures
[b]   Luke 11:38-55

[c]   Dictionary - Fool
[d]   Dictionary - Tithe
[e]   Dictionary - Love
[f]   Dictionary - Hypocrite

48 Woe unto you! For you build the [a]sepulchers of the prophets, and your fathers killed them.

49 Truly ye bear witness that ye allow the deeds of your fathers; for they indeed killed them, and ye build their sepulchers.

50 Therefore also said the wisdom of God, I will send them prophets, and apostles, and some of them they shall slay and persecute;

51 That the blood of all the prophets, which was shed from the foundation of the world, may be required of this generation; from the blood of [b]Abel unto the blood of [c]Zacharias, who perished between the altar and the temple.

52 Verily I say unto you, It shall be required of this generation.

53 Woe unto you, lawyers! For ye have taken away the key of knowledge, the fullness of the scriptures; ye enter not in yourselves into the kingdom; and those who were entering in, ye hindered.

54 And as he said these things unto them, the scribes and Pharisees began to be angry, and to urge [d]vehemently, endeavoring to provoke him to speak of many things;

55 Laying wait for him, and seeking to catch something out of his mouth, that they might accuse him.

Jesus warns of the hypocrisy of the Pharisees

[e]1 In the mean time, when there were gathered together an innumerable multitude of people, insomuch that they trod one upon another, he began to say unto his disciples first of all, Beware ye of the [f]leaven of the Pharisees, which is hypocrisy.

2 For there is nothing covered which shall not be revealed; neither hid which shall not be known.

3 Therefore, whatsoever ye have spoken in darkness, shall be heard in the light; and that which ye have spoken in the ear in closets, shall be proclaimed upon the house tops.

4 And I say unto you my friends, Be not afraid of them who kill the body, and after that have no more that they can do.

5 But I will forewarn you whom ye shall fear; fear him, who after he hath killed, hath power to cast into [g]hell; yea, I say unto you, Fear him.

6 Are not five sparrows sold for two [h]farthings, and not one of them is forgotten before God?

7 But even the very hairs of your head are all numbered. Fear

---

a   place of burial, tomb
b   Easy Ref. Genesis 5:5
c   Dictionary - Zacharias
d   great energy, feeling or passion

e   Luke 12:1-7
f   Dictionary - Leaven
g   Dictionary - Hell
h   Dictionary - Money

not therefore; ye are of more value than many sparrows.

All sins forgiven except the sin against the Holy Ghost

[a]8 Also I say unto you, Whosoever shall confess me before men, him shall the Son of Man also confess before the angels of God;

9 But he who denieth me before men, shall be denied before the angels of God.

10 Now his disciples knew that he said this, because they had spoken evil against him before the people; for they were afraid to confess him before men.

11 And they reasoned among themselves, saying, He knoweth our hearts, and he speaketh to our condemnation, and we shall not be forgiven. But he answered them, and said unto them,

12 Whosoever shall speak a word against the Son of Man, and repenteth, it shall be forgiven him; but unto him who blasphemeth against the Holy Ghost, it shall not be forgiven him.

13 And again I say unto you, They shall bring you into the synagogues, and before magistrates, and powers; when they do this, take ye no thought how, or what things ye shall answer, or what ye shall say;

14 For the Holy Ghost shall teach you in the same hour what ye ought to say.

Parable of the unclean spirit

[b]37 Then came some of the scribes and said unto him, Master, it is written that, Every sin shall be forgiven; but ye say, Whosoever speaketh against the Holy Ghost shall not be forgiven. And they asked him, saying, How can these things be?

38 And he said unto them, When the unclean spirit is gone out of a man, he walketh through dry places, seeking rest and findeth none; but when a man speaketh against the Holy Ghost, then he saith, I will return into my house from whence I came out; and when he is come, he findeth him empty, swept and garnished; for the good spirit leaveth him unto himself.

39 Then goeth the evil spirit, and taketh with him seven other spirits more wicked than himself: and they enter in and dwell there; and the last end of the man is worse than the first. Even so shall it be also unto this wicked generation.

[c]28 And it came to pass, as he spake these things, a certain woman of the company, lifted up her voice, and said unto him, Blessed is the womb which bear thee, and the

---

[a]   Luke 12:8-14

[b]   Matthew 12:37-39
[c]   Luke 11:28

paps which thou hast sucked.

Beware of covetousness

[a]15 And one of the company said unto him, Master, speak to my brother, that he divide the inheritance with me.

16 And he said unto him, Man, who made me a judge, or a divider over you?

17 And he said unto them, Take heed, and beware of covetousness; for a man's life consisteth not in the abundance of the things which he possesseth.

Parable of the rich man

[b]18 And he spake a parable unto them, saying, The ground of a certain rich man brought forth plentifully;

19 And he thought within himself, saying, What shall I do, because I have no room where to [c]bestow my fruits?

20 And he said, This will I do; I will pull down my barns, and build greater; and there will I bestow all my fruits, and my goods.

21 And I will say to my soul, Soul, thou hast much goods laid up for many years; take thine ease, eat, drink, and be merry.

22 But God said unto him, Thou fool! This night thy [d]soul

shall be required of thee; then whose shall those things be which thou hast provided?

23 So shall it be with him who layeth up treasure for himself, and is not rich toward God.

Nicodemus comes to Jesus at night

[e]1 There was a man of the Pharisees named [f]Nicodemus, a ruler of the Jews;

2 The same came to Jesus by night, and said unto him, Rabbi, we know that thou art a teacher come from God; for no man can do these miracles which thou doest, except God be with him.

3 Jesus answered and said unto him, Verily, verily, I say unto thee, Except a man be [g]born again, he cannot see the kingdom of God.

4 Nicodemus saith unto him, How can a man be born when he is old? Can he enter the second time into his mother's womb and be born?

5 Jesus answered, Verily, verily, I say unto thee, Except a man be born of water, and the Spirit, he cannot enter into the kingdom of God.

6 That which is born of the flesh, is flesh; and that which is born of the Spirit, is spirit.

7 Marvel not that I say unto

---

[a] Luke 12:15-17
[b] Luke 12:18-23
[c] put, store
[d] Dictionary - Soul

---

[e] John 3:1-22
[f] Dictionary - Nicodemus
[g] Dictionary - Baptism

thee, Ye must be born again.

8 The wind bloweth where it [a]listeth, and thou hearest the sound thereof, but canst not tell whence it cometh, and whither it goeth; so is everyone who is born of the Spirit.

9 Nicodemus answered and said unto him, How can these things be?

10 Jesus answered and said, Art thou a master of Israel, and knowest not these things?

11 Verily, verily, I say unto thee, We speak that we do know, and testify that we have seen; and ye receive not our witness.

12 If I have told you earthly things, and ye believe not, how shall ye believe if I tell you heavenly things?

13 I tell you, No man hath ascended up to heaven, but he who came down from heaven, even the Son of Man who is in heaven.

14 And as Moses lifted up the serpent in the wilderness, even so must the Son of Man be lifted up;

15 That whosoever believeth on him should not perish, but have eternal life.

16 For God so loved the world, that he gave his Only Begotten Son, that whosoever believeth on him should not perish; but have everlasting life.

17 For God sent not his Son into the world to condemn the world; but that the world through him might be saved.

18 He who believeth on him is not condemned; but he who believeth not is condemned already, because he hath not believed on the name of the Only Begotten Son of God, which before was preached by the mouth of the holy prophets; for they testified of me.

19 And this is the condemnation, that light is come into the world, and men love darkness rather than light, because their deeds are evil.

20 For everyone who doeth evil hateth the light, neither cometh to the light, lest his deeds should be reproved.

21 But he who loveth truth, cometh to the light, that his deeds may be made manifest.

22 And he who obeyeth the truth, the works which he doeth they are of God.

Jesus tarries in Judea

[b]23 After these things came Jesus and his disciples into the land of Judea; and there he [c]tarried with them, and baptized;

24 And John also was baptizing in Enon, near to Salim, because there was much water there; and they came and were baptized;

25 For John was not yet cast

---

[a]   goes

[b]   John 3:23-36
[c]   stayed

into prison.

26 Then there arose a question between some of John's disciples, and the Jews, about purifying.

27 And they came unto John, and said unto him, Rabbi, he who was with thee beyond Jordan, to whom thou barest witness, behold, the same baptizeth, and he receiveth of all people who come unto him.

28 John answered and said, A man can receive nothing, except it be given him from heaven.

29 Ye yourselves bear me witness that I said, I am not the Christ, but that I am sent before him.

30 He who hath the bride, is the bridegroom; but the friend of the bridegroom, who standeth and heareth him, rejoiceth greatly because of the bridegroom's voice; this my joy therefore is fulfilled.

31 He must increase, but I must decrease.

32 He who cometh from above is above all; he who is of the earth is earthly, and speaketh of the earth; he who cometh from heaven is above all. And what he hath seen and heard, that he testifieth; and but few men receive his testimony.

33 He who hath received his testimony, hath set to his seal that God is true.

34 For he whom God hath sent, speaketh the words of God; for God giveth him not the Spirit by measure, for he dwelleth in him,

even the fullness.

35 The Father loveth the Son, and hath given all things into his hands.

36 And he who believeth on the Son hath everlasting life; and shall receive of his fullness. But he who believeth not the Son, shall not receive of his fullness; for the wrath of God is upon him.

John is cast into prison

[a]26 But Herod, the tetrarch, being reproved of him for [b]Herodias, [c]his brother Philip's wife, and for all the evils which Herod had done;

27 Added yet this above all, that he shut up John in prison.

[d]11 And now Jesus knew that John was cast into prison, and he sent angels, and, behold, they came and ministered unto him.

Jesus testifies of John the Baptist

[e]18 And the disciples of John showed him of all these things.

19 And John calling two of his disciples, sent them to Jesus, saying, Art thou he that should come, or look we for another?

20 When the men were come unto him, they said, John Baptist hath sent us unto thee, saying, Art

---

a   Luke 3:26-27
b   Dictionary - Herodias
c   adultery
d   Matthew 4:11
e   Luke 7:18-28

thou he [a][of whom it is written in the prophets] who should come, or look we for another?

21 And in the same hour he cured many of infirmities, and plagues, and of evil spirits, and unto many blind he gave sight.

22 Then Jesus, answering, said unto them, Go your way, and tell John what things ye have seen and heard; how that the blind see, the lame walk, the lepers are cleansed, the deaf hear, the dead are raised, and to the poor the gospel is preached;

23 And blessed are they, who shall not be offended in me.

24 And when the messengers of John were departed, he began to speak unto the people concerning John; What went ye out into the wilderness to see? A reed shaken with the wind? [b][And they answered him, No]. Or a man clothed in soft raiment?

25 Behold, they who are gorgeously appareled, and live delicately, are in king's courts.

26 But what went ye out for to see? A prophet? Yea, I say unto you, and much more than a prophet.

27 This is the one of whom it is written, Behold I send my messenger before thy face, who shall prepare thy way before thee.

28 For I say unto you, Among those who are born of women, there is not a greater prophet than John the Baptist; but he who is least in the kingdom of God is greater than he.

[c]12 And from the days of John the Baptist until now, the kingdom of heaven suffereth violence, and the violent take it by force.

13 But the day will come, when the violent shall have no power; for all the prophets and the law prophesied that it should be thus until John.

14 Yea, as many as have prophesied have foretold of these days.

15 And if ye will receive it, verily, he was the Elias, who was for to come and prepare all things.

16 [d]He that hath ears to hear, let him hear.

[e]29 And all the people who heard him, and the publicans, justified God, being baptized with the baptism of John.

30 But the Pharisees, and lawyers, rejected the counsel of God against themselves, not being baptized of him.

31 And the Lord said, Whereunto then shall I liken the men of this generation? And to what are they like?

32 They are like unto children sitting in the market place, call-

---

[a] Matthew 11:3
[b] Matthew 11:7

[c] Matthew 11:12-16
[d] Dictionary - Conundrum
[e] Luke 7:29-35

ing one to another, and saying, We have piped for you, and ye have not danced; we have mourned for you, and ye have not wept.

33 For John the Baptist came neither eating bread nor drinking wine; and ye say he hath a devil.

34 The Son of man is come, eating and drinking; and ye say, Behold a gluttonous man, and a wine bibber, a friend of publicans and sinners!

35 But wisdom is justified of all her children.

Jesus talks with the woman at the well in Samaria

[a]1 When therefore the Pharisees had heard that Jesus made and baptized more disciples than John,

2 They sought more diligently some means that they might put him to death; for many received John as a prophet, but they believed not on Jesus.

3 Now the Lord knew this, though he himself baptized not so many as his [b]disciples,

4 For he suffered them for an example, preferring one another.

5 And he left Judea, and departed again into Galilee,

6 And he said unto his disciples, I must needs go through [c]Samaria.

7 Then he cometh to the city of Samaria which is called [d]Sychar, near to the parcel of ground which Jacob gave to his son Joseph; the place where Jacob's well was.

8 Now Jesus being weary with the journey, it being about the [e]sixth hour, sat down on the well;

9 And there came a woman of Samaria to draw water; Jesus said unto her, Give me to drink.

10 Now his disciples were gone away into the city to buy meat.

11 Wherefore he being alone, the woman of Samaria said unto him, How is it that thou being a Jew, askest drink of me, who am a woman of Samaria? The Jews have no dealings with the [f]Samaritans.

12 Jesus answered and said unto her, [g]If thou knewest the gift of God, and who it is that saith to thee, Give me to drink; thou wouldest have asked of him, and he would have given thee living water.

13 The woman said unto him, Sir, thou hast nothing to draw with, and the well is deep; from whence then hast thou that living water?

14 Art thou greater than our father Jacob, who gave us the well, and drank thereof himself, and his children, and his cattle?

15 Jesus answered and said unto

---

[a] John 4:1-32
[b] apostles
[c] Dictionary - Samaria

[d] see Map 1
[e] Dictionary - Day
[f] Dictionary - Samaritans
[g] Dictionary - Conundrum

her, Whosoever shall drink of this well, shall thirst again;

16 But whosoever drinketh of the water which I shall give him shall never thirst; but the water I shall give him shall be in him a well of water springing up into everlasting life.

17 The woman said unto him, Sir, give me of this water that I thirst not, neither come hither to draw.

18 Jesus said unto her, Go, call thy husband and come hither.

19 The woman answered and said, I have no husband. Jesus said unto her, Thou hast well said, I have no husband.

20 For thou hast had five husbands, and he whom thou now hast, is not thy husband; in that saidst thou truly.

21 The woman said unto him, Sir, I perceive that thou art a prophet.

22 Our fathers worshipped in this mountain; and ye say that in Jerusalem is the place where men ought to worship.

23 Jesus said unto her, Woman, believe me, the hour cometh, when ye shall neither in this mountain, nor yet at Jerusalem, worship *the* Father.

24 Ye worship ye know not what; we know what we worship; and salvation is of the Jews.

25 And the hour cometh, and now is, when the true worshipers shall worship *the* Father in spirit and in truth; for *the* Father seeketh such to worship him.

26 For unto such hath God promised his Spirit. And they who worship him, must worship in spirit and in truth.

27 The woman said unto him, I know that Messias cometh, who is called Christ; when he is come, he will tell us all things.

28 Jesus said unto her, I who speak unto thee am the Messias.

29 And upon this came his disciples, and marveled that he talked with the woman; yet no man said, What seeketh thou? or, Why talkest thou with her?

30 The woman then left her water pot, and went her way into the city, and said to the men,

31 Come see a man who told me all things that I have ever done. Is not this the Christ?

32 Then they went out of the city, and came unto him.

Jesus teaches the Apostles the law of the harvest

[a]33 In the meantime his disciples prayed him, saying, Master, eat.

34 But he said unto them, I have meat to eat that ye know not of.

35 Therefore said the disciples one to another, Hath any man

---

[a]   John 4:33-45

brought him meat to eat?

36 Jesus said unto them, My meat is to do the will of him who sent me, and to finish his work.

37 Say not ye there are yet [a]four months, then cometh harvest? Behold, I say unto you, Lift up your eyes, and look on the fields; for they are white already to harvest.

38 And he who reapeth, receiveth wages, and gathereth fruit unto life eternal; that both he who soweth, and he who reapeth, may rejoice together.

39 And herein is that saying true, One soweth and another reapeth.

40 I have sent you to reap that thereon ye bestowed no labor; the prophets have labored, and ye have entered into their labors.

41 And many of the Samaritans of that city believed on him for the saying of the woman, who testified, saying, He told me all things I have ever done.

42 So when the Samaritans were come unto him, they besought him that he would tarry with them; and he abode there two days.

43 And many more believed on his own word;

44 And said unto the woman, Now we believe, not because of thy sayings; we have heard for ourselves, and know that this is indeed the Christ, the Savior of the world.

45 Now after two days he departed thence, and went into Galilee.

Jesus returns to Nazareth

[b]16 And he came to Nazareth, where he had been brought up; and as his custom was he went into the synagogue on the Sabbath day, and stood up to read.

17 And there was delivered unto him, the book of the prophet Esaias. And when he had opened the book, he found the place where it was written,

18 [c]The Spirit of the Lord is upon me, because he hath anointed me to preach the gospel to the poor; he hath sent me to heal the broken hearted, to preach deliverance to the captives, and the recovering of sight to the blind; to set at liberty them who are bruised;

19 To preach the acceptable year of the Lord.

20 And he closed the book, and he gave it again to the minister, and he sat down.

21 And the eyes of all those who were in the synagogue, were fastened on him, And he began to say unto them, This day is this scripture fulfilled in your ears.

22 And all bear him witness, and wondered at the gracious words which proceeded out of his

---

[a] Dictionary - Sabbatical Year
[b] Luke 4:16-30
[c] compare Isaiah 61:1-2 in E.R.

mouth. And they said, Is not this Joseph's son?

23 And he said unto them, Ye will surely say unto me this ᵃproverb, Physician, heal thyself. Whatsoever we have heard was done in Capernaum, do also here in thy country.

24 And he said, verily I say unto you, No prophet is accepted in his own country.

25 But I tell you the truth, many widows were in Israel in the days of Elias, when the heaven was shut up three years and six months, and great famine was throughout all the land;

26 But unto none of them was Elias sent, save unto Sarepta, of Sidon, unto a woman who was a widow.

27 And many lepers were in Israel, in the time of ᵇEliseus the prophet; and none of them were cleansed, save Naaman the Syrian.

28 And all they in the synagogue, when they heard these things, were filled with wrath,

29 And rose up, and thrust him out of the city, and led him unto the brow of the hill, whereon the city was built, that they might cast him down headlong.

30 But he, passing through the midst of them, went his way,

Jesus returns to Galilee

ᶜ12 Jesus departed into Galilee, and leaving Nazareth, in ᵈZebulon, he came and dwelt in Capernaum, which is upon the sea coast, in the borders of Nephthalim,

13 That it might be fulfilled which was spoken by Esaias the prophet, saying,

14 ᵉThe land of Zebulon, and the land of Nephthalim, in the way of the sea, beyond Jordan, Galilee of the Gentiles;

15 The people which sat in darkness saw a great light, and unto them that sat in the region and shadow of death, light is sprung up.

16 From that time, Jesus began to preach, and to say, Repent; for the kingdom of heaven is at hand.

ᶠ47 Then when he had come into Galilee, the Galileans received him, having seen all the things that he did at Jerusalem at the feast; for they also went unto the feast.

Jesus heals nobleman's son

ᵍ48 So Jesus came again into Cana of Galilee, where he made the water wine. And there was a certain ʰnobleman, whose son was sick at Capernaum.

ᵃ   Dictionary - Proverb
ᵇ   Greek for Elisha

ᶜ   Matthew 4:12-16
ᵈ   see Map 1
ᵉ   Easy Ref. Isaiah 9:1-2
ᶠ   John 4:47
ᵍ   John 4:48-56
ʰ   Smiths' - a man of high rank

49 When he heard that Jesus was come out of Judea into Galilee, he went unto him, and besought him that he would come down, and heal his son; for he was at the point of death.

50 Then said Jesus unto him, Except ye see signs and wonders, ye will not believe.

51 The nobleman said unto him, Sir, come down before my child die.

52 Jesus said unto him, Go thy way, thy son liveth. And the man believed the word which Jesus had spoken unto him, and he went his way.

53 And as he was going down to his house, his servants met him, and spake, saying, Thy son liveth.

54 Then inquired he of them the hour when he began to mend. And they said unto him, Yesterday at the seventh hour the fever left him.

55 So the father knew that his son was healed in the same hour in the which Jesus said unto him, Thy son liveth; and himself believed, and his whole house;

56 This being the second miracle which Jesus had done when he had come out of Judea into Galilee.

Jesus heals a leper

[a]34 And he said unto them, Let us go into the next towns, that I may preach there also; for therefore came I forth.

35 And he preached in their synagogues throughout all Galilee, and cast out devils.

36 And there came a [b]leper to him, beseeching him, and kneeling down to him, said, If thou wilt, thou canst make me clean.

37 And Jesus, moved with compassion, put forth his hand and touched him; and saith unto him, I will; be thou clean.

38 And as soon as he had spoken, immediately the leprosy departed from him, and he was cleansed.

39 And he straitly charged him, and forthwith sent him away; and said unto him, See thou say nothing to any man; but go thy way, show thyself to the priests, and offer for thy cleansing, those things which Moses commanded, for a testimony unto them.

40 But he went out, and began to publish it much, and to blaze abroad the matter, insomuch that Jesus could no more openly enter into the city, but was without in solitary places; and they came to him from every quarter.

Jesus heals a man with palsy

[c]1 And again, he entered into Capernaum after many days; and it was noised abroad that he was in

---

[a] Mark 1:34-40

[b] Dictionary - Leper
[c] Mark 2:1-7

the house.

2 And straightway many were gathered together, insomuch that there was no room to receive the multitude; no, not so much as about the door; and he preached the word unto them.

3 And they came unto him, bringing one sick of the [a]palsy, which was [b]borne of four persons.

4 And they could not come nigh unto him, for the press, they uncovered the roof where he was; and when they had broken it up, they let down the bed wherein the sick of the palsy lay.

5 When Jesus saw their faith, he said unto the sick of the palsy, Son, [c][be of good cheer;] thy sins be forgiven thee. [Go thy way and sin no more.]

6 But there were certain of the scribes sitting there, and reasoning in their hearts, Why doth this man thus speak [d]blasphemies? Who can forgive sins but God only?

7 And immediately, when Jesus perceived in his spirit, that they so reasoned within themselves, he said unto them, Why reason ye these things in your hearts? . . .

[e]23 Does it require more power to forgive sins than to make the sick rise up and walk?

[f]8 But that ye may know that the Son of Man has power on earth to forgive sins, (he said to the sick of the palsy,) I say unto thee, Arise, and take up thy bed, and go thy way into thy house.

9 And immediately he arose, took up the bed, and went forth before them all; insomuch that they were all amazed, and many glorified God, saying, We never saw the power of God after this manner.

[g]22 And Jesus went about all Galilee teaching in their synagogues, and preaching the gospel of the kingdom; and healing all manner of sickness, and all manner of diseases among the people which believed on his name.

23 And his fame went throughout all Syria; and they brought unto him all sick people that were taken with diverse diseases, and torments, and those who were possessed with devils, and those who were lunatic, and those that had the palsy; and he healed them.

24 And there followed him great multitudes of people from Galilee, and [h]Decapolis, and Jerusalem, and Judea, and beyond Jordan, [i][and from the seacoasts of [j]Tyre and Sidon, who came to hear him, and

---

[a] Dictionary - Palsy
[b] carried by
[c] Matthew 9:2
[d] Dictionary - Blasphemy
[e] Luke 5:23

[f] Mark 2:8-9
[g] Matthew 4:22-24
[h] Dictionary - Decapolis
[i] Luke 6:17
[j] see Map 1

to be healed of their diseases.]

[a]19 And the whole multitude sought to touch him; for there went virtue out of him and healed them all.

Sermon on the Mount

[b]1 And Jesus, seeing the multitude, went up into a mountain; and when he was set down, his disciples came unto him;

2 And he opened his mouth, and taught them, saying,

3 [c]Blessed are they who shall believe on me; and again, more blessed are they who shall believe on your words, when ye shall testify that ye have seen me and that I am.

4 [d]Yea, blessed are they who shall believe on your words, and come down into the depth of humility, and be baptized in my name; for they shall be visited with fire and the Holy Ghost, and shall receive a remission of their sins.

5 Yea, blessed are the poor in spirit, who come unto me; for theirs is the [e]kingdom of heaven.

6 And again, blessed are they that mourn; for they shall be comforted.

7 And blessed are the meek; for they shall inherit the earth.

[f]25 Woe unto you who are full! For ye shall hunger. Woe unto you who laugh now! For ye shall mourn and weep.

[g]8 And blessed are all they that do hunger and thirst after righteousness; for they shall be filled with the Holy Ghost.

9 And blessed are the merciful; for they shall obtain mercy.

10 And blessed are all the pure in heart; for they shall see God.

11 And blessed are all the peacemakers; for they shall be called the children of God.

[h]26 Woe unto you, when all men shall speak well of you! For so did their fathers to the false prophets.

[i]12 Blessed are all they that are persecuted for my name's sake; for theirs is the kingdom of heaven.

13 And blessed are ye when men shall revile you, and persecute you, and shall say all manner of evil against you falsely, for my sake.

14 For you shall have great joy, and be exceeding glad; for great shall be your reward in heaven; for so persecuted they the prophets which were before you.

15 Verily, verily, I say unto you, I give unto you to be the salt of the earth; but if the salt shall lose its savor, wherewith shall the earth be

---

a   Luke 6:19
b   Matthew 5:1-7
c   Dictionary - Beatitudes
d   compare 3 Nephi 12:1-2 in E.R.
e   Dictionary - Kingdom of Heaven

---

f   Luke 6:25
g   Matthew 5:8-11
h   Luke 6:26
i   Matthew 5:12-33

salted? the salt shall thenceforth be good for nothing, but to be cast out, and to be trodden under foot of men.

16 Verily, verily, I say unto you, I give you to be the light of the world; a city that is set on a hill cannot be hid.

17 Behold, do men light a candle and put it under a bushel? Nay, but on a candlestick; and it giveth light to all that are in the house.

18 Therefore, let your light so shine before this world, that they may see your good works, and glorify *your* Father who is in heaven.

19 Think not that I am come to destroy the law, or the prophets; I am not come to destroy, but to fulfil.

20 For verily I say unto you, Heaven and earth must pass away, but one ᵃjot or one tittle shall in no wise pass from the law, until all be fulfilled.

21 Whosoever, therefore, shall break one of these least commandments, and shall teach men so to do, he shall in no wise be saved in the kingdom of heaven; but whosoever shall do and teach these commandments of the law until it be fulfilled, the same shall be called great, and shall be saved in the kingdom of heaven.

22 For I say unto you, except your righteousness shall exceed that of the Scribes and Pharisees, ye shall in no case enter into the kingdom of heaven.

23 Ye have heard that it hath been said by them of old time that, Thou shalt not kill; and whosoever shall kill, shall be in danger of the judgment of God.

24 But I say unto you, that whosoever is angry with his brother, shall be in danger of his judgment; and whosoever shall say to his brother, ᵇRaca, or Rabcah, shall be in danger of the council; and whosoever shall say to his brother, Thou fool, shall be in danger of hell fire.

25 Therefore, if ye shall come unto me, or shall desire to come unto me, or if thou bring thy gift to the altar, and there rememberest that thy brother hath ᶜaught against thee,

26 Leave thou thy gift before the altar, and go thy way unto thy brother, and first be reconciled to thy brother, and then come and offer thy gift.

27 Agree with thine adversary quickly, while thou art in the way with him; lest at any time thine adversary deliver thee to the judge, and the judge deliver thee to the officer, and thou be cast into prison.

28 Verily I say unto thee, thou shalt by no means come out thence,

---

ᵃ   Dictionary - Jot or Tittle

ᵇ   devoid of intelligence
ᶜ   anything

until thou hast paid the uttermost ᵃfarthing.

29 Behold, it is written by them of old time, that thou shalt not commit adultery.

30 But I say unto you, that whosoever looketh on a woman to lust after her, hath committed adultery with her in his heart already.

31 Behold, I give unto you a commandment, that ye suffer none of these things to enter into your heart, for it is better that ye should deny yourselves of these things, wherein ye will take up your cross, than that ye should be cast into hell.

32 Therefore, if thy right eye offend thee, pluck it out and cast it from thee; for it is profitable for thee that one of thy members should perish, and not that thy whole body should be cast into hell.

33 Or if thy right hand offend thee, cut it off and cast it from thee; for it is profitable for thee that one of thy members should perish, and not that thy whole body should be cast into hell.

ᵇ9 And a man's hand is his friend, and his foot, also; and a man's eye, are they of his own household.

ᶜ34 And now this I speak, a parable concerning your sins; wherefore, cast them from you, that ye may not be hewn down and cast into the fire.

35 It hath been written that, Whosoever shall put away his wife, let him give her a writing of ᵈdivorcement.

36 Verily, verily, I say unto you, that whosoever shall put away his wife, saving for the cause of fornication, causeth her to commit adultery; and whosoever shall marry her that is divorced, committeth adultery.

37 Again, it hath been written by them of old time, Thou shalt not forswear thyself, but shall perform unto the Lord thine oaths.

38 But I say unto you, swear not at all; neither by heaven, for it is God's throne; nor by the earth, for it is his footstool; neither by Jerusalem, for it is the city of the great King; neither shalt thou swear by thy head, because thou canst not make one hair white or black.

39 But let your communication be, Yea, yea; Nay, nay: for whatsoever is more than these cometh of evil.

40 Ye have heard that it hath been said, An eye for an eye, and a tooth for a tooth.

41 But I say unto you, that ye resist not evil; but whosoever shall smite thee on thy right cheek, turn to him the other also ᵉ[or, in other

---

ᵃ   Dictionary - Farthing
ᵇ   Matthew 18:9
ᶜ   Matthew 5:34-42

ᵈ   Dictionary - Divorce
ᵉ   Luke 6:29

words, it is better to offer the other, than to revile again.]

42 And if any man will sue thee at the law, and take away thy coat, let him have it; and if he sue thee again, let him have thy ᵃcloak also.

ᵇ30 For it is better that thou suffer thine enemy to take these things, than to contend with him. Verily I say unto you, *Your* heavenly Father who seeth in secret, shall bring that wicked one into judgment.

ᶜ24 But woe unto you that are rich! For ye have received your consulation.

ᵈ43 And whosoever shall compel thee to go a mile, go with him a mile; and whosoever shall compel thee to go with him twain, thou shalt go with him twain.

44 Give to him that asketh of thee; and from him that would borrow of thee, turn not thou away; ᵉ[and of him who taketh away thy goods, ask them not again.]

ᶠ32 And as ye would that men should do to you, do ye also to them likewise.

ᵍ34 And if ye lend to them of whom ye hope to receive, what reward have you? for sinners also lend to sinners, to receive as much again.

35 But love ye your enemies, and do good, and lend, hoping for nothing again; and your reward shall be great; and ye shall be the children of the Highest; for he is kind unto the unthankful, and to the evil.

ʰ45 Ye have heard that it hath been said, Thou shalt love thy neighbor, and hate thine enemy.

46 But I say unto you, love your enemies; bless them that curse you; do good to them that hate you; and pray for them which despitefully use you and persecute you;

47 That ye may be the children of *your* Father who is in heaven; for he maketh his sun to rise on the evil and on the good, and sendeth rain on the just and on the unjust.

48 For if you love only them which love you, what reward have you? Do not even the publicans the same?

49 And if ye salute your brethren only, what do ye more than others? Do not even the publicans the same?

50 Ye are therefore commanded to be perfect, ⁱeven as *your* Father who is in heaven is perfect.

Jesus teaches His disciples

ʲ1 And it came to pass that, as

ᵃ   loose outer garment
ᵇ   Luke 6:30
ᶜ   Luke 6:24
ᵈ   Matthew 5:43-44
ᵉ   Luke 6:31
ᶠ   Luke 6:32
ᵍ   Luke 6:34-35

ʰ   Matthew 5:45-50
ⁱ   Compare 3 Nephi 12:48 in E.R.
ʲ   Matthew 6:1-9

Jesus taught his disciples, he said unto them, Take heed that ye do not your alms before men, to be seen of them; otherwise ye have no reward of *your* Father who is in heaven.

2 Therefore, when thou doest alms, do not sound a trumpet before thee, as the hypocrites do, in the synagogues and in the streets, that they may have glory of men. Verily I say unto you, they have their reward.

3 But when thou doest alms, let it be unto thee as thy left hand not knowing what thy right hand doeth;

4 That thine alms may be in secret; and *thy* Father who seeth in secret, himself shall reward thee openly.

5 And when thou prayest, thou shalt not be as the hypocrites; for they love to pray standing in the synagogues and in the corners of the streets, that they may be seen of men; for, verily, I say unto you, they have their reward.

6 But thou, when thou prayest, enter into thy closet, and when thou hast shut the door, pray to *thy* Father who is in secret; and *thy* Father who seeth in secret shall reward thee openly.

7 But when ye pray, use not vain repetitions, as the hypocrites do; for they think that they shall be heard for their much speaking.

8 Therefore be ye not like unto them; for *your* Father knoweth

what things ye have need of, before ye ask him.

9 Therefore after this manner shall ye pray, saying,

The Lord's Prayer

[a]10 [b]*Our* Father who art in heaven, Hallowed be thy name.

11 Thy kingdom come. Thy will be done on earth, as it is done in heaven.

12 Give us this day, our daily bread.

13 And [c]forgive us our trespasses, as we forgive those who trespass against us.

14 And suffer us not to be led into temptation, but deliver us from evil.

15 For thine is the kingdom, and the power, and the glory, forever and ever, [d]Amen.

16 For if ye forgive men their trespasses, who trespass against you, *your* heavenly Father will also forgive you; but if ye forgive not men their trespasses, neither will *your* heavenly Father forgive your trespasses.

Parable of the importuned friend

[e]5 And he said unto them, *Your* heavenly Father will not fail to give

---

a   Matthew 6:10-16
b   Dictionary - *Son of God*
c   Dictionary - Forgiveness
d   Dictionary - Amen
e   Luke 11:5-9

unto you whatsoever ye ask of him. And he spake a parable, saying,

6 Which of you shall have a friend, and shall go unto him at midnight, and say unto him, Friend, lend me three loaves;

7 For a friend of mine has come to me in his journey, and I have nothing to set before him;

8 And he from within shall answer and say, Trouble me not; the door is now shut, and my children are with me in bed; I cannot rise and give thee.

9 I say unto you, Though he will not rise and give him because he is his friend, yet because of his ªimportunity, he will rise and give him as many as he needeth.

Ask and ye shall receive

ᵇ10 And I say unto you, Ask, and it shall be given you; seek, and ye shall find; knock, and it shall be opened unto you.

11 For everyone who asketh, receiveth; and he that seeketh, findeth; and to him who knocketh, it shall be opened.

ᶜ17 Moreover, when ye fast, be not as the hypocrites, of a sad countenance; for they disfigure their faces, that they may appear unto men to fast. Verily, I say unto you, they have their reward.

18 But thou, when thou fastest, anoint thy head and wash thy face, that thou appear not unto men to fast, but unto *thy* Father who is in secret; and *thy* Father who seeth in secret, shall reward thee openly.

19 Lay not up for yourselves treasures upon the earth, where moth and rust doth corrupt, and where thieves break through and steal.

20 But lay up for yourselves treasure in heaven, where neither moth nor rust doth corrupt, and where thieves do not break through nor steal.

21 For where your treasure is, there will your heart be also.

22 The light of the body is the eye; if therefore thine eye be single to the glory of God, thy whole body shall be full of light.

23 But if thine eye be evil, thy whole body shall be full of darkness. If therefore the light which is in thee be darkness, how great shall that darkness be.

24 No man can serve two masters; for either he will hate the one, and love the other; or else he will hold to the one and despise the other. Ye cannot serve God and ᵈmammon.

25 And, again, I say unto you, go ye into the world, and care not for the world; for the world will hate you, and will persecute you, and will turn you out of their

---

ª   troublesome persistence
ᵇ   Luke 11:10-11
ᶜ   Matthew 6:17-35

ᵈ   Dictionary - Mammon

synagogues.

26 Nevertheless, ye shall go forth from house to house, teaching the people; and I will go before you.

27 And *your* heavenly Father will provide for you, whatsoever things ye need for food, what you shall eat: and for raiment, what ye shall wear or put on.

28 Therefore I say unto you, take no thought for your life, what ye shall eat, or what ye shall drink; nor yet for your bodies, what ye shall put on. Is not the life more than meat, and the body than raiment?

29 Behold the fowls of the air, for they sow not, neither do they reap, nor gather into barns; yet *your* heavenly Father feedeth them. Are ye not much better than they? How much more will he not feed you?

30 Wherefore take no thought for these things, but keep my commandments wherewith I have commanded you.

31 For which of you by taking thought can add one [a]cubit unto his stature.

32 And why take ye thought for raiment? Consider the lilies of the field, how they grow; they toil not, neither do they spin.

33 And yet I say unto you, that even Solomon, in all his glory, was not arrayed like one of these.

34 Therefore, if God so clothe the grass of the field, which today is, and tomorrow is cast into the oven, how much more will he not provide for you, if ye are not of little faith.

35 Therefore take no thought, saying What shall we eat? or, What shall we drink? or, Wherewithal shall we be clothed? [b][neither be ye of doubtful mind;]

[c]33 And ye are sent unto them to be their ministers, and the laborer is worthy of his hire; for the law sayeth, That a man shall not muzzle the ox that treadeth out the corn.

[d]37 Behold, I say unto you, that *your* heavenly Father knoweth that ye have need of all these things.

38 Wherefore, seek not the things of this world; but seek ye first to build up the kingdom of God, and to establish his righteousness, and all these things shall be added unto you.

39 Take, therefore, no thought for the morrow; for the morrow shall take thought for the things of itself. Sufficient unto the day shall be the evil thereof.

[e]35 Fear not, little flock; for it is *your* Father's good pleasure to give you the kingdom.

---

[a] Smith's - about 18 inches

[b] Luke 12:31
[c] Luke 12:33
[d] Matthew 6:37-39
[e] Luke 12:35

Jesus teaches His disciples what to say

[a]1 Now these are the words which Jesus taught his disciples that they should say unto the people.

2 Judge not unrighteously, that ye be not judged; but judge righteous judgment.

3 For with what judgment ye shall judge, ye shall be judged; and with that measure ye mete, it shall be measured to you again.

4 And again, ye shall say unto them, Why is it that thou beholdest the [b]mote that is in thy brother's eye, but considerest not the beam that is in thine own eye?

5 Or how wilt thou say to thy brother, Let me pull out the mote out of thine eye; and canst not behold a beam in thine own eye?

6 And Jesus said unto his disciples, Beholdest thou the Scribes, and the Pharisees, and the Priests, and the Levites? They teach in their synagogues, but do not observe the law, nor the commandments; and all have gone out of the way, and are under sin.

7 Go thou and say unto them, Why teach ye men the law and the commandments, when ye yourselves are the children of corruption?

8 Say unto them, Ye hypocrites, first cast out the beam out of thine own eyes, and then shalt thou see clearly to cast out the mote out of thy brother's eye.

9 Go ye into the world, saying unto all, Repent, for the kingdom of heaven has come nigh unto you.

10 And the mysteries of the kingdom ye shall keep within yourselves; for it is not meet to give that which is holy unto the dogs; neither cast ye your pearls unto swine, lest they trample them under their feet.

11 For the world cannot receive that which ye, yourselves, are not able to bear; wherefore ye shall not give your pearls unto them, lest they turn again and rend you.

12 Say unto them, Ask of God; ask, and it shall be given you; seek, and ye shall find; knock, and it shall be opened unto you.

13 For every one that asketh receiveth; and he that seeketh, findeth; and to him that knocketh, it shall be opened.

14 And then said his disciples unto him, They will say unto us, We ourselves are righteous, and need not that any man should teach us. God, we know, heard Moses and some of the prophets; but us he will not hear.

15 And they will say, We have the law for our salvation, and that is sufficient for us.

16 Then Jesus answered, and said unto his disciples, Thus shall ye say unto them,

---

[a]   Matthew 7:1-19
[b]   Dummelow - small twig

17 What man among you, having a son, and he shall be standing out, and shall say, Father, open thy house that I may come in and ᵃsup with thee, will not say, Come in, my son; for mine is thine, and thine is mine?

18 Or what man is there among you, who, if his son ask bread, will give him a stone?

19 Or if he ask a fish, will he give him a serpent?

ᵇ13 Or if he ask an egg, will he offer him a scorpion?

ᶜ20 If ye then, being evil, know how to give good gifts unto your children, how much more shall *your* Father who is in heaven, give good things to them that ask him?

21 Therefore, all things whatsoever ye would that men should do unto you, do ye even so to them; for this is the law and the prophets.

22 Repent, therefore, and enter ye in at the strait gate; for wide is the gate, and broad is the way that leadeth to destruction, and many there be who go in thereat.

23 Because strait is the gate, and narrow is the way that leadeth unto life, and few there be that find it.

24 And, again, beware of false prophets, who come to you in sheep's clothing; but inwardly they are ravening wolves.

25 Ye shall know them by their fruits; for do men gather grapes of thorns, or figs of thistles?

26 Even so every good tree bringeth forth good fruit; but a corrupt tree bringeth forth evil fruit.

27 A good tree cannot bring forth evil fruit; neither a corrupt tree bring forth good fruit.

28 Every tree that bringeth not forth good fruit, is ᵈhewn down, and cast into the fire.

29 Wherefore by their fruits ye shall know them.

30 Verily I say unto you, it is not everyone that saith unto me, Lord, Lord, that shall enter into the kingdom of heaven; but he that doeth the will of *my* Father who is in heaven.

31 For the day soon cometh, that men shall come before me to judgment, to be judged according to their works.

32 And many shall say unto me in that day, Lord, Lord, have we not prophesied in thy name; and in thy name cast out devils; and in thy name done many wonderful works?

33 And then will I say, Ye never knew me; depart from me ye that work iniquity.

34 Therefore, whosoever heareth these sayings of mine and doeth them, I will liken him unto

---

ᵃ eat

ᵇ Luke 11:13

ᶜ Matthew 7:20-37

ᵈ cut

a wise man, who built his house upon a rock, and the rains descended, and the floods came, and the winds blew, and beat upon that house, and it fell not; for it was founded upon a rock.

35 And everyone that heareth these sayings of mine, and doeth them not, shall be likened unto a foolish man, who built his house upon the sand; and the rains descended, and floods came, and the winds blew, and beat upon that house, and it fell; and great was the fall of it.

36 And it came to pass when Jesus had ended these sayings with his disciples, the people were astonished at his doctrine;

37 For he taught them as one having authority from God, and not as having authority from the Scribes.

Jesus heals the centurion's servant

[a]1 Now when he had ended all these sayings in the audience of the people, he entered into Capernaum.

2 And a certain [b]centurion's servant, who was dear unto him, was sick and ready to die.

3 And when he heard of Jesus, he sent unto him the [c]elders of the Jews, beseeching him that he would come and heal his servant.

4 And when they came to Jesus, they besought him instantly, saying, That he was worthy for whom he should do this;

5 For he loveth our nation, and he hath built us a synagogue.

6 Then Jesus went with them. And when he was now not far from the house, the centurion sent friends to him, saying unto him, Lord, trouble not thyself; for I am not worthy that thou shouldest enter under my roof.

7 Wherefore, neither thought I myself worthy to come unto thee; but say the word, and my servant shall be healed.

8 For I also am a man set under authority, having under me soldiers, and I say unto one, Go, and he goeth; and to another, Come, and he cometh; and to my servant, Do this, and he doeth it.

9 When Jesus heard these things, he marveled at him, and turned him about, and said unto the people who followed him, I say unto you, I have not found so great faith, no, not in Israel.

[d]11 And I say unto you, that many shall come from the east, and the west, and shall sit down with Abraham, and Isaac, and Jacob, in the kingdom of heaven.

12 But the children of the wicked one shall be cast out into outer

---

[a]   Luke 7:1-9
[b]   Dictionary - Centurion
[c]   Dictionary - Elder

[d]   Matthew 8:11-12

darkness; there shall be weeping and gnashing of teeth.

ᵃ10 And they who were sent, returning to the house, found the servant whole who had been sick.

Jesus heals a man with dropsy

ᵇ1 And it came to pass, as he went into the house of one of the chief Pharisees to eat bread on the Sabbath day, that they watched him.

2 And, behold, there was a certain man before him, who had the ᶜdropsy.

3 And Jesus spake unto the lawyers, and Pharisees, saying, Is it lawful to heal on the Sabbath day?

4 And they held their peace. And he took the man, and healed him, and let him go;

5 And spake unto them again, saying, Which of you shall have an ass or an ox fallen into a pit, and will not straightway pull him out on the Sabbath day?

6 And they could not answer him to these things.

Parable of the honored guest

ᵈ7 And he put forth a parable unto them concerning those who were ᵉbidden to a wedding; for he knew how they chose out the chief rooms, and exalted themselves one above another; wherefore he spake unto them, saying;

8 But when thou art bidden of any man to a wedding, sit not down in the highest room, lest a more honorable man than thou be bidden of him;

9 And he who bade thee, with him who is more honorable, come, and say to thee; Give this man place; and thou begin with shame to take the lowest room.

10 When thou art bidden, go and sit down in the lowest room; that when he who bade thee, cometh, he may say unto thee, Friend, go up higher; then shalt thou have honor of God, in the presence of them who sit at meat with thee.

11 For whosoever exalteth himself shall be abased; and he who humbleth himself shall be exalted.

12 Then said he also concerning him who bade to the wedding, When thou makest a dinner, or a supper, call not thy friends, nor thy brethren, neither thy kinsmen, nor rich neighbors; lest they also bid thee again, and a recompense be made thee.

13 But when thou makest a feast, call the poor, the maimed, the lame, the blind,

---

ᵃ Luke 7:10
ᵇ Luke 14:1-6
ᶜ edema - fluid in connective
    tissue
ᵈ Luke 14:7-15

ᵉ invited

14 And thou shalt be blessed; for they cannot recompense thee; for thou shalt be recompensed at the resurrection of the just.

15 And when one of them who sat at meat with him, heard these things, he said unto him, Blessed is he who shall eat bread in the kingdom of God.

Whosoever does not bear his cross cannot be my disciple

[a]25 And when he had finished these sayings, he departed thence, and there went great multitudes with him, and he turned and said unto them,

26 If any man come to me, and hate not his father, and mother, and wife, and children, and brethren, and sisters, or husband, yea and his own life also; or in other words, is afraid to lay down their life for my sake, he cannot be my disciple.

27 And whosoever doth not bear his cross, and come after me, cannot be my disciple.

28 Wherefore, settle this in your hearts, that ye will do the things which I shall teach, and command you.

Parable of the tower

[b]29 For which of you intending to build a tower, sitteth not down first, and counteth the cost, whether he have money to finish his work?

30 Lest, unhappily, after he has laid the foundation and is not able to finish his work, all who behold, begin to mock him,

31 Saying, This man began to build, and was not able to finish. And this he said, signifying there should not any man follow him, unless he was able to continue; saying,

Parable of the king going to war

[c]32 Or what king, going to make war against another king, sitteth not down first, and consulteth whether he be able with ten thousand, to meet him who cometh against him with twenty thousand.

33 Or else, while the other is yet a great way off, he sendeth an embassage, and desireth conditions of peace.

34 So likewise, whosoever of you forsaketh not all that he hath he cannot be my disciple.

35 Then certain of them came to him, saying, Good Master, we have Moses and the prophets, and whosoever shall live by them, shall he not have life?

36 And Jesus answered, saying, Ye know not Moses, neither the

---

[a]   Luke 14:25-28
[b]   Luke 14:29-31

[c]   Luke 14:32-38

prophets; for if ye had known them, ye would have believed on me; for to this intent they were written. For I am sent that ye might have life. Therefore I will liken it unto salt which is good;

37 But if the salt has lost its savor, wherewith shall it be seasoned?

38 It is neither fit for the land, nor yet for the dung hill; men cast it out. [a]He who hath ears to hear, let him hear. These things he said, signifying; that which was written, verily must all be fulfilled.

Parable of the husbandman

[b]1 And there were present at that time, some who spake unto him of the Galileans, whose blood Pilate had mingled with their sacrifices.

2 And Jesus said unto them, Suppose ye that these Galileans were sinners above all the Galileans, because they suffered such things?

3 I say unto you, nay; but except you repent, you shall all likewise perish.

4 Or those eighteen, on whom the tower in Siloam fell, and slew them; think ye that they were sinners above all men that dwelt in Jerusalem?

5 I tell you, nay; but except ye repent, you shall all likewise perish.

6 He spake also this parable, A certain husbandman had a fig tree planted in his vineyard. He came and sought fruit thereon and found none.

7 Then said he to the dresser of his vineyard, Behold, these three years I come seeking fruit on this fig tree, and find none. Cut it down, why cumbereth it the ground?

8 And he, answering, said unto him, Lord, let it alone this year also, till I shall dig about, and [c]dung it;

9 And if it bear fruit, the tree is saved; and if not, after that thou shalt cut it down. And many other parables spake he unto the people.

Jesus heals a woman of an infirmity

[d]10 And after this, as he was teaching in one of the synagogues on the Sabbath;

11 Behold, there was a woman who had a spirit of infirmity eighteen years, and was bowed together, and could in no wise straighten up.

12 And when Jesus saw her, he called and said unto her, Woman, thou art loosed from thine infirmities.

13 And he laid hands on her; and immediately she was made straight, and glorified God.

14 And the ruler of the synagogue was filled with indignation, because that Jesus had healed on the Sabbath day, and said unto the

---

[a]   Dictionary - Conundrum
[b]   Luke 13:1-9

[c]   fertilize
[d]   Luke 13:10-17

people, There are six days in which men ought to work; in them therefore come and be healed, and not on the Sabbath day.

15 The Lord then said unto him, O hypocrite! Doth not each one of you on the Sabbath, loose an ox or an ass from the stall, and lead him away to watering?

16 And ought not this woman, being a daughter of Abraham, whom Satan hath bound, lo, these eighteen years, be loosed from this bond on the Sabbath day?

17 And when he had said these things, all his adversaries were ashamed; and all his disciples rejoiced for all the glorious things which were done by him.

Are there few that be saved?

[a]23 And there said one unto him, Lord, are there few only that be saved? And he answered him, and said,

24 Strive to enter in at the strait gate; for I say unto you, Many shall seek to enter in, and shall not be able; for the Lord shall not always strive with man.

25 Therefore, when once the Lord of the kingdom is risen up, and hath shut the door of the kingdom, then ye shall stand without, and knock at the door, saying, Lord, Lord, open unto us. But the Lord shall answer and say unto you, I will not receive you, for [b]ye know not from whence ye are.

26 Then shall ye begin to say, We have eaten and drunk in thy presence, and thou hast taught in our streets.

27 But he shall say, I tell you, ye know not from whence ye are; depart from me, all workers of iniquity.

28 There shall be weeping and gnashing of teeth among you, when ye shall see Abraham, and Isaac, and Jacob, and all the prophets, in the kingdom of God, and you are thrust out.

29 And verily I say unto you, They shall come from the east, and the west; and from the north, and the south, and shall sit down in the kingdom of God;

30 And, behold, there are last which shall be first, and there are first which shall be last, and shall be saved therein.

Pharisees warn Jesus of Herod

[c]31 And as he was thus teaching, there came to him certain of the Pharisees, saying unto him, Get thee out, and depart hence; for Herod will kill thee.

32 And he said unto them, Go ye and tell Herod, Behold, I cast out devils, and do cures today and

---

[a] Luke 13:23-30

[b] Dictionary - Conundrum
[c] Luke 13:31-36

tomorrow, and the third day I shall be perfected.

33 Nevertheless, I must walk today, and tomorrow, and the third day; for it cannot be that a prophet perish out of Jerusalem.

34 This he spake, signifying of his death. And in this very hour he began to weep over Jerusalem,

35 Saying, O Jerusalem, Jerusalem, thou who killest the prophets, and stonest them who are sent unto thee; how often would I have gathered thy children together, as a hen her brood under her wings, and ye would not.

36 Behold, your house is left unto you desolate. And verily I say unto you, Ye shall not know me, until ye have received from the hand of the Lord a just recompense for all your sins; until the time come when ye shall say, Blessed is he who cometh in the name of the Lord.

a22 And he went through the cities and villages, teaching, and journeying toward Jerusalem.

Jesus brings a widow's son back to life

b11 And it came to pass the day after, that he went into a city called cNain; and many of his disciples went with him, and much people.

12 Now, when he was come nigh to the gate of the city, behold, there was a dead man carried out, the only son of his mother, and she was a widow; and many people of the city were with her.

13 And now the Lord saw her, and had compassion on her, and he said unto her, Weep not.

14 And he came and touched the dbier; and they who bear it stood still, and he said, Young man, I say unto thee, Arise.

15 And he who was dead, sat up, and began to speak; and he delivered him to this mother.

16 And there came a fear on all; and they glorified God, saying, That a great prophet is risen up among us; and, That God hath visited his people.

17 And this rumor of him went forth throughout all Judea, and throughout all the region round about.

Jesus eats with Simon the Pharisee

e36 And one of the Pharisees desired him that he would eat with him. And he went into the Pharisee's house, and sat down to meat.

37 And behold, a fwoman in the city, who was a sinner, when

---

a   Luke 13:22
b   Luke 7:11-17
c   see Map 1

d   a stand on which the coffin is placed
e   Luke 7:36-40
f   Mary - see John 11:2

she knew that Jesus was at meat in the Pharisee's house, brought an alabaster box of ointment.

38 And stood at his feet weeping, and began to wash his feet with tears, and did wipe them with the hairs of her head, and kissed his feet, and anointed them with the ointment.

39 Now when the Pharisee who had bidden him saw this, he spake within himself, saying, This man, if he were a prophet, would have known who or what manner of woman this is who toucheth him; for she is a sinner.

40 And Jesus answering, said unto him, Simon, I have somewhat to say unto thee. And he said, Master, say on.

Parable of the two debtors

[a]41 And Jesus said, There was a certain creditor, who had two debtors; the one owed him five hundred pence, and the other fifty.

42 And when he found they had nothing to pay, he frankly forgave them both. Tell me therefore, which of them will love him most?

43 Simon answered and said, I suppose the man to whom he forgave most. And he said unto him, Thou hast rightly judged.

44 And he turned to the woman, and said unto Simon, Seest thou this woman? I entered into thy house, thou gavest me no water for my feet; but she hath washed my feet with tears, and wiped them with the hairs of her head.

45 Thou gavest me no kiss; but this woman since the time I came in, hath not ceased to kiss my feet.

46 My head with oil thou didst not anoint; but this woman hath anointed my feet with ointment.

47 Wherefore I say unto thee, Her sins, which are many, are forgiven; for she loved much. But to whom little is forgiven, the same loveth little.

48 And he said unto her, Thy sins are forgiven.

49 And they that sat at meat with him, began to say within themselves, Who is this that forgiveth sins also?

50 And he said to the woman, Thy faith hath saved thee; go in peace.

Jesus goes to Bethesda and heals a man on the sabbath

[b]1 After this there was a [c]feast of the Jews; and Jesus went up to Jerusalem.

2 Now there is at Jerusalem, by the sheep market, a pool which is called in the Hebrew tongue, [d]Bethesda, having five porches.

---

[a] Luke 7:41-50

[b] John 5:1-9
[c] may be Feast of Tabernacles - John 7:2
[d] means house of mercy – see

3 In these porches lay a great many impotent folk, of blind, halt, withered, waiting for the moving of the water.

4 For an angel went down at a certain season into the pool, and troubled the water; whosoever then first after the troubling of the water stepped in, was made whole of whatsoever disease he had.

5 And a certain man was there, who had an infirmity thirty and eight years.

6 And Jesus saw him lie, and knew that he had been now a long time afflicted; and he said unto him, Wilt thou be made whole?

7 The impotent man answered him, Sir, I have no man when the water is troubled, to put me into the pool; but while I am coming, another steppeth down before me.

8 Jesus said unto him, Rise, take up thy bed and walk.

9 And immediately the man was made whole, and took up his bed, and walked; and it was on the Sabbath day.

Jews find fault with Jesus for healing on the sabbath

[a]10 The Jews therefore said unto him who was cured, It is the Sabbath day; it is not lawful for thee to carry thy bed.

11 He answered them, He who made me whole, said unto me, Take up thy bed and walk.

12 Then answered they him, saying, What man is he who said unto thee, Take up thy bed and walk?

13 And he that was healed knew not who it was; for Jesus had conveyed himself away, a multitude being in that place.

14 Afterward Jesus findeth him in the temple, and said unto him, Behold, thou art made whole; sin no more, lest a worse thing come unto thee.

15 The man departed, and told the Jews that it was Jesus who had made him whole;

16 And therefore did the Jews persecute Jesus, and sought to slay him, because he had done these things on the Sabbath day.

17 But Jesus answered them, *My* Father worketh hitherto, and I work.

18 Therefore the Jews sought the more to kill him, because he not only had broken the Sabbath, but said also that God was *his* father, making himself equal with God.

19 Then answered Jesus and said unto them, Verily, verily, I say unto you, The Son can do nothing of himself, but what he seeth *the* Father do; for what things soever he doeth, these also doeth the Son likewise.

20 For *the* Father loveth the Son, and showeth him all things

---

Map 2
[a] John 5:10-48

that himself doeth; and he will show him greater works than these, that ye may marvel.

21 For as *the* Father riseth up the dead, and quickeneth them; even so the Son quickeneth whom he will.

22 So *the* Father judgeth no man; but hath committed all judgment unto the Son;

23 That all men should honor the Son, even as they honor *the* Father. He who honoreth not the Son, honoreth not *the* Father who hath sent him.

24 Verily, verily, I say unto you, he who heareth my words, and believeth on him who sent me, hath everlasting life, and shall not come into condemnation; but is passed from ᵃdeath into life.

25 Verily, verily, I say unto you, The hour is coming, and now is, when the dead shall hear the voice of the Son of God; and they who hear shall live.

26 For as *the* Father hath life in Himself; so hath he given to the Son to have life in himself;

27 And hath given him authority to execute judgment also, because he is the Son of man.

28 Marvel not at this; for the hour is coming, in the which all who are in their graves shall hear his voice,

29 And shall come forth; they who have done good, in the ᵇresurrection of the just; and they who have done evil, in the resurrection of the unjust,

30 And all shall be judged of the Son of Man. For as I hear, I judge, and my judgment is just;

31 For I can of mine own self do nothing; because I seek not mine own will, but the will of *the* Father who hath sent me.

32 Therefore if I bear witness of myself, yet my witness is true.

33 For I am not alone, there is another who beareth witness of me, and I know that the testimony which he giveth of me is true.

34 Ye sent unto John, and he bear witness also unto the truth.

35 And he received not his testimony of man, but of God, and ye yourselves say that he is a prophet, therefore you ought to receive his testimony. These things I say that ye might be saved.

36 He was a burning and a shining light; and ye were willing for a season to rejoice in his light.

37 But I have a greater witness than the testimony of John; for the works which *the* Father hath given me to finish, the same works that I do, bear witness of me, that *the* Father hath sent me.

38 And *the* Father himself who hath sent me, hath borne witness of me. And verily I testify unto you,

---

ᵃ   Dictionary - Death

ᵇ   Dictionary - Resurrection

that ye have never heard his voice at any time, nor seen his shape;

39 For you have not his word abiding in you; and him whom he hath sent, ye believe not.

40 Search the scriptures; for in them ye think ye have eternal life; and they are they which testify of me.

41 And ye will not come to me that ye might have life, lest ye should honor me.

42 I receive not honor from men.

43 But I know you, that ye have not the love of God in you.

44 I am come in *my* Father's name, and ye receive me not; if another shall come in his own name, him ye will receive.

45 How can ye believe, who seek honor one of another, and seek not the honor which cometh of God only?

46 Do not think that I will accuse you to *the* Father; there is Moses who accuseth you, in whom ye trust.

47 For had ye believed Moses, ye would have believed me; for he wrote of me.

48 But if ye believe not his writings, how shall ye believe my words?

Jesus withdraws to the sea

[a]13 But Jesus knew it when they took [b]counsel, and he withdrew himself from thence; [c][with his disciples, to the sea;] and great multitudes followed him, and he healed their sick, and charged them that they should not make him known;

14 That it might be fulfilled which was spoken by Esaias the prophet, saying, [d]Behold my servant, whom I have chosen; my beloved, in whom my soul is well pleased.

15 I will put my spirit upon him, and he shall show judgment to the Gentiles. He shall not strive, nor cry; neither shall any man hear his voice in the streets.

16 A bruised reed shall he not break, and smoking flax shall he not quench; [e]till he send forth judgment unto victory.

17 And in his name shall the Gentiles trust.

[f]9 And he spake unto his disciples, that a small ship should wait on him, because of the multitude, lest they should throng him.

10 For he had healed many; insomuch that they pressed upon him for to touch him. As many as had plagues and unclean spirits, when they saw him, fell down before him, and cried, saying, Thou art the Son of God.

[a] Matthew 12:13-17
[b] Dictionary - Sanhedrin
[c] Mark 3:8
[d] Easy Ref. Isaiah 42:1-3
[e] Compare D&C 52:11 in E.R.
[f] Mark 3:9-10

Parable of the sower

[a]1 And he began again to teach them by the sea side; and there was gathered unto him a great multitude; so that he entered into a ship and sat in the sea; and the whole multitude was by the sea on the land.

2 And he taught them many things by parables.

3 And he said unto them in his doctrine, Harken; Behold, there went out a sower to sow;

4 And it came to pass as he sowed, some fell by the way side, and the fowls of the air came and devoured it up.

5 And some fell on stony ground, where it had not much earth; and immediately it sprang up, because it had no depth of earth: but when the sun was up, it scorched; and because it had no root, it withered away.

6 And some fell among thorns, and the thorns grew up and choked it; and it [b][bring no fruit to perfection.]

7 And other seed fell on good ground, and did yield fruit, that sprang up and increased, and brought forth, some thirty fold, and some sixty, and some an hundred.

8 And he said unto them, He that hath ears to hear, let him hear.

---

^a   Mark 4:1-8
^b   Luke 8:14

Parable of the candle

[c]18 And he said unto them, Is a candle brought to be put under a bushel, or under a bed, and not to be set on a candlestick? I say unto you, Nay; [d][but setteth it on a candlestick, that they who enter in may see the light.]

[e]35 The light of the body is the eye; therefore when thine eye is single, thy whole body also is full of light; but when thine eye is evil, thy body also is full of darkness.

36 Take heed therefore, that the light which is in thee be not darkness.

37 If thy whole body therefore is full of light, having no part dark, the whole shall be full of light, as when the bright shining of a candle lighteneth a room, and doth give thee light in all the room.

[f]19 For there is nothing hid which shall not be manifested; neither was anything kept secret, but that it should in due time [g][go] abroad. If any man have ears to hear, let him hear.

20 And he said unto them, Take heed what you hear; for with what measure ye mete, it shall be measured to you; and unto you that continue to receive, shall more be

---

^c   Mark 4:18
^d   Luke 8:16
^e   Luke 11:35-37
^f   Mark 4:19-20
^g   Luke 8:17

given; for he that receiveth, to him shall be given; but he that continueth not to receive, from him shall be taken even that which he hath.

Parable of the wheat and the tares

[a]22 Another parable put he forth unto them, saying, The kingdom of heaven is likened unto a man who sowed good seed in his field;

23 But while he slept, his enemy came and sowed [b]tares among the wheat, and went his way.

24 But when the blade sprung up, and brought forth fruit, then appeared the tares also.

25 So the servants of the householder came and said unto him, Sir, didst not thou sow good seed in thy field? whence then hath it tares?

26 He said unto them, An enemy hath done this.

27 And the servants said unto him, Wilt thou then that we go and gather them up?

28 But he said, Nay; lest while ye gather up the tares, ye root up also the wheat with them.

29 Let both grow together until the harvest, and in the time of harvest, I will say to the reapers, Gather ye together first the wheat into my barn; and the tares are bound in bundles to be burned.

Parable of the mustard seed

[c]24 And he said, Whereunto shall I liken the kingdom of God? Or with what comparison shall we compare it?

[d]30 And another parable put he forth unto them, saying, The kingdom of heaven is like unto a grain of mustard seed, which a man took and sowed in his field;

31 Which indeed is the least of all seeds; but when it is grown, it is the greatest among herbs, and becometh a tree, so that the birds of the air come and lodge in the branches thereof.

Parable of the leaven

[e]32 Another parable spake he unto them, The kingdom of heaven is like unto [f]leaven, which a woman took and hid in three measures of meal, till the whole was leavened.

33 All these things spake Jesus unto the multitudes in parables; and without a parable spake he not unto them,

34 That it might be fulfilled which was spoken by the prophets, saying, [g]I will open my mouth in parables; I will utter things which have been kept secret from the foundation of the world.

Parable of the seed

---

[a]   Matthew 13:22-29
[b]   Dictionary - Tares

[c]   Mark 4:24
[d]   Matthew 13: 30-31
[e]   Matthew 13:32-34
[f]   Dummelow - yeast
[g]   Easy Ref. Psalms 78:2

[a]21 And he said, So is the kingdom of God; as if a man should cast seed into the ground; and should sleep and rise, night and day, and the seed should spring and grow up, he knoweth not how;

22 For the earth bringeth forth fruit of herself, first the blade, then the ear, after that the full corn in the ear.

23 But when the fruit is brought forth, immediately he putteth in the sickle, because the harvest is come.

Why Jesus taught in parables

[b]8 Then the disciples came and said unto him, Why speakest thou unto them in parables?

9 He answered and said unto them, because it is given unto you to know the [c]mysteries of the kingdom of heaven, but to them it is not given.

10 For whosoever receiveth, to him shall be given, and he shall have more abundance;

11 But whosoever continueth not to receive, from him shall be taken away even that he hath.

12 Therefore speak I to them in parables; because they, seeing, see not; and hearing, they hear not; neither do they understand.

13 And in them is fulfilled the prophecy of Esaias concerning them, which saith, [d]By hearing, ye shall hear and shall not understand; and seeing, ye shall see and shall not perceive.

14 For this people's heart is waxed gross, and their ears are dull of hearing, and their eyes they have closed, lest at any time they should see with their eyes and hear with their ears, and should understand with their hearts, and should be converted, and I should heal them.

15 But blessed are your eyes, for they see; and your ears, for they hear. And blessed are you because these things are come unto you, that you might understand them.

16 And verily, I say unto you, many righteous prophets have desired to see these days which you see, and have not seen them; and to hear that which you hear, and have not heard.

Jesus explains the parable of the sower to the Apostles

[e]12 And he said unto them, Know ye not this parable? And how then will ye know all parables?

[f]17 Hear ye therefore the parable of the sower.

18 When anyone heareth the word of the kingdom, and understandeth not, then cometh the

---

a   Mark 4:21-23
b   Matthew 13:8-16
c   Dictionary - Mystery
d   Easy Ref. Jeremiah 5:21
e   Mark 4:12
f   Matthew 13:17-21

wicked one, and taketh away that which was sown in his heart; this is he who receiveth seed by the way side.

19 But he that receiveth the seed into stony places, the same is he that heareth the word and ready with joy receiveth it, yet he hath not root in himself, and endureth but for a while; for when tribulation or persecution ariseth because of the word, by and by he is offended.

20 He also who received seed among the thorns, is he that heareth the word; and the care of this world and the deceitfulness of riches, [a][and lusts of other things enter in,] choke the word, and he becometh unfruitful.

21 But he who received seed into the good ground, is he who heareth the word and understandeth and endureth; which also beareth fruit, and bringeth forth, some an hundred fold, some sixty, and some thirty.

Jesus explains parables to His Apostles

[b]28 And the same day, when the even was come, [c][he gave commandment to depart unto the other side of the sea.]

29 And when they had sent away the multitude, they took

---

[a]   Mark 4:16
[b]   Mark 4:28-29
[c]   Matthew 8:18

him, even as he was, in the ship. And there were also with him other little ships.

[d]35 . . . And his disciples came unto him, saying, Declare unto us the parable of the tares of the field.

36 He answered and said unto them, He that soweth the good seed is the Son of Man.

37 The field is the world; the good seed are the children of the kingdom; but the tares are the children of the wicked.

38 The enemy that sowed them is the devil.

39 The harvest is the end of the world, or the destruction of the wicked.

40 The reapers are the angels, or the messengers sent of heaven.

41 As, therefore, the tares are gathered and burned in the fire, so shall it be in the end of this world, or the destruction of the wicked.

42 For in that day, before the Son of Man shall come, he shall send forth his angels and messengers of heaven.

43 And they shall gather out of his kingdom all things that offend, and them which do iniquity, and shall cast them out among the wicked; and there shall be wailing and gnashing of teeth.

44 For the world shall be burned with fire.

---

[d]   Matthew 13:35-45

45 Then shall the righteous shine forth as the sun in the kingdom of their Father. Who hath ears to hear, let him hear.

Parable of the treasure hid in a field

[a]46 Again, the kingdom of heaven is like unto a treasure hid in a field. And when a man hath found a treasure which is hid, he secureth it, and straightway, for joy thereof, goeth and selleth all that he hath, and buyeth that field.

Parable of the pearl of great price

[b]47 And again, the kingdom of heaven is like unto a merchantman, seeking goodly pearls, who, when he had found one pearl of great price, he went and sold all that he had and bought it.

Parable of the gospel net

[c]48 Again, the kingdom of heaven is like unto a net that was cast into the sea, and gathered of every kind, which, when it was full, they drew to shore, and sat down, and gathered the good into vessels; but cast the bad away.

49 So shall it be at the end of the world.

50 And the world is the children of the wicked.

51 The angels shall come forth, and sever the wicked from among the just, and shall cast them out into the world to be burned. There shall be wailing and gnashing of teeth.

52 Then Jesus said unto them, Have ye understood all these things? They say unto him, Yea, Lord.

53 Then said he unto them, Every scribe well instructed in the things of the kingdom of heaven, is like unto a householder; a man, therefore, which bringeth forth out of his treasure that which is new and old.

Jesus calms the sea

[d]23 But as they sailed he fell asleep; [e][and he was in the hinder part of the ship asleep on a pillow;] and there came down a storm of wind on the lake; and they were filled with fear, and were in danger.

24 And they came to him and awoke him, [f][and said unto him, Master, carest thou not that we parish?] Then he arose, and rebuked the wind [and said unto the sea, Peace, be still. And the wind ceased,] and there was a [great] calm.

25 And he said unto them, Where is your faith? and they being afraid, wondered, saying one to another, What manner of man is

---

a   Matthew 13:46
b   Matthew 13:47
c   Matthew 13:48-53
d   Luke 8:23-25
e   Mark 4:30
f   Mark 4:30, 31

this? For he commandeth even the winds and waters, and they obey him.

Jesus heals a man with many devils

[a]29 And when he was come to the other side, into the country of the [[b]Gadarenes], there met him a man possessed of devils, coming out of the tombs, exceeding fierce, so that no man could pass by that way.

[c]3 And no man could bind him, no, not with chains; because that he had been often bound with fetters and chains, and the chains had been plucked asunder by him, and the fetters broken in pieces; neither could any man tame him.

4 And always, night and day, he was in the mountains, and in the tombs, crying, and cutting himself with stones.

[d]30 And, behold, he cried out, saying, What have we to do with thee, Jesus, thou Son of God? Art thou come hither to torment us before the time? [e][I [f]adjure thee by God, that thou torment me not.]

[g]6 And he commanded him saying, Declare thy name. And he answered, saying, My name is Legion; for we are many.

[h]31 And there was there a herd of many swine, feeding on the mountain.

32 And they besought him that he would suffer them to enter into the swine, and he suffered them.

33 And they besought him also, that he would not command them to go out into the deep. And he said unto them, Come out of the man.

34 Then went the devils out of the man, and entered into the swine; and the herd ran violently down a steep place into the lake, [i][they were about two thousand,] and were choked.

35 When they who fed the swine saw what was done, they fled, and went and told the people of the city and in the country.

36 Then they went out to see what was done; and came to Jesus, and found the man, out of whom the devils were departed, sitting at the feet of Jesus, clothed, and in his right mind; and they were afraid.

37 They also who saw the miracle, told them by what means he who was possessed of the devils was healed.

38 Then the whole multitude of the country of the Gadarenes

a   Matthew 8:29
b   Mark 5:1
c   Mark 5:3-4
d   Matthew 8:30
e   Mark 5:5
f   command as if under penalty of a curse
g   Mark 5:6

h   Luke 8:31-40
i   Mark 5:10

round about, besought Jesus to depart from them; for they were taken with great fear. And Jesus went up into the ship, and returned back again.

39 Now the man out of whom the devils were departed, besought him that he might be with him. But Jesus sent him away, saying,

40 Return to thine own house, and show how great things God hath done unto thee. And he went his way, and published throughout the whole city, how great things Jesus had done unto him.

[a]17 And he departed, and began to publish in Decapolis, how great things Jesus had done for him; and all that heard him did marvel.

Woman healed by touching Jesus' garment

[b]41 And it came to pass, that, when Jesus was returned, the people received him; for they were all waiting for him.

42 And Behold, there came a man named Jairus, and he was a ruler of the synagogue; and he fell down at Jesus' feet, and besought him that he would come into this house;

43 For he had an only daughter, about twelve years of age, and she lay a dying. [c][And Jesus arose and followed him, and also his disciples.] But as he went, the people thronged him.

[d]21 And a certain woman, which had an issue of blood twelve years, and had suffered many things of many physicians, and had spent all that she had, and was nothing bettered but rather grew worse; when she had heard of Jesus, she came in the press behind, and touched his garment; for she said, If I may touch but his clothes, I shall be whole.

22 And straightway the fountain of her blood was dried up; and she felt in her body that she was healed of that plague.

23 And Jesus, immediately knowing in himself that virtue had gone out of him, turned him about in the press, and said, Who touched my clothes?

24 And his disciples said unto him, Thou seest the multitude thronging thee, and sayest thou, Who touched me?

25 And he looked round about to see her that had done this thing; but the woman, fearing and trembling, knowing what was done in her, came and fell down before him, and told him all the truth.

26 And he said unto her, Daughter, thy faith hath made thee whole; go in peace, and be whole of thy plague.

---

[a] Mark 5:17
[b] Luke 8:41-43
[c] Matthew 9:25

[d] Mark 5:21-26

Jesus brings Jairus' daughter back to life

[a]27 While he yet spake, there came from the ruler of the synagogue's house, a man who said, Thy daughter is dead; why troublest thou the Master any further?

28 As soon as he spake, Jesus heard the word that was spoken, and said unto the ruler of the synagogue, Be not afraid, only believe.

29 And he suffered no man to follow him, save Peter, and James, and John the brother of James.

30 And he cometh to the house of the ruler of the synagogue, and seeth the [b]tumult, and them that wept and wailed greatly.

31 And when he was come in he said unto them, Why make ye this ado, and weep? The damsel is not dead, but sleepeth. And they laughed him to [c]scorn.

32 But when he had put them all out, he taketh the father and the mother of the damsel, and them that were with him, and entered in where the damsel was lying;

33 And he took the damsel by the hand, and said unto her, Talitha cumi; which is, being interpreted, Damsel, I say unto thee, arise.

34 And straightway the damsel arose and walked; for she was twelve years old. And they were astonished with a great astonishment.

35 And he charged them straitly that no man should know it; and commanded that something should be given her to eat.

[d]32 And the fame of Jesus went abroad into all that land.

Jesus heals the blind and the dumb

[e]33 And when Jesus departed thence, two blind men followed him, crying, and saying, Jesus, thou Son of David, have mercy on us.

34 And when he was come into the house, the blind men came to him; and Jesus said unto them, Believe ye that I am able to do this? They said unto him, Yea, Lord.

35 Then touched he their eyes, saying, According to your faith, be it unto you.

36 And their eyes were opened; and straitly he charged them, saying, Keep my commandments, and see ye tell no man in this place, that no man know it.

37 But they, when they were departed, spread abroad his fame in all that country.

38 And as they went out, behold, they brought to him a dumb man possessed with a devil.

---

[a] Mark 5:27-35
[b] disorderly, confusion
[c] emotion involving anger and disgust

---

[d] Matthew 9:32
[e] Matthew 9:33-39

39 And when the devil was cast out, the dumb man spake, And the multitudes marveled, saying, It was never so seen in Israel.

Jesus' second rejection at Nazareth

[a]1 And he went out from thence, and came into his own country; and his disciples followed him.

2 And when the Sabbath day was come, he began to teach in the synagogue; and many hearing, were astonished at his words, saying, From whence hath this man these things?

3 And what wisdom is this that is given unto him, that even such mighty works are wrought by his hands?

4 Is not this the carpenter, the son of Mary, the brother of James and Joses, and of Judah and Simon?

5 And are not his sisters here with us? And they were offended at him.

6 But Jesus said unto them, A prophet is not without honor, save in his own country, and among his own kin, and in his own house.

7 And he could do no mighty work there, save that he laid his hands upon a few sick folks and they were healed.

8 And he marveled because of their unbelief . . .

[b]41 And Jesus went about all the cities and villages, teaching in their synagogues, and preaching the gospel of the kingdom, and healing every sickness and disease among the people.

42 But when he saw the multitudes, he was moved with compassion on them, because they fainted, and were scattered abroad, as [c]sheep having no shepherd.

43 Then said he unto his disciples, The harvest truly is plenteous, but the laborers are few.

44 Pray ye therefore the Lord of the harvest, that he will send forth laborers into his harvest.

Jesus sends the Apostles out to teach the gospel

[d]1 And when he had called unto him his twelve disciples, he gave them power over unclean spirits, to cast them out, and to heal all manner of sickness and all manner of disease.

2 Now the names of the twelve apostles are these; the first Simon, who is called Peter, and Andrew his brother; James the son of Zebedee, and John his brother; Philip, and Bartholomew; Thomas, and Matthew the publican; James the son of Alpheus, and Lebbeus, whose surname was Thaddeus; Simon the Canaanite, and Judas

---

[b]   Matthew 9:41-44
[c]   Dictionary - Sheep
[d]   Matthew 10:1-38

[a]   Mark 6:1-8

Iscariot, who also betrayed him.

3 These twelve Jesus [a][began to send them forth by two and two;] and commanded them, saying,

4 Go not into the way of the Gentiles, and enter ye not into any city of the Samaritans.

5 But rather go to the lost sheep of the house of Israel.

6 And as ye go, preach, saying, The kingdom of heaven is at hand.

7 Heal the sick; cleanse the lepers; raise the dead; cast out devils; freely ye have received, freely give.

8 Provide neither gold, nor silver, nor brass in your purses.

9 Nor [b]script for your journey, neither two coats, neither shoes, nor yet staves; for the workman is worthy of his meat.

10 And into whatsoever town or city ye shall enter, inquire who in it is worthy, and there abide till ye go thence.

11 And when ye come into a house, salute it; and if the house be worthy, let your peace come upon it; but if it be not worthy, let your peace return to you.

12 And whosoever shall not receive you, nor hear your words, when ye depart out of that house, or city, shake off the dust of your feet for a testimony against them.

13 And, verily, I say unto you, it shall be more tolerable for the land of Sodom and Gomorrah in the day of judgment, than for that city.

14 Behold, I send you forth as sheep in the midst of wolves; be ye therefore wise servants, and as harmless as doves.

15 But, beware of men; for they will deliver you up to the councils, and they will [c]scourge you in their synagogues.

16 And ye shall be brought before governors and kings for my sake, for a testimony against them and the Gentiles.

17 But when they deliver you up, take no thought how or what ye shall speak; for it will be given you in that same hour what ye shall speak; for it is not ye that speak, but the Spirit of *your* Father which speaketh in you.

18 And the brother shall deliver up the brother to death, and the father the child; and the children shall rise up against their parents and cause them to be put to death.

19 And ye shall be hated of all the world for my name's sake; but he that endureth to the end shall be saved.

20 But when they persecute you in one city, flee ye into another; for verily, I say unto you, Ye shall not have gone over the cities of Israel, till the Son of Man has come.

---

[a] Mark 6:9
[b] Smith's - knapsack to carry food in

[c] Dictionary - Scourge

21 Remember, the disciple is not above his master; nor the servant above his lord. It is enough that the disciple be as his master, and the servant as his lord.

22 If they have called the master of the house ᵃBeelzebub, how much more shall they call them of his household?

23 Fear them not, therefore; for there is nothing covered, that shall not be revealed; and hid, that shall not be known.

24 What I tell you in darkness, preach ye in light; and what ye hear in the ear, preach ye upon the housetops.

25 And fear not them who are able to kill the body, but are not able to kill the soul; but rather fear him who is able to destroy both soul and body in hell.

26 Are not two sparrows sold for a farthing? And one of them shall not fall to the ground without *your* Father knoweth it.

27 And the very hairs of your head are all numbered. Fear ye not, therefore; ye are of more value than many sparrows.

28 Whosoever, therefore, shall confess me before men, him will I confess also before *my* Father who is in heaven.

29 But whosoever shall deny me before men, him will I also deny before *my* Father who is in heaven.

30 Think not that I am come to send peace on earth; I came not to send peace, but a sword.

31 For I am come to set a man at variance against his father, and the daughter against her mother, and the daughter-in-law against her mother-in-law; and a man's foes are they of his own household.

32 He who loveth father and mother more than me, is not worthy of me; and he who loveth son or daughter more than me, is not worthy of me.

33 And he who taketh not his cross and followeth after me, is not worthy of me.

34 He who seeketh to save his life shall lose it; and he who loseth his life for my sake shall find it.

35 He who receiveth you, receiveth me; and he who receiveth me, receiveth him who sent me.

36 He that receiveth a prophet, in the name of a prophet, shall receive a prophet's reward.

37 He that receiveth a righteous man, in the name of a righteous man, shall receive a righteous man's reward.

38 And whosoever shall give to drink unto one of these little ones, a cup of water only in the name of a disciple, verily, I say unto you, he shall in no wise lose his reward.

Death of John the Baptist

ᵃ   Chief of the demons, or Satan

[a]15 And King Herod heard of Jesus; for his name was spread abroad; and he said, That John the Baptist was risen from the dead, and therefore, mighty works do show forth themselves in him.

16 Others said, That it is Elias; and others said, That it is a prophet, or as one of the prophets.

17 But when Herod heard of him, he said, It is John whom I beheaded; he is risen from the dead.

18 For Herod himself had sent forth and laid hold upon John, and bound him in prison for Herodias' sake, his brother Philip's wife; for he had married her.

19 For John had said unto Herod, It is not lawful for thee to have thy brother's wife.

20 Therefore Herodias had a quarrel against him, and would have killed him; but she could not.

21 For Herod feared John, knowing that he was a just man, and a holy man, and one who feared God and observed to worship him; and when he heard him he did many things for him, and heard him gladly.

22 But when Herod's birthday was come, he made a supper for his lords, high captains, and the chief priests of Galilee.

23 And when the [b]daughter of Herodias came in, and danced, and pleased Herod and them that sat with him, the king said unto the damsel, Ask of me whatsoever thou wilt, and I will give it thee.

24 And he swear unto her Whatsoever thou shalt ask of me, I will give it thee, unto the half of my kingdom.

25 And she went forth, and said unto her mother, What shall I ask? And she said, The head of John the Baptist.

26 And she came in straightway with haste unto the king, and asked, saying, I will that thou give me, by and by, in a [c]charger, the head of John the Baptist.

27 And the king was exceeding sorry; but for his oath's sake, and for their sakes which sat with him, he would not reject her.

28 And immediately the king sent an executioner, and commanded his head to be brought; and he went and beheaded him in prison.

29 And brought his head in a charger, and gave it to the damsel; and the damsel gave it to her mother.

30 And when John's disciples heard of it, they came and took up his [d][body] and laid it in a tomb.

Jesus feeds five thousand men besides women and children

---

[a]   Mark 6:15-30
[b]   Dictionary - Salome (2)

[c]   platter for carrying meat
[d]   Matthew 14:11

[a]4 And the Passover, a feast of the Jews, was nigh.

[b]31 Now the apostles gathered themselves together unto Jesus, and told him all things; both what they had done, and what they had taught. [c][And they cast out many devils, and anointed with oil many that were sick, and they were healed.]

32 And he said unto them, Come ye yourselves apart into a solitary place, [d][belonging to the city called Bethsaida] and rest awhile; for there were many coming and going, and they had no leisure, not so much as to eat.

33 And they departed into a solitary place by ship, privately.

34 And the people saw them departing; and many knew Jesus, and ran afoot thither out of the cities, and outran them, and came together unto him.

35 And Jesus when he came out, saw much people, and was moved with compassion towards them, because they were as sheep not having a shepherd; and he began to teach them many things.

36 And when [e][the day began to wear away,] his disciples came unto him and said, This is a solitary place, and now the time for departure is come, send them away, that they may go into the country round about, and into the villages, and buy themselves bread; for they have nothing to eat.

[f]5 When Jesus then lifted up his eyes, and saw a great company come unto him, he saith unto Philip, Whence shall we buy bread, that these may eat?

6 And this he said to prove him; for he himself knew what he would do.

7 Philip answered him, Two hundred pennyworth of bread is not sufficient for them, that every one of them may take a little.

8 One of his disciples, Andrew, Simon Peter's brother, saith unto him,

9 There is a lad here, which hath five barley loaves, and two small fishes; but what are they among so many? [g][and except we should go and buy meat, we can provide no more food for all this multitude.]

[h]41 And he commanded them to make all sit down by companies, upon the green grass.

42 And they sat down in ranks, by hundreds, and by fifties.

43 And when he had taken the five loaves and two fishes, he looked up to heaven, and blessed, and break the loaves, and gave to his disciples to set before the multitude; and the two fishes divided he

---

a   John 6:4
b   Mark 6:31-36
c   Mark 6:14
d   Luke 9:10
e   Luke 9:12

f   John 6:5-9
g   Luke 9:13
h   Mark 6:41-43

among them all.

[a]12 When they had eaten and were satisfied, he said unto his disciples, Gather up the fragments that remain, that nothing be lost.

13 Therefore they gathered them together, and filled twelve baskets with the fragments of the five barley loaves, which remained over and above unto them that had eaten.

[b]46 And they that did eat of the loaves, were about five thousand men.

[c]14 Then those men, when they had seen the miracle that Jesus did, said, This is of a truth that prophet that should come into the world.

15 When Jesus therefore perceived that they would come and take him by force, to make him a king . . .

[d]47 . . . he constrained his disciples to get into the ship, and to go to the other side before him, unto [e][Capernaum] while he sent away the people.

Jesus walks upon the sea

[f]48 And when he had sent them away, he departed into a mountain to pray.

49 And when even was come,

the ship was in the midst of the sea, and he alone on the land, and he saw them toiling in rowing; for the wind was contrary to them.

50 And about the fourth [g]watch of the night he cometh unto them, walking upon the sea, as if he would have passed by them.

51 And when they saw him walking upon the sea, they supposed it had been a [h]spirit, and cried out;

52 For they all saw him, and were troubled.

53 And immediately he talked with them, and said unto them, Be of good cheer; it is I; be not afraid.

[i]24 And Peter answered him and said, Lord, if it be thou, bid me come unto thee on the water. And he said, Come.

25 And When Peter was come down out of the ship, he walked on the water, to go to Jesus. But when he saw the wind boisterous, he was afraid; and, beginning to sink, he cried, saying, Lord, save me.

26 And immediately Jesus stretched forth his hand, and caught him, and said unto him, O thou of little faith, wherefore didst thou doubt?

27 And when they were come into the ship, the wind ceased.

28 Then they that were in the ship, came and worshipped him,

---

a   John 6:12-13
b   Mark 6:46
c   John 6:14-15
d   Mark 6:47
e   John 6:17
f   Mark 6:48-53

g   Dictionary - Watch
h   Dictionary - Spirit
i   Matthew 14:24-28

saying, Of a truth thou art the Son of God.

The bread of life sermon

[a]22 The day following, when the people, which stood on the other side of the sea, saw that there was none other boat there, save that one whereinto his disciples were entered, and that Jesus went not with his disciples into the boat, but that his disciples were gone away alone;

23 Howbeit there came other boats from [b]Tiberias nigh unto the place where they did eat bread, after that the Lord had given thanks;

24 When the people therefore saw that Jesus was not there, neither his disciples, they also took shipping, and came to Capernaum, seeking for Jesus.

25 And when they had found him on the other side of the sea, they said unto him, [c]Rabbi, how camest thou hither?

26 Jesus answered them and said, Verily, verily, I say unto you, Ye seek me, not because ye desire to keep my sayings, neither because ye saw the miracles, but because ye did eat of the loaves and were filled.

27 Labor not for the meat which perishes, but for that meat which endureth unto everlasting life, which the Son of Man hath power to give unto you; for him

hath God *the* Father sealed.

28 Then said they unto him, What shall we do, that we might work the works of God?

29 Jesus answered and said unto them, This is the work of God, that ye believe on him whom he hath sent.

30 They said therefore unto him, What sign showest thou then, that we may see, and believe thee? What dost thou work?

31 Our Fathers did eat manna in the desert; as it is written, He gave them bread from heaven to eat.

32 Then said Jesus unto them, Verily, verily, I say unto you, Moses gave you not that bread from heaven; but *my* Father giveth you the true bread from heaven.

33 For the bread of God is he which cometh down from heaven, and giveth life unto the world.

34 Then said they unto him, Lord, evermore give us this bread.

35 And Jesus said unto them, I am the bread of life; he that cometh to me shall never hunger; and he that believeth on me shall never thirst.

36 But I said unto you, That ye also have seen me, and believe not.

37 All that *the* Father giveth me shall come to me; and him that cometh to me I will in no wise cast out.

38 For I came down from heaven, not to do mine own will, but

---

[a]   John 6:22-71
[b]   Map 1, also Dictionary
[c]   means Master

the will of him that sent me.

39 And this is *the* Father's will which hath sent me, that of all which he hath given me I should lose nothing, but should raise it up again at the last day.

40 And this is the will of him that sent me, that everyone which seeth the Son, and believeth on him, may have everlasting life; and I will raise him up in the resurrection of the just, at the last day.

41 The Jews then murmured at him, because he said, I am the bread which came down from heaven.

42 And they said, Is not this Jesus, the son of Joseph, whose father and mother we know? how is it then that he saith, I came down from heaven?

43 Jesus therefore answered and said unto them, Murmur not among yourselves.

44 No man can come to me, except he doeth the will of *my* Father who hath sent me. And this is the will of him who hath sent me, that ye receive the Son; for *the* Father beareth record of him; and he who receiveth the testimony, and doeth the will of him who sent me, I will raise up in the resurrection of the just.

45 For it is written in the prophets, And these shall all be taught of God. Every man therefore that hath heard, and hath learned of *the* Father, cometh unto me.

46 Not that any man hath seen *the* Father, save he which is of God, he hath seen *the* Father.

47 Verily, verily, I say unto you, He that believeth on me hath everlasting life.

48 I am that bread of life.

49 This is the bread which cometh down from heaven, that a man may eat thereof, and not ᵃdie.

50 Your fathers did eat manna in the wilderness, and are dead.

51 But I am the living bread which came down from heaven; if any man eat of this bread, he shall live forever; and the bread that I will give is my flesh, which I will give for the life of the world.

52 The Jews therefore strove among themselves, saying, How can this man give us his flesh to eat?

53 Then Jesus said unto them, Verily, verily, I say unto you, ᵇExcept ye eat the flesh of the Son of Man, and drink his blood, ye have no life in you.

54 Whoso eateth my flesh, and drinketh my blood, hath eternal life; and I will raise him up in the resurrection of the just; at the last day.

55 For my flesh is meat indeed, and my blood is drink indeed.

56 He that eateth my flesh, and drinketh my blood, dwelleth in me, and I in him.

ᵃ   Dictionary - Spiritual Death
ᵇ   Dictionary - Conundrum

57 As *the* living Father hath sent me, and I live by *the* Father; so he that eateth me, even he shall live by me.

58 This is that bread which came down from heaven; not as your fathers did eat manna, and are dead; he that eateth of this bread shall live for ever.

59 These things said he in the synagogue, as he taught in Capernaum.

60 Many therefore of his disciples, when they had heard this, said, This is an hard saying; who can ªhear it?

61 When Jesus knew in himself that his disciples murmured at it, he said unto them, Doth this offend you?

62 What if ye shall see the Son of Man ascend up where he was before?

63 It is the spirit that quickeneth; the flesh profiteth nothing; the words that I speak unto you, they are spirit, and they are life.

64 But there are some of you that believe not. For Jesus knew from the beginning who they were that believed not, and who should betray him.

65 And he said, therefore said I unto you, that no man can come unto me, except he doeth the will of *my* Father who hath sent me.

66 From that time many of his disciples went back, and walked no more with him.

67 Then said Jesus unto the twelve, Will ye also go away?

68 Then Simon Peter answered him, Lord, to whom shall we go? thou hast the words of eternal life.

69 And we believe and are sure that thou art that Christ, the Son of the living God.

70 Jesus answered them, Have not I chosen you twelve, and one of you is a devil?

71 He spake of Judas Iscariot the son of Simon; for he it was that should betray him, being one of the twelve.

Jesus returns not openly to Jerusalem

ᵇ1 After these things Jesus walked in Galilee; for he would not walk in Jewry, because the Jews sought to kill him.

2 Now the Jews' feast of tabernacles was at hand.

3 ᶜHis brethren therefore said unto him, Depart hence, and go into Judea, that thy disciples there also may see the works that thou doest.

4 For there is no man that doeth anything in secret, and he himself seeketh to be known openly. But if thou do these things, show thyself

---

ª   understand

ᵇ   John 7:1-53
ᶜ   Jesus' half brothers - Mark 6:4

to the world.

5 For neither did his brethren believe in him.

6 Then Jesus said unto them, My time is not yet come; but your time is always ready.

7 The world cannot hate you; but me it hateth, because I testify of it, that the works thereof are evil.

8 Go ye up unto this feast; I go not up yet unto this feast; for my time is not yet full come.

9 When he had said these words unto them, he continued still in Galilee.

10 But after his brethren were gone up, then went he also up unto the feast, not openly, but as it were in secret.

11 Then the Jews sought him at the feast, and said, Where is he?

12 And there was much murmuring among the people concerning him; for some said, He is a good man; others said, Nay; but he deceiveth the people.

13 Howbeit no man spake openly of him for fear of the Jews.

14 Now about the midst of the feast Jesus went up into the temple, and taught.

15 And the Jews marveled, saying, How knoweth this man letters, ªhaving never learned?

16 Jesus answered them, and said, My doctrine is not mine, but his that sent me.

17 If any man will do his will, he shall know of the doctrine, whether it be of God, or whether I speak of myself.

18 He that speaketh of himself seeketh his own glory; but he that seeketh his glory that sent him, the same is true, and no unrighteousness is in him.

19 Did not Moses give you the law, and yet none of you keepeth the law? Why go ye about to kill me?

20 The people answered and said, Thou hast a devil; who goeth about to kill thee?

21 Jesus answered and said unto them, I have done one work, and ye all marvel.

22 Moses therefore gave unto you circumcision; (not because it is of Moses, but of the fathers;) and ye on the Sabbath day circumcise a man.

23 If a man on the sabbath day receive circumcision, that the law of Moses should not be broken; are ye angry at me, because I have made a man every whit whole on the Sabbath day?

24 Judge not according to your traditions, but judge righteous judgment.

25 Then said some of them of Jerusalem, Is not this he, whom they seek to kill?

26 But, lo, he speaketh boldly,

ª Dummelow - no Rabbinical training

and they say nothing unto him. Do the rulers know indeed that this is the very Christ?

27 Howbeit we know this man whence he is; but when Christ cometh, no man knoweth whence he is.

28 Then cried Jesus in the temple as he taught, saying, Ye both know me, and ye know whence I am; and I am not come of myself, but he that sent me is true, whom ye know not.

29 But I know him; for I am from him, and he hath sent me.

30 Then they sought to take him; but no man laid hands on him, because his hour was not yet come.

31 And many of the people believed on him, and said, When Christ cometh, will he do more miracles that these which this man hath done?

32 The Pharisees heard that the people murmured such things concerning him; and the Pharisees and the chief priests sent officers to take him.

33 Then said Jesus unto them, Yet a little while I am with you, and then I go unto him that sent me.

34 Ye shall seek me, and shall not find me; and where I am, thither ye cannot come.

35 Then said the Jews among themselves, Whither will he go, that we shall not find him? will he go unto the dispersed among the Gentiles, and teach the Gentiles?

36 What manner of saying is this that he said, Ye shall seek me, and shall not find me; and where I am thither ye cannot come?

37 In the last day, that great day of the feast, Jesus stood and cried, saying, If any man thirst, let him come unto me, and drink.

38 He that believeth on me, as the Scripture hast said, out of his belly shall flow rivers of living water.

39 (But this spake he of the Spirit, which they that believe on him should receive; for the Holy Ghost was promised unto them who believe, after that Jesus was glorified.)

40 Many of the people therefore, when they heard this saying, said, Of a truth this is the Prophet.

41 Others said, This is the Christ. But some said, Shall Christ come out of Galilee?

42 Hath not the scripture said, That Christ cometh of the seed of David, and out of the town of Bethlehem, where David was?

43 So there was a division among the people because of him.

44 And some of them would have taken him; but no man laid hands on him.

45 Then came the officers to the chief priests and Pharisees; and they said unto them, Why have ye not brought him?

46 The officers answered, Never man spake like this man.

47 Then answered them the Pharisees, Are ye also deceived?

48 Have any of the rulers or of the Pharisees believed on him?

49 But this people who knoweth not the law are cursed.

50 Nicodemus saith unto them, (he that came to Jesus by night being one of them,)

51 Doth our law judge any man, before it hear him, and know what he doeth?

52 They answered and said unto him, Art thou also of Galilee? Search, and look; for out of Galilee ariseth no prophet.

53 And every man went home to his own house.

[a]1 And Jesus went unto the [b]mount of Olives.

Woman taken in adultery

[c]2 Early in the morning he came again into the temple, and all the people came unto him; and he sat down, and taught them.

3 And the scribes and Pharisees brought unto him a woman taken in adultery; and when they had set her in the midst of the people,

4 They say unto him, Master, this woman was taken in adultery, in the very act.

5 Now Moses in the law commanded us, that such should be stoned; but what sayest thou?

6 This they said, tempting him, that they might have to accuse him. But Jesus stooped down, and with his finger wrote on the ground, as though he heard them not.

7 So when they continued asking him, he lifted up himself, and said unto them, He that is without sin among you, let him first cast a stone at her.

8 And again he stooped down, and wrote on the ground.

9 And they which heard it, being convicted by their own conscience, went out one by one, beginning at the eldest, even unto the last; and Jesus was left alone, and the woman standing in the midst [d][of the temple].

10 When Jesus had raised up himself, and saw none of her accusers, and the woman standing, he said unto her, Woman, where are those thine accusers? Hath no man condemned thee?

11 She said, No man, Lord. And Jesus said unto her, Neither do I condemn thee; go, and sin no more. And the woman glorified God from that hour, and believed on his name.

Jesus bears testimony of Himself

a   John 8:1
b   Dictionary - Mount of Olives
c   John 8:2-11
d   JST p. 459

[a]12 Then spake Jesus again unto them, saying, I am the light of the world; he that followeth me shall not walk in darkness, but shall have the light of life.

13 The Pharisees therefore said unto him, Thou bearest record of thyself; thy record is not true.

14 Jesus answered and said unto them, Though I bear record of myself, yet my record is true; for I know whence I came, and whither I go; but ye cannot tell whence I come, and whither I go.

15 Ye judge after the flesh; I judge no man.

16 And yet if I judge, my judgment is true; for I am not alone, but I and *the* Father that sent me.

17 It is also written in your law, that the testimony of two men is true.

18 I am one that bear witness of myself, and *the* Father that sent me beareth witness of me.

19 Then said they unto him, Where is *thy* Father? Jesus answered, Ye neither know me, nor *my* Father; if ye had known me, ye should have known *my* Father also.

20 These words spake Jesus in the treasury, as he taught in the temple; and no man laid hands on him; for his hour was not yet come.

21 Then said Jesus again unto them, I go my way, and ye shall seek me, and shall die in your sins; whither I go, ye cannot come.

22 Then said the Jews, Will he kill himself? Because he saith, Whither I go, ye cannot come.

23 And he said unto them, Ye are from beneath; I am from above; ye are of this world; I am not of this world.

24 I said therefore unto you, that ye shall die in your sins; for if ye believe not that I am he, ye shall die in your sins.

25 Then said they unto him, Who art thou? And Jesus saith unto them, Even the same that I said unto you from the beginning.

26 I have many things to say and to judge of you: but he that sent me is true; and I speak to the world those things which I have heard of him.

27 They understood not that he spake to them of *the* Father.

28 Then said Jesus unto them, When ye have lifted up the Son of Man, than shall ye know that I am he, and that I do nothing of myself; but as *my* Father hath taught me, I speak these things.

29 And he that sent me is with me; *the* Father hath not left me alone; for I do always those things that please him.

30 As he spake these words, many believed on him.

31 Then said Jesus to those Jews which believed on him, If ye continue in my word, then are ye my disciples indeed;

---

[a]   John 8:12-59

32 And ye shall know the truth, and the truth shall make you free.

33 They answered him, We be Abraham's seed, and were never in bondage to any man; how sayest thou, Ye shall be made free?

34 Jesus answered them, Verily, verily, I say unto you, Whosoever committeth sin is the servant of sin.

35 [a]And the servant abideth not in the house for ever, but the Son abideth ever.

36 If the son therefore shall make you free, ye shall be free indeed.

37 I know that ye are Abraham's seed; but ye seek to kill me because my word hath no place in you.

38 I speak that which I have seen with *my* Father; and ye do that which ye have seen with your father.

39 They answered and said unto him, Abraham is our father. Jesus saith unto them, If ye were Abraham's children, ye would do the works of Abraham.

40 But now ye seek to kill me, a man that hath told you the truth, which I have heard of God: this did not Abraham.

41 Ye do the deeds of your father. Then said they to him, We be not born of fornication; we have one Father, even God.

42 Jesus said unto them, If God were *your* Father, ye would love me; for I proceeded forth and came from God; neither came I of myself, but he sent me.

43 Why do ye not understand my speech? even because ye cannot bear my word.

44 Ye are of your father the devil, and the lusts of your father ye will do; he was a murderer from the beginning, and abode not in the truth, because there is no truth in him. When he speaketh a lie, he speaketh of his own; for he is a liar, and the father of it.

45 And because I tell you the truth, ye believe me not.

46 Which of you convinceth me of sin? And if I say the truth, why do ye not believe me?

47 He that is of God receiveth God's words; ye therefore receive them not, because ye are not of God.

48 Then answered the Jews, and said unto him, Say we not well that thou art a Samaritan, and hast a devil?

49 Jesus answered, I have not a devil; but honor *my* Father, and ye do dishonor me.

50 And I seek not mine own glory; there is one that seeketh and judgeth.

51 Verily, verily, I say unto you, If a man keep my saying, [b]he shall

---

[a]   Dictionary - Conundrum

[b]   Dictionary - Conundrum

never see death.

52 Then said the Jews unto him, Now we know that thou hast a devil. Abraham is dead, and the prophets; and thou sayest, If a man keep my saying, he shall never taste of death.

53 Art thou greater than our father Abraham, which is dead? and the prophets are dead; whom makest thou thyself?

54 Jesus answered, if I honor myself, my honor is nothing; it is *my* Father that honoreth me; of whom ye say, he is your God;

55 Yet ye have not known him; but I know him; and if I should say, I know him not, I should be a liar like unto you; but I know him, and keep his saying.

56 Your father Abraham rejoiced to see my day; and he saw it, and was glad.

57 Then said the Jews unto him, Thou art not yet fifty years old, and hast thou seen Abraham?

58 Jesus said unto them, Verily, verily, I say unto you, [a]Before Abraham was, I am.

59 Then took they up stones to cast at him; but Jesus hid himself, and went out of the temple, going through the midst of them, and so passed by.

Pharisees accuse Jesus of breaking the sabbath

[b]1 And it came to pass on the second Sabbath after this, that he went through the cornfield; and his disciples plucked the ears of corn, and did eat, rubbing them in their hands.

2 And certain of the Pharisees said unto them, Why do ye that which is not lawful to do on the Sabbath days?

3 Jesus answering them, said, Have ye not read so much as this, what David did, when he himself was an hungered, and they who were with him;

4 How he went into the house of God, [c][in the days of Abiathar the high priest,] and did take and eat the [d]shewbread, and gave also to them who were with him, which it is not lawful to eat, but for the priests alone?

[e]4 Or have ye not read in the law, how that on the Sabbath day the priests in the temple [f]profane the Sabbath, and ye say they are blameless?

5 But I say unto you, that in this place is one greater than the temple.

[g]26 Wherefore the Sabbath was given unto man for a day of rest; and also that man should glorify

---

[a]   Dictionary - Conundrum

[b]   Luke 6:1-4
[c]   Mark 2:24
[d]   Dictionary - Shewbread
[e]   Matthew 12:4-5
[f]   treat with irreverence
[g]   Mark 2:26

God, and not that man should not eat;

[a]6 But if ye had known what this meaneth, [b]I will have mercy and not sacrifice, ye would not have condemned the guiltless. For the Son of Man is Lord even of the Sabbath.

Jesus restores a man's withered hand on the sabbath

[c]6 And it came to pass also on another Sabbath, that he entered into the synagogue and taught. And there was a man whose right hand was withered;

7 And the scribes and Pharisees watched him, whether he would heal on the Sabbath day; that they might find an accusation against him.

[d]9 And he said unto them, What man shall there be among you that shall have one sheep, and if it fall into a pit on the Sabbath day, will he not lay hold on it, and lift it out?

10 How much then is a man better than a sheep?

[e]8 But he knew their thoughts, and said to the man who had the withered hand, Rise up, and stand forth in the midst. And he arose and stood forth.

9 Then said Jesus unto them, I will ask you one thing; is it lawful on the Sabbath days to do good, or to do evil? To save life, or to destroy? [f][But they held their peace.]

[g]5 And when he had looked round about on them with anger, being grieved for the hardness of their hearts, he said unto the man, Stretch forth thy hand.

6 And he stretched out his hand; and his hand was restored whole as the other.

7 And the Pharisees went forth, and straightway took counsel with the Herodians against him how they might destroy him.

Jesus goes to Gennesaret

[h]56 And when they had passed over, they came into the land of [i]Gennesaret, and drew to the shore.

57 And when they were come out of the ship, straightway the people knew him, and ran through that whole region round about, and began to carry about in beds, those that were sick, where they heard he was.

58 And whithersoever he entered, into villages, or cities, or country, they laid the sick in the streets, and besought him that they might touch if it were but the border of his garments; and as many as touched him were made whole.

---

[a] Matthew 12:6
[b] Dictionary - Conundrum
[c] Luke 6:6-7
[d] Matthew 12:9-10
[e] Luke 6:8-9

[f] Mark 3:4
[g] Mark 3:5-7
[h] Mark 6:56-58
[i] Dictionary - Gennesaret

[a]28 And Jesus departed from thence, and came nigh unto the [b]sea of Galilee; and went up into a mountain, and sat down there.

29 And great multitudes came unto him, having with them some lame, blind, dumb, maimed, and many others, and cast them down at Jesus' feet; and he healed them; insomuch that the multitude wondered, when they saw the dumb to speak, the maimed to be whole, the lame to walk, and the blind to see. And they glorified the God of Israel.

Jesus feeds four thousand men besides women and children

[c]30 Then Jesus called his disciples and said, I have compassion on the multitude, because they continue with me now three days, and have nothing to eat; and I will not send them away fasting, lest they faint in the way; [d][for [e]diverse of them came from far].

31 And his disciples say unto him, Whence should we have so much bread in the wilderness, so as to fill so great a multitude.

32 And Jesus said unto them, How many loaves have ye? And they said, Seven, and a few little fishes.

33 And he commanded the multitude to sit down on the ground.

34 And he took the seven loaves, and the fishes, and gave thanks, and brake the bread, and gave to his disciples, and the disciples, to the multitude.

35 And they did all eat, and were filled. And they took up of the broken meat seven baskets full.

36 And they that did all eat, were four thousand men, besides women and children.

37 And he sent away the multitude, and took ship, and came into the coast of Magdala.

Jesus goes to Magdala

[f]1 And it came to pass afterward, that he went throughout every city and village, preaching and showing the glad tidings of the kingdom of God; and the twelve who were ordained of him, were with him,

2 And certain women who had been healed of evil spirits and infirmities, [g]Mary called Magdalene, out of whom went seven devils;

3 And [h]Joanna the wife of Chuza, Herod's steward, and Susanna, and many others, who ministered unto him with their substance.

---

[a]   Matthew 15:28-29
[b]   Dictionary - Sea of Galilee
[c]   Matthew 15:30-37
[d]   Mark 8:2
[e]   various

[f]   Luke 8:1-3
[g]   Dictionary - Mary (2)
[h]   Dictionary - Joanna

Traditions can defile

[a]1 Then came together unto him, the Pharisees, and certain of the scribes, which came from Jerusalem.

2 And when they saw some of his disciples eat bread with defiled, (that is to say, with unwashen) hands; they found fault.

3 For the Pharisees, and all the Jews, except they wash their hands oft, eat not; holding the traditions of the elders.

4 And when they come from the market, except they wash their bodies, they eat not.

5 And many other things there be, which they have received to hold, as the washing of cups, and pots, brazen vessels, and of tables.

6 And the Pharisees and scribes asked him, Why walk not thy disciples according to the traditions of the elders, but eat bread with unwashen hands?

7 He answered and said unto them, Well hath Isaiah prophesied of you hypocrites, as it is written, [b]This people honoreth me with their lips, but their heart is far from me. Howbeit, in vain do they worship me, teaching the doctrines and commandments of men.

8 For laying aside the commandment of God, ye hold the tradition of men; the washing of pots and of cups; and many other such like things ye do.

9 And he said unto them, Yea, altogether ye reject the commandment of God, that ye may keep your own traditions.

10 Full well it is written of you, by the prophets whom you have rejected.

11 They testified these things of a truth, and their blood shall be upon you.

12 Ye have kept not the ordinances of God; for Moses said, Honor thy father and thy mother; and whoso curseth father or mother, let him die the death of the transgressor, as it is written in your law; but ye keep not the law.

13 Ye say, If a man shall say to his father or mother, [c]Corban, that is to say, a gift, by whatsoever thou mightest be profited by me, he is of age. And ye suffer him no more to do aught for his father or his mother; making the word of God of none effect through your tradition, which ye have delivered; and many such like things do ye.

14 And when he had called all the people, he said unto them, Hearken unto me every one, and understand;

15 There is nothing from without, that entering into a man, can defile him, which is food; but the things which come out of him;

---

[a]   Mark 7:1-16
[b]   Easy Ref. Isaiah 29:26

[c]   Dictionary - Corban

those are they that defile the man, that proceedeth forth out of the heart.

16 If any man have ears to hear, let him hear.

[a]11 Then came his disciples and said unto him, Knowest thou that the Pharisees were offended, after they heard this saying?

12 But he answered and said, Every plant which *my* heavenly Father hath not planted, shall be rooted up.

13 Let them alone; they be blind leaders of the blind; and if the blind lead the blind, both shall fall into the ditch.

14 Then answered Peter and said unto him, Declare unto us this parable.

15 And Jesus said, Are ye also yet without understanding?

16 Do ye not yet understand, that whatsoever entereth in at the mouth goeth into the belly, and is cast into the draught?

17 But those things which proceed out of the mouth, come forth from the heart; and they defile the man.

18 For out of the heart proceed evil thoughts, murders, adulteries, fornications, thefts, false witness, blasphemies;

19 These are the things which defile a man. But to eat with unwashen hands defileth not a man.

Jesus warns the twelve of the leaven of the Pharisees and the Sadducees

[b]9 And straightway he entered into a ship with his disciples, and came into the parts of Dalmanutha.

[c]1 The Pharisees also, with the Sadducees, came, and tempting Jesus, desired him that he would show them a sign from heaven.

[d]11 And he sighed deeply in his spirit, and said, Why doth this generation seek after a sign?

[e]2 And he answered and said unto them, When it is evening ye say, The weather is fair; and in the morning, ye say, The weather is foul today; for the sky is red and lowering.

3 O hypocrites! ye can discern the face of the sky; but ye cannot tell the [f]signs of the times.

4 A wicked and adulterous generation seeketh after a sign; and there shall no sign be given unto it, but the [g]sign of the prophet Jonas.

[h]13 And he left them, and entering into the ship again, departed to the other side.

[i]6 And when his disciples were come to the other side, they had

---

[a]   Matthew 15:11-19

[b]   Mark 8:9
[c]   Matthew 16:1
[d]   Mark 8:11
[e]   Matthew 16:2-4
[f]   Dictionary - Signs of the times
[g]   Easy Ref. Jonah 1:17
[h]   Mark 8:13
[i]   Matthew 16:6-13

forgotten to take bread.

7 Then Jesus said unto them, Take heed and beware of the leaven of the Pharisees and of the Sadducees.

8 And they reasoned among themselves, saying, He said this because we have taken no bread.

9 And when they reasoned among themselves, Jesus perceived it; and he said unto them, O ye of little faith! why reason ye among yourselves, because ye have brought no bread?

10 Do ye not understand, neither remember the five loaves of the five thousand, and how many baskets ye took up?

11 Neither the seven loaves of the four thousand, and how many baskets ye took up?

12 How is it that ye do not understand, that I spoke not unto you concerning bread, that ye should beware of the leaven of the Parisees and of the Sadducees?

13 Then understood they, how that he bade them not beware of the leaven of bread, but of the doctrine of the Pharisees and of Sadducees.

Jesus heals a blind man in stages

[a]23 And he cometh to Bethsaida; and they bring a blind man unto him, and besought him

to touch him.

24 And he took the blind man by the hand, and led him out of the town; and when he had spit upon his eyes, and put his hands upon him, he asked if he saw aught?

25 And he looked up and said, I see men as trees walking.

26 After that he put his hands again upon his eyes, and made him look up, and he was restored and saw every man clearly.

27 And he sent him away to his house, saying, Neither go into the town, nor tell what is done, to any in the town.

Jesus heals a Canaanite woman's daughter

[b]20 Then Jesus went thence, and departed into the coasts of Tyre and Sidon.

21 And, behold, a woman of [c]Canaan [d][a Syrophenecian by Nation;] came out of the same coasts, and cried unto him, saying, Have mercy on me, O Lord, thou Son of David; my daughter is grievously vexed with a devil.

22 But he answered her not a word. And his disciples came and besought him, saying, Send her away; for she crieth after us.

23 He answered, I am not sent but unto the lost sheep of the house of Israel.

_____

[b] Matthew 15:20-24
[c] Dictionary - Canaanite
[d] Mark 7:25

_____

[a] Mark 8:23-27

24 Then came she and wor-shipped him, saying, Lord, help me.

[a]26 But Jesus said unto her, Let the children of the kingdom first be filled; for it is not meet to take the children's bread, and to cast it unto the dogs.

[b]26 And she said, Truth, Lord; yet the dogs eat the crumbs that fall from the master's table.

27 Then Jesus answered and said unto her, O woman, great is thy faith; be it unto thee even as thou wilt. And her daughter was made whole from that very hour.

Peter bears testimony of Jesus as the Christ

[c]18 And it came to pass, as he went alone with his disciples to pray . . .

[d]14 And when Jesus came into the coasts of [e]Caesarea Philippi, he asked his disciples, saying, Whom do men say that I, the Son of Man, am?

15 And they said, Some say John the Baptist; some Elias; and others Jeremias; or one of the prophets.

16 He said unto them, But whom say ye that I am?

17 And Simon Peter answered and said, Thou art the Christ, the Son of the living God.

18 And Jesus answered and said unto him, Blessed art thou, Simon [f]Barjona; for flesh and blood hath not revealed this unto thee, but *my* Father who is in heaven.

19 And I say unto thee, That thou art Peter; and upon this [g]rock I will build my church, and the gates of hell shall not prevail against it.

20 And I will give unto thee the keys of the kingdom of heaven; and whatsoever thou shalt bind on earth, shall be bound in heaven; and whatsoever thou shalt loose on earth, shall be loosed in heaven.

21 Then charged he his disciples that they should tell no man that he was Jesus, the Christ.

Jesus foretells His crucifixion

[h]22 From that time forth began Jesus to show unto his disciples, how that he must go to Jerusalem, and suffer many things of the el-ders, and chief priests, and Scribes, and be killed, and be raised again the third day.

23 Then Peter took him, and began to rebuke him, saying, Be it far from thee, Lord; this shall not be done unto thee.

24 But he turned and said unto Peter, Get thee behind me, Satan; thou art an offence unto me; for

---

[a]   Mark 7:26
[b]   Matthew 15:26-27
[c]   Luke 9:18
[d]   Matthew 16:14-21
[e]   see Map 1

[f]   son of Jona
[g]   revelation from God
[h]   Matthew 16:22-26

thou savorest not the things which be of God, but those that be of men.

25 Then said Jesus unto his disciples, If any man will come after me, let him deny himself, and take up his cross and follow me.

26 And now for a man to take up his cross, is to deny himself all ungodliness, and every worldly lust, and keep my commandments.

[a]37 For whosoever will save his life, shall lose it; or whosoever will save his life, shall be willing to lay it down for my sake; and if he is not willing to lay it down for my sake, he shall lose it.

[b]28 And whosoever will lose his life in this world, for my sake [c][and the gospel's,] shall find it in the world to come.

29 Therefore, forsake the world, and save your souls; for what is a man profited, if he shall gain the whole world, and lose his own soul? Or what shall a man give in exchange for his soul?

[d]40 Therefore deny yourselves of these, and be not ashamed of me.

41 Whosoever shall be ashamed of me, and of my words, in this adulterous and sinful generation, of him also shall the Son of Man be ashamed, when he cometh in the glory of *his* Father with the holy angels; [e][and then shall reward every man according to his works.]

42 And they shall not have part in that resurrection when he cometh.

43 For verily I say unto you, That he shall come; and he that layeth down his life for my sake and the gospel's, shall come with him, and shall be clothed with his glory in the cloud, on the right hand of the Son of Man.

44 And he said unto them again, Verily I say unto you, That there be some of them that stand here, which shall not taste of death, till they have seen the kingdom of God come with power.

Mount of Transfiguration

[f]1 And after six days, Jesus taketh Peter, James, and John his brother, and bringeth them up into a high [g]mountain, apart, and was [h]transfigured before them; and his face did shine as the sun, and his raiment was white as the light.

2 And, behold, there appeared unto them Moses and [i]Elias, talking with him.

[j]31 Who appeared in glory, and

---

a   Mark 8:37
b   Matthew 16:28-29
c   Mark 8:38
d   Mark 8:40-44

e   Matthew 16:30
f   Matthew 17:1-2
g   Dictionary - Mount of Transfiguration
h   change in appearance, exalted, glorified
i   John the Baptist - Matt. 17:14
j   Luke 9:31-32

spake of this death, and also his resurrection, which he should accomplish at Jerusalem.

32 And Peter and they who were with him were heavy with sleep; and when they were awake they saw his glory, and the two men who stood with him.

^a3 Then answered Peter, and said unto Jesus, Lord, it is good for us to be here; if thou wilt, let us make here three ^btabernacles; one for thee, one for Moses, and one for Elias.

4 While he yet spake, behold, a light cloud overshadowed them; and behold, a voice out of the cloud, which said, This is my beloved Son, in whom I am well pleased; hear ye him.

5 And when the disciples heard the voice, they ^cfell on their faces, and were sore afraid.

6 And Jesus came and touched them, and said, Arise; be not afraid.

7 And when they lifted up their eyes, they saw no man, save Jesus only.

8 And as they came down from the mountain, Jesus charged them, saying, Tell the vision to no man, until the Son of Man be risen again from the dead.

^d8 And they kept that saying with themselves, questioning one with another what the rising of the dead should mean.

^e9 And his disciples asked him saying, Why then say the scribes that Elias must first come?

10 And Jesus answered and said unto them, Elias truly shall first come, and restore all things, as the prophets have written.

11 And again I say unto you that Elias has come already, concerning whom it is written, Behold, I will send you my messenger, and he shall prepare the way before me; and they knew him not, and have done unto him, whatsoever they listed.

12 Likewise shall the Son of Man suffer of them.

13 But I say unto you, Who is Elias? Behold, this is Elias, whom I sent to prepare the way before me.

14 Then the disciples understood that he spake unto them of John the Baptist, and also another who should come and restore all things, as it is written by the prophets.

Jesus casts out a devil from a boy

^f12 And when he came to the disciples, he saw a great multitude about them, and the scribes questioning with them.

13 And straightway all the people, when they beheld him, were

---

^a   Matthew 17:3-8
^b   Dictionary - Tabernacle
^c   kneeled down with their faces to the ground
^d   Mark 9:8

^e   Matthew 17:9-14
^f   Mark 9:12-25

greatly amazed, and running to him, saluted him.

14 And Jesus asked the scribes, What questioned ye with them?

15 And one of the multitude answered, and said, Master, I have brought unto thee my son, ᵃ[for he is mine only child] who hath a dumb spirit that is a devil; and when he seizeth him, he teareth him; and he foameth and gnasheth with his teeth, and pineth away; and I spake to thy disciples that they might cast him out, and they could not.

16 Jesus spake unto him and said, O faithless generation! How long shall I be with you? How long shall I suffer you? Bring him unto me. And they brought him unto Jesus.

17 And when the man saw him, immediately he was torn by the spirit; and he fell on the ground and wallowed, foaming.

18 And Jesus asked his father, How long a time is it since this came unto him? and his father said, When a child;

19 And ᵇofttimes it hath cast him into the fire and into the water, to destroy him, but if thou canst, I ask thee to have compassion on us, and help us.

20 Jesus said unto him, If thou wilt believe all things I shall say unto you, this is possible to him that believeth.

21 And immediately the father of the child cried out, and said, with tears, Lord, I believe; help thou mine unbelief.

22 When Jesus saw that the people came running together, he rebuked the foul spirit, saying unto him, I charge thee to come out of him, and enter no more into him.

23 Now the dumb and deaf spirit cried, and rent him sore, and came out of him; and he was as one dead, insomuch that many said, He is dead.

24 But Jesus took him by the hand, and lifted him up; and he arose.

25 When Jesus came into the house, his disciples asked him privately, Why could not we cast him out?

ᶜ20 And Jesus said unto them, Because of your unbelief; for, verily, I say unto you, If ye have faith as a grain of mustard seed, ye shall say unto this mountain, Remove to yonder place, and it shall remove; and nothing shall be impossible unto you.

21 Howbeit, this kind goeth not out but by prayer and fasting.

Jesus heals a deaf and dumb man

ᵈ30 And again, departing from

ᵃ Luke 9:38
ᵇ often times

ᶜ Matthew 17:20-21
ᵈ Mark 7:30-36

the coasts of Tyre and Sidon, he came unto the sea of Galilee, through the midst of the coasts of Decapolis.

31 And they brought unto him one that was deaf, and had an impediment in his speech; and they besought him to put his hand upon him.

32 And he took him aside from the multitude, and put his fingers into his ears, and he spit, and touched his tongue;

33 And looking up to heaven, he sighed, and said unto him, Ephphatha, that is, Be opened.

34 And straightway his ears were opened, and the string of his tongue was loosed; and he spake plain.

35 And he charged them that they should tell no man; but the more he charged them, so much the more a great deal they published him;

36 And were beyond measure astonished, saying, He hath done all things well; he maketh both the deaf to hear, and the dumb to speak.

Who is greatest among them

[a]30 And he came to Capernaum; and being in the house, he asked them, Why was it that ye disputed among yourselves by the way?

31 But they held their peace, being afraid, for by the way they had disputed among themselves, who was the greatest among them.

32 Now Jesus sat down and called the twelve, and said unto them, If any man desire to be first, he shall be last of all, and servant of all.

33 And he took a child, and sat in the midst of them; and when he had taken the child in his arms, he said unto them, [b][Verily, I say unto you, Except ye be converted, and become as little children, ye shall not enter into the kingdom of heaven.]

34 Whosoever shall humble himself like one of these children, and receiveth me, ye shall receive in my name.

35 And whosoever shall receive me, receiveth not me only, but him that sent me, even *the* Father.

36 And John spake unto him, saying, Master, we saw one casting out devils in thy name, and he followed not us; and we forbade him, because he followed not us.

37 But Jesus said, Forbid him not; for there is no man which shall do a miracle in my name, that can speak evil of me. For he that is not against us is on our part.

38 And whosoever shall give you a cup of water to drink, in my name, because ye belong to Christ, verily I say unto you, He shall not lose his reward.

---

a   Mark 9:30-39

b   Matthew 18:2

39 And whosoever shall offend one of these little ones that believe in me, it were better for him that a millstone were hanged about his neck, and he were cast into the sea.

[a]10 Take heed that ye despise not one of these little ones; for I say unto you, that in heaven their angels do always behold the face of *my* Father who is in heaven.

11 For the Son of Man is come to save that which is lost, and to call sinners to repentance; but these little ones have no need of repentance, and I will save them.

Parable of the lost sheep

[b]12 How think ye? If a man have an hundred sheep, and one of them be gone astray, doth he not leave the ninety and nine, [c][and goeth into the wilderness after that which is lost, until he find it?]

[d]5 And when he hath found it, he layeth it on his shoulders, rejoicing.

6 And when he cometh home, he calleth together his friends and neighbors, and saith unto them, Rejoice with me; for I have found my sheep which was lost.

[e]13 And if it so be that he find it, verily, I say unto you, he rejoiceth more over that which was lost, than over the ninety and nine which went not astray.

14 Even so, it is not the will of *your* Father which is in heaven, that one of these little ones should perish.

Parable of the lost coin

[f]8 Either, what woman having ten pieces of silver, if she lose one piece, doth not light a candle, and sweep the house, and seek diligently till she find it?

9 And when she hath found it, she calleth her friends and her neighbors together, saying, Rejoice with me; for I have found the piece which I had lost.

10 Likewise I say unto you, there is joy in the presence of the angels of God over one sinner who repenteth.

Parable of the prodigal son

[g]11 And he said, A certain man had two sons;

12 And the younger of them said to his father, Father, give me the portion of goods which falleth to me. And he divided unto them his living.

13 And not many days after, the younger son gathered all together, and took his journey into a far country, and there wasted his substance with riotous living.

---

[a] Matthew 18:10-11
[b] Matthew 18:12
[c] Luke 15:4
[d] Luke 15:5-6
[e] Matthew 18:13-14

[f] Luke 15:8-10
[g] Luke 15:11-32

14 And when he had spent all, there arose a mighty famine in that land; and he began to be in want.

15 And he went and joined himself with a citizen of the country; and he sent him into his fields to feed swine.

16 And he would ªfain have filled his belly with the husks which the swine did eat; and no man gave unto him.

17 And when he came to himself he said, How many hired servants of my father's have bread enough and to spare, and I perish with hunger!

18 I will rise and go to my father, and will say unto him, Father, I have sinned against heaven, and before thee;

19 And am no more worthy to be called thy son; make me as one of thy hired servants.

20 And he arose and came to his father. But when he was yet a great way off, his father saw him, and had compassion, and ran, and ᵇfell on his neck, and kissed him.

21 And the son said unto him, Father, I have sinned against heaven, and in thy sight, and am no more worthy to be called thy son.

22 But the father said unto his servants, Bring forth the best robe, and put it on him; and put a ring on his finger, and shoes on his feet;

23 And bring hither the fatted calf, and kill it; and let us eat and be merry;

24 For this my son was dead, and is alive again; he was lost, and is found. And they began to be merry.

25 Now his elder son was in the field; and as he came, and drew nigh to the house, he heard music and dancing.

26 And he called one of the servants, and asked what these things meant?

27 And he said unto him, Thy brother is come; and thy father hath killed the fatted calf, because he hath received him safe and sound.

28 And he was angry, and would not go in: therefore came his father out and ᶜentreated him.

29 And he answering, said to his father, Lo these many years do I serve thee, neither transgressed I at any time thy commandment; and thou never gavest me a kid, that I might make merry with my friends;

30 But as soon as this thy son was come, who hath devoured thy living with harlots, thou hast killed for him the fatted calf.

31 And he said unto him, Son, thou art ever with me; and all that I have is thine.

ª willingly
ᵇ embraced

ᶜ entreat - deal or plead with

32 It was ᵃmeet that we should make merry, and be glad; for this thy brother was dead, and is alive again; was lost, and is found.

How oft shall I forgive my brother?

ᵇ15 Moreover, if thy brother shall trespass against thee, go and tell him his fault between thee and him alone; ᶜ[rebuke him; and if he repent, forgive him,] thou hast gained thy brother.

16 But if he will not hear thee, then take with thee one or two more, that in the mouth of two or three witnesses every word may be established.

17 And if he neglect to hear them, tell it unto the church; but if he neglect to hear the Church, let him be unto you as a heathen man and a publican.

18 Verily, I say unto you, Whatsoever ye shall bind on earth, shall be bound in heaven; and whatsoever ye shall loose on earth, shall be loosed in heaven.

19 Again, I say unto you, that if two of you shall agree on earth as touching anything that they shall ask, that they may not ask amiss, it shall be done for them of *my* Father who is in heaven.

20 For where two or three are gathered together in my name,

there am I in the midst of them.

21 Then came Peter to him and said, Lord, how oft shall my brother sin against me, and I forgive him? Till seven times?

22 Jesus saith unto him, I say not unto thee, until seven times; but, until seventy times seven.

ᵈ4 And if he trespass against you seven times in a day, and seven times in a day turn to you again, saying, I repent; you shall forgive him.

Parable of the unmerciful servant

ᵉ23 Therefore is the kingdom of heaven likened unto a certain king, who would take account of his servants.

24 And when he had begun to reckon, one was brought unto him who owed ten thousand ᶠtalents.

25 But forasmuch as he had not to pay, his lord commanded him to be sold, and his wife, and his children, and all that he had, and payment to be made.

26 And the servant besought him, saying, Lord, have patience with me, and I will pay thee all.

27 Then the lord of that servant was moved with compassion, and loosed him, and forgave him the debt. The servant, therefore, fell

---

ᵃ important to settle the matter
ᵇ Matthew 18:15-22
ᶜ Luke 17:3
ᵈ Luke 17:4
ᵉ Matthew 18:23-34
ᶠ Roman coin worth a large sum of money

down and worshiped him.

28 But the same servant went out, and found one of his fellow servants, which owed him a hundred ᵃpence; and he laid hands on him, and took him by the throat, saying, Pay me that thou owest.

29 And his fellow servant fell down at his feet, and besought him, saying, Have patience with me, and I will pay thee all.

30 And he would not; but went and cast him into prison, till he should pay the debt.

31 So when his fellow servants saw what was done, they were very sorry, and came and told unto their lord all that was done.

32 Then his lord, after that he had called him, said unto him, O thou wicked servant! I forgave thee all the debt; because thou desiredst me; shouldest not thou also have had compassion on thy fellow servant, even as I had pity on thee?

33 And his lord was wroth, and delivered him to the tormentors, till he should pay all that was due unto him.

34 So likewise shall *my* heavenly Father do also unto you, if ye from your hearts forgive not every one his brother their trespasses.

The coin in the fish's mouth

ᵇ23 And when they were come to Capernaum, they that received tribute came to Peter, and said, Doth not your master pay tribute? He said, Yea.

24 And when he was come into the house, Jesus rebuked him, saying,

25 What thinkest thou, Simon? Of whom do the kings of the earth take custom, or tribute? Of their own children, or of strangers?

26 Peter said unto him, Of strangers. Jesus said unto him, Then are the children free. Notwithstanding, lest we should offend them, go thou to the sea, and cast a hook, and take up the fish, that first cometh up; and when thou hast opened his mouth, thou shalt find a piece of money; that take and give unto them for me and thee.

Jesus calls Chorazin, Bethsaida, and Capernaum to repentance

ᶜ22 Then began he to upbraid the cities wherein most of his mighty works were done, because they repented not:

23 Woe unto thee, ᵈChorazin! Woe unto thee, Bethsaida! For if the mighty works which were done in you, had been done in Tyre and Sidon, they would have repented long since in ᵉsackcloth and ashes.

24 But I say unto you, It shall

ᵃ   small sum of money
ᵇ   Matthew 17:23-26

ᶜ   Matthew 11:22-30
ᵈ   see Map 1
ᵉ   Dictionary - Sackcloth

be more tolerable for Tyre and Sidon at the day of judgment, than for you.

25 And thou, Capernaum, which art exalted unto heaven, shalt be brought down to hell; for if the mighty works, which have been done in thee, had been done in ªSodom, it would have remained until this day.

26 But I say unto you, It shall be more tolerable for the land of Sodom in the day of judgment, than for thee.

27 And at that time, there came a voice out of heaven, and Jesus answered and said, I thank thee, O Father, Lord of heaven and earth, because thou hast hid these things from the wise and prudent, and hast revealed them unto babes. Even so, Father, for so it seemed good in thy sight!

28 All things are delivered unto me of *my* Father; and no man knoweth the Son, but *the* Father; neither knoweth any man *the* Father, save the Son, ᵇand they to whom the Son will reveal himself; they shall see *the* Father also.

29 Then spake Jesus, saying, Come unto me, all ye that labor and are heavy laden, and I will give you rest.

30 Take my yoke upon you, and learn of me; for I am meek and lowly in heart; and ye shall find rest unto your souls; for my yoke is easy and my burden is light.

The Lord appoints other seventy

ᶜ1 After these things the Lord appointed other ᵈseventy also, and sent them two and two before his face, into every city and place where he himself would come.

2 And he said unto them, The harvest truly is great, but the laborers few; pray ye therefore the Lord of the harvest, that he would send forth laborers into his harvest.

3 Go your ways: behold I send you forth as lambs among wolves.

4 Carry neither purse, nor scrip, nor shoes; nor salute any man by the way.

5 And into whatsoever house ye enter, first say, Peace to this house.

6 And if the son of peace be there, your peace shall rest upon it; if not, it shall turn to you again.

7 And into whatsoever house they receive you, remain, eating and drinking such things as they give; for the laborer is worthy of his hire. Go not from house to house.

8 And into whatsoever city ye enter, and they receive you, eat such things as are set before you;

9 And heal the sick that are

ª Easy Ref. - Genesis 13:8
ᵇ Dictionary - Conundrum

ᶜ Luke 10:1-12
ᵈ Dictionary - Seventy

there in, and say, The kingdom of God is come nigh unto you.

10 But into whatsoever city ye enter, and they receive you not, go your ways out into the streets of the same, and say,

11 Even the very dust of your city which cleaveth on us, we do wipe off against you; notwithstanding, be sure of this, that the kingdom of God is nigh unto you.

12 But I say unto you, that it shall be more tolerable in the day of judgment for Sodom, than for that city.

Parable if thy eye offend thee

[a]6 Woe unto the world because of offences! For it must needs be that offences come; but woe unto that man by whom the offence cometh!

[b]40 Therefore, if thy hand offend thee, cut it off; or if thy brother offend thee and confess not and forsake not, he shall be cut off. For it is better for thee to enter into life maimed, than having two hands, to go into hell.

41 For it is better for thee to enter into life without thy brother, than for thee and thy brother to be cast into hell; into the fire that never shall be quenched, where their worm dieth not, and the fire is not quenched.

42 And again, if thy foot offend thee, cut it off; for he that is thy standard, by whom thou walkest, if he become a transgressor, he shall be cut off.

43 It is better for thee, to enter halt into life, than having two feet to be cast into hell; into the fire that never shall be quenched.

44 Therefore, let every man stand or fall, by himself, and not for another; or not trusting in another.

45 [c]Seek unto *my* Father, and it shall be done in that very moment what ye shall ask, if ye ask in faith, believing that ye shall receive.

46 And if thine eye which seeth for thee, him that is appointed to watch over thee to show thee light, become a transgressor and offend thee, pluck him out.

47 It is better for thee to enter into the kingdom of God, with one eye, than having two eyes to be cast into hell fire.

48 For it is better that thyself should be saved, than to be cast into hell with thy brother, where their worm dieth not, and where the fire is not quenched.

49 For everyone shall be [d]salted with fire; and every sacrifice shall be salted with salt; but the salt

---

[a]   Matthew 18:6
[b]   Mark 9:40-50

[c]   pray
[d]   Dictionary - Sanctify

must be good.

50 For if the salt have lost his saltiness, wherewith will ye season it? (the sacrifice;) therefore it must needs be that ye have salt in yourselves, and have peace one with another.

Jesus goes to Judea, heals ten lepers

[a]11 And it came to pass, as he went to Jerusalem, that he passed through the midst of Galilee and Samaria.

12 And as he entered into a certain village, there met him ten men who were lepers, who stood afar off;

13 And they lifted up their voices, and said, Jesus, Master, have mercy on us.

14 And he said unto them, Go show yourselves to the priests. And it came to pass, as they went, they were cleansed.

15 One of them, when he saw he was healed, turned back, and with a loud voice glorified God,

16 And fell down on his face at Jesus' feet, giving him thanks; and he was a Samaritan.

17 And Jesus answering, said, Were there not ten cleansed? But where are the nine?

18 There are not found that returned to give glory to God, save this [b]stranger.

19 And he said unto him, Arise, go thy way; thy faith hath made thee whole.

Pharisees ask when the kingdom of God should come?

[c]20 And when he was demanded of the Pharisees, when the kingdom of God should come, he answered them, and said, The kingdom of God cometh not with observation;

21 Neither shall they say, Lo, here! or, Lo, there! For, behold, the kingdom of God has already come unto you.

22 And he said unto his disciples, The days will come, when they will desire to see one of the days of the Son of Man, and they shall not see it.

23 And if they shall say to you, See here! or, See there! Go not after them, nor follow them.

24 For as the light of the morning, that shineth out of the one part of heaven, and lighteneth to the other part under heaven; so shall also the Son of Man be in his day.

25 But first he must suffer many things, and be rejected of this generation.

Parable of the widow and the judge

---

[a] Luke 17:11-19
[b] Dictionary - Stranger

[c] Luke 17:20-25

[a]1 And he spake unto them, saying, that men ought always to pray and not faint.

2 Saying, There was in a city a judge, who feared not God, nor regarded man.

3 And there was a widow in that city; and she came unto him, saying, Avenge me of mine adversary.

4 And he would not for a while; but afterward, he said within himself, Though I fear not God, nor regard man;

5 Yet because this widow troubleth me, I will avenge her; lest by her continual coming she weary me.

6 And the Lord said, Hear what the unjust judge saith.

7 And shall not God avenge his own elect, who cry day and night unto him, though he bear long with men?

8 I tell you that he will come, and when he does come, he will avenge his [b]saints speedily. Nevertheless, when the Son of Man cometh, shall he find faith on the earth?

Parable of the Pharisee and the Publican who prayed

[c]9 He spake this parable unto certain men, who trusted in themselves that they were righteous, and despised others.

10 Two men went up into the temple to pray; the one a Pharisee, and the other a publican.

11 The Pharisee stood and prayed thus with himself; God, I thank thee, that I am not as other men, extortioners, unjust, adulterers; or even as this publican.

12 I fast twice in the week; I give tithes of all that I possess.

13 But the publican, standing afar off, would not lift up so much as his eyes unto heaven, but smote upon his breast, saying, God, be merciful to me a sinner.

14 I tell you, this man went down to his house justified, rather than the other; for everyone who exalteth himself, shall be abased; and he who humbleth himself, shall be exalted.

Jesus rejected by the Samaritans

[d]51 And it came to pass, when the time was come that he should be received up, he steadfastly set his face to go to Jerusalem;

52 And sent [e]messengers before his face; and they went and entered into a village of the Samaritans to make ready for him.

53 And the Samaritans would not receive him, because his face was turned as though he would go to Jerusalem.

---

a   Luke 18:1-8
b   Dictionary - Saint
c   Luke 18:9-14
d   Luke 9: 51-56
e   Seventy

54 And when his disciples, James and John, saw that they would not receive him, they said, Lord, wilt thou that we command fire to come down from heaven and consume them, [a]even as Elias did?

55 But he turned and rebuked them, and said, Ye know not what manner of spirit ye are of.

56 For the Son of man is not come to destroy men's lives, but to save them. And they went to another village.

No man looking back is fit for the kingdom of God

[b]57 And it came to pass, as they went in the way, a certain [c][scribe] said unto him, Lord, I will follow thee whithersoever thou goest,

58 And Jesus said unto him, Foxes have holes, and birds of the air have nests; but the Son of Man hath not where to lay his head.

59 And he said unto another, Follow me. But he said, Lord, suffer me first to go and bury my father.

60 Jesus said unto him, Let the dead bury their dead; but go thou and preach the kingdom of God.

61 And another also said, Lord, I will follow thee; but let me first go and bid them farewell who are at my house.

62 And Jesus said unto him, No man having put his hand to the plough, and looking back, is fit for the kingdom of God.

Pharisees ask Jesus why Moses permitted divorce

[d]1 And he arose from thence and cometh into the coasts of Judea by the farther side of Jordan; and the people resort unto him again; and as he was accustomed to teach, he also taught them again.

2 And the Pharisees came to him and asked him, Is it lawful for a man to put away his wife [e][for every cause]? This they said, thinking to tempt him.

3 And he answered and said unto them, What did Moses command you?

4 And they said, Moses suffered to write a bill of divorcement, and to put her away.

5 Jesus answered and said unto them, For the hardness of your hearts he wrote you this precept; [f][but from the beginning it was not so.]

6 But from the beginning of the creation, God made them male and female.

7 For this cause shall a man leave his father, and mother, and cleave to his wife; and they two shall be one flesh; so then they are

---

a   Easy Ref. 2 Kings 1:10
b   Luke 9:57-62
c   Matthew 8:19

d   Mark 10:1-7
e   Matthew 19:2
f   Matthew 19:8

no more two, but one flesh; what therefore God hath joined together, let not man put asunder.

Jesus explains the higher law and divorce to the twelve

[a]8 And in the house his disciples asked him again of the same matter.

9 And he said unto them, Whosoever shall put away his wife, [b][except for fornication,] and marry another, committeth adultery against her.

10 And if a woman shall put away her husband, and be married to another, she committeth adultery.

[c]10 His disciples say unto him, If the case of the man be so with a wife, it is not good to marry.

11 But he said unto them, All cannot receive this saying; it is not for them save to whom it is given.

12 For there are some [d]eunuchs, which were so born from their mother's womb; and there are some eunuchs which were made eunuchs of men; and there be eunuchs, which have made themselves eunuchs for the kingdom of heaven's sake. He that is able to receive, let him receive my sayings.

Suffer the little children to come unto Me

[e]11 And they brought young children to him, that he should touch them; and the disciples rebuked those that brought them, [f][saying, There is no need, for Jesus hath said, Such shall be saved.]

12 But when Jesus saw and heard them, he was much displeased, and said unto them, Suffer the little children to come unto me, and forbid them not; for of such is the kingdom of God.

13 Verily I say unto you, Whosoever shall not receive the kingdom of God as a little child, he shall not enter therein.

14 And he took them up in his arms, put his hands upon them, and blessed them.

A rich man told to sell his possessions and give to the poor

[g]15 And when he was gone forth into the way, there came one running, and kneeled to him, and asked him, Good Master, what shall I do that I may inherit eternal life?

16 And Jesus said unto him, why callest thou me good? None is good but one, that is God; [h][but if

---

[a] Mark 10:8-10
[b] Matthew 19:9
[c] Matthew 19:10-12
[d] Dictionary - Eunuch

[e] Mark 10:11-14
[f] Matthew 19:13
[g] Mark 10:15-16
[h] Matthew 19:17

thou wilt enter into life, keep the commandments.]

ª18 He said unto him, Which? Jesus said, Thou shalt not kill. Thou shalt not commit adultery. Thou shalt not steal. Thou shalt not bear false witness.

19 Honor thy father and mother. And, Thou shalt love thy neighbor as thyself.

20 The young man saith unto him, All these things have I kept from my youth up; what lack I yet?

ᵇ19 Then Jesus beholding him, loved him, and said unto him, One thing thou lackest;

ᶜ21 . . . If thou wilt be perfect, go, sell that thou hast, and give to the poor, and thou shalt have treasure in heaven, and come ᵈ[take up the cross,] and follow me.

ᵉ21 And the man was sad at that saying, and went away grieved; for he had great possessions.

22 And Jesus looked round about, and said unto his disciples, How hardly shall they that have riches enter into the kingdom of *my* Father!

23 And the disciples were astonished at his words. But Jesus spake again and said unto them, Children, how hard is it for them who trust in riches to enter into the kingdom of God!

24 It is easier for a camel to go through the eye of a ᶠneedle, than for a rich man to enter into the kingdom of God.

25 And they were astonished out of measure, saying among themselves, Who then can be saved?

26 And Jesus, looking upon them, said, With men that trust in riches, it is impossible; but not impossible with men who trust in God and leave all for my sake, for with such, all things are possible.

Peter says they have left all

ᵍ27 Then Peter began to say unto him, Lo, we have left all, and have followed thee.

28 And Jesus answered and said, Verily I say unto you, There is no man that hath left house, or brethren, or sisters, or father, or mother, or wife, or children, or lands, for my sake and the gospel's,

29 But he shall receive an hundred fold now in this time, houses, and brethren, and sisters, and mothers, and children, and lands, with persecutions; and in the world to come eternal life.

ʰ28 And Jesus said unto them, Verily I say unto you, that ye who have followed me, shall, in the res-

---

ª Matthew 19:18-20
ᵇ Mark 10:19
ᶜ Matthew 19:21
ᵈ Mark 10:20
ᵉ Mark 10:21-26
ᶠ Smith's - narrow door, gateway.
ᵍ Mark 10:27-29
ʰ Matthew 19:28

urrection, when the Son of Man shall come sitting on the throne of his glory, ye shall also sit upon twelve thrones, judging the twelve tribes of Israel.

[a]30 But there are many who make themselves first, that shall be last; and the last first.

31 This he said, rebuking Peter; and they were in the way going up to Jerusalem; and Jesus went before, and they were amazed; and as they followed, they were afraid.

Parable of the laborers in the vineyard

[b]1 For the kingdom of heaven is like unto a man, an householder, who went out early in the morning to hire laborers into his vineyard.

2 And when he had agreed with the laborers for a [c]penny a day, he sent them into his vineyard.

3 And he went out about the third hour, and found others standing idle in the market place,

4 And he said unto them, Go ye also into the vineyard, and whatsoever is right, I will give you, and they went their way.

5 And again he went out about the sixth and ninth hour and did likewise.

6 And about the eleventh hour he went out, and found others standing idle, and saith unto them, Why stand ye here all the day idle?

7 They said unto him, Because no man hath hired us.

8 He said unto them, Go ye also into the vineyard; and whatsoever is right ye shall receive.

9 So when the [d]even was come, the lord of the vineyard said unto his steward, Call the laborers and give them their hire, beginning from the last unto the first.

10 And when they came that began about the eleventh hour, they received every man a penny.

11 But when the first came, they supposed that they should have received more; and they likewise received every man a penny. And when they had received a penny, they murmured against the good man of the house, saying, These last have wrought one hour only, and thou hast made them equal unto us, who have borne the burden and heat of the day.

12 But he answered one of them, and said, Friend, I do thee no wrong; didst not thou agree with me for a penny?

13 Take thine and go thy way; I will give unto this last even as unto thee. Is it not lawful for me to do what I will with mine own?

14 Is thine eye evil, because I am good?

15 So the last shall be first, and

---

a   Mark 10:30-31
b   Matthew 20:1-15
c   Dictionary - Penny

d   evening

the first last; and [a]many are called, but few are chosen.

Jesus again foretells His death

[b]31 Then he took the twelve, and said unto them, Behold, we go up to Jerusalem, and all things which are written by the prophets concerning the Son of Man, shall be accomplished.

32 For he shall be delivered unto the Gentiles, and shall be mocked, and spitefully entreated, and spitted on.

33 And they shall scourge and put him to death; and the third day he shall rise again.

34 And they understood none of these things; and this saying was hid from them; neither remembered they the things which were spoken.

Parable of the unjust steward

[c]1 And he said unto his disciples, There was a certain rich man who had a steward; and the same was accused unto him, that he had wasted his goods.

2 And he called him, and said unto him, How is it that I hear this of thee? Give an account of thy stewardship; for thou mayest be no longer steward.

3 Then the steward said within himself, What shall I do? for my Lord taketh away from me the stewardship. I cannot dig; to beg I am ashamed.

4 I am resolved what to do, that, when I am put out of the stewardship, they may receive me into their houses.

5 So he called every one of his Lord's debtors, and said unto the first, How much owest thou unto my lord?

6 And he said, an hundred measures of oil. And he said unto him, Take thy bill, and sit down quickly, and write fifty.

7 Then he said to another, And how much owest thou? And he said, A hundred measures of wheat. And he said unto him, Take thy bill, and write four score.

8 And the lord commended the unjust steward, because he had done wisely; for the children of this world are wiser in their generation, than the children of light.

9 And I say unto you, Make to yourselves friends, of the [d]mammon of unrighteousness; that, when ye fail, they may receive you into everlasting habitations.

10 He who is faithful in that which is least, is faithful also in much; and he who is unjust in the least, is also unjust in much.

---

[a]   Dictionary - Conundrum
[b]   Luke 18:31-34
[c]   Luke 16:1-13

[d]   Smith's - riches

11 If therefore ye have not been faithful in the unrighteous mammon, who will commit to your trust the true riches?

12 And if ye have not been faithful in that which is another man's, who shall give unto you that which is your own?

13 No servant can serve two masters; for either he will hate the one, and love the other; or else he will hold to the one, and despise the other. Ye cannot serve God and mammon.

Jesus calls Pharisees adulterers

[a]14 And the Pharisees also who were covetous, heard these things; and they derided him.

15 And he said unto them, Ye are they who justify yourselves before men; but God knoweth your hearts; for that which is lightly esteemed among men, is an abomination in the sight of God.

16 And they said unto him, We have the law, and the prophets; but as for this man we will not receive him to be our ruler; for he maketh himself to be a judge over us.

17 Then said Jesus unto them, The law and the prophets testify of me; yea, and all the prophets who have written, even unto John, have foretold of these days.

18 Since that time, the kingdom of God is preached, and every man who seeketh truth presseth into it.

19 And it is easier for heaven and earth to pass, than for one tittle of the law to fail.

20 And why teach ye the law, and deny that which is written; and condemn him whom *the* Father hath sent to fulfill the law, that ye might all be redeemed?

21 O fools! for you have said in your hearts, There is no God. And you pervert the right way; and the kingdom of heaven suffereth violence of you; and you persecute the meek; and in your violence you seek to destroy the kingdom; and ye take the children of the kingdom by force. Woe unto you, ye adulterers!

22 And they [b]reviled him again, being angry for the saying, that they were adulterers.

Parable of the rich man and Lazarus

[c]23 But he continued, saying, Whosoever putteth away his wife, and marrieth another, committeth adultery; and whosoever marrieth her who is put away from her husband, committeth adultery. Verily I say unto you, I will liken you unto the rich man.

24 For there was a certain rich man, who was clothed in purple,

---

[a] Luke 16:14-22

[b] subjected him to verbal abuse
[c] Luke 16:23-36

and fine linen, and fared [a]sumptuously every day.

25 And there was a certain beggar named Lazarus, who was laid at his gate, full of sores,

26 And desiring to be fed with the crumbs which fell from the rich man's table; moreover the dogs came and licked his sores.

27 And it came to pass, that the beggar died, and was carried of the angels into Abraham's bosom. The rich man also died, and was buried.

28 And in hell he lifted up his eyes, being in torments, and saw Abraham afar off, and Lazarus in his bosom.

29 And he cried, and said, Father Abraham, have mercy on me, and send Lazarus that he may dip the tip of his finger in water, and cool my tongue; for I am tormented in this flame.

30 But Abraham said, Son, remember that thou in thy lifetime receivedst thy good things, and likewise Lazarus evil things; but now he is comforted, and thou art tormented.

31 And beside all this, between us and you, there is a great gulf fixed; so that they who would pass from hence to you, cannot; neither can they pass to us that would come from thence.

32 Then he said, I pray thee therefore, father, that thou wouldest send him to my father's house,

33 For I have five brethren, that he may testify unto them, lest they also come into this place of torment.

34 Abraham said unto him, They have Moses and the prophets; let them hear them.

35 And he said, Nay, father Abraham; but if one went unto them from the dead, they will repent.

36 And he said unto him, If they hear not Moses and the prophets, neither will they be persuaded, though one should rise from the dead.

Mother of James and John asks a question

[b]18 Then came to him the mother of Zebedee's children with her sons, worshiping Jesus, and desiring a certain thing of him.

19 And he said unto her, What wilt thou that I should do?

20 And she said unto him, Grant that these my two sons may sit, the one on thy right hand, and the other on thy left, in thy kingdom.

21 But Jesus answered and said, Ye know not what ye ask. Are ye able to drink of the cup I shall drink of, and to be baptized with the baptism that I am baptized with?

---

[a]   large outlay of expense, lavish

[b]   Matthew 20:18-28

22 They say unto him, We are able.

23 And he said unto them, Ye shall drink indeed of my cup, and be baptized with the baptism I am baptized with; but to sit on my right hand, and on my left, is for whom it is prepared of *my* Father, but not mine to give, [a][but they shall receive it for whom it is prepared.]

24 And when the ten heard this, they were moved with indignation against the two brethren.

25 But when Jesus called them, and said, Ye know that princes of the Gentiles exercise dominion over them, and they that are great exercise authority upon them; but it shall not be so among you.

26 But whosoever will be great among you, let him be your minister;

27 And whosoever will be chief among you, let him be your servant;

28 Even as the Son of Man came, not to be ministered unto, but to minister; and to give his life a ransom for many.

Jesus heals blind Bartimaeus

[b]35 And it came to pass, as he was come nigh unto [c]Jericho, [d][blind Bartimaeus, the son of Timaeus, sat by the highway side begging].

36 And hearing the multitude pass by, he asked what it meant.

37 And they told him that Jesus of Nazareth passed by.

38 And he cried, saying, Jesus, son of David, have mercy on me.

39 And they who went before, rebuked him, telling him that he should hold his peace; but he cried so much the more, saying, Son of David, have mercy on me.

40 And Jesus stood, and commanded him to be brought unto him; and when he was come near, he asked him,

41 Saying, What wilt thou that I shall do unto thee? And he said, Lord, that I may receive my sight.

42 And Jesus said unto him, Receive thy sight; thy faith hath saved thee.

43 And immediately he received his sight; and he followed him, glorifying God. And all the disciples when they saw this, gave praise unto God.

Jesus stays at Zacchaeus' house

[e]1 And Jesus entered, and passed through Jericho.

2 And behold, there was a man named Zacchaeus, who was chief among publicans; and he was rich.

3 And he sought to see Jesus,

---

[a]   Mark 10:40
[b]   Luke 18:35-43
[c]   see Map 1
[d]   Mark 10:46

[e]   Luke 19:1-10

who he was; and could not for the press, because he was little of stature.

4 And he ran before, and climbed up into a sycamore tree to see him; for he was to pass that way.

5 And when Jesus came to the place, he looked up, and saw him, and said unto him, Zacchaeus, make haste, and come down; for to day I must abide at thy house.

6 And he made haste, and came down, and received him joyfully.

7 And when the disciples saw it, they all murmured, saying, That he was gone to be guest with a man who is a sinner.

8 And Zacchaeus stood, and said unto the Lord, Behold, Lord, the half of my goods I give to the poor; and if I have taken anything from any man by unjust means, I restore fourfold.

9 And Jesus said unto him, This day is salvation come to this house, forasmuch as he also is a son of Abraham;

10 For the Son of man is come to seek and to save that which was lost.

Parable of the pounds

^a11 And as they heard these things, he added and spake a parable, because he was nigh to Jerusalem, and because the Jews taught that the kingdom of God should immediately appear.

12 He said therefore, A certain nobleman went into a far country to receive for himself a kingdom, and to return.

13 And he called his ten servants, and delivered them ten ^bpounds, and said unto them, Occupy till I come.

14 But his citizens hated him, and sent a messenger after him, saying, We will not have this man to reign over us.

15 And it came to pass, that when he was returned, having received the kingdom, then he commanded these servants to be called unto him, to whom he had given the money, that he might know how much every man had gained by trading.

16 Then came the first, saying, Lord, thy pound hath gained ten pounds.

17 And he said unto him, Well done, thou good servant; because thou hast been faithful in a very little, have thou authority over ten cities.

18 And the second came, saying, Lord, thy pound hath gained five pounds.

19 And he said likewise to him, Be thou also over five cities.

20 And another came, saying, Lord, behold thy pound which I have kept laid up in a napkin;

---

^a Luke 19:11-26

^b Dictionary - Gifts of the Spirit

21 For I feared thee, because thou art an ªaustere man; thou takest up that thou layedst not down, and reapest that which thou didst not sow.

22 And he said unto him, Out of thine own mouth will I judge thee, O wicked servant. Thou knewest that I was an austere man, taking up that I laid not down, and reaping that I did not sow.

23 Wherefore then, gavest not thou my money into the bank, that at my coming I might have received my own with ᵇusury?

24 And he said unto them who stood by, Take from him the pound, and give it to him who hath ten pounds.

25 For I say unto you, That unto everyone who occupieth, shall be given; and from him who occupieth not, even that he hath received shall be taken away from him.

26 But those mine enemies, who would not that I should reign over them, bring them hither, and slay them before me.

A blind man from birth is healed

ᶜ1 And as Jesus passed by, he saw a man which was blind from his birth.

2 And his disciples asked him saying, Master, who did sin, this man, or his parents, that he was born blind?

3 Jesus answered, Neither hath this man sinned, nor his parents; but that the works of God should be made manifest in him.

4 I must work the works of him that sent me, while I am with you; the time cometh when I shall have finished my work, than I go unto *the* Father.

5 As long as I am in the world, I am the light of the world.

6 When he had thus spoken, he spat on the ground, and made clay of the spittle, and he anointed the eyes of the blind man with the clay,

7 And said unto him, Go, wash in the pool of Siloam, (which is by interpretation, Sent.) He went his way therefore, and washed, and came seeing.

8 The neighbors therefore, and they which before had seen him that he was blind, said, Is not this he that sat and begged?

9 Some said, This is he; others said, He is like him: but he said, I am he.

10 Therefore said they unto him, How were thine eyes opened?

11 He answered and said, A man that is called Jesus made clay, and anointed mine eyes, and said unto me, Go to the pool Siloam, and wash; and I went and washed, and I received sight.

12 Then said they unto him, Where is he? He said, I know not.

ª   severe or harsh
ᵇ   Smith's - interest
ᶜ   John 9:1-41

13 And they brought him who had been blind to the Pharisees.

14 And it was the sabbath day when Jesus made the clay, and opened his eyes.

15 Then again the Pharisees also asked him how he had received his sight. He said unto them, He put clay upon mine eyes, and I washed, and do see.

16 Therefore said some of the Pharisees, This man is not of God, because he keepeth not the sabbath day. Others said, How can a man that is a sinner do such miracles? And there was a division among them.

17 They said unto the blind man again, What sayest thou of him who hath opened thine eyes? He said, He is a prophet.

18 But the Jews did not believe concerning him, that he had been blind, and received his sight, until they called his parents of him that had received his sight.

19 And they asked them, saying, Is this your son, who ye say was born blind? how then doth he now see?

20 His parents answered them and said, We know that this is our son, and that he was born blind;

21 But by what means he now seeth, we know not; or who hath opened his eyes, we know not; he is of age; ask him: he shall speak for himself.

22 These words spake his parents, because they feared the Jews; for the Jews had agreed already, that if any man did confess that he was Christ, he should be put out of the synagogue.

23 Therefore said his parents, He is of age; ask him.

24 Then again called they the man that was blind, and said unto him, Give God the praise; we know that this man is a sinner.

25 He answered and said, Whether he be a sinner or no, I know not; one thing I know, that, whereas I was blind, now I see.

26 Then said they to him again, What did he to thee? how opened he thine eyes?

27 He answered them, I have told you already, and ye did not believe; wherefore would you believe if I should tell you again? and would you also be his disciples?

28 Then they reviled him, and said, Thou art his disciple; but we are Moses' disciples.

29 We know that God spake unto Moses; as for this man we know not from whence he is.

30 The man answered and said unto them, Why herein is a marvelous thing, that ye know not from whence he is, and yet he hath opened mine eyes.

31 Now we know that God heareth not sinners; but if any man be a worshipper of God, and doeth his will, him he heareth.

32 Since the world began was

it not heard that any man opened the eyes of one that was born blind, except he be of God.

33 If this man were not of God, he could do nothing.

34 They answered and said unto him, Thou wast altogether born in sins, and dost thou teach us? And they cast him out.

35 Jesus heard that they had cast him out; and when he had found him, he said unto him, Dost thou believe on the Son of God?

36 He answered and said, Who is he, Lord, that I might believe on him?

37 And Jesus said unto him, Thou hast both seen him, and it is he that talketh with thee.

38 And he said, Lord, I believe. And he worshipped him.

39 And Jesus said, For judgment I am come into the world, that they which see not might see; and that they which see might be made blind.

40 And some of the Pharisees which were with him heard these words, and said unto him, Are we blind also?

41 Jesus said unto them, If ye were blind, ye should have no sin; but now ye say, We see; therefore your sin remaineth.

Parable His sheep know His voice

[a]1 Verily, verily, I say unto you, He that entereth not by the door into the sheepfold, but climbeth up some other way, the same is a thief and a robber.

2 But he that entereth in by the door is the shepherd of the sheep.

3 To him the [b]porter openeth; and the sheep hear his voice; and he calleth his own sheep by name, and leadeth them out.

4 And when he putteth forth his own sheep, he goeth before them, and the sheep follow him; for they know his voice.

5 And a stranger will they not follow, but will flee from him; for they know not the voice of strangers.

6 This parable spake Jesus unto them; but they understood not what things they were which he spake unto them.

7 Then said Jesus unto them again, Verily, verily, I say unto you, I am the door of the sheepfold.

8 All that ever came before me who testified not of me are thieves and robbers; but the sheep did not hear them.

9 I am the door; by me if any man enter in, he shall be saved, and shall go in and out, and find pasture.

10 The thief cometh not, but

---

[a]   John 10:1-16
[b]   Smith's - gate keeper

for to steal, and to kill, and to destroy; I am come that they might have life, and that they might have it more abundantly.

11 I am the good shepherd; the good shepherd giveth his life for his sheep.

12 And the shepherd that is not as a hireling, whose own the sheep are not, who seeth the wolf coming, and leaveth the sheep, and fleeth; and the wolf catcheth the sheep and scattereth them.

13 For I am the good shepherd, and know my sheep, and am known of mine.

14 But he who is a hireling fleeth, because he is a hireling, and which careth not for the sheep.

15 As *the* Father knoweth me, even so know I *the* Father; and I lay down my life for the sheep.

16 And ªother sheep I have, which are not of this fold; them also I must bring, and they shall hear my voice; and there shall be one fold, and one shepherd.

Jesus will give His life voluntarily

ᵇ17 Therefore doth *my* Father love me, because I lay down my life, that I might take it again.

18 No man taketh it from me, but I lay it down of myself. I have power to lay it down, and I have power to take it again. This commandment have I received of *my* Father.

19 There was a division therefore again among the Jews for these sayings.

20 And many of them said, He hath a devil, and is mad; why hear ye him?

21 Others said, These are not the words of him that hath a devil. Can a devil open the eyes of the blind?

The Jews want to stone Jesus

ᶜ22 And it was at Jerusalem the feast of the dedication, and it was winter.

23 And Jesus walked in the temple in Solomon's porch.

24 Then came the Jews round about him, and said unto him, How long dost thou make us to doubt? If thou be the Christ, tell us plainly.

25 Jesus answered them, I told you, and ye believed not; the works that I do in *my* Father's name, they bear witness of me.

26 But ye believe not, because ye are not of my sheep, as I said unto you.

27 My sheep hear my voice, and I know them, and they follow me;

28 And I give unto them eternal life; and they shall never perish, neither shall any man pluck them out of my hand.

ª   Compare 3 Nephi 15:12-24 E.R.
ᵇ   John 10:17- 21

ᶜ   John 10:22-42

29 *My* Father, which gave them me, is greater than all; and no man is able to pluck them out of *my* Father's hand.

30 I and *my* Father are one.

31 Then the Jews took up stones again to stone him.

32 Jesus answered them, Many good works have I showed you from *my* Father; for which of those works do ye stone me?

33 The Jews answered him, saying, For a good work we stone thee not; but for blasphemy; and because that thou, being a man, makest thyself God.

34 Jesus answered them, Is it not written in your law, I said, Ye are gods?

35 If he called them gods, unto whom the word of God came, and the Scripture cannot be broken;

36 Say ye of him, whom *the* Father hath sanctified, and sent into the world, Thou blasphemest; because I said, I am the *Son of God*?

37 If I do not the works of *my* Father, believe me not.

38 But if I do, though ye believe not me, believe the works; that ye may know, and believe, that *the* Father is in me, and I in him.

39 Therefore they sought again to take him; but he escaped out of their hand,

40 And went away again beyond Jordan into the place where John at first baptized; and there he abode.

41 And many resorted unto him, and said, John did no miracle; but all things that John spake of this man were true.

42 And many believed on him there.

Jesus raises Lazarus from the dead

[a]1 Now a certain man was sick, whose name was [b]Lazarus, of the town of [c]Bethany;

2 And Mary, his sister, who anointed the Lord with ointment and wiped his feet with her hair, lived with her sister [d]Martha, in whose house her brother Lazarus was sick.

3 Therefore his sister sent unto him, saying, Lord, behold, he whom thou lovest is sick.

4 And when Jesus heard he was sick, he said, This sickness is not unto death, but for the glory of God, that the Son of God, might be glorified thereby.

5 Now Jesus loved Martha, and her sister, and Lazarus.

6 And Jesus tarried two days, after he heard that Lazarus was sick, in the same place where he was.

7 After that he said unto his disciples, Let us go into Judea again.

8 But his disciples said unto

---

[a]   John 11:1-46
[b]   Dictionary - Lazarus
[c]   House of the poor
[d]   Dictionary - Martha

him, Master, the Jews of late sought to stone thee; and goest thou thither again?

9 Jesus answered, Are there not twelve hours in a day? If any man walk in the day, he stumbleth not, because he seeth the light of the world.

10 But if a man walk in the night, he stumbleth, because there is no light in him.

11 These things said he; and after that he saith unto them, Our friend Lazarus sleepeth; but I go, that I may awake him out of sleep.

12 Then said his disciples, Lord, if he sleep, he shall do well.

13 Howbeit Jesus spake of his death; but they thought that he had spoken of taking of rest in sleep.

14 Then said Jesus unto them plainly, Lazarus is dead.

15 And I am glad for your sakes that I was not there, to the intent ye may believe; nevertheless let us go unto him.

16 Then said Thomas, which is called [a]Didymus, unto his fellow disciples, Let us also go, that we may die with him; for they feared lest the Jews should take Jesus and put him to death, for as yet they did not understand the power of God.

17 And when Jesus came to Bethany, to Martha's house, Lazarus had already been in the grave four days.

18 Now Bethany was nigh unto Jerusalem, about fifteen [b]furlongs off;

19 And many of the Jews came to Martha and Mary, to comfort them concerning their brother.

20 Then Martha, as soon as she heard that Jesus was coming, went and met him; but Mary sat still in the house.

21 Then said Martha unto Jesus, Lord, if thou hadst been here, my brother had not died.

22 But I know, that even now, whatsoever thou wilt ask of God, God will give it thee.

23 Jesus saith unto her, Thy brother shall rise again.

24 Martha saith unto him, I know that he shall rise again in the resurrection at the last day.

25 Jesus said unto her, I am the resurrection, and the life; he that believeth in me, though he were dead, yet shall he live;

26 And whosoever liveth and believeth in me shall never die. Believest thou this?

27 She said unto him, Yea, Lord; I believe that thou art the Christ, the Son of God, which should come into the world.

28 And when she had so said, she went her way, and called Mary her sister secretly, saying, The

[a] Smith's - meaning twin

[b] Smith's - 220 yards, less than ¼ mile

Master is come, and calleth for thee.

29 As soon as Mary heard Jesus was come, she arose quickly, and came unto him.

30 Now Jesus was not yet come into the town, but was in the place where Martha met him.

31 The Jews then which were with her in the house, and comforted her, when they saw Mary, that she rose up hastily and went out, followed her, saying, She goeth unto the grave to weep there.

32 Then when Mary was come where Jesus was, and saw him, she fell down at his feet, saying unto him, Lord, if thou hadst been here, my brother had not died.

33 When Jesus therefore saw her weeping, and the Jews also weeping which came with her, he groaned in the spirit, and was troubled,

34 And said, Where have ye laid him? They said unto him, Lord, come and see.

35 Jesus wept.

36 Then said the Jews, Behold how he loved him!

37 And some of them said, Could not this man, which opened the eyes of the blind, have caused that even this man should not have died?

38 Jesus therefore again groaning in himself cometh to the grave. It was a cave, and a stone lay upon it.

39 Jesus said, Take ye away the stone. Martha, the sister of him that was dead, saith unto him, Lord, by this time he stinketh; for he hath been dead four days.

40 Jesus saith unto her, Said I not unto thee, that, if thou wouldst believe, thou shouldest see the glory of God?

41 Then they took away the stone from the place where the dead was laid. And Jesus lifted up his eyes, and said, Father, I thank thee that thou hast heard me.

42 And I know that thou hearest me always; but because of the people which stand by I said it, that they may believe that thou hast sent me.

43 And when he thus had spoken, he cried with a loud voice, Lazarus, come forth.

44 And he that was dead came forth, bound hand and foot with grave clothes; and his face was bound about with a napkin. Jesus saith unto them, Loose him, and let him go.

45 Then many of the Jews which came to Mary, and had seen the things which Jesus did, believed on him.

46 But some of them went their ways to the Pharisees, and told them what things Jesus had done.

Caiaphas prophesies

[a]47 Then gathered the chief

---

priests and the Pharisees a council, and said, What shall we do? for this man doeth many miracles.

48 If we let him thus alone, all men will believe on him; and the Romans shall come and take away both our place and nation.

49 And one of them, named Caiaphas, being the high priest that same year, said unto them, Ye know nothing at all,

50 Nor consider that it is expedient for us, that one man should die for the people, and that the whole nation perish not.

51 And this he spake not of himself; but being high priest that year, he prophesied that Jesus should die for that nation;

52 And not for that nation only, but that also he should gather together in one the children of God that were scattered abroad.

53 Then from that day forth they took counsel together for to put him to death.

54 Jesus therefore walked no more openly among the Jews; but went thence unto a country near the wilderness, into a city called ᵃEphraim, and there continued with his disciples.

The seventy return

ᵇ18 And the seventy returned again with joy, saying, Lord, even the devils are subject to us through thy name.

19 And he said unto them, As lightning falleth from heaven, I beheld Satan also falling.

20 Behold, I will give unto you power over serpents and scorpions, and over all the power of the enemy; and nothing shall by any means hurt you.

21 Notwithstanding, in this rejoice not, that the spirits are subject unto you; but rather rejoice, because your names are written in heaven.

22 In that hour Jesus rejoiced in spirit, and said, I thank thee, O Father, Lord of heaven and earth, that thou hast hid these things from them who think they are wise and prudent, and hast revealed them unto babes; even so, Father; for so it seemed good in thy sight.

23 All things are delivered to me of *my* Father; ᶜand no man knoweth that the Son is the Father, and the Father is the Son, but him to whom the Son will reveal it.

24 And he turned him unto the disciples, and said privately, Blessed are the eyes which see the things that ye see.

25 For I tell you, That many prophets and kings have desired to see those things which ye see, and

---

ᵃ   Map number 1
ᵇ   Luke 10:18-25

ᶜ   Dictionary - Conundrum

have not seen them; and to hear those things which ye hear, and have not heard them.

Jesus returns to Bethany

[a]55 And the Jews passover was nigh at hand; and many went out of the country up to Jerusalem before the Passover, to purify themselves.

56 Then sought they for Jesus, and spake among themselves, as they stood in the temple, What think ye of Jesus? Will he not come to the feast?

57 Now both the chief priests and the Pharisees had given a commandment, that, if any man knew where he was, he should show them, that they might take him.

[b]1 Then Jesus six days before the passover came to Bethany, where Lazarus was which had been dead, whom he raised from the dead.

[c]39 . . . and a certain woman named Martha received him into her house.

40 And she had a sister, called Mary, who also sat at Jesus' feet, and heard his words.

41 But Martha was cumbered about much serving, and came to him, and said, Lord, dost thou not care that my sister hath left me to serve alone? Bid her therefore that she help me.

42 And Jesus answered and said unto her, Martha, Martha, thou art careful and troubled about many things;

43 But one thing is needful; and Mary hath chosen that good part, which shall not be taken away from her.

[d]2 There they made him a supper; and Martha served; but Lazarus was one of them that sat at the table with him.

[e]9 Much people of the Jews therefore knew that he was there; and they came not for Jesus' sake only, but that they might see Lazarus also, whom he had raised from the dead.

10 But the chief priests consulted that they might put Lazarus also to death;

11 Because that by reason of him many of the Jews went away, and believed on Jesus.

Jesus' triumphal entry

[f]1 And when Jesus drew nigh unto Jerusalem, and they were come to [g]Bethphage, on the mount of Olives, then sent Jesus two disciples,

2 Saying unto them, Go into the village over against you, and straightway ye shall find a colt tied; [h][whereon yet never man sat;] loose

---

a   John 11:55-57
b   John 12:1
c   Luke 10:39-43
d   John 12:2
e   John 12:9-11
f   Matthew 21:1-4
g   Map number 1 - house of figs
h   Luke 19:29

it, and bring it unto me; and if any shall say aught unto you, ye shall say, The Lord hath need of it; and straightway he will send it.

3 All this was done, that it might be fulfilled which was spoken by the prophets, saying,

4 Tell ye the daughter of ᵃZion, Behold, thy king cometh unto thee, and he is meek, and he is ᵇsitting upon an ass, and a colt, the foal of an ass.

ᶜ4 And they went their way, and found the colt tied by the door without, in a place where two ways met; and they loosed him.

5 And certain of them who stood by, said unto the disciples, Why loose ye the colt?

6 And they said unto them even as Jesus had commanded; and they let them go.

7 And they brought the colt to Jesus, and cast their garments on it; and Jesus sat upon it.

ᵈ16 These things understood not his disciples at the first; but when Jesus was glorified, then remembered they that these things were written of him, and that they had done these things unto him.

17 The people therefore that was with him when he called Lazarus out of his grave, and raised him from the dead, bear record.

18 For this cause the people also met him, for they heard that he had done this miracle.

ᵉ6 And a very great multitude spread their garments in the way; others cut down branches ᶠ[of palm] trees, and strewed in the way.

7 And the multitudes that went before, and also that followed after, cried, saying, ᵍHosanna to the Son of David; blessed is ʰ[the king] who cometh in the name of the Lord! Hosanna in the highest!

8 And when he was come into Jerusalem, all the city was moved, saying, Who is this?

9 And the multitude said, This is Jesus of Nazareth, the prophet of Galilee.

ⁱ19 The Pharisees therefore said among themselves, Perceive ye how ye prevail nothing? behold, the world is gone after him.

Jesus weeps over Jerusalem

ʲ40 And when he was come near, he beheld the city, and wept over it;

41 Saying, if thou hadst known, even thou, at least in this thy day,

---

ᵃ Dictionary - Zion
ᵇ Easy Ref. Zechariah 9:9
ᶜ Mark 11:4-7
ᵈ John 12:16-18
ᵉ Matthew 21:6-9
ᶠ John 12:13
ᵍ Smith's - save now
ʰ Luke 19:37
ⁱ John 12:19
ʲ Luke 19:40-43

the things which belong unto thy peace! But now they are hid from thine eyes.

42 For the days shall come upon thee, that thine enemies shall cast a trench about thee, and compass thee round, and keep thee in on every side;

43 And shall lay thee even with the ground, and thy children within thee, and they shall not leave in thee, one stone upon another; because thou knewest not the time of thy visitation.

Second cleansing of the Temple

[a]17 And they came to Jerusalem. And Jesus went into the temple, and began to cast out them that sold and bought in the temple, and overthrew the tables of the money changers and the seats of them who sold doves;

18 And would not suffer that any man should carry a [b]vessel through the temple.

19 And he taught, saying unto them, Is it not written, My house shall be called of all nations the house of prayer? But ye have made it a den of thieves.

20 And the scribes and chief priests heard him, and sought how they might destroy him; for they feared him because all the people were astonished at his doctrine.

Out of the mouths of babes

[c]12 And the blind and the lame came to him in the temple; and he healed them.

13 And when the chief priests and Scribes saw the wonderful things that he did, and the children of the kingdom crying in the temple, and saying, Hosanna to the Son of David! they were sore displeased, and said unto him, Hearest thou what these say?

[d]38 And some of the Pharisees from among the multitude, said unto him, Master, rebuke thy disciples.

39 And he answered and said unto them, If these should hold their peace, the stones would immediately cry out.

[e]14 And Jesus said unto them, Yea; have ye never read the scriptures which saith, [f]Out of the mouths of babes and sucklings, O Lord, thou hast perfected praise?

Greeks ask to see Jesus

[g]20 And there were certain Greeks among them that came up to worship at the feast;

21 The same came therefore to

---

a   Mark 11:17-20
b   Smith's - cup
c   Matthew 21:12-13
d   Luke 19:38-39
e   Matthew 21:14
f   Easy Ref. Psalms 8:2
g   John 12:20-50

Philip, which was of Bethsaida of Galilee, and desired him, saying, Sir, we would see Jesus.

22 Philip cometh and telleth Andrew; and again Andrew and Philip tell Jesus.

23 And Jesus answered them, saying, The hour is come, that the Son of Man should be glorified.

24 Verily, verily, I say unto you, Except a corn of wheat fall into the ground and die, it abideth alone; but if it die, it bringeth forth much fruit.

25 He that loveth his life shall lose it; and he that hateth his life in this world shall keep it unto life eternal.

26 If any man serve me, let him follow me; and where I am, there shall also my servant be; if any man serve me, him will *my* Father honor.

27 Now is my soul troubled; and what shall I say? Father, save me from this hour; but for this cause came I unto this hour.

28 Father, glorify thy name. Then came there a voice from heaven, saying, I have both glorified it and will glorify it again.

29 The people therefore that stood by, and heard it, said that it thundered; others said, An angel spake to him.

30 Jesus answered and said, This voice came not because of me, but for your sakes.

31 Now is the judgment of this world; now shall the prince of this world be cast out.

32 And I, if I be lifted up from the earth, will draw all men unto me.

33 This he said, signifying what death he should die.

34 The people answered him, We have heard out of the law that the Christ abideth for ever; and how sayest thou, The Son of Man must be lifted up? who is this Son of Man?

35 Then said Jesus unto them, Yet a little while is the light with you. Walk while ye have light, lest darkness come upon you; for he that walketh in darkness knoweth not whither he goeth.

36 While ye have light, believe in the light, that ye may be the children of light . . .

37 But though he had done so many miracles before them, yet they believed not on him;

38 That the saying of Esaias the prophet might be fulfilled, which he spake, ªLord, who hath believed our report? and to whom hath the arm of the Lord been revealed?

39 Therefore they could not believe, because that Esaias said again,

40 He hath blinded their eyes, and hardened their heart; that they should not see with their eyes, nor understand with their heart, and be converted, and I should heal

---

ª   Easy Ref. Isaiah 53:1

them.

41 These things said Esaias, when he saw his glory, and spake of him.

42 Nevertheless among the chief rulers also many believed on him; but because of the Pharisees they did not confess him, lest they should be put out of the synagogue;

43 For they loved the praise of men more than the praise of God.

44 Jesus cried and said, He that believeth on me, believeth not on me, but on him that sent me.

45 And he that seeth me seeth him that sent me.

46 I am come a light into the world, that whosoever believeth on me should not abide in darkness.

47 And if any man hear my words, and believe not, I judge him not; for I came not to judge the world, but to save the world.

48 He that rejecteth me, and receiveth not my words, hath one that judgeth him; the word that I have spoken, the same shall judge him in the last day.

49 For I have not spoken of myself; but *the* Father which sent me, he gave me a commandment, what I should say, and what I should speak.

50 And I know that his commandment is life everlasting; whatsoever I speak therefore, even as *the* Father said unto me, so I speak.

[a]13 . . . And when he had looked round about upon all things, and blessed the disciples, the eventide was come; and he went out unto Bethany with the twelve.

A fig tree is cursed

[b]14 And on the morrow, when they came from Bethany he was hungry; and seeing a fig tree afar off having leaves, he came to it with his disciples; and as they supposed, he came to it to see if he might find anything thereon.

15 And when he came to it, there was nothing but leaves; for as yet the figs were not ripe.

16 And Jesus spake and said unto it, No man eat fruit of thee hereafter, forever. And his disciples heard him;

The baptism of John, was it from heaven or of men?

[c]21 And when he was come into the temple, the chief priests and the elders of the people came unto him as he was teaching, and said, By what authority doest thou these things? And who gave thee this authority?

22 And Jesus answered and said unto them, I also will ask you one thing, which if ye tell me, I, likewise, will tell you by what authority I do these things.

---

[a]   Mark 11:13
[b]   Mark 11:14-16
[c]   Matthew 21:21-25

23 The baptism of John, whence was it? From heaven, or of men?

24 And they reasoned with themselves, saying, If we shall say, From heaven; he will say unto us, Why did ye not then believe him? But if we say, Of men; a[all the people will stone us; for they] held John as a prophet. And they answered Jesus and said, We cannot tell.

25 And he said, Neither tell I you by what authority I do these things.

Parable of the two sons

b26 But what think ye? A man had two sons; and he came to the first, saying, Son, go work today in my vineyard.

27 He answered and said, I will not; but afterwards he repented, and went.

28 And he came to the second, and said likewise. And he answered and said, I will serve; and went not.

29 Whether of these twain did the will of their father?

30 They say unto him, The first.

31 Jesus said unto them, Verily I say unto you, That the publicans and the harlots shall go into the kingdom of God before you.

32 For John came unto you in the way of righteousness, and bore record of me, and ye believed him not; but the publicans and the harlots believed him; and ye, afterward; when ye had seen me, repented not, that ye might believe him.

33 For he that believed not John concerning me, cannot believe me, except he first repent.

34 And except ye repent, the preaching of John shall condemn you in the day of judgment; And again, hear another parable; for unto you that believe not, I speak in parables; that your unrighteousness may be rewarded unto you.

Parable of the wicked husbandmen

c35 Behold, there was a certain householder, who planted a vineyard, and hedged it round about, and digged a winepress in it; and built a tower, and let it out to husbandmen, and went into a far country.

36 And when the d[season of harvest] drew near, he sent his servants to the husbandmen, that they might receive the fruits of it.

37 And the husbandmen took his servants, and beat one, and killed another, and stoned another.

38 Again, he sent other servants, more than the first; and they did unto them likewise.

39 But last of all, he sent unto

---

a   Luke 20:6
b   Matthew 21:26-34

c   Matthew 21:35-43
d   Luke 20:10

them his son, saying, They will reverence my son.

40 But when the husbandmen saw the son, they said among themselves, This is the [a]heir; come, let us kill him, and let us seize on his inheritance.

41 And they caught him, and cast him out of the vineyard, and slew him.

42 And Jesus said unto them, When the Lord therefore of the vineyard cometh, what will he do unto those husbandmen?

43 They said unto him, He will destroy those miserable, wicked men, and will let out the vineyard unto other husbandmen, who shall render him the fruits in their seasons.

The kingdom shall be taken from the Jews

[b]44 Jesus said unto them, Did ye never read in the Scriptures, [c]The stone which the builders rejected, the same is become the head of the corner; this is the Lord's doings, and it is marvelous in our eyes?

45 Therefore say I unto you, The kingdom of God shall be taken from you, and given to a nation bringing forth the fruits thereof.

46 For whosoever shall fall on this stone, shall be broken; but on whomsoever it shall fall, it will grind him to powder.

47 And when the chief priests and Pharisees had heard his parables, they perceived that he spake of them.

48 And they said among themselves, Shall this man think that he alone can spoil this great kingdom? And they were angry with him.

49 But when they sought to lay hands on him, they feared the multitude, because they learned that the multitude took him for a prophet.

50 And now his disciples came to him, and Jesus said unto them, Marvel ye at the words of the parable which I spake unto them?

51 Verily, I say unto you, I am the stone, and those wicked ones reject me.

52 I am the head of the corner. These Jews shall fall upon me, and shall be broken.

53 And the kingdom of God shall be taken from them, and shall be given to a nation bringing forth the fruits thereof; (meaning the Gentiles.)

54 Wherefore, on whomsoever this stone shall fall, it shall grind him to powder.

55 And when the Lord therefore of the vineyard cometh, he will destroy those miserable, wicked men, and will let again his vineyard unto other husbandmen, even in the last

---

[a]   one who inherits property or an endowment
[b]   Matthew 21:44-56
[c]   Easy Ref. Psalms 118:22

days, who shall render him the fruits in their seasons.

56 And then understood they the parable which he spake unto them, that the Gentiles should be destroyed also, when the Lord should descend out of heaven to reign in his vineyard, which is the earth and the inhabitants thereof.

Parable of the marriage of the king's son

[a]1 And Jesus answered the people again, and spake unto them in parables, and said,

2 The kingdom of heaven is like unto a certain king, who made a marriage for his son.

3 And when the marriage was ready, he sent forth his servants to call them which were bidden to the wedding; and they would not come.

4 Again he sent forth other servants, saying, Tell them that are bidden, Behold, I have prepared my oxen, and my fatlings have been killed, and my dinner is ready, and all things are prepared; therefore come unto the marriage.

5 But they made light of the servants, and went their ways; one to his farm, another to his merchandise;

6 And the remnant took his servants, and entreated them spite-fully, and slew them.

7 But when the king heard that his servants were dead, he was wroth; and he sent forth his armies, and destroyed those murderers, and burned up their city.

8 Then said he to his servants, The wedding is ready; but they who were bidden were not worthy.

9 Go ye therefore into the highways, and as many as ye find, bid to the marriage.

10 So those servants went out into the highways, and gathered together all, as many as they found, both bad and good; and the wedding was furnished with guests.

11 But when the king came in to see the guests, he saw there a man who had not a wedding garment.

12 And he said unto him, Friend, how camest thou in hither, not having a wedding garment? And he was speechless.

13 Then said the king unto his servants, Bind him hand and foot, and take and cast him away into outer darkness; there shall be weeping and gnashing of teeth.

14 For many are called, but few chosen; wherefore all do not have on the wedding garment.

Is it lawful to give tribute unto Caesar?

[b]15 Then went the Pharisees and took counsel how they might

---

a   Matthew 22:1-14

b   Matthew 22:15-21

entangle him in talk.

16 And they sent out unto him their disciples with the [a]Herodians, saying, Master, we know that thou art true, and teachest the way of God in truth, neither carest thou for any; for thou regardest not the person of men.

17 Tell us, therefore, What thinkest thou? Is it lawful to give tribute unto Caesar, or not?

18 But Jesus perceived their wickedness, and said, Ye hypocrites! Why tempt ye me? Show me the tribute money.

19 And they brought unto him a penny.

20 He said unto them, Whose image is this, and superscription?

21 They said unto him, Caesar's. Then said he unto them, Render therefore unto Caesar, the things which are Caesar's; and unto God the things which are God's.

[b]26 And they could not take hold of his words before the people, and they marveled at his answer, and held their peace.

Whose wife shall she be?

[c]23 The same day came the Sadducees to him, who say that there is no resurrection, and asked him, saying, Master, Moses said, If a man die, having no children, his brother shall marry his wife, and raise up seed unto his brother.

24 Now there were with us, seven brethren; and the first, when he had married a wife, deceased; and, having no issue, he left his wife unto his brother.

25 Likewise the second also, and the third, and even unto the seventh.

26 And last of all the woman died also.

27 Therefore, in the resurrection, whose wife shall she be of the seven? For they all had her.

28 Jesus answered and said unto them, Ye do [d]err, [e][because ye know not, and understand not the scriptures,] nor the power of God.

29 For in the resurrection, they neither marry, nor are given in marriage; [f][neither can they die any more; for they are equal unto] the angels of God in heaven.

30 But as touching the resurrection of the dead, have ye not read that which was spoken unto you of God, saying,

31 I am the God of Abraham, and the God of Isaac, and the God of Jacob? God is not the God of the dead, but of the living; [g][for he raiseth them up out of their graves. Ye therefore do greatly err.]

32 And when the multitude heard him, they were astonished at

---

a   servants of Herod
b   Luke 20:26
c   Matthew 22:23-32

d   error
e   Mark 12:28
f   Luke 20:36
g   Mark 12:32

his doctrine.

Which is the great commandment?

[a]33 But when the Pharisees heard that he had put the Sadducees to silence, they were gathered together.

34 Then one of them, a [b]lawyer, tempting him, asked, saying,

35 Master, which is the great commandment in the law?

[c]27 He said unto him, What is written in the law? How readest thou?

28 And he answering, said, Thou shalt love the Lord thy God with all thy heart, and with all thy soul, and with all thy strength, and with all thy mind; and thy neighbor as thyself.

29 And he said unto him, Thou hast answered right; this do and thou shalt live.

[d]39 On these two commandments hang all the law and the prophets.

[e]30 But he, willing to justify himself, said unto Jesus, And who is my neighbor?

Parable of the Good Samaritan

[f]31 And Jesus answering, said, A certain man went down from Jerusalem to Jericho, and fell among thieves, which stripped him of his raiment and wounded him, and departed, leaving him half dead.

32 And by chance, there came down a certain priest that way; and when he saw him, he passed by on the other side of the way.

33 And likewise a Levite, when he was at the place, came and looked upon him, and passed by on the other side of the way; for they desired in their hearts that it might not be known that they had seen him.

34 But a certain Samaritan, as he journeyed, came where he was; and when he saw him, he had compassion on him,

35 And went to him, and bound up his wounds, pouring in oil and wine, and set him on his beast, and brought him to an inn, and took care of him.

36 And on the [g]morrow, when he departed, he took money and gave to the host, and said unto him, Take care of him, and whatsoever thou spendest more, when I come again, I will repay thee.

37 Who now of these three, thinkest thou, was neighbor unto him that fell among the thieves?

38 And he said, He who showed mercy on him. Then said Jesus

---

[a] Matthew 22:33-35
[b] Dictionary - Lawyer
[c] Luke 10:27-29
[d] Matthew 22:39
[e] Luke 10:30
[f] Luke 10:31-38

---

[g] next day

unto him, Go, and do likewise.

[a]37 And the scribe said unto him, Well, Master, thou hast said the truth; for there is one God, and there is none other but him.

38 And to love him with all the heart, and with all the understanding, and with all the soul, and with all the strength; and to love his neighbor as himself, is more than all whole burnt offerings and sacrifices.

39 And when Jesus saw that he answered discreetly, he said unto him, Thou art not far from the kingdom of God.

40 And no man after that durst ask him [b][any question at all.]

[c]21 And when even was come he went out of the city.

The fig tree dried up

[d]22 And in the morning as they passed by, they saw the fig tree dried up from the roots.

23 And Peter calling to remembrance, said unto him, Master, behold, the fig tree which thou cursedst is withered away.

24 And Jesus spake and said unto him, Have faith in God.

[e]5 And the apostles said unto him, Lord, increase our faith.

6 And the Lord said, If you had faith as a grain of mustard seed, you might say unto this sycamore tree, Be thou plucked up by the roots, and be thou planted in the sea; [f][and shall not doubt in his heart, but shall believe that those things which he saith shall come to pass;] and it should obey you.

[g]26 Therefore I say unto you, Whatsoever things ye desire, when ye pray, believe that ye receive, and ye shall have whatsoever ye ask.

27 And when ye stand praying, forgive if ye have aught against any; that *your* Father also who is in heaven, may forgive you your trespasses.

28 But if ye do not forgive, neither will *your* Father who is heaven forgive your trespasses.

Jesus asks the Pharisees a question

[h]40 While the Pharisees were gathered together, [i][he taught in the temple,] Jesus asked them, saying, What think ye of Christ? Whose son is he?

41 They say unto him, The Son of David.

42 He saith unto them, How then doth David [j][by the Holy Ghost,] [k][saith in the book of

---

[a]   Mark 12:37-40
[b]   Luke 20:40
[c]   Mark 11:21
[d]   Mark 11:22-24
[e]   Luke 17:5-6
[f]   Mark 11:25
[g]   Mark 11:26-28
[h]   Matthew 22:40-44
[i]   Mark 12:41
[j]   Mark 12:42
[k]   Luke 20:42

Psalms,] The Lord said unto my Lord, Sit thou on my right hand, till I make thine enemies thy footstool?

43 [a]If David called him Lord, how is he his son?

44 And no man was able to answer him a word, neither durst any man from that day forth ask him any more questions.

[b]44 And the common people heard him gladly; but the high priests and the elders were offended at him.

Jesus warns the people of the Scribes and the Pharisees

[c]1 Then spake Jesus to the multitude, and to his disciples, saying, The Scribes and the Pharisees sit in Moses' seat.

2 All, therefore, whatsoever they bid you observe, they will make you observe and do; for they are ministers of the law, and they make themselves your judges. But do not ye after their works; for they say, and do not.

3 For they bind heavy burdens and lay on men's shoulders, and they are grievous to be borne; but they will not move them with one of their fingers.

4 And all their works they do to be seen of men. They make broad

their [d]phylacteries, and enlarge the boarders of their garments, and love the uppermost rooms at feasts, and the chief seats in the synagogues, and greetings in the markets, and to be called of men, Rabbi, Rabbi, (which is master.)

5 But be not ye called Rabbi; for one is your master, which is Christ; and ye are brethren.

6 And call no one your creator upon the earth, or *your* heavenly Father; for one is *your* creator and heavenly Father, even he who is in heaven.

7 Neither be ye called Master; for one is your master, even he whom *your* heavenly Father sent, which is Christ; for he hath sent him among you that ye might have life.

8 But he that is greatest among you shall be your servant.

9 And whosoever shall exalt himself shall be abased of him; and he that shall humble himself shall be exalted of him.

10 But [e]woe unto you, Scribes and Pharisees, hypocrites! For ye shut up the kingdom of heaven against men; for ye neither go in yourselves, neither suffer ye them that are entering to go in.

11 Woe unto you, Scribes and Pharisees! for ye are hypocrites! Ye devour widows' houses, and for a pretense make long prayers; there-

---

[a]   Dictionary - Conundrum
[b]   Mark 12:44
[c]   Matthew 23:1-41

[d]   Dictionary - Phylactery
[e]   condition of deep suffering
       or calamity

fore ye shall receive the greater punishment.

12 Woe unto you, Scribes and Pharisees, hypocrites! For ye compass sea and land to make one ᵃproselyte; and when he is made, ye make him two fold more the child of hell than he was before, like unto yourselves.

13 Woe unto you, blind guides, who say, Whosoever shall swear by the temple, it is nothing; but whosoever shall swear by the gold of the temple, he committeth sin, and is a debtor.

14 You are fools and blind; for which is the greatest, the gold, or the temple that sanctifieth the gold?

15 And ye say, Whosoever sweareth by the ᵇaltar, it is nothing; but whosoever sweareth by the gift that is upon it, he is guilty.

16 O fools, and blind! For which is the greatest, the gift, or the altar that sanctifieth the gift?

17 Verily I say unto you, Whoso, therefore, sweareth by it, sweareth by the altar, and by all things thereon.

18 And whoso shall swear by the temple, sweareth by it, and by him who dwelleth therein.

19 And he that swear by heaven, sweareth by the throne of God,

and by him who sitteth thereon.

20 Woe unto you, Scribes and Pharisees, hypocrites! For you pay tithe of mint, and anise, and cummin; and have omitted the weightier things of the law; judgment, mercy, and faith; these ought ye to have done, and not to leave the other undone.

21 You blind guides, who strain at a gnat, and swallow a camel; who make yourselves appear unto men that ye would not commit the least sin, and yet you, yourselves, transgress the whole law.

22 Woe unto you, Scribes and Pharisees, hypocrites! For you make clean the outside of the cup, and of the platter; but within ye are full of extortion and excess.

23 Ye blind Pharisees! Cleanse first the cup and platter within, that the outside of them may be clean also.

24 Woe unto you, Scribes and Pharisees, hypocrites! For ye are like unto whited sepulchers, which indeed appear beautiful outwardly, but are within full of the bones of the dead, and of all uncleanness.

25 Even so, you also outwardly appear righteous unto men, but within ye are full of hypocrisy and iniquity.

26 Woe unto you, Scribes and Pharisees, hypocrites! Because you build the tombs of the prophets, and garnish the sepulchers of the righteous,

---

ᵃ   Dictionary - Proselyte
ᵇ   raised structure on which sacrifices are offered

27 And say, If we had been in the days of our fathers, we would not have been partakers with them in the blood of the prophets;

28 Wherefore, you are witnesses unto yourselves of your own wickedness; and ye are the children of them who killed the prophets;

29 And will fill up the measure then of your fathers; for you, yourselves, kill the prophets like unto your fathers.

30 You serpents, and generation of vipers! How can ye escape the damnation of hell?

31 Wherefore, behold, I send unto you prophets, and wise men, and scribes; and of them you shall kill and crucify; and of them you shall scourge in your synagogues, and persecute them from city to city;

32 That upon you may come all the righteous blood shed upon the earth, from the blood of righteous Abel, unto the blood of Zacharias son of Barachias, whom ye slew between the temple and the altar.

33 Verily I say unto you, All these things shall come upon this generation.

34 Ye bear testimony against your fathers, when you, yourselves, are partakers of the same wickedness.

35 Behold your fathers did it through ignorance, but ye do not; wherefore, their sins shall be upon your heads.

36 Then Jesus began to weep over Jerusalem, saying,

37 O Jerusalem! Jerusalem! You who will kill the prophets, and will stone them who are sent unto you; how often would I have gathered your children together, even as a hen gathers her chickens under her wings, and ye would not.

38 Behold, your house is left unto you desolate!

39 For I say unto you, that you shall not see me henceforth, and know that I am he of whom it is written by the prophets, until ye shall say,

40 Blessed is he who cometh in the name of the Lord, in the clouds of heaven, and all the holy angels with him.

41 Then understood his disciples that he should come again on the earth, after that he was glorified and crowned on the right hand of God.

The widow's mites

[a]47 And after this, Jesus sat over against the treasury, and beheld how the people cast money into the treasury; and many that were rich cast in much.

48 And there came a certain poor widow, and she cast in two [b]mites, which make a farthing.

49 And Jesus called his disci-

---

[a]   Mark 12:47-50
[b]   Dictionary - Mite

ples, and said unto them, Verily I say unto you, that this poor widow hath cast more in, than all they who have cast into the treasury;

50 For all the rich did cast in of their abundance; but she, notwithstanding her want, did cast in all she had; yea, even all her living.

Jesus prophesies of the destruction of the Temple

a5 And as some spake of the temple, how it was adorned with goodly stones, and gifts, he said,

6 These things which ye behold, the days will come, in the which there shall not be left one stone upon another, which shall not be thrown down.

b1 And as Jesus went out of the temple, his disciples came to him for to hear him, saying, Master, show us concerning the buildings of the temple.

2 And Jesus said unto them, Behold ye these stones of the ctemple, and all this great work, and buildings of the temple?

3 Verily I say unto you, they shall be thrown down and left unto the Jews desolate.

4 And Jesus said unto them, See ye not all these things, and do ye not understand them?

5 Verily I say unto you, There shall not be left here upon this temple, one stone upon another, which shall not be thrown down.

6 And Jesus left them and went upon the mount of Olives.

7 And as he sat upon the mount of Olives, the disciples came unto him privately, saying,

8 Tell us, when shall these things be which thou hast said, concerning the destruction of the temple, and the Jews?

9 And what is the sign of thy coming, and of the end of the world, (or the destruction of the wicked, which is the end of the world?)

Signs of the second coming

d5 And Jesus answered and said unto them, Take heed that no man deceive you.

6 For many shall come in my name, saying, I am Christ; and shall deceive many.

e11 But before all these things shall come, they shall lay their hands on you, and persecute you; delivering you up to the synagogues, and into prisons; being brought before kings and rulers for my name's sake.

12 Settle this therefore in your hearts, not to meditate before what ye shall answer;

13 For I will give you a mouth and wisdom, which all your adver-

---

a   Luke 21:5-6
b   Mark 13:1-9
c   Dictionary – Temple of Herod

d   Matthew 24:5-6
e   Luke 21:11-18

saries shall not be able to ᵃgainsay nor resist.

14 And it shall turn to you for a testimony.

15 And ye shall be betrayed both by parents, and brethren, and kinsfolk, and friends; and some of you they cause to be put to death.

16 And ye shall be hated of all the world for my name's sake.

17 But there shall not a hair of your head perish.

18 In your patience possess ye your souls.

ᵇ8 And then shall many be offended, and shall betray one another.

9 And many false prophets shall rise, and shall deceive many.

10 And because iniquity shall abound, the love of many shall wax cold.

11 But he that remaineth steadfast, and is not overcome, the same shall be saved.

12 When you, therefore, shall see the abomination of desolation, spoken of by Daniel the prophet, concerning the destruction of Jerusalem, then you shall ᶜstand in the ᵈholy place. (Whoso readeth let him understand.)

13 Then let them who are in Judea, flee unto the mountains.

14 Let him who is on the house-top, flee, and not return to take anything out of his house.

15 Neither let him who is in the field, return back to take his clothes.

16 And woe unto them that are with child, and unto them that give suck in those days! ᵉ[For there shall be great distress in the land, and wrath upon this people.]

ᶠ23 And they shall fall by the edge of the sword, and shall be led away captive into all nations; and Jerusalem shall be trodden down of the Gentiles, until the times of the Gentiles be fulfilled.

ᵍ17 Therefore, pray ye the Lord, that your flight be not in the winter, neither on the Sabbath day.

18 For then, in those days, shall be great tribulations on the Jews, and upon the inhabitants of Jerusalem; such as was not before sent upon Israel, of God, since the beginning of their kingdom until this time; no, nor ever shall be sent again upon Israel.

19 All these things which have befallen them, are only the beginning of the sorrows which shall come upon them; and except those days should be shortened, there should none of their flesh be saved.

20 But for the elect's sake, according to the covenant, those days shall be shortened.

ᵃ   deny or dispute
ᵇ   Matthew 24:8-16
ᶜ   Dictionary - Conundrum
ᵈ   Dictionary - Holy Place

ᵉ   Luke 21:22
ᶠ   Luke 21:23
ᵍ   Matthew 24:17-34

21 Behold these things I have spoken unto you concerning the Jews.

22 And again, after the tribulation of those days which shall come upon Jerusalem, if any man shall say unto you, Lo! here is Christ, or there; believe him not.

23 For in those days, there shall also arise false Christs, and false prophets, and shall show great signs and wonders; insomuch that, if possible, they shall deceive the very elect, who are the ᵃelect according to the covenant.

24 Behold, I speak these things unto you for the elect's sake.

25 And you also shall hear of wars, and rumors of wars; see that ye be not troubled; for all I have told you must come to pass. But the end is not yet.

26 Behold, I have told you before, Wherefore, if they shall say unto you, Behold, he is in the desert; go not forth. Behold, he is in the secret chambers; believe it not.

27 For as the light of the morning cometh out of the east, and shineth even unto the west, and covereth the whole earth; so shall also the coming of the Son of Man be.

28 And now I show unto you a parable. Behold, wheresoever the carcass is, there will the eagles be gathered together; so likewise shall mine elect be gathered from the four quarters of the earth.

29 And they shall hear of wars, and rumors of wars. Behold, I speak for mine elect's sake.

30 For nation shall rise against nation, and kingdom against kingdom; there shall be famine and pestilences, and earthquakes in diverse places.

31 And again, because iniquity shall abound, the love of men shall wax cold; but he that shall not be overcome, the same shall be saved.

32 And again, this gospel of the kingdom shall be preached in all the world, for a witness unto all nations, and then shall the end come, or the destruction of the wicked.

33 And again shall the abomination of desolation, spoken of by Daniel the prophet, be fulfilled.

34 And immediately after the tribulation of those days, the sun shall be darkened, and the moon shall not give her light, and the stars shall fall from heaven, and the powers of heaven shall be shaken.

ᵇ25 . . . And upon the earth distress of nations with perplexity, like the sea and the waves roaring. The earth also shall be troubled, and the waters of the great deep;

26 Men's hearts failing them for fear, and for looking after those things which are coming on the

---

ᵃ   Dictionary - Elect

ᵇ   Luke 21:25-26

earth. For the powers of heaven shall be shaken.

[a]35 Verily I say unto you, this generation, in which these things shall be shown forth, shall not pass away until all I have told you shall be fulfilled.

36 Although the days will come that heaven and earth shall pass away, yet my word shall not pass away; but all shall be fulfilled.

37 And as I said before, after the tribulation of those days, and the powers of the heavens shall be shaken, then shall appear the sign of the Son of Man in heaven; and then shall all the tribes of the earth mourn.

38 And they shall see the Son of Man coming in the clouds of heaven, with power and great glory.

39 And whoso treasureth up my words, shall not be deceived.

40 For the Son of Man shall come, and he shall send his angels before him with the great sound of a trumpet, and they shall gather together the remainder of his elect from the four winds; from one end of heaven to the other.

41 Now learn a parable of the fig tree, When its branches are yet tender, and it begins to put forth leaves, you know that summer is nigh at hand.

42 So likewise mine elect, when they shall see all these things, they shall know that he is near, even at the doors.

43 But of that day and hour no one knoweth; no, not the angels of God in heaven, but *my* Father only.

44 But as it was written in the days of Noah, so it shall be also at the coming of the Son of Man.

45 For it shall be with them as it was in the days which were before the flood; for until the day that Noah entered into the ark, they were eating and drinking, marrying and giving in marriage, and knew not until the flood came and took them all away; so shall also the coming of the Son of Man be.

46 Then shall be fulfilled that which is written, that, In the last days,

[b]34 I tell you, in that night there shall be two in one bed; the one shall be taken, and the other left.

[c]47 Two shall be in the field; the one shall be taken and the other left.

48 Two shall be grinding at the mill; the one taken and the other left.

[d]36 And they answered and said unto him, Where, Lord, shall they be taken.

37 And he said unto them, Wheresoever the body is gathered; or, in other words, whithersoever the saints are gathered; thither will the eagles be gathered together; or,

---

[a] Matthew 24:35-46

[b] Luke 17:34
[c] Matthew 24:47-48
[d] Luke 17:36-40

thither will the remainder be gathered together.

38 This he spake, signifying the gathering of his saints; and of angels descending and gathering the remainder unto them; the one from the bed, the other from the grinding, and the other from the field, whithersoever he listeth.

39 For verily there shall be new heavens, and a new earth, wherein dwelleth righteousness.

40 And there shall be no unclean thing; for the earth becoming old, even as a garment, having waxed in corruption, wherefore it vanisheth away, and the footstool remaineth sanctified, cleansed from all sin.

[a]36 And what I say unto one, I say unto all, Watch ye therefore, and pray always, and keep my commandments, that ye may be counted worthy to escape all these things which shall come to pass, and to stand before the Son of Man when he shall come clothed in the glory of *his* Father.

[b]50 But know this, if the good man of the house had known in what watch the thief would come, he would have watched, and would not have suffered his house to have been broken up; but would have been ready.

51 Therefore be ye also ready; for in such an hour as ye think not, the Son of Man cometh.

Who then is a wise servant?

[c]52 Who then is a faithful and a wise servant, whom his lord hath made ruler over his household, to give them meat in due season?

53 Blessed is that servant, whom his lord when he cometh shall find so doing;

54 And, verily I say unto you, he shall make him ruler over all his goods.

55 But if that evil servant shall say in his heart, My Lord delayeth his coming; and shall begin to smite his fellow servants, and to eat and drink with the drunken; the Lord of that servant shall come in a day when he looketh not for him, and in an hour that he is not aware of, and shall cut him asunder, and shall appoint him his portion with the hypocrites; there shall be weeping and gnashing of teeth.

56 And thus cometh the end of the wicked according to the prophecy of Moses, saying, They should be cut off from among the people. But the end of the earth is not yet; but bye and bye.

Parable of the ten virgins

[d]1 And then, at that day, before the Son of Man comes, the kingdom

---

a   Luke 21:36
b   Matthew 24:50-51
c   Matthew 24:52-56
d   Matthew 25:1-12

of heaven shall be likened unto ten virgins, who took their lamps, and went forth to meet the bridegroom.

2 And five of them were wise, and five of them were foolish.

3 They that were foolish took their lamps and took no oil with them; but the wise took oil in their vessels with their lamps.

4 While the bridegroom tarried, they all slumbered and slept.

5 And at midnight there was a cry made, Behold, the bridegroom cometh; go ye out to meet him.

6 Then all those virgins arose, and trimmed their lamps.

7 And the foolish said unto the wise, Give us of your oil; for our lamps are gone out.

8 But the wise answered, saying, Lest there be not enough for us and you, go you rather to them that sell, and buy for yourselves.

9 And while they went to buy, the bridegroom came; and they that were ready went in with him to the marriage; and the door was shut.

10 Afterward came also the other virgins, saying, Lord, Lord, open unto us.

11 But he answered and said, Verily I say unto you, You know me not.

12 Watch therefore; for you know neither the day nor the hour wherein the Son of Man cometh.

Parable of the talents

[a]13 Now I will liken these things unto a parable.

14 For it is like a man traveling into a far country, who called his own servants, and delivered unto them his goods.

15 And unto one he gave five [b]talents, to another two, and to another one; to every man according to his several ability; and straightway went on his journey.

16 Then he that had received the five talents, went and traded with the same; and gained other five talents.

17 And likewise he who received two talents, he also gained other two.

18 But he who had received one, went and digged in the earth and hid his lord's money.

19 After a long time the lord of those servants cometh, and reckoneth with them.

20 And so he that had received the five talents came, and brought other five talents, saying, Lord, thou deliveredst unto me five talents; behold, I have gained besides them, five talents more.

21 His lord said unto him, Well done, good and faithful servant; thou hast been faithful over a few things, I will make thee ruler over many things; enter thou into the

---

[a]   Matthew 25:13-31
[b]   gifts of the spirit

joy of thy lord.

22 He also that had received two talents came and said, Lord, thou deliveredst unto me two talents; behold, I have gained two talents besides them.

23 His lord said unto him, Well done, good and faithful servant; thou hast been faithful over a few things; I will make thee ruler over many things; enter into the joy of thy lord.

24 Then he who had received the one talent came, and said, Lord, I knew thee that thou art a hard man, reaping where thou hast not sown, and gathering where thou hast not scattered.

25 And I was afraid, and went and hid thy talent in the earth; and lo, here is thy talent; take it from me as thou hast from thine other servants, for it is thine.

26 His Lord answered and said unto him, O wicked and slothful servant; thou knewest that I reap where I sowed not, and gather where I have not scattered.

27 Having known this, therefore, thou oughtest to have put my money to the exchangers, and at my coming I should have received mine own with usury.

28 I will take, therefore, the talent from you, and give it unto him who hath ten talents.

29 For unto everyone who hath obtained other talents, shall be given, and he shall have in abundance.

30 But from him that hath not obtained other talents, shall be taken away even that which he hath received.

31 And his lord shall say unto his servants, Cast ye the unprofitable servant into outer darkness; there shall be weeping and gnashing of teeth.

Sheep and the goats

[a]32 When the Son of Man shall come in his glory, and all the holy angels with him, then he shall sit upon the throne of his glory;

33 And before him shall be gathered all nations; and he shall separate them one from another, as a shepherd divideth sheep from the goats; the sheep on his right hand, but the goats on his left.

34 And he shall sit upon his throne, and the twelve apostles with him.

I was an hungered, and ye gave me meat

[b]35 Then shall the King say unto them on his right hand, Come, ye blessed of *my* Father, inherit the kingdom prepared for you from the foundation of the world.

36 For I was an hungered, and ye gave me meat; I was thirsty, and ye gave me drink; I was a stranger, and ye took me in; naked, and ye

---

[a]   Matthew 25:32-34
[b]   Matthew 25:35-47

clothed me;

37 I was sick, and ye visited me; I was in prison, and ye came unto me.

38 Then shall the righteous answer him, saying, Lord, when saw we thee an hungered, and fed thee? or thirsty, and gave thee drink?

39 When saw we thee a stranger, and took thee in; or naked, and clothed thee?

40 Or when saw we thee sick, or in prison, and came unto thee?

41 And the King shall answer and say unto them, Verily I say unto you, inasmuch as ye have done it unto one of the least of these my brethren, ye have done it unto me.

42 Then shall he say also unto them on the left hand, Depart from me, ye cursed, into everlasting fire, prepared for the devil and his angels.

43 For I was an hungered, and ye gave me no meat; I was thirsty, and ye gave me no drink;

44 I was a stranger, and ye took me not in; naked, and ye clothed me not; sick, and in prison, and ye visited me not.

45 Then shall they also answer him, saying, Lord, when saw we thee an hungered, or athirst, or a stranger, or naked, or sick, or in prison, and did not minister unto thee?

46 Then he shall answer them, saying, Verily I say unto you,

Inasmuch as ye did it not unto one of the least of these my brethren, ye did it not unto me.

47 And these shall go away into everlasting punishment; but the righteous into life eternal.

[a]1 And it came to pass, when Jesus had finished all these sayings, he said unto his disciples,

2 Ye know that after two days is the passover, and then the Son of Man is betrayed to be crucified.

Mary anoints Jesus with spikenard

[b]4 And Jesus being in Bethany, in the house of Simon the leper, as he sat at meat, there came a [c]woman having an alabaster box of ointment of [d]spikenard, very precious; and she brake the box, and poured the ointment on his head.

5 And there were some among the disciples who had indignation within themselves, and said, Why was this waste of the ointment made? for it might have been sold for more than three hundred pence, and have been given to the poor. And they murmured against her.

6 And Jesus said unto them, Let her alone; why trouble ye her? [e][and from whence is this evil in

---

a   Matthew 26:1-2
b   Mark 14:4-9
c   Mary of Bethany - John 12:3
d   Dictionary - Spikenard
e   JST p. 224

your hearts. For verily I say unto you] she hath wrought a good work on me.

7 Ye have the poor with you always, and whensoever ye will, ye may do them good; but me ye have not always.

8 She has done what she could, and this which she has done unto me, shall be in remembrance in generations to come, wheresoever my gospel shall be preached; for verily she has come beforehand to anoint my body to the burying.

9 Verily I say unto you, Wheresoever this gospel shall be preached throughout the whole world, what she hath done shall be spoken of also for a memorial of her a[for in that she hath done for me she hath obtained a blessing of *my* Father.]

Judas meets with the high priests

b2 And the chief Priests, and the Scribes, sought how they might kill him; but they feared the people.

c11 Then one of the twelve, called Judas Iscariot, went unto the chief Priests, and said, What will ye give me, and I will deliver him unto you? d[And they were glad,] And they covenanted with him for thirty pieces of silver.

e3 Then assembled together the chief Priests, and Scribes, and the Elders of the people, unto the palace of the high Priest, who was called Caiaphas, and consulted that they might take Jesus by subtlety and kill him.

4 But they said, Not on the feast day, lest there be an uproar among the people.

f12 And from that time he sought opportunity to betray Jesus g[unto them in the absence of the multitude.]

Preparations for the Passover

h13 Now on first day of the feast of unleavened bread, i[when the passover must be killed,] the disciples came to Jesus, saying unto him, Where wilt thou that we prepare for thee to eat the passover?

j8 And he sent Peter and John, saying, Go, and prepare us the passover, that we may eat.

9 And they said unto him, Where wilt thou that we prepare?

10 And he said unto them, Behold, when ye have entered into the city, there shall a man meet you bearing a pitcher of water; follow him unto the house where he entereth in.

---

a   JST p. 225
b   Luke 22:2
c   Matthew 26:11
d   Luke 22:5
e   Matthew 26:3-4
f   Matthew 26:12
g   Luke 22:6
h   Matthew 26:13
i   Luke 22:7
j   Luke 22:8-13

11 And ye shall say unto the good man of the house, The Master saith unto you, Where is the guest chamber, where I shall eat the passover with my disciples?

12 And he shall show you a large upper room furnished; there make ready.

13 And they went, and found as he had said unto them; and they made ready the passover.

Passover supper

[a]16 Now when the evening was come, he sat down with the twelve.

[b]15 And he said unto them, With desire I have desired to eat this passover with you before I suffer;

[c]21 When Jesus had thus said, he was troubled in spirit, and testified, and said, Verily, verily, I say unto you, that one of you shall betray me.

22 Then the disciples looked one on another, doubting of whom he spake.

23 Now there was leaning on Jesus' bosom one of his disciples, whom Jesus loved.

24 Simon Peter therefore beckoned to him, that he should ask who it should be of whom he spake.

25 He then lying on Jesus' breast said unto him, Lord, who is it?

26 Jesus answered, He it is, to whom I shall give a sop, when I have dipped it. And when he had dipped the sop, he gave it to Judas Iscariot, the son of Simon.

27 And after the sop Satan entered into him. Then said Jesus unto him, That thou doest, do quickly; [d][but beware of innocent blood.]

[e]31 Nevertheless, Judas Iscariot, even one of the twelve, went unto the chief priests to betray Jesus unto them; for he turned away from him, and was offended because of his words.

[f]28 Now no man at the table knew for what intent he spake this unto him.

29 For some of them thought, because Judas held the bag, that Jesus had said unto him, Buy those things that we have need of against the feast; or, that he should give something to the poor.

30 He then having received the sop, went immediately out; and it was night.

31 Therefore, when he was gone out, Jesus said, Now is the Son of Man glorified, and God is glorified in him.

32 If God be glorified in him, God shall also glorify him in himself, and shall straightway glorify him.

a   Matthew 26:16
b   Luke 22:15
c   John 13:21-27
d   Mark 14:30
e   Mark 14:31
f   John 13:28-32

Who is greatest among them?

[a]24 There was also a strife among them, who of them should be accounted the greatest.

25 And he said unto them, The kings of the Gentiles exercise lordship over them, and they who exercise authority upon them, are called benefactors.

26 But it ought not to be so with you; but he who is greatest among you, let him be as the younger; and he who is chief, as he who doth serve.

27 For whether is he greater, who sitteth at meat, or he who serveth? I am not as he who sitteth at meat, but I am among you as he who serveth.

Jesus washes the Apostle's feet

[b]2 And supper being ended, the devil having now put into the heart of Judas Iscariot, Simon's son, to betray him;

3 Jesus knowing that *the* Father had given all things into his hands, and that he was come from God, and went to God;

4 He riseth from supper, and laid aside his garments; and took a towel, and girded himself.

5 After that he poureth water into a basin, and began to [c]wash the disciples' feet, and to wipe them with the towel wherewith he was girded.

6 Then cometh he to Simon Peter; and Peter saith unto him, Lord, dost thou wash my feet?

7 Jesus answered and said unto him, What I do thou knowest not now; but thou shalt know hereafter.

8 Peter saith unto him, Thou needest not to wash my feet. Jesus answered him, If I wash thee not, thou hast no part with me.

9 Simon Peter saith unto him, Lord, not my feet only, but also my hands and my head.

10 Jesus saith unto him, He that has washed his hands and his head, needeth not save to wash his feet, but is clean every whit; and ye are clean, but not all. Now this was the custom of the Jews under their law; wherefore, Jesus did this that the law might be fulfilled.

11 For he knew who should betray him; therefore said he, Ye are not all clean.

12 So after he had washed their feet, and had taken his garments, and was set down again, he said unto them, Know ye what I have done to you?

13 Ye call me Master and Lord; and ye say well; for so I am.

14 If I then, your Lord and

---

a   Luke 22:24-27
b   John 13:2-20
c   Dictionary - Washing the Hands and the Feet

Master, have washed your feet; ye also ought to wash one another's feet.

15 For I have given you an example, that ye should do as I have done to you.

16 Verily, verily, I say unto you, The servant is not greater than his Lord; neither he that is sent greater than he that sent him.

17 If ye know these things, [a]happy are ye if ye do them.

18 I speak not of you all; I know whom I have chosen; but that the Scripture may be fulfilled, He that eateth bread with me hath lifted up his heel against me.

19 Now I tell you before it come, that, when it is come to pass, ye may believe that I am the Christ.

20 Verily, verily, I say unto you, He that receiveth whomsoever I send receiveth me; and he that receiveth me receiveth him that sent me.

Jesus institutes the sacrament

[b]20 And as they did eat, Jesus took bread and blessed it, and brake, and gave to them, and said, Take it, and eat.

21 Behold, this is for you to do in remembrance of my body; [c][which I give a ransom for you,]

for as oft as ye do this ye will remember this hour that I was with you.

22 And he took the cup, and when he had given thanks, he gave it to them: and they all drank of it.

[d]24 For this is in remembrance of my blood of the new [e]testament, which is shed for as many as shall believe on my name, for the remission of their sins.

[f]24 And as oft as ye do this ordinance, ye will remember me in this hour that I was with you, and drank with you of this cup, even the last time in my ministry.

[g]25 And I give unto you a commandment, that ye shall observe to do the things which ye have seen me do, and bear record of me even unto the end.

26 But I say unto you, I will not drink henceforth of this fruit of the vine, until that day when I drink it new with you in *my* Father's kingdom.

[h]26 And now they were grieved, and wept over him.

Jesus tells Peter he will deny Him thrice

[i]28 Ye are they who have continued with me in my temptations;

---

a   Dictionary - Happiness
b   Mark 14:20-22
c   Matthew 26:22
d   Matthew 26:24
e   means covenant with God
f   Mark 14:24
g   Matthew 26:25-26
h   Mark 14:26
i   Luke 22:28-30

29 And I appoint unto you a kingdom, as *my* Father hath appointed unto me;

30 That you may eat and drink at my table in my kingdom; and sit on twelve thrones, judging the twelve tribes of Israel.

[a]33 Little children, yet a little while I am with you. Ye shall see me; and as I said unto the Jews, Whither I go, ye cannot come; so now I say to you.

34 A new commandment I give unto you, That ye love one another; as I have loved you, that ye also love one another.

35 By this shall all men know that ye are my disciples, if ye have love one to another.

36 Simon Peter said unto him, Lord, whither goest thou? Jesus answered him, Whither I go, thou canst not follow me now; but thou shalt follow me afterwards.

37 Peter said unto him, Lord, why cannot I follow thee now? I will lay down my life for thy sake.

[b]31 And the Lord said, Simon, Simon, behold Satan hath desired to have you, that he may sift the children of the kingdom as wheat.

32 But I have prayed for you, that your faith fail not; and when you are converted strengthen your brethren.

33 And he said unto him, being aggrieved, Lord, I am ready to go with you, both into prison, and unto death.

34 And the Lord said, I tell you, Peter, that the cock shall not crow this day, before that you will [c]thrice deny that you know me.

[d]32 Peter said unto him, Though I should die with thee, yet will I not deny thee. Likewise also said all the disciples.

Jesus comforts the Apostles

[e]1 Let not your heart be troubled; ye believe in God, believe also in me.

2 In *my* Father's house are many mansions; if it were not so, I would have told you. I go to prepare a place for you.

3 And when I go, I will prepare a place for you, and come again, and receive you unto myself; that where I am, ye may be also.

4 And whither I go ye know, and the way ye know.

5 Thomas saith unto him, Lord, we know not whither thou goest; and how can we know the way?

6 Jesus saith unto him, I am the way, the truth, and the life; no man cometh unto *the* Father, but by me.

7 If ye had known me, ye should have known *my* Father also; and from henceforth ye know him, and have seen him.

---

[a]   John 13:33-37
[b]   Luke 22:31-34
[c]   three times
[d]   Matthew 26:32
[e]   John 14:1-31

8 Philip saith unto him, Lord, show us *the* Father, and it sufficeth us.

9 Jesus saith unto him, Have I been so long time with you, and yet hast thou not known me, Philip? [a]he that hath seen me hath seen *the* Father; and how sayest thou then, Show us *the* Father?

10 Believest thou not that I am in *the* Father, and *the* Father in me? the words that I speak unto you I speak not of myself; but *the* Father that dwelleth in me, he doeth the works.

11 Believe me that I am in *the* Father, and *the* Father in me; or else believe me for the very works' sake.

12 Verily, verily, I say unto you, He that believeth on me, the works that I do shall he do also; and greater works than these shall he do; because I go unto *my* Father.

13 And whatsoever ye shall ask in my name, that will I do, that *the* Father may be glorified in the Son.

14 If ye shall ask any thing in my name, I will do it.

15 If ye love me, keep my commandments.

16 And I will pray *the* Father, and he shall give you another [b]Comforter, that he may abide with you for ever;

17 Even the spirit of truth; whom the world cannot receive, because it seeth him not, neither knoweth him; but ye know him; for he dwelleth with you, and shall be in you.

18 I will not leave you comfortless; I will come to you.

19 Yet a little while, and the world seeth me no more; but ye see me; because I live, ye shall live also.

20 At that day ye shall know that I am in *my* Father, and ye in me, and I in you.

21 He that hath my commandments, and keepeth them, he it is that loveth me; and he that loveth me shall be loved of *my* Father, and I will love him, and will manifest myself to him.

22 Judas saith unto him, (not Iscariot,) Lord, how is it that thou wilt manifest thyself unto us, and not unto the world?

23 Jesus answered and said unto him, If a man love me, he will keep my words; and *my* Father will love him, and we will come unto him, and make our abode with him.

24 He that loveth me not keepeth not my sayings; and the word which ye hear is not mine, but *the* Father's which sent me.

25 These things have I spoken unto you, being yet present with you.

26 But the Comforter, which is the Holy Ghost, whom *the* Father will send in my name, he shall teach you all things, and bring

---

[a] Dictionary - Conundrum
[b] Dictionary - Comforter

all things to your remembrance, whatsoever I have said unto you.

27 [a]Peace I leave with you, my peace I give unto you; not as the world giveth, give I unto you. Let not your heart be troubled, neither let it be afraid.

28 Ye have heard how I said unto you, I go away, and come again unto you. If ye loved me, ye would rejoice, because I said, I go unto *the* Father; for *my* Father is greater than I.

29 And now I have told you before it come to pass, that, when it is come to pass, ye might believe.

30 Hereafter I will not talk much with you; for the prince of darkness, who is of this world, cometh, but hath no power over me, but he hath power over you.

31 I tell you these things, that ye may know that I love *the* Father; and as *the* Father gave me commandment, even so I do. . .

Jesus teaches He is the true vine

[b]1 I am the true vine, and *my* Father is the husbandman.

2 Every branch in me that beareth not fruit he taketh away; and every branch that beareth fruit, he [c]purgeth it, that it may bring forth more fruit.

3 Now ye are clean through the word which I have spoken unto you.

4 Abide in me, and I in you. As the branch cannot bear fruit of itself, except it abide in the vine; no more can ye, except ye abide in me.

5 I am the vine, ye are the branches. He that abideth in me, and I in him, the same bringeth forth much fruit; for without me ye can do nothing.

6 If a man abide not in me, he is cast forth as a branch, and is withered; and men gather them, and cast them into the fire, and they are burned.

7 If ye abide in me, and my words abide in you, ye shall ask what ye will, and it shall be done unto you.

8 Herein is *my* Father glorified, that ye bear much fruit; so shall ye be my disciples.

9 As *the* Father hath loved me, so have I loved you; continue ye in my love.

10 If ye keep my commandments, ye shall abide in my love; even as I have kept *my* Father's commandments, and abide in his love.

11 These things I have spoken unto you, that my joy might remain in you, and that your joy might be full.

12 This is my commandment, That ye love one another, as I have loved you.

---

[a] Dictionary - Peace
[b] John 15:1-27
[c] Prune or eliminate things standing in the way of doing his work

13 Greater love hath no man than this, that a man lay down his life for his friends.

14 Ye are my friends, if ye do whatsoever I command you.

15 Henceforth I call you not servants; for the servant knoweth not what his lord doeth; but I have called you friends; for all things that I have heard of *my* Father I have made known unto you.

16 Ye have not chosen me, but I have chosen you, and ordained you, that ye should go and bring forth fruit, and that your fruit should remain; that whatsoever ye shall ask of *the* Father in my name, he may give it you.

17 These things I command you, that ye love one another.

18 If the world hate you, ye know that it hated me before it hated you.

19 If ye were of the world, the world would love his own; but because ye are not of the world, but I have chosen you out of the world, therefore the world hateth you.

20 Remember the word that I said unto you, The servant is not greater than his lord. If they have persecuted me, they will also persecute you; if they have kept my saying, they will keep yours also.

21 But all these things will they do unto you for my name's sake, because they know not him that sent me.

22 If I had not come and spoken unto them, they had not had sin; but now they have no cloak for their sin.

23 He that hateth me hateth *my* Father also.

24 If I had not done among them the works which none other man did, they had not had sin; but now have they both seen and hateth both me and *my* Father.

25 But this cometh to pass, that the word might be fulfilled that is written in their law, They hated me without a cause.

26 But when the Comforter is come, whom I will send unto you from *the* Father, even the spirit of truth, which proceedeth from *the* Father, he shall testify of me;

27 And ye also shall bear witness, because ye have been with me from the beginning.

Jesus teaches about the Holy Ghost

[a]1 These things have I spoken unto you, that ye should not be offended.

2 They shall put you out of the synagogues; yea, the time cometh, that whosoever killeth you will think that he doeth God service.

3 And these things will they do unto you, because they have not known *the* Father, nor me.

4 But these things have I told

---

a   John 16:1-15

you, that when the time shall come, ye may remember that I told you of them. And these things I said not unto you at the beginning, because I was with you.

5 But now I go my way to him that sent me; and none of you ask me, Whither goest thou?

6 But because I have said these things unto you, sorrow hath filled your heart.

7 Nevertheless I tell you the truth; it is expedient for you that I go away; for if I go not away, the Comforter will not come unto you; but if I depart, I will send him unto you.

8 And when he is come, he will reprove the world of sin, and of righteousness, and of judgment;

9 Of sin, because they believe not on me;

10 Of righteousness, because I go to *my* Father, and they see me no more;

11 Of judgment, because the prince of this world is judged.

12 I have yet many things to say unto you, but ye cannot bear them now.

13 Howbeit when he, the Spirit of truth, is come, he will guide you into all truth; for he shall not speak of himself; but whatsoever he shall hear, that shall he speak; and he will show you things to come.

14 He shall glorify me; for he shall receive of mine, and shall show it into you.

15 All things that *the* Father

hath are mine; therefore said I, that he shall take of mine, and shall show it unto you.

Jesus prophesies of His resurrection

[a]16 A little while, and ye shall not see me; and again, a little while, and ye shall see me, because I go to *the* Father.

17 Then said some of his disciples among themselves, What is this that he saith unto us, A little while, and ye shall not see me; and again, a little while, and ye shall see me; and, Because I go to *the* Father?

18 They say therefore, What is this that he saith, A little while? we cannot tell what he saith.

19 Now Jesus knew that they were desirous to ask him, and said unto them, Do ye inquire among yourselves of that I said, A little while, and ye shall not see me; and again, a little while, and ye shall see me?

20 Verily, verily, I say unto you, That ye shall weep and lament, but the world shall rejoice; and ye shall be sorrowful, but your sorrow shall be turned into joy.

21 A woman when she is in travail hath sorrow, because her hour is come; but as soon as she is delivered of the child, she remembereth no more the anguish, for joy that a

---

[a]   John 16:16-33

man is born into the world.

22 And ye now therefore have sorrow; but I will see you again, and your heart shall rejoice, and your joy no man taketh from you.

23 And in that day ye shall ask me nothing but it shall be done unto you. Verily, verily, I say unto you, Whatsoever ye shall ask *the* Father in my name, he will give it you.

24 Hitherto have ye asked nothing in my name; ask, and ye shall receive, that your joy may be full.

25 These things I have spoken unto you in proverbs; but the time cometh, when I shall no more speak unto you in proverbs, but I shall show you plainly of *the* Father.

26 At that day ye shall ask in my name; and I say not unto you, that I will pray *the* Father for you;

27 For *the* Father himself loveth you, because ye have loved me, and have believed that I came out from God.

28 I came forth from *the* Father, and am come into the world; again, I leave the world, and go to *the* Father.

29 His disciples said unto him, Lo, now speakest thou plainly, and speakest no proverb.

30 Now are we sure that thou knowest all things, and needest not that any man should ask thee; by this we believe that thou camest from God.

31 Jesus answered them, Do ye now believe?

32 Behold, the hour cometh, yea, is now come, that ye shall be scattered, every man to his own, and shall leave me alone; and yet I am not alone, because *the* Father is with me.

33 These things I have spoken unto you, that in me ye might have peace. In the world ye shall have tribulation; but be of good cheer; I have overcome the world.

The intercessory prayer

[a]1 These words spake Jesus, and lifted up his eyes to heaven, and said, Father, the hour is come; glorify thy Son, that thy Son also may glorify thee;

2 As thou hast given him power over all flesh, that he should give [b]eternal life to as many as thou hast given him.

3 And this is life eternal, that they might know thee the only true God, and Jesus Christ, whom thou hast sent.

4 I have glorified thee on the earth; I have finished the work which thou gavest me to do.

5 And now, O Father, glorify thou me with thine own self with the glory which I had with thee before the world was.

6 I have manifested thy name unto the men which thou gavest

---

[a] John 17:1-26
[b] Dictionary - Eternal life

me out of the world; thine they were, and thou gavest them me; and they have kept thy word.

7 Now they have known that all things whatsoever thou hast given me are of thee.

8 For I have given unto them the words which thou gavest me; and they have received them, and have known surely that I came out from thee, and they have believed that thou didst send me.

9 I pray for them; I pray not for the world, but for them which thou hast given me; for they are thine.

10 And all mine are thine, and thine are mine; and I am glorified in them.

11 And now I am no more in the world, but these are in the world, and I come to thee. Holy Father, keep through thine own name those whom thou hast given me, that they may be one, as we are.

12 While I was with them in the world, I kept them in thy name; those that thou gavest me I have kept, and none of them is lost, but the ᵃson of perdition; that the scripture might be fulfilled.

13 And now I come to thee; and these things I speak in the world, that they might have my joy fulfilled in themselves.

14 I have given them thy word; and the world hath hated them, because they are not of the world, even as I am not of the world.

15 I pray not that thou shouldest take them out of the world, but that thou shouldest keep them from the evil.

16 They are not of the world, even as I am not of the world.

17 Sanctify them through thy truth; thy word is truth.

18 As thou hast sent me into the world, even so have I also sent them into the world.

19 And for their sakes I sanctify myself, that they also might be sanctified through the truth.

20 Neither pray I for these alone, but for them also which shall believe on me through their word;

21 That they all may be one; as thou, Father, art in me, and I in thee, that they also may be one in us; that the world may believe that thou hast sent me.

22 And the glory which thou gavest me I have given them; that they may be one, even as we are one;

23 I in them, and thou in me, that they may be made perfect in one; and that the world may know that thou hast sent me, and hast loved them, as thou hast loved me.

24 Father, I will that they also, whom thou hast given me, be with me where I am; that they may behold my glory, which thou hast given me; for thou lovedst me be-

---

ᵃ   as used here; a follower of Satan

fore the [a]foundation of the world.

25 O righteous Father, the world hath not known thee; but I have known thee, and these have known that thou hast sent me.

26 And I have declared unto them thy name, and will declare it; that the love wherewith thou hast loved me may be in them, and I in them.

They go to the Mount of Olives

[b]27 And when they had sung a hymn, they went out into the mount of Olives.

[c]35 And he said unto them, When I sent you without purse and scrip, or shoes, lacked ye anything? And they said, Nothing.

36 Then said he unto them, I say unto you again, He who hath a purse, let him take it, and likewise his scrip; and he who hath no sword, let him sell his garment and buy one.

37 For I say unto you, This that is written must be accomplished in me, And he was reckoned among the transgressors; for the things concerning me have an end.

38 And they said, Lord, behold, here are two swords. And he said unto them, It is enough.

[d]1 When Jesus had spoken these words, he went forth with his disciples over the brook [c]Cedron, where was a garden, into the which he entered, and his disciples.

Gethsemane

[f]36 And they came to a place which was named [g]Gethsemane, which was a garden; and the disciples began to be sore amazed, and to be very heavy, and to complain in their hearts, wondering if this be the Messiah.

37 And Jesus knowing their hearts, said to his disciples, Sit you here, while I shall pray.

38 And he taketh with him, Peter, and James, and John, and rebuked them, and said unto them, My soul is exceeding sorrowful, even unto death; tarry ye here and watch.

39 . . . [h][And he was withdrawn from them about a stones cast,] and fell on the ground, and prayed, that if it were possible the hour might pass from him.

40 And he said, Abba, Father, all things are possible unto thee; take away this cup from me; nevertheless, not my will, but thine be done.

[i]43 And there appeared an angel unto him from heaven, strengthen-

---

[a] Dictionary - Plan of salvation
[b] Matthew 26:27
[c] Luke 22:35-38
[d] John 18:1
[e] Map 2 also Dictionary - Kidron
[f] Mark 14:36-40
[g] Dictionary - Gethsemane
[h] Luke 22:41
[i] Luke 22:43-44

ing him.

44 And being in agony, he prayed more earnestly; and he sweat as it were great drops of blood falling down to the ground.

[a]41 And he cometh and findeth them sleeping, and said unto Peter, Simon, sleepest thou? Couldest not thou watch one hour?

42 Watch ye and pray, lest ye enter into temptation.

43 And they said unto him, The spirit truly is ready, but the flesh is weak.

44 And again he went away and prayed, and spake the same words.

45 And when he returned, he found them asleep again, for their eyes were heavy; neither knew they what to answer him.

46 And he cometh to them the third time, and said unto them, Sleep on now and take rest; it is enough, the hour is come; behold, the Son of Man is betrayed into the hands of sinners.

Judas betrays Jesus with a kiss

[b]2 And Judas also, which betrayed him, knew the place; for Jesus ofttimes resorted thither with his disciples.

3 Judas then, having received a band of men and officers from the chief priests and Pharisees, cometh thither with lanterns and torches and weapons.

[c]43 And after they had slept, he said unto them, Arise, and let us be going. Behold, he is at hand that doth betray me.

44 And while he yet spake, lo, Judas, one of the twelve, came, and with him a great multitude with swords and staves, from the chief priests and elders of the people.

[d]4 Jesus therefore, knowing all things that should come upon him, went forth, and said unto them, Whom seek ye?

5 They answered him, Jesus of Nazareth. Jesus saith unto them, I am he. And Judas also, which betrayed him, stood with them.

6 As soon then as he had said unto them, I am he, they went backward, and fell to the ground.

7 Then asked he them again, Whom seek ye? And they said, Jesus of Nazareth.

8 Jesus answered, I have told you that I am he; if therefore ye seek me, let these go their way;

9 That the saying might be fulfilled, which he spake, Of them which thou gavest me have I lost none.

[e]45 Now he that betrayed him gave them a sign, saying, Whomsoever I shall kiss, that same

---

[a] Mark 14:41-46
[b] John 18:2-3
[c] Matthew 26:43-44
[d] John 18:4-9
[e] Matthew 26:45-47

is he; hold him fast.

46 And forthwith he came to Jesus, and said, Hail, Master! and kissed him.

47 And Jesus said unto him, Judas, wherefore art thou come to betray me with a kiss?

ª49 When they who were about him, saw what would follow, they said unto him, Lord, shall we smite with a sword?

ᵇ10 Then Simon Peter having a sword drew it, and smote the high priest's servant, and cut off his right ear. The servant's name was Malchus.

ᶜ50 Then said Jesus unto him, Put up again thy sword into its place; for all they that take the sword shall perish with the sword, ᵈ[And he put forth his finger and healed the servant of the high priest.]

51 Thinkest thou that I cannot now pray to *my* Father, and he shall presently give me more than twelve legions of angels?

52 ᵉ[The cup which *my* Father hath given me, shall I not drink it?] But how then shall the scriptures be fulfilled, that thus it must be?

53 In that same hour said Jesus unto the multitudes, Are ye come out as against a thief, with swords and staves, for to take me? I sat dai-ly with you in the temple, teaching, and ye laid no hold on me.

54 But all this was done, that the scriptures of the prophets might be fulfilled.

55 Then all the disciples forsook him, and fled.

ᶠ48 Then came they, and laid hands on Jesus, and took him.

ᵍ57 And there followed him a certain young man, a disciple, having a linen cloth cast about his naked body; and the young men laid hold on him, and he left the linen cloth and fled from them naked, and saved himself out of their hands.

Jesus is led away to Annas

ʰ12 Then the band and the captain and officers of the Jews took Jesus, and bound him,

13 And led him away to Annas first; for he was father-in-law to Caiaphas, which was the high priest that same year.

ⁱ19 The high priest then asked Jesus of his disciples, and of his doctrine.

20 Jesus answered him, I spake openly to the world; I ever taught in the synagogue, and in the temple, whither the Jews always resort; and in secret have I said nothing.

21 Why askest thou me? ask

ª   Luke 22:49
ᵇ   John 18:10
ᶜ   Matthew 26:50-55
ᵈ   Mark 14:53
ᵉ   John 18:11

ᶠ   Matthew 26:48
ᵍ   Mark 14:57
ʰ   John 18:12-13
ⁱ   John 18:19-24

them which heard me, what I have said unto them; behold, they know what I said.

22 And when he had thus spoken, one of the officers which stood by struck Jesus with the palm of his hand, saying, Answerest thou the high priest so?

23 Jesus answered him, If I have spoken evil, bear witness of the evil; but if well, why smitest thou me?

24 Now Annas had sent him bound unto Caiaphas the high priest.

Peter denies knowing Jesus

[a]56 And they that had laid hold on Jesus, led him away to Caiaphas the high priest, where the Scribes and the elders were assembled.

[b]14 Now Caiaphas was he, which gave counsel to the Jews, that it was expedient that one man should die for the people.

15 And Simon Peter followed Jesus, [c][afar off,] and so did another disciple; that disciple was known unto the high priest, and went in with Jesus into the palace of the high priest.

16 But Peter stood at the door without. Then went out that other disciple, which was known unto the high priest, and spake unto her that kept the door, and brought in Peter.

[d]18 And the servants and officers stood there, who had made a fire of coals, for it was cold; and they warmed themselves; and Peter stood with them, and warmed himself.

[e]56 But [f][the damsel that kept the door] beheld him, as he [stood] by the fire, and earnestly looked upon him, and said, This man was also with him.

57 And he denied him, saying, Woman, I know him not.

[g]26 One of the servants of the high priest, being his kinsman whose ear Peter cut off, saith, Did not I see thee in the garden with him?

[h]72 And again he denied with an oath, saying, I do not know the man.

[i]59 [j][And when he was gone out into the porch,] And about the space of one hour, another confidently affirmed, saying, Of a truth, this man was also with him; for he is a Galilean, [k][for thy speech betrayeth thee.]

60 And Peter [l][began . . . to curse and to swear, saying, I know not the man.] And immediately,

---

a   Matthew 26:56
b   John 18:14-16
c   Mark 14:59

d   John 18:18
e   Luke 22:56-57
f   John 18:17
g   John 18:26
h   Matthew 26:72
i   Luke 22:59-62
j   Matthew 26:71
k   Matthew 26:73
l   Matthew 26:74

while he yet spake, the cock crew.

61 And the Lord turned, and looked upon Peter. And Peter remembered the word of the Lord, how he had said unto him, Before the cock crow, thou shalt deny me thrice.

62 And Peter went out, [a][and fell upon his face,] and wept bitterly.

Chief priests seek false witness

[b]58 Now the chief priests, and elders, and all the council, sought false witness against Jesus, to put him to death; but found none.

59 Yea, though many false witnesses came, they found none that could accuse him.

60 At the last came two false witnesses, and said, This man said, I am able to destroy the temple of God, and to build it in three days.

61 And the high priest arose and said unto him, Answerest thou nothing? Knowest thou what these witness against thee?

62 But Jesus held his peace.

63 And the high priest answered and said unto him,

64 I adjure thee by the living God, that thou tell us whether thou be the Christ, the Son of God.

65 Jesus said unto him, Thou hast said. Nevertheless, I say unto you, hereafter shall ye see the Son of Man sitting on the right hand of power, and coming in the clouds of heaven.

66 Then the high priest rent his clothes, saying, He hath spoken blasphemy; what further need have we of witnesses? Behold, now, ye have heard his blasphemy. What think ye?

67 They answered and said, He is guilty, and worthy of death.

[c]63 And the men who held Jesus, mocked him, and smote him.

[d]71 And some began to spit on him, [e][And when they had blindfolded him, they struck him on the face, and asked him, saying, Prophesy, who is it who smote thee?]

[f]65 And many other things blasphemously spake they against him.

Judas hangs himself

[g]1 When the morning was come, all the chief priests and elders of the people took counsel against Jesus, to put him to death:

2 And when they had bound him, they led him away, and delivered him to Pontius Pilate, the governor.

3 Then Judas, who had betrayed

---

him, when he saw that he was condemned, repented himself, and brought again the thirty pieces of silver to the chief priests and elders.

4 Saying, I have sinned in that I have betrayed the innocent blood.

5 And they said unto him, What is that to us? See thou to it; thy sins be upon thee.

6 And he cast down the pieces of silver in the temple, and departed, and went, and hanged himself on a tree. And straightway he fell down, and his bowels gushed out, and he died.

7 And the chief priests took the silver pieces, and said, It is not lawful for us to put them in the treasury, because it is the price of blood.

8 And they took counsel, and bought with them the ᵃpotter's field, to bury strangers in. Wherefore that field was called, The field of blood, unto this day.

9 Then was fulfilled that which was spoken by Jeremy, the prophet, saying, And they took the thirty pieces of silver, the price of him that was valued, whom they of the children of Israel did value.

Jesus is brought before Pilate

ᵇ28 Then led they Jesus from Caiaphas unto the hall of judgment; and it was early; and they themselves went not into the judgment hall, lest they should be ᶜdefiled; but that they might eat the passover.

29 Pilate then went out unto them, and said, What accusation bring ye against this man?

30 And they answered and said unto him, If he were not a ᵈmalefactor, we would not have delivered him up unto thee.

ᵉ2 And they began to accuse him, saying, We found this man perverting the nation, and forbidding to give tribute to Caesar, saying, that he himself is Christ, a king.

ᶠ31 Then said Pilate unto them, Take ye him, and judge him according to your law. The Jews therefore said unto him, It is not lawful for us to put any man to death;

32 That the saying of Jesus might be fulfilled, which he spake signifying what death he should die.

ᵍ13 And when he was accused of the chief priests and the elders, he answered nothing.

14 Then said Pilate unto him, Hearest thou not how many things they witness against thee?

ᵃ   Easy Ref. Zechariah 11:13
ᵇ   John 18:28-30

ᶜ   Dictionary - Defiled
ᵈ   one who commits an offence against the law
ᵉ   Luke 23:2
ᶠ   John 18:31-32
ᵍ   Matthew 27:13-15

15 And he answered him not to his questions; yea, never a word, insomuch that the governor marveled greatly.

[a]33 Then Pilate entered into the judgment hall again, and called Jesus, and said unto him, Art thou the king of the Jews?

34 Jesus answered him, Sayest thou this thing of thyself, or did others tell it thee of me?

35 Pilate answered, Am I a Jew? Thine own nation and the chief priests have delivered thee unto me; what hast thou done?

36 Jesus answered, My kingdom is not of this world; if my kingdom were of this world, then would my servants fight, that I should not be delivered to the Jews; but now is my kingdom not from hence.

37 Pilate therefore said unto him, Art thou a king then? Jesus answered, Thou sayest that I am a king. To this end was I born, and for this cause came I into the world, that I should bear witness unto the truth. Every one that is of the truth heareth my voice.

38 Pilate saith unto him, What is truth? And when he had said this, he went out again unto the Jews, and saith unto them, I find in him no fault at all.

[b]5 And they were the more fierce, saying, He stirreth up the people, teaching throughout all Jewry, beginning from Galilee to this place.

6 When Pilate heard of Galilee, he asked whether the man were a Galilean.

7 And as soon as he knew that he belonged unto Herod's jurisdiction, he sent him to Herod, who himself also was at Jerusalem at that time.

Jesus is brought before Herod

[c]8 And when Herod saw Jesus, he was exceeding glad; for he was desirous to see him, of a long time, because he had heard many things of him; and hoped to have seen some miracle done by him.

9 Then he questioned with him in many words; but he answered him nothing.

10 And the chief priests and scribes stood and vehemently accused him.

11 And Herod with his men of war set him at naught, and mocked him, and arrayed him in a gorgeous robe, and sent him away to Pilate.

12 And the same day Pilate and Herod were made friends together; for before this they were at [d]enmity between themselves.

[a] John 18:33-38
[b] Luke 23:5-7
[c] Luke 23:8-12
[d] hostility, antagonism, or animosity

Jesus is brought before Pilate a second time

[a]13 And Pilate, when he had called together the chief priests, and the rulers, and the people,

14 Said unto them, You have brought this man unto me, as one who perverteth the people; and behold, I, having examined him before you, have found no fault in this man, touching those things whereof ye accuse him.

15 No, nor yet Herod; for I sent you to him; and, lo, nothing worthy of death is done unto him;

16 I will therefore chastise him, and release him.

[b]8 Now it was common at the feast, for Pilate to release unto them one prisoner, whomsoever they desired.

[c]19 And the soldiers led him away into the hall, called Praetorium; and then called together the whole band;

20 And they clothed him with purple, and platted a crown of thorns, and put it about his head;

21 And began to salute him, saying, Hail, King of the Jews.

22 And they smote him on the head with a reed, and did spit upon him, and bowing their knees worshipped him.

[d]4 Pilate therefore went forth again, and saith unto them, Behold, I bring him forth to you, that ye may know that I find no fault in him.

5 Then came Jesus forth, wearing the crown of thorns, and the purple robe. And Pilate saith unto them, [e][Behold your King]!

[f]15 But they cried out, Away with him, away with him, crucify him. Pilate saith unto them, Shall I crucify your King? The chief priests answered, We have no king but Caesar.

[g]39 But ye have a custom, that I should release unto you one at the Passover; will ye therefore that I release unto you the king of the Jews?

[h]12 For he knew that the chief priests had delivered him for envy.

13 But the chief priests moved the people that he should rather release [i]Barabbas unto them, as he had done before unto them.

[j]40 Then cried they all again, saying, Not this man, but Barabbas,[k][Who for a certain sedition made in the city, and for murder, was cast into prison.]

[l]20 Pilate therefore, willing to

---

a   Luke 23:13-16
b   Mark 15:8
c   Mark 15:19-22

d   John 19:4-5
e   John 19:14
f   John 19:15
g   John 18:39
h   Mark 15:12-13
i   Dictionary - Barabbas
j   John 18:40
k   Luke 23:19
l   Luke 23:20

release Jesus, spake again to them, [a][What will ye then that I shall do with him whom ye call the King of the Jews?]

[b]15 And they cried out again, Deliver him unto us to be [c]crucified. Away with him. Crucify him.

[d]22 And when he said unto them the third time, Why, what evil hath he done? I have found no cause of death in him; I will therefore chastise him, and let him go.

[e]7 The Jews answered him, We have a law, and by our law he ought to die, because he made himself the Son of God.

8 When Pilate therefore heard that saying, he was the more afraid;

Pilate's wife has a vision

[f]20 When he was set down on the judgment seat, his wife sent unto him, saying, Have thou nothing to do with that just man, for I have suffered many things this day in a vision because of him.

[g]9 And [he] went into the judgment hall, and saith unto Jesus, Whence art thou? But Jesus gave him no answer.

10 Then saith Pilate unto him, Speakest thou not unto me? knowest thou not that I have power to crucify thee, and have power to release thee?

11 Jesus answered, Thou couldest have no power at all against me, except it were given thee from above; therefore he that delivered me unto thee hath the greater sin.

12 And from thenceforth Pilate sought to release him; but the Jews cried out, saying, If thou let this man go, thou art not Caesar's friend; whosoever maketh himself a king speaketh against Caesar.

Jesus is crucified

[h]13 When Pilate therefore heard that saying, he brought forth, and sat down in the judgment seat in a place called the [i]Pavement, but in the Hebrew, Gabbatha.

[j]23 And they were instant in loud voices, requiring that he might be crucified; and the voices of them, and of the chief priests, prevailed.

[k]26 When Pilate saw that he could prevail nothing, but rather that a tumult was made, he took water, and washed his hands before the multitude, saying, I am innocent of the blood of this just person; see that ye do nothing unto him.

[a] Mark 15:14
[b] Mark 15:15
[c] Dictionary - Crucifixion
[d] Luke 23:22
[e] John 19:7-8
[f] Matthew 27:20
[g] John 19:9-12

[h] John 19:13
[i] courtyard made with many exquisite gems
[j] Luke 23:23
[k] Matthew 27:26-27

27 Then answered all the people, and said, His blood come upon us and our children.

[a]18 And now Pilate, willing to content the people, released Barabbas unto them, and delivered Jesus, when he had scourged him, to be crucified.

[b]23 And when they had mocked him, they took off the purple from him, and put his own clothes on him, and led him out to crucify him.

24 And they compelled one Simon, a Cyrenian, who passed by, coming out of the country, the father of Alexander and Rufus, to bear his cross.

[c]27 There followed him a great company of people, and of women, who also bewailed and lamented him.

28 But Jesus turned unto them and said, Daughters of Jerusalem, weep not for me, but weep for yourselves, and for your children.

29 For behold, the days are coming, in the which they shall say, Blessed are the barren, and the wombs which never bear, and the paps which never gave suck.

30 Then shall they begin to say to the mountains, Fall on us; and to the hills, Cover us.

31 And if these things are done in the green tree, what shall be done in the dry tree?

32 This he spake, signifying the scattering of Israel, and the desolation of the heathen, or in other words, the Gentiles.

33 And there were also two others, malefactors, led with him to be put to death.

34 And when they were come to the place, which is called [d][eGolgotha, which is, (being interpreted,) The place of burial,] they crucified him, and the malefactors; one on the right hand, and the other on the left, [f][and Jesus in the midst.]

[g]33 And the scripture was fulfilled which said, [h]And he was numbered with the transgressors

[i]28 And it was the third hour, when they crucified him.

[j]23 Then the soldiers, when they had crucified Jesus, took his garments, and made four parts, to every soldier a part; and also his coat; now the coat was without seam, woven from the top throughout.

24 They said therefore among themselves, Let us not rend it, but cast lots for it, whose it shall be; that the scripture might be fulfilled, which saith, [k]They parted

---

d   Mark 15:25
e   Dictionary - Golgotha
f   John 19:18
g   Mark 15:33
h   Easy Ref. Isaiah 53:12
i   Mark 15:28
j   John 19:23-24
k   Easy Ref. Psalms 22:18

my raiment among them, and for my vesture they did cast lots. These things therefore the soldiers did.

[a]35 Then said Jesus, Father, forgive them; for they know not what they do. (Meaning the soldiers who crucified him,) . . .

[b]44 And they that passed by reviled him, wagging their heads, and saying, Thou that destroyest the temple, and buildest it again in three days, save thyself. If thou be the Son of God come down from the cross.

45 Likewise also the chief Priests mocking with the Scribes and the elders, said, He saved others, himself he cannot save. If he be the King of Israel, let him now come down from the cross, and we will believe him.

46 He trusted in God; let him deliver him now; if he will save him, let him save him; for he said, I am the Son of God.

[c]38 And sitting down they watched him there;

The two thieves

[d]40 And one of the malefactors who was crucified with him, railed on him, saying, If thou be the Christ, save thyself and us.

41 But the other answering, rebuked him, saying, Dost thou not fear God, seeing thou art in the same condemnation?

42 And we indeed justly; for we receive the due reward of our deeds; but this man hath done nothing amiss [e][and hath not sinned].

43 And he said unto Jesus, Lord, remember me when thou comest into thy kingdom.

44 And he said unto him, Verily I say unto thee; To day shalt thou be with me in [f]paradise.

King of the Jews

[g]19 And Pilate wrote a title, and put it on the cross. And the writing was, JESUS OF NAZARETH THE KING OF THE JEWS.

20 This title then read many of the Jews; for the place where Jesus was crucified was nigh to the city; and it was written in Hebrew, and Greek, and Latin.

21 Then said the chief priests of the Jews to Pilate, Write not, The King of the Jews; but that he said, I am King of the Jews.

22 Pilate answered, What I have written I have written, [h][let it alone.]

Behold thy mother

[i]25 Now there stood by the

---

[a]   Luke 23:35
[b]   Matthew 27:44-46
[c]   Matthew 27:38
[d]   Luke 23:40-44

[e]   Matthew 27:47
[f]   the world of spirits - T to the F p.111 E.R.
[g]   John 19:19-22
[h]   Matthew 27:42
[i]   John 19:25-27

cross of Jesus his mother, and his mother's sister, Mary the wife of Cleophas, and Mary Magdalene.

26 When Jesus therefore saw his mother, and the disciple standing by, whom he loved, he saith unto his mother, Woman, behold thy son!

27 Then saith he to his disciple, Behold thy mother! And from that hour that disciple took her unto his own home.

Jesus thirsts

[a]28 After this, Jesus knowing that all things were now accomplished, [b]that the scripture might be fulfilled, saith, I thirst.

29 Now there was a vessel full of [c]vinegar, mingled with [d]gall, and they filled a sponge with it, and put upon [e]hyssop, and put to his mouth; [f][and when he had tasted the vinegar, he would not drink.]

30 When Jesus therefore had received the vinegar, he said, It is finished . . .

Jesus dies

[g]45 And it was about the sixth hour, and there was darkness over all the earth until the ninth hour.

[h]39 And at the ninth hour, Jesus cried with a loud voice, saying, Eloi, Eloi, lama sabachthani? which is, (being interpreted,) My God, my God, why hast thou forsaken me?

40 And some of them who stood by, when they heard him, said, Behold, he calleth Elias.

[i]53 The rest said, Let him be, let us see whether Elias will come to save him.

54 Jesus when he had cried again with a loud voice saying, Father, it is finished, thy will is done, [j][into thy hands I commend my spirit;] [k][he bowed his head, and gave up the ghost.]

55 And behold, the [l]veil of the temple was rent in twain from the top to the bottom; and the earth did quake, and the rocks rent;

[m]44 And when the centurion who stood over against him, [n][and they that were with him, watching Jesus, heard the earthquake, and saw those things which were done, they feared greatly, saying,] Truly, this man is the Son of God.

[o]49 And all the people who came together to that sight, beholding

---

[a]   John 19:28-30
[b]   Easy Ref. Psalms 69:21
[c]   Dictionary - Wine
[d]   Dictionary - Gall
[e]   Dictionary - Hyssop
[f]   Mark 15:26
[g]   Luke 23:45

[h]   Mark 15:39-40
[i]   Matthew 27:53-55
[j]   Luke 23:47
[k]   John 19:30
[l]   Dictionary - Veil of the Temple
[m]   Mark 15:44
[n]   Matthew 27:58
[o]   Luke 23:49-50

the things which were done, smote their breasts, and returned.

50 And all his acquaintance, and women who followed him from Galilee, [a][ministering unto him for his burial;] stood afar off, beholding these things.

The soldiers pierce His side

[b]31 The Jews therefore, because it was the preparation, that the bodies should not remain upon the cross on the Sabbath day, (for that sabbath day was a high day,) besought Pilate that their legs might be broken, and that they might be taken away.

32 Then came the soldiers, and brake the legs of the first, and of the other which was crucified with him.

33 But when they came to Jesus, and saw that he was dead already, [c]they brake not his legs;

34 But one of the soldiers with a spear pierced his side, and forthwith came there out blood and water.

35 And he that saw it bear record, and his record is true; and he knoweth that he saith true, that ye might believe.

36 For these things were done, that the scripture should be fulfilled, [d]A bone of him shall not be broken.

37 And again another scripture saith, [e]They shall look on him whom they pierced.

Jesus is laid in the tomb

[f]51 And, behold, a [g][rich] man named [h]Joseph, a counselor; a good man and a just one; [i][being a disciple of Jesus, but secretly for fear of the Jews,]

52 The same day had not consented to the counsel and deed of them; a man of Arimathea, a city of the Jews; who also himself waited for the kingdom of God.

53 He went [j][in boldly] unto Pilate, and begged the body of Jesus. [k][And Pilate marveled, and asked if he were already dead.]

[l]48 And calling the centurion, he asked him, If he had been any while dead?

49 And when he knew it of the centurion, he gave the body to Joseph.

[m]39 And there came also Nicodemus, (which at the first came to Jesus by night,) and brought a mixture of myrrh and aloes, about

---

a   Matthew 27:59
b   John 19:31-37
c   Easy Ref. Psalms 34:20
d   Easy Ref. Exodus 12:46 and
     Numbers 9:12
e   Easy Ref. Zechariah 12:10
f   Luke 23:51-53
g   Matthew 27:60
h   Dictionary - Joseph of
     Arimathaea
i   John 19:38
j   Mark 15:47
k   Mark 15 47
l   Mark 15:48-49
m   John 19:39-42

an hundred pound weight.

40 Then took they the body of Jesus, and wound it in linen clothes with the spices, as the manner of the Jews is to bury.

41 Now in the place where he was crucified there was a garden; and in the garden a new sepulcher, wherein was never man yet laid.

42 There laid they Jesus therefore because of the Jews' preparation day; for the sepulcher was nigh at hand.

[a]56 And [b][Mary Magdalene, and Mary the mother of James and Joses, and the mother of Zebedee's children,] also, who came with him from Galilee, followed after, and beheld the sepulcher, and how his body was laid.

[c]62 . . . and he rolled a great stone to the door of the sepulcher,[d][and the sabbath drew on.]

63 And there was Mary Magdalene, and the other Mary, sitting over against the sepulcher.

[e]57 And they returned, and prepared spices and ointments; and rested the Sabbath day according to the commandment.

Jews ask Pilate for a watch

[f]64 Now the next day that followed the day of the preparation, the chief priests and Pharisees came together unto Pilate, saying, Sir, we remember that that deceiver said, while he was yet alive, After three days I will rise again.

65 Command therefore, that the sepulcher be made sure until the third day, lest his disciples come by night, and steal him away, and say unto the people, He is risen from the dead; so this last [g]imposture will be worse than the first.

66 Pilate said unto them, Ye have a watch; go your way, make it as sure as you can.

67 So they went, and made the sepulcher sure, sealing the stone and setting a watch.

He is risen

[h]1 And when the Sabbath was past, Mary Magdalene, and Mary the mother of James and Salome, brought sweet spices, that they might come and anoint him.

2 And very early in the morning, the first day of the week, they came unto the sepulcher at the rising of the sun; and they said among themselves, Who shall roll us away the stone from the door of the sepulcher? [i][for it was very great.]

[j]2 And behold, there had been

---

a   Luke 23:56
b   Matthew 27:59
c   Matthew 27:62-63
d   Luke 23:55
e   Luke 23:57
f   Matthew 27:64-67

g   a counterfeit action passed off as genuine
h   Mark 16:1-2
i   Mark 16:3
j   Matthew 28:2

a great earthquake; [a][and the rocks rent;]

[b]56 And the graves were opened; and the bodies of the saints which slept, arose, who were many, and came out of their graves.

57 And after his resurrection, went into the holy city and appeared unto many.

[c]2 . . . for two angels of the Lord descended from heaven, and came and rolled back the stone from the door, and sat upon it; [d][clothed in long white garments.]

3 And their countenance was like lightning, and their raiment white as snow; and for fear of them the keepers did shake, and became as though they were dead.

[e]4 And [the women] were affrighted, and bowed down their faces to the earth. But behold the angels said unto them. [f][Fear not ye; for we know that ye seek Jesus who was crucified.] Why seek ye the living among the dead?

[g]5 He is not here; for he is risen, as he said. Come, see the place where the Lord lay; [h][Remember how he spake unto you when he was yet in Galilee,]

[i]6 Saying, The Son of man must be delivered into the hands of sinful men, and be crucified, and the third day rise again?

7 And they remembered his words.

[j]6 And they, entering into the sepulcher, saw the place where they laid Jesus.

[k]5 And go your way, tell his disciples and Peter, that he goeth before you into Galilee; there shall ye see him as he said unto you.

[l]6 And they departed quickly from the sepulcher, with fear and great joy; and did run to bring his disciples word.

Elders give money to the soldiers to lie

[m]10 Now when they were going, behold, some of the watch came into the city, and showed unto the chief priests all the things that were done.

11 And when they were assembled with the elders, and had taken counsel, they gave large money unto the soldiers,

12 Saying, Say ye, His disciples came by night, and stole him while we slept.

13 And if this comes to the governor's ears, we will persuade him,

---

[a]   Matthew 27:55
[b]   Matthew 27:56-57
[c]   Matthew 28:2-3
[d]   Mark 16:3
[e]   Luke 24:4
[f]   Matthew 28:4
[g]   Matthew 28:5
[h]   Luke 24:5

[i]   Luke 24:6-7
[j]   Mark 16:6
[k]   Mark 16:5
[l]   Matthew 28:6
[m]   Matthew 28:10-14

and secure you.

14 So they took the money, and did as they were taught; and this saying is commonly reported among the Jews until this day.

The women tell the Apostles

[a]9 It was Mary Magdalene, and Joanna, and Mary the mother of James, and other women who were with them, who told these things unto the apostles; [b][and saith unto them, They have taken away the Lord out of the sepulcher, and we know not where they have laid him.]

10 And their words seemed to them as idle tales, and they believed them not.

[c]3 Peter therefore went forth, and that other disciple, and came to the sepulcher,

4 So they ran together; and the other disciple did outrun Peter, and came first to the sepulcher.

5 And stooping down, and looking in, saw the linen clothes lying; yet went he not in.

6 Then cometh Simon Peter following him, and went into the sepulcher, and seeth the linen clothes lie,

7 And the napkin, that was about his head, not lying with the linen clothes, but wrapped

together in a place by itself, [d][and he beheld the linen clothes laid by themselves.]

8 Then went in also that other disciple, which came first to the sepulcher, and he saw, and believed.

9 For as yet they knew not the scripture, that he must rise again from the dead.

10 Then the disciples went away again unto their own homes.

Jesus appears to Mary Magdalene

[e]11 But Mary stood without at the sepulcher weeping; and as she wept, she stooped down, and looked into the sepulcher,

12 And seeth two angels in white sitting, the one at the head, and the other at the feet, where the body of Jesus had lain.

13 And they said unto her, Woman, why weepest thou? She saith unto them, Because they have taken away my Lord, and I know not where they have laid him.

14 And when she had thus said, she turned herself back, and saw Jesus standing, and knew not that it was Jesus.

15 Jesus saith unto her, Woman, why weepest thou? whom seekest thou? She, supposing him to be the gardener, saith unto him, Sir, if thou hast borne him hence, tell

[a]   Luke 24:9-10
[b]   John 20:2
[c]   John 20:3-10

[d]   Luke 24:11
[e]   John 20:11-16

me where thou hast laid him, and I will take him away.

16 Jesus saith unto her, Mary. She turned herself, and said unto him, [a]Rabboni; which is to say, Master.

[b]8 And [she] came and held him by the feet, and worshipped him.

[c]17 Jesus saith unto her, [d]hold me not; for I am not yet ascended to *my* Father; but go to my brethren, and say to them, I ascend unto *my* Father, and *your* Father; and to *my* God, and *your* God.

Mary tells the Apostles

[e]18 Mary Magdalene came and told the disciples, [f][as they mourned and wept,] that she had seen the Lord, and that he had spoken these things unto her.

[g]10 And they, when they had heard that he was alive, and had been seen of her, believed not.

Jesus appears to two others

[h]12 And behold, two of them went that same day to a village called [i]Emmaus, which was from Jerusalem [j]three score furlongs.

13 And they talked together of all these things which had happened.

14 And it came to pass, that while they communed together, and reasoned, Jesus himself drew near, and went with them.

15 But their eyes were holden, or covered, that they could not know him.

16 And he said unto them, What manner of communications are these which you have one with another, as ye walk and are sad?

17 And one of them, whose name was [k]Cleopas, answering, said unto him, Art thou a stranger in Jerusalem, and hast not known the things which are come to pass there in these days?

18 And he said unto them, What things? And they said unto him, Concerning Jesus of Nazareth, who was a prophet mighty in deed and word before God and all the people;

19 And how the chief priests and our rulers delivered him to be condemned to death, and have crucified him.

20 But we trusted that it had been he who should have redeemed Israel. And besides all this, to day is the third day since these things were done;

21 Yea, and certain women

---

[a] Smith's - great Master
[b] Matthew 28:8
[c] John 20:17
[d] hold me not - JST p. 467
[e] John 20:18
[f] Mark 16:9
[g] Mark 16:10
[h] Luke 24:12-31
[i] see Map 1
[j] Smith's - 13,200 feet or 2 ½ miles
[k] Dictionary - Cleopas

also of our company made us astonished, who were early at the sepulcher;

22 And when they found not his body, they came, saying, that they had also seen a vision of angels, who said that he was alive.

23 And certain of them who were with us, went to the sepulcher, and found it even so as the women had said; but him they saw not.

24 Then he said unto them, O fools, and slow of heart to believe all that the prophets have spoken!

25 Ought not Christ to have suffered these things, and to enter into his glory?

26 And beginning at Moses and all the prophets, he expounded unto them all the scriptures the things concerning himself.

27 And they drew nigh unto the village whither they went; and he made as though he would have gone farther.

28 But they constrained him, saying, Abide with us; for it is toward evening, and the day is far spent. And he went in to tarry with them.

29 And it came to pass, as he sat at meat with them, he took bread, and blessed, and brake, and gave to them.

30 And their eyes were opened, and they knew him; and he was taken up out of their sight.

31 And they said one to another, Did not our hearts burn within

us, while he talked with us by the way, and while he opened to us the scriptures?

The two tell the Apostles

[a]32 And they rose up that same hour and returned to Jerusalem, and found the eleven gathered together, and those who were with them,

34 And they told what things they saw and heard in the way, and how he was known to them, in breaking of bread, [b][neither believed they them.]

Jesus appears to ten of the Apostles

[c]19 Then the same day at evening, being the first day of the week, when the doors were shut where the disciples were assembled for fear of the Jews, came Jesus and stood in the midst, and saith unto them, Peace be unto you.

[d]36 But they were terrified and affrighted, and supposed that they had seen a spirit.

37 And he said unto them, Why are you troubled, and why do thoughts arise in your hearts?

38 Behold my hands and my feet, that it is I, myself. Handle me, and see; for a spirit hath not flesh and bones, as ye see me have.

---

[a]   Luke 24:32, 34
[b]   Mark 16:12
[c]   John 20:19
[d]   Luke 24:36-42

39 When he had thus spoken, he showed them his hands and his feet.

40 And while they yet wondered and believed not for joy, he said unto them, Have ye here any meat?

41 And they gave him a piece of broiled fish, and a honey comb.

42 And he took it and did eat before them.

[a]13 Afterward he . . . upbraided them with their unbelief, and hardness of heart, because they believed not them which had seen him after he was risen.

[b]43 And he said unto them, These are the words which I spake unto you while I was yet with you, that all things must be fulfilled which were written in the law of Moses, and in the prophets, and in the Psalms, concerning me.

44 Then opened he their understanding, that they might understand the scriptures,

45 And said unto them, Thus it is written, and thus it behooved Christ to suffer, and to rise from the dead the third day;

46 And that repentance and remission of sins should be preached in his name among all nations, beginning at Jerusalem.

[c]20 And when he had so said, he showed unto them his hands and his side. Then were the disciples glad, when they saw the Lord.

21 Then said Jesus to them again, Peace be unto you; as *my* Father hath sent me, even so send I you.

22 And when he had said this, he breathed on them, and saith unto them, Receive ye the Holy Ghost;

23 Whosesoever sins ye remit, they are remitted unto them; and whosesoever sins ye retain, they are retained.

Thomas does not believe

[d]24 But Thomas, one of the twelve, called Didymus, was not with them when Jesus came.

25 The other disciples therefore said unto him, We have seen the Lord. But he said unto them, Except I shall see in his hands the print of the nails, and put my finger into the print of the nails, and thrust my hand into his side, I will not believe.

26 And after eight days again his disciples were within, and Thomas with them; then came Jesus, the doors being shut, and stood in the midst, and said, Peace be unto you.

27 Then saith he to Thomas, Reach hither thy finger, and behold my hands; and reach hither

---

[a]   Mark 16:13
[b]   Luke 24:43-46
[c]   John 20:20-23

[d]   John 20:24-29

thy hand, and thrust it into my side; and be not faithless, but believing.

28 And Thomas answered and said unto him, My Lord and my God.

29 Jesus saith unto him, Thomas, because thou hast seen me, thou hast believed; blessed are they that have not seen, and yet have believed.

Jesus tells them to stay in Jerusalem

[a]4 And, being with them when they were assembled together, commanded them that they should not depart from Jerusalem, but wait for the promise of *the* Father, which, saith he, ye have heard of me.

5 For John truly baptized with water; but ye shall be baptized with the Holy Ghost not many days hence.

6 When they therefore were come together, they asked him, saying, Lord, wilt thou at this time restore again the kingdom to Israel?

7 And he said unto them, It is not for you to know the times or the seasons, which *the* Father hath put into his own power.

8 But ye shall receive power, after that the Holy Ghost is come upon you; and ye shall be witnesses unto me both in Jerusalem, and in all Judea, and in Samaria, and unto the uttermost part of the earth.

[b]48 And, behold, I send the promise of *my* Father upon you; but tarry ye in the city of Jerusalem, until ye be [c]endued with power from on high.

49 And he led them out as far as Bethany, and he lifted up his hands and blessed them.

The first ascension

[d]50 And it came to pass, while he blessed them, he was taken from them, and carried up into heaven [e][and a cloud received him out of their sight].

[f]10 And while they looked stedfastly toward heaven as he went up, behold, two men stood by them in white apparel;

11 Which also said, Ye men of Galilee, why stand ye gazing up into heaven? this same Jesus, which is taken up from you into heaven, shall so come in like manner as ye have seen him go into heaven.

[g]51 And they worshipped him, and returned to Jerusalem, [h][from the mount called Olivet,] with great joy.

52 And were continually in

---

[a] Acts 1:4-8

[b] Luke 24:48-49
[c] bring in or introduce - Webster's
[d] Luke 24:50
[e] Acts 1:9
[f] Acts 1:10 -11
[g] Luke 24:51-52
[h] Acts 1:12

the temple, praising and blessing God.

Jesus appears to the Apostles in Galilee

[a]1 After all these things Jesus showed himself again to his disciples at the sea of Tiberias; and on this wise showed he himself.

2 There were together Simon Peter, and Thomas called Didymus, and Nathanael of Cana in Galilee, and the sons of Zebedee, and two other of his disciples.

3 Simon Peter saith unto them, I go a fishing. They say unto him, We also go with thee. They went forth, and entered unto a ship immediately; and that night they caught nothing.

4 But when morning was now come, Jesus stood on the shore; but the disciples knew not that it was Jesus.

5 Then Jesus saith unto them, Children, have ye any meat? They answered him, No.

6 And he said unto them, Cast the net on the right side of the ship, and ye shall find. They cast therefore, and now they were not able to draw it for the multitude of fishes.

7 Therefore that disciple whom Jesus loved saith unto Peter, It is the Lord. Now when Simon Peter heard that it was the Lord, he girt his fisher's coat unto him, (for he was naked,) and did cast himself into the sea.

8 And the other disciples came in a little ship, (for they were not far from land, but as it were two hundred cubits,) dragging the net with fishes.

9 As soon as they were come to land, they saw a fire of coals there, and fish laid thereon, and bread.

10 Jesus said unto them, Bring of the fish which ye have now caught.

11 Simon Peter went up, and drew the net to land full of great fishes, an hundred and fifty three; and for all there were so many, yet was not the net broken.

12 Jesus saith unto them, Come and dine. And none of the disciples durst ask him, Who art thou? knowing that it was the Lord.

13 Jesus then cometh, and taketh bread, and giveth them, and fish likewise.

14 This is now the third time that Jesus showed himself to his disciples, after that he was risen from the dead.

Lovest thou Me?

[b]15 So when they had dined, Jesus saith to Simon Peter, Simon, son of Jonas, lovest thou me more than these? He saith unto him, Yea, Lord; thou knowest that I love thee. He saith unto him, Feed my lambs.

---

a   John 21:1-14

b   John 21:15-19

16 He saith unto him again the second time, Simon, son of Jonas, lovest thou me? He saith unto him, Yea, Lord; thou knowest that I love thee. He saith unto him, Feed my sheep.

17 He saith unto him the third time, Simon, son of Jonas, lovest thou me? Peter was grieved because he said unto him the third time, Lovest thou me? And he said unto him, Lord, thou knowest all things; thou knowest that I love thee. Jesus saith unto him, Feed my sheep.

18 Verily, verily, I say unto thee, When thou wast young, thou girdedst thyself, and walkedst whither thou wouldest; but when thou shalt be old, thou shalt stretch forth thy hands, and another shall gird thee, and carry thee whither thou wouldest not.

19 This spake he, signifying by what death he should glorify God. And when he had spoken this, he saith unto him, Follow me.

John will tarry till Jesus returns

ᵃ20 Then Peter, turning about, seeth the disciple whom Jesus loved following; which also leaned on his breast at supper, and said, Lord, which is he that betrayeth thee?

21 Peter seeing him saith to Jesus, Lord, and what shall this man do?

22 Jesus saith unto him, If I will that he tarry till I come, what is that to thee? follow thou me.

23 Then went this saying abroad among the brethren, that that disciple should not die; yet Jesus said not unto him, He shall not die; but If I will that he tarry till I come, what is that to thee?ᵇ

Jesus teaches the Apostles on a mountain

ᶜ15 Then the eleven disciples went away into Galilee, into a mountain where Jesus had appointed them.

16 And when they saw him, they worshipped him; but some doubted.

17 And Jesus came and spake unto them, saying, All power is given unto me in heaven and in earth.

ᵈ14 And he said unto them, Go ye into all the world, ᵉ[and teach all nations] and preach the gospel to every creature.

ᶠ19 Teaching them to observe all things whatsoever I have commanded you; . . .

ᵍ15 He that believeth and is baptized ʰ[in the name of *the* Father,

---

ᵃ   John 21:20-23

ᵇ   Compare D&C 7:1-8 E.R.
ᶜ   Matthew 28:15-17
ᵈ   Mark 16:14
ᵉ   Matthew 28:18
ᶠ   Matthew 28:19
ᵍ   Mark 16:15-19
ʰ   Matthew 28:18 - also see
     Dictionary - Godhead

and of the Son, and of the Holy Ghost;] shall be saved; but he that believeth not, shall be damned.

16 And these signs shall follow them that believe;

17 In my name they shall cast out devils; they shall speak with new tongues;

18 They shall take up serpents; and if they drink any deadly thing, it shall not hurt them;

19 They shall lay hands on the sick, and they shall recover.

[a]47 And ye are witnesses of these things [b][and, lo, I am with you always, unto the end of the world . . .]

The final ascension

[c]20 So then, after the Lord had spoken unto them, he was received up into heaven, and sat on the right hand of God.

21 And they went forth and preached everywhere, the Lord working with them, and confirming the word with signs following . . .

[d]30 And many other signs truly did Jesus in the presence of his disciples, which are not written in this book;

31 But these are written, that ye might believe that Jesus is the Christ, the Son of God; and that believing ye might have life through his name.

[e]24 This is that disciple which testifieth of these things, and wrote these things; and we know that his testimony is true.

25 And there are also many other things which Jesus did, the which, if they should be written every one, I suppose that even the world itself could not contain the books that should be written. Amen.

a   Luke 24:47
b   Matthew 28:19
c   Mark 16:20-21
d   John 20:30-31

e   John 21:24-25

Map 1 - Holy Land At The Time Of Jesus

Skype: Photography by Digiwisdom   ©Larry Ward 2011

1. **Region of Galilee:** Jesus spent most of his life and ministry in Galilee. At the Sea of Galilee he gave the Sermon on the Mount (Matthew 5); chose, ordained, and sent forth the Twelve Apostles, all of whom were Galilean except Judas Iscariot, who was Judean. In Galilee the risen Christ appeared to the Apostles before the final ascension (Matthew 28:16-20).

2. **Nazareth:** After returning from Egypt, Jesus grew up here and remained until the beginning of his ministry (Matthew 2:19-23; Luke 2:51-52). It was in Nazareth that he announced his divine Sonship, and was rejected by his own (Luke 4:14-32).

3. **Wilderness of Judea:** Jesus fasted 40 days and was tempted there (Matthew 4:1-11). John the Baptist also preached in the wilderness of Judea (Matthew 3:1-4).

4. **Bethlehem:** Is also known as the city of David. This is where Jesus was born and was laid in a manger (Luke 2:1-7). Angels announced to the shepherds the birth of Jesus (Luke 2:8-20) and wise men were directed by a star to Bethlehem (Matthew 2:1-12). Herod slew all the children two years of age and younger (Matthew 2:16-18).

5. **Jerusalem:** City of peace, first mentioned in Genesis 14:7. This is where Jesus taught in the temple, performed many miracles, and would eventually be crucified.

6. **Bethabara:** John the Baptist testified that he was the "voice of one crying in the wilderness" (John 1:19-28). John baptized Jesus in the Jordan River and testified that Jesus is the Lamb of God (John 1:28-34).

7. **Cana:** Jesus performed his first miracle by turning water into wine (John 2:1-11). Cana was also the home of Nathanael the Apostle (John 21:2).

8. **Sea of Galilee:** Jesus taught from Peter's boat (Luke 5:1-3) and called Peter, Andrew, James, and John to be fishers of men (Matthew 4:18-22; Luke 5:1-11). He also stilled the tempest (Luke 8:22-25), taught parables from a boat (Matthew 13), walked on the sea (Matthew 14:22-32), and appeared to his disciples after his resurrection (John 21).

9. **Capernaum:** This was Peter's and Andrew's home (Matthew 8:5, 14). Jesus called Matthew to be one of his Apostles here (Matthew 9:9). It

was in Capernaum that he gave the bread of life sermon (John 6:22-65).

10. **Bethsaida:** Peter, Andrew, and Philip were born in Bethsaida (John 1:44). It was near Bethsaida that Jesus fed the 5,000 (Luke 9:10-17; John 6:1-14).

11. **Sychar:** A city of Samaria named from the false worship on Mt. Gerizim.

12. **Magdala:** This was the home of Mary Magdalene (Mark 16:9). Jesus came here soon after feeding the 4,000 (Matthew 15:38-39).

13. **Tyre and Sidon:** Jesus healed the daughter of a Canaanite woman (Matthew 15:21-28). He compared Chorazin and Bethsaida to Tyre and Sidon, stating that if his works had been done in them that they would have repented a long time ago (Matthew 11:20-22).

14. **Caesarea Philippi:** It was near here that Peter testified that Jesus is the Christ and was promised the keys of the kingdom (Matthew 16:13-20).

15. **Bethany:** Home of Mary, Martha, and Lazarus (John 11:1). It was here that Mary anointed Jesus' head (Matthew 26:6-13, John 12:1-8). Jesus raised Lazarus from the dead (John 11:1-44).

16. **Jericho:** Jesus gave sight to Bartimaeus (Luke 18:35-43). He also dined with Zacchaeus, "chief among the publicans" (Luke 19:1-10).

17. **Bethphage:** Located on the Mt. of Olives near Jerusalem. His apostles brought Jesus a colt on which he began his triumphal entry into Jerusalem (Matthew 21:1-11). It was here that the fig tree withered (Mark 10:14-16).

18. **Emmaus:** The resurrected Lord walked on the road to Emmaus with Cleopas and his companion (Luke 24:13-32).

Map 2 - Jerusalem At The Time Of Jesus

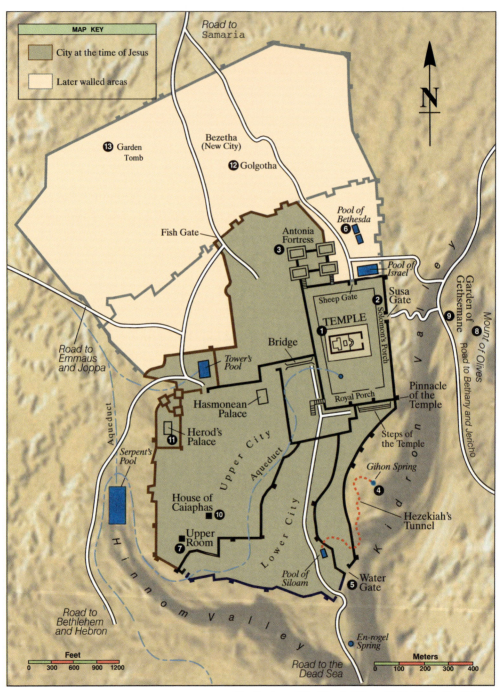

Map Courtesy of The Chruch of Jesus Christ of Latter-Day Saints

1. **Temple:** First built by Solomon (1 Kings 6:1-10). This is where Gabriel promised Zacharias that Elizabeth would bear a son (Luke 1:5-25). Jesus was presented here as a baby (Luke 2:22-39). At age twelve, Jesus taught in the temple (Luke 2:41-50). Jesus cleansed the temple twice (Matthew 21:10-14 and John 2:13-17) and taught here on several occasions. The veil of the temple was rent at His death (Matthew 27:55). It was destroyed by the Romans in A.D. 70.

2. **Solomon's Porch:** Jesus proclaimed that He was the Son of God and the Jews attempted to stone Him (John 10:22-39).

3. **Antonia Fortress:** Where the Roman guards were stationed. Jesus may have been condemned, mocked, and scourged at this site (John 18:28-19:6).

4. **Gihon Spring:** Where Solomon was anointed king (1 Kings 1:38-39). Hezekiah had a tunnel dug to bring water from the spring into the city (2 Chronicles 32:30).

5. **Water Gate:** Ezra read and interpreted the Law of Moses to the people here (Nehemiah 8:1-8).

6. **Pool of Bethesda:** Jesus healed an invalid on the Sabbath (John 5:2-9).

7. **Upper Room:** The traditional location where Jesus ate the Passover meal and instituted the sacrament (Matthew 26:16-27). He also washed the feet of the apostles, (John 13:4-17) taught, and prayed for them (John 13:18, 17:26).

8. **Mount of Olives:** Jesus foretold the destruction of Jerusalem and the temple. He also prophesied of His Second Coming (Matthew 24:3-56).

9. **Garden of Gethsemane:** Where Jesus suffered and atoned for mankind, was betrayed, and arrested (Matthew 26:33-43 and Luke 22:39-54).

10. **House of Caiaphas:** Jesus was taken before Caiaphas (Matthew 26:56-68). It was here that Peter denied that he knew Jesus (Matthew 26:69-76).

11. **Herod's Palace:** Jesus was taken before Herod (Luke 23:7-11).

12. **Golgotha:** Where Jesus was crucified (Matthew 27:35-39).

13. **Garden Tomb:** Jesus was buried here (John 19:38-42). The risen Christ appeared to Mary Magdalene in the garden (John 20:1-7). The traditional site is located north west of temple mount, a distance greater than is shown on the map. More recent archeological discoveries put in question its exact location.

EASY REFERENCE

Old Testament

Genesis 5:5 And she again conceived, and bare his brother Abel. And Abel hearkened unto the voice of the Lord. And Abel was a keeper of sheep, but Cain was a tiller of the ground.

Genesis 7:85 And Noah was four hundred and fifty years old, and begat Japheth, and forty-two years afterwards, he begat Shem, of her who was the mother of Japheth, and when he was five hundred years old, he begat Ham.

Genesis 11:15 And Terah lived seventy years, and begat Abram, Nahor, and Haran.

Genesis 13:8 And Lot lifted up his eyes, and beheld all the plain of Jordan, that it was well watered everywhere, before the Lord destroyed Sodom and Gomorrah, like as the garden of the Lord, like the land of Egypt.

Genesis 38:29 And it came to pass, as he drew back his hand, that, behold, his brother came out: and she said, How hast thou broken forth? this breach be upon thee: therefore his name was called Pharez.

Exodus 12:46 In one house shall be eaten; thou shalt not carry for ought of the flesh abroad out of the house; neither shall ye break a bone thereof.

Exodus 13:2 Sanctify unto me all the firstborn, whatsoever openeth the womb among the children of Israel, both of man and of beast; it is mine.

Leviticus 1:14 And if the burnt sacrifice for his offering to the Lord be of fowls, then he shall bring his offering of turtledoves, or of young pigeons.

Leviticus 8:33 And ye shall not go out of the door of the tabernacle of the congregation in seven days, until the days of your consecration be at an end: for seven days shall he consecrate you.

Numbers 9:12 They shall leave none of it unto the morning, nor break any bone of it: according to all the ordinances of the Passover they shall keep it.

2 Kings 1:10 And Elijah answered and said to the captain of fifty, If I be a man of God, then let fire come down out of heaven, and consume thee and thy fifty. And there came down fire from heaven, and consumed him and his fifty.

Psalms 8:2 Out of the mouth of babes and sucklings hast thou ordained strength because of thine enemies, that thou mightiest still the enemy and the avenger.

Psalms 22:18 They part my garments among them, and cast lots upon my vesture.

Psalms 34:20 He keepeth all his bones: not one of them is broken.

Psalms 69:9 For the zeal of thine house hath eaten me up; and the reproaches of them that reproached thee are fallen upon me.

Psalms 69:21 They gave me also gall for my meat; and in my thirst they gave me vinegar to drink.

Psalms 78:2 I will open my mouth in a parable: I will utter dark sayings of old:

Psalms 118:22 The stone which the builders refused is become the head stone of the corner.

Isaiah 7:14 Therefore the Lord himself shall give you a sign; Behold, a virgin shall conceive, and shall bear a son, and shall call his name Immanuel.

Isaiah 9:1-2; 1 Nevertheless the dimness shall not be such as was in her vexation, when at the first he lightly afflicted the land of Zebulun, and the land of Naphtali, and afterward did more grievously afflict her by the way of the Red sea, beyond Jordan, in Galilee of the nations. **2** The people that walked in darkness have seen a great light: they that dwell in the land of the shadow of death, upon them hath the light shined.

Isaiah 29:26 And again it shall come to pass, that the Lord shall say unto him that shall read the words that shall be delivered him, Forasmuch, as this people draw near unto me with their mouth, and with their lips do honor me, but have removed their hearts far from me and their fear toward me is taught by the precepts of men, therefore I will proceed to do a marvelous work among this people; yea, a marvelous work and a wonder; for the wisdom of their wise and learned shall perish, and the understanding of their prudent shall be hid.

Isaiah 40:3 The voice of him that crieth in the wilderness, Prepare ye the way of the Lord, make straight in the desert a highway for our God.

Isaiah 42:1-3; 1 Behold my servant, whom I upheld; mine elect, in whom my soul delighteth; I have put my spirit upon him: he shall bring forth judgment to the Gentiles. **2** He shall not cry, nor lift up, nor cause his voice to be heard in the street. **3** A bruised reed shall he not break, and the smoking flax shall he not quench: he shall bring judgment unto truth.

Isaiah 53:1 Who hath believed our report? And to whom is the arm of the Lord revealed?

Isaiah 53:12 Therefore I will divide him a portion with the great, and he shall divide the spoil with the strong; because he hath poured out his soul unto death: and he was numbered with the transgressors; and he bare the sin of many, and made intercession for the transgressors.

Isaiah 61:1-2; 1 The Spirit of the Lord God is upon me; because the Lord hath anointed me to preach good tidings unto the meek; he hath sent me to bind up the broken hearted, to proclaim liberty to the captives, and the opening of the prison to them that are bound. **2** To proclaim the acceptable year of the Lord, and the day of vengeance of our God; to comfort all that mourn;

Jeremiah 5:21 Hear now this, O foolish people, and without understanding; which have eyes, and see not; which have ears, and hear not:

Jeremiah 31:15 Thus saith the Lord; A voice was heard in Ramah, lamentation, and bitter weeping; Rachel weeping for her children refused to be comforted for her children, because they were not.

Hosea 11:1 When Israel was a child, then I loved him, and called my son out of Egypt.

Jonah 1:17 Now the Lord had prepared a great fish to swallow up Jonah. And Jonah was in the belly of the fish three days and three nights.

Jonah 2:10 And the Lord spake unto the fish, and it vomited out Jonah upon the dry land.

Micah 4:7 And I will make her that halted a remnant, and her that was cast far off a strong nation: and the Lord shall reign over them in mount Zion from henceforth, even for ever.

Micah 5:2 But thou, Bethlehem Ephratah, though thou be little among the thousands of Judah, yet out of thee shall come forth unto me that is to be the ruler in Israel; whose goings forth have been from of old, from everlasting.

Zechariah 9:9 Rejoice greatly, O daughter of Zion; shout, O daughter of Jerusalem: behold, thy King cometh unto thee: he is just, and having salvation; lowly, and riding upon an ass, and upon a colt the foal of an ass.

Zechariah 11:12-13; 12 And I said unto them, If ye think good, give me my price; and if not, forebear. So they weighed for my price thirty pieces of silver. **13** And the Lord said unto me, Cast it unto the potter: a goodly price that I was prised at of them. And I took the thirty pieces of silver, and cast them to the potter in the house of the lord.

Zechariah 12:10 And I will pour upon the house of David, and upon the inhabitants of Jerusalem, the spirit of grace and of supplications: and they shall look upon me whom they have pierced, and they shall mourn for him, as one mourneth for his only son, and shall be in bitterness for him, as one that is in bitterness for his firstborn.

New Testament

Hebrews 1:2 Hath in these last days spoken unto us by his Son, whom he hath appointed heir of all things, by whom he also made the worlds.

Book of Mormon

3 Nephi 12:1-2; 1 And it came to pass that when Jesus had spoken these words unto Nephi, and to those who had been called, (now the number of them who had been called, and received power and authority to baptize, was twelve) and behold, he stretched forth his hand unto the multitude, and cried unto them, saying: Blessed are ye if ye shall give heed unto the words of these twelve whom I have chosen from among you to minister unto you, and to be your servants; and unto them I have given power that they may baptize you with water; and after that ye are baptized with water, behold, I will baptize you with fire and with the Holy Ghost; therefore blessed are ye if ye shall believe in me and be baptized, after that ye have seen me and know that I am. **2** And again, more blessed are they who shall believe in your words because that ye shall testify that ye have seen me, and that ye know that I am. Yea, blessed are they who shall believe in your words, and come down into the depths of humility and be baptized, for they shall be visited with fire and the Holy Ghost, and shall receive a remission of their sins.

3 Nephi 12:48 Therefore I would that ye should be perfect even as I, or your Father in heaven is perfect.

3 Nephi 15:12-24; 12 Ye are my disciples; and ye are a light unto this people, who are a remnant of the house of Joseph. **13** And behold this is the land of your inheritance; and the Father hath given it unto you. **14** And not at any time hath the Father given me commandment that I should tell it unto your brethren at Jerusalem. **15** Neither at any time hath the Father given me commandment that I should tell unto them concerning the other tribes of the house of Israel, whom the Father hath led away out of the land. **16** This much did the Father command me, that I should tell unto them: **17** That other sheep I have which are not of this fold; them also I must bring, and they shall hear my voice; and there shall be one fold, and one shepherd. **18** And now, because of stiffneckedness and unbelief they understood not my word; therefore I was commanded to say no more of the Father concerning this thing unto them. **19** But, verily, I say unto you that the Father hath commanded me, and I tell it unto you, that ye were separated from among them because of their iniquity; therefore it is because of their iniquity that they know not of you. **20** And verily, I say unto you again that the other tribes hath the Father separated from them; and it is because of their iniquity that they know not of them. **21** And verily I say unto you, that ye are they of whom I said: Other sheep I have which are not of this fold; them also I must bring, and they shall hear my voice; and there shall be one fold, and one shepherd. **22** And they understood me not, for they supposed it had been the Gentiles; for they understood not that the Gentiles should be converted through their preaching. **23** And they understood me not that I said they shall hear my voice; and they understood me not that the Gentiles should not at any time hear my voice – that I should not manifest myself unto them save it were by the Holy Ghost. **24** But behold, ye have both heard my voice, and seen me; and ye are my sheep, and ye are numbered among those whom the Father hath given me.

Doctrine and Covenants

D&C 7:1-8; 1 And the Lord said unto me: John, my beloved, what desirest thou? For if you shall ask what you will, it shall be granted unto you. **2** And I said unto him: Lord, give unto me power over death, that I may live long and brings souls unto thee. **3** And the Lord said unto me: Verily, verily, I say unto thee, because thou desirest this thou shalt tarry until I come in my glory, and shalt prophesy before nations, kindreds, tongues and people. **4** And for this cause the Lord said unto Peter: If I will that he tarry till I come, what is that to thee? For he desired of me that he might bring souls unto me, but thou desiredst that thou mightiest speedily come unto me in my kingdom. **5** I say unto thee, Peter, this was a good desire; but my beloved has desired that he might do more, or a greater work yet among men than what he has before done. **6** Yea, he has undertaken a greater work; therefore I will make him as flaming fire and a ministering angel; he shall minister for those who shall be heirs of salvation who dwell on the earth. **7** And I will make thee to minister for him and for thy brother James; and unto you three I will give this power and the keys of this ministry until I come. **8** Verily I say unto you, ye shall both have according to your desires, for ye both joy in that which ye have desired.

D&C 52:11 For thus saith the Lord, I will cut my work short in righteousness, for the days come that I will send forth judgment unto victory.

D&C 93:6-17; 6 And John saw and bore record of the fullness of my glory, and the fullness of John's record is hereafter to be revealed. **7** And he bore record, saying: I saw his glory, that he was in the beginning, before the world was; **8** Therefore, in the beginning the Word was, for he was the Word, even the messenger of salvation—**9** The light and the Redeemer of the world; the spirit of truth, who came into the world, because the world was made by him, and in him was the life of men and the light of men. **10** The worlds were made by him; men were made by him; all things were made by him, and through him, and of him. **11** And I, John, bear record that I beheld his glory, as the glory of the Only Begotten of the Father, full of grace and truth, even the spirit of truth, which came and dwelt in the flesh, and dwelt among us. **12** And I, John, saw that he received not of the fullness at the first, but received grace for grace. **13** And he received not of the fullness at first, but continued from grace to grace, until he received a fullness; **14** And thus he was called the Son of God, because he received not of the fullness at the first. **15** And I, John, bear record, and lo, the heavens were opened, and the Holy Ghost descended upon him in the form of a dove, and sat upon him, and there came a voice out of heaven saying: This is my beloved Son. **16** And I, John, bear record that he received a fullness of the glory of the Father; **17** And he received all power, both in heaven and on earth, and the glory of the Father was with him, for he dwelt in him.

D&C 93:19 I give unto you these sayings that you may understand and know how to worship, and know what you worship, that you may come unto the Father in my name, and in due time receive of his fullness.

True to the Faith

p.111 A second use of the word paradise is found in Luke's account of the Savior's crucifixion. When Jesus was on the cross, a thief who also was being crucified said, "Lord, remember me when thou comest into they kingdom" (Luke 23:43). According to Luke 23:44, the Lord replied, "Verily I say unto thee, Today shalt thou be with me in paradise". The Prophet Joseph Smith explained that this is a mistranslation; the Lord actually said that the thief would be with him in the world of spirits.

DICTIONARY

Preface

This dictionary is a compilation from the LDS Bible Dictionary along with, True to the Faith, Smith's Bible Dictionary, Webster's Seventh Collegiate Dictionary, The Bible Commentary, The Holy Scriptures as translated by Joseph Smith as well as other sources listed under Sources. It has been greatly abbreviated in its scope and deals mainly with the life and time period of Jesus Christ as presented in the four gospels. This dictionary was added as a ready reference.

A significant difference between this dictionary and other dictionaries is that all of the scriptural references given are referencing the Joseph Smith Translation of the Bible. While some of the scriptures may be the same as the King James Version of the Bible, most will not be. It is recommended that the reader have access to a complete JST of the Bible.

| A

Abraham: *Father of a multitude.* He was the son of Terah, born in Ur of the Chaldees (Gen. 11:26-28) B.C. 1996. He had two elder brothers; Haran and Nahor, and a half sister, Sarah, (Iscah), who was his wife and the mother of Isaac. Besides Sarah he had a wife, Keturah, who bore him several sons; and a handmaid, Hagar, whose son was named Ishmael. He is regarded as a great patriarch in the house of Israel as the 'father of the faithful'. Latter-day revelation has clarified the significance of the Abrahamic covenant and other aspects of Abraham's life and ministry.

Amen: Hebrew word meaning *truth.* Used at the end of a sentence not translated, means: so be it. It is used as a word of confirmation, and as the closing of a prayer.

Annas: Served as a high priest A.D. 7 – A.D. 15 but according to Jewish custom he kept the title "High Priest" after he was deposed from office. The New Testament (NT) authors, the Dead Sea scrolls' authors, and Josephus, all provide a negative portrait of Annas. Some scholars associate him with greed and an insatiable desire for wealth which may account for why he was deposed from office. Annas continued to have great influence in the Sanhedrin (John

18:13) after his son-in-law, Caiaphas, became the next high priest.

Andrew the Apostle: Peter's brother (Matt: 10:2). He and John were disciples of John the Baptist before they became disciples of Jesus (John 1:40) and went on to become one of the Twelve. Tradition states he was killed in Patras, Greece on an X shaped cross, now called St. Andrews cross. Early writers mention the 'Acts of Andrew' and the 'Gospel of St. Andrew' but they were rejected and are now lost.

Apostle: Means *sent forth*. An apostle is a special witness of Jesus Christ's divinity and is sent to teach the gospel to the world. Just as there were twelve apostles during the time of Jesus, today there are also twelve apostles in The Church of Jesus Christ of Latter-day Saints. See individual names of apostles for character descriptions.

Archelaus: Son of Herod by Malthace, a Samaritan, brought up in Rome. He was appointed by Augustus Ethnarch after his father's death. He had a reputation for cruelty and oppression. He was banished to Gaul of Vienne where he also died.

| B

Baptism: The first saving ordinance of the gospel of Jesus Christ, Jesus, Himself, being baptized to "fulfill all righteousness" (Matt: 3:41-44). It must be done by one holding priesthood authority and by immersion (D&C 20:73-74). Immersion is symbolic of the death of a person's sinful life and rebirth into a spiritual life dedicated to the service of God and His children. All who are accountable and seek eternal life must follow the Lord's example and be baptized. Little children do not need baptism (Moroni 8:4-14) until the age of accountability defined as the age of eight (D&C 68:25). Those who have died without baptism, by priesthood authority, will have the opportunity to have this ordinance done for them by proxy (1 Corinthians 15:29).

Barabbas: Means *son of the father*. A "notable prisoner" held at the time of the feast of the Passover. He was an insurrectionist, robber, and a murderer (Luke 23:19; John 18:40). Barabbas was released (a Roman tradition at the time of the Passover) instead of Jesus per the people's request.

Bartholomew the Apostle: (Also Nathanael) was from Cana in Galilee and called by Jesus to be an apostle. Philip first told Nathanael of Jesus to which he responded,

"Can there any good thing come out of Nazareth?" (John 1:46). This one sentence gives us a sense of the separation of the people of Nazareth from the rest of the people of Galilee. When Jesus saw Nathanael coming to him, he said of him, "Behold an Israelite indeed, in whom is no guile!" (John 1:47). Nathanael is named only in the gospel of John while the other three gospel writers call him Bartholomew (Matt. 10:2; Mark 3:14; Luke 6:14).

Beatitudes: Name given to certain declarations of blessedness in the Sermon on the Mount (Matt. 5:3-14; Luke 6:20-22). They describe qualities of character and those blessings associated with them. Rather than being isolated statements the beatitudes are interrelated and progressive in their arrangement. A more comprehensive and accurate listing is found in 3 Nephi 12 and Matthew 5, where greater spiritual emphasis is given.

Beelzebub: Used as a title for the 'chief of the demons,' or Satan. The Pharisees accused Jesus of casting out devils by Beelzebub the prince of the devils (Matthew 12:20), see Lucifer.

Beth: Hebrew for *house.*

Bethabara; house of the ford,

Bethany; house of the poor, **Bethel**; house of God, **Bethesda**; house of mercy or house of grace, **Bethhoron**; house of caves, **Bethlehem**; house of bread, **Bethphage**; house of figs, **Bethsaida**; house of fish, **Bethshan**, or **Bethshean**; house of safety. **Bethshemesh**; house of the sun.

Blasphemy: Generally denotes *contemptuous speech concerning God*, or concerning something that is in sacred relation to God, such as his commandments, the prophets, or the temple. Our Lord was charged with blasphemy because he called himself the Son of God and claimed the right to forgive sins. These charges would have been true had he not been who he said he was. The punishment for blasphemy was death (Lev. 24:11-16).

| C

Caesar: The title by which a roman emperor was known. The emperors during the time covered in the NT, with dates of their accessions, were as follows: Augustus, 31 B.C.; Tiberius A.D. 14; Caligula A.D. 37; Claudius A.D. 41; Nero A.D. 54. Tiberius became Tiberius Julius Caesar and ruled during most of Jesus' life. Conflicts with his mother (widow of Augustus) added to the political intrigue in

Rome and led him to leave the capital for the island of Capri, in a self imposed exile, from where he governed through lieutenants.

Caiaphas: His full name was Joseph Caiaphas and he was high priest from A.D. 18 to A.D. 36; a son-in-law to Annas. He belonged to the Sadducee party and took part in the judgment of blasphemy made against Jesus (Matt. 26:66). He unknowingly prophesied of Jesus' death (John 11:49-52). Caiaphas was removed from office the same year as Pilate suggesting that his tenure was closely linked with that of Pilate.

Calendar: The NT Jews called their months by names which they learned while in Babylon: **(1)** Nissan (March-April), **(2)** Iyar (April-May), **(3)** Sivan (May-June), **(4)** Tammuz (June-July), **(5)** Av (July-August), **(6)** Elul (August-September), **(7)** Tishri (September-October), **(8)** Heshvan (October-November), **(9)** Kislev (November-December), **(10)** Tevet (December- January), **(11)** Shevat (January-February, **(12)** Adar 1, leap years only (February-March). A month consisted of 29 or 30 days. The Jewish calendar is based on the rotation of the earth (a day); the revolution of the moon around the earth (29½ days or a month); and the revolution of the earth around the sun (365¼ days or a year) and coordinates all three of these events. Since there are 12.4 lunar months in a solar year, an intercalary month called Adar 1 was added by observation of the Sanhedrin. In such years it preceded the regular month of Adar, and is called Adar Beit. The Jewish new year was on the first of Tishri (the seventh month) accompanied by the Feast of the Trumpets. A corresponding example is our year starts on January first but some school years start in September. Understanding this helps to reconcile many of the events listed in the gospels.

Camel's Hair: Is clipped from the animal's neck, back, and hump and woven into a course, durable, rough, and often itchy cloth like material and used for clothing. The camel's hair garment worn by John the Baptist (Mark 1:5) may have been used to separate him from the soft raiment of the kings and Jewish leaders.

Canaanite: Refers to *land of origin* or *lineage through Canaan*, fourth son of Ham (Genesis 10:4, 9-11, 12:4-5; Abraham 1:21). Canaanite was sometimes used as a general name for all non-Israelite inhabitants of the country west of Jordan. Canaanite also came to denote merchant (Isaiah 23:8; Ezekiel

17:4; Hosea 12:7). They were dwellers of the lowlands in the plains by the sea and in the Jordan valley.

Centurion: Officer in the Roman army, in command of one hundred men, forming one-sixtieth part of a Roman legion. In NT time the legions were not up to their full strength. A centurion was in charge of fifty up to one hundred men.

Cephas: Aramaic word meaning *a stone* (petros is the corresponding Greek word). Given by Jesus to Peter when he was called to be a disciple (John 1:42).

Christ: English word for the Greek *Khristo's* meaning the 'anointed one'. It is the Hebrew equivalent of Messiah.

Chronology: Deals with fixing exact dates with various events recorded. There is not sufficient evidence in the gospels to put in exact order many events. Some of the parables and teachings of Jesus were taught more than once in different locations. And the gospel writers do not always agree on certain events. One example is the anointing of Jesus by Mary. Luke records this event much earlier in his narration than the other three writers. A careful study of all four accounts indicates that there were two different occasions in which Mary first washed Jesus feet with her tears and anointed his feet with 'ointment' and later, just before his crucifixion, anointed his head with 'spikenard' in preparation for his burial. Because of the differences between the gospels, some of the earliest efforts to make one gospel were first done by Marcion in the second century, who only accepted the gospel of Luke. Another was Tatian who also lived in the second century, who composed a gospel harmony called the Diatessaron. This was a single narrative containing about 72 percent of all four gospels. It was successful for a long time because it eliminated conflicts of passages within the gospels. It should be noted that The Fifth Gospel also incorporates about 72 percent of the four gospels (a higher percent if portions of verses added to other verses are counted). By word count, The Fifth Gospel contains 108 percent. Great care was taken to include the smallest of details. The intent was to bring all of the details given about an event together for a more complete understanding.

Circumcision: As part of the Law of Moses, circumcision was practiced in OT and NT times on Israelite males when eight days old in connection with the giving of a name. It was done away with in the early church after the death and resurrection of Jesus Christ (3 Nephi 15:1-4; Mormon 8:8).

Cleopas: or Cleophas mentioned in (John 19:25). He was one of the two who met Jesus on the road to Emmaus (Luke 24:17). He and his companion (assumed to be his wife Mary), along with Mary Magdalene, fulfill the law of two or three witnesses (Matt. 18:16). According to John, Cleophas would have been an uncle-in-law to Jesus which may account for why Jesus appeared to him, out of respect for patriarchal order in his earthly family assuming Joseph had already died.

Comforter: Two comforters are spoken of. The first is the Holy Ghost (John 14:16-27, Moroni 8:26; D&C 21:9, 42:17, 90:11) also see Holy Ghost. The second comforter is the Lord Jesus Christ himself. "When any man obtains this last comforter, he will have the personage of Jesus Christ to attend him, or appear unto him from time to time, and He will manifest the Father unto him" (D&C 88:3-4, 130:3; HC 3:381)

Conundrum: *A confusing question or difficult problem having a conjectural answer; riddle. A question asked for amusement.* As with parables and other methods used in teaching the people, Jesus used conundrums so that the spiritually inclined would be able to find the deeper meaning.

Corban: Means *given to God.* The utterance of it was held to constitute a binding vow regarded by the Pharisees as an even deeper obligation than the duty to parents (Mark 7:13; Matt. 15:5). It appears that the Pharisees misused the opportunity of dedicating their material possessions to God, in order to avoid responsibility to care for their parents.

Crucifixion: *A Roman form of punishment,* usually inflicted on slaves and the lowest criminals. Our Lord was condemned to it on request of the Jewish mob. Crucifixion was preceded by scourging, and then made to carry his own cross to the place of execution. The cross was put into the ground so that the feet of the condemned were a foot or two above the surface. The cross was watched by four soldiers at a time until death took place, which was sometimes not until the third day.

Cubit: 18 U.S. inches. The sacred cubit is 19.05 inches.

| D

Damnation: The opposite of eternal life, and exists in varying degrees. All who do not obtain the fullness of celestial exaltation will in some degree be limited in their progress and privileges, and hence be damned to that extent.

Darkness: Symbol of spiritual blindness or ignorance.

David: Means *beloved*. Born in Bethlehem of Judea B.C. 1084. He showed his faith and courage as a youth by slaying Goliath. He served as Israel's second king uniting the twelve tribes of Israel and his reign was considered to be one of the most brilliant in Israel's history. His strength was in his dependence upon God and he was loved by the Lord. He had Uriah murdered and took Bathsheba, his wife, to be his own. Because of his transgression he has fallen from his exaltation (D&C 132:39) but has received a promise that the Lord would not leave his soul in hell. It was prophesied that the Messiah would be born through the linage of David. Those who understood this called our Lord 'Son of David'.

Day: Began and ended at sunset. The hours of the day were usually counted from sunrise, the hours of the night from sunset. There were four watches during the night (Matthew 14:21; Mark 6:50). The first day of the week was Sunday on which our resurrected Lord appeared to several of his disciples and the apostles. The

day of Pentecost in that year also fell on the first day. The seventh day of the week, called the Lord's Day, was the Sabbath. It was a day of rest and a day of rejoicing. The morning and evening sacrifices for the temple were doubled and the shewbread was replaced with new. The seventh day of the seventh month of the seventh year began the Sabbatical year (see Sabbatical year).

Death: There are two kinds of death spoken of in the scriptures. One is the *death of the body*, which is caused by the separation of the spirit from the body. The other is *spiritual death* which is to be separated from the things of God by consequence of our own sins. The result of physical death is the grave; the result of spiritual death is hell.

Decapolis: Means *ten cities*. This district was southeast of the Sea of Galilee, containing a mixed population of Greeks, Syrians, Arabs, and Jews, the Greek element being the greatest.

Defiled: *To make ceremonially unclean.* As used in this instance (John 18:28), the Jews had a law that to have entered into a Gentile home or building, would have made them unclean. This would have required them to remain in seclusion until evening and then to wash their body. In doing so they would have missed the Passover feast. In some cases, a sin offering of a kid or young goat (Numbers 28:15) was also necessary.

Devil(s): Are disembodied spirits who follow Satan (see Satan).

Didymus: Means *twin* (see Thomas).

Disciple: A *student* or *learner*. Also a name used to denote **(1)** one of the Twelve Apostles, **(2)** all followers of Jesus. We also read that John the Baptist had disciples as well as the Pharisees (Mark 2:16).

Divorce: The dissolution of marrage was permitted under some circumstances in NT times because of the hardness of the people's hearts. But as explained by Jesus, "from the beginning it was not so" (Matt. 19:3-12). One school, (Shammai) limited it to moral misconduct, and the other school, (Hillel) included many other offences such as snoring, burning the food, and even bad breath. Jesus taught that the party who permits the divorce is guilty of adultery if he or she re-marry and causes the other party to commit adultery should they re-marry. Paul taught that separation of a believer from an unbeliever was permitted but that they should not remarry but seek reconciliation and reunion.

Dove, sign of: The prearranged means by which John the Baptist would recognize the Messiah at Jesus' baptism (John 1:32-34). "The sign of the dove was instituted before the creation of the world, a witness for the Holy Ghost, and the devil cannot come in the sign of the dove" (HC 5:261).

E

El: In Hebrew and related languages designates the *divine being*. Many biblical names employ El with other words, such as **Bethel**, the house of God; **Eleazar**, God has helped, **Michael**, who is like God; **Ezekiel**, God will strengthen; **Israel**, to prevail with God or let God prevail; **Elyon**, the most high God; **Eliakim**, God raiseth up; **Elijah**, Jehovah is my God; **Elisha**, God of salvation or God shall save. **Elohim** is plural denoting Gods, or the Father, meaning collectively. The prophet Joseph taught, "In the beginning God (Elohim) created the heaven and the earth, should more properly be translated, in the beginning the head of the Gods brought forth the Gods and they created the heavens and the earth" (Teachings of the Prophet Joseph Smith p. 370-71).

Elder: The term elder is used in

various ways. It may refer to older men entrusted with governmental affairs (Matthew 15:2; Acts 4:5). Elder is also an ordained office in the Melchizedek Priesthood mentioned in the OT, NT, Book of Mormon and modern revelation. The detailed duties of an Elder in the church today are defined in (D&C 20:42-45, 42:44-52, 46:2, 107:12).

Elect: The elect of God is a very select group of baptized members of His church. If male, it requires the Melchizedek Priesthood be conferred upon them. They must also be endowed in the temple, entered into the new and everlasting covenant of marriage, and are those who have overcome all things through their faith. In addition they must magnify their callings, keep the commandments, and be sanctified by the Spirit (D&C 84:33-41).

Eli: *My God* (Matt. 27:50). Mark 15:39 renders the word Eloi, which is perhaps a Galilean form.

Elias: The NT Greek name for the OT Hebrew name *Elijah* (Luke 4:25-26). The term Elias generally is used as a title of one who prepares or restores. For example John the Baptist was the forerunner or preparer and Jesus the restorer to the Jews in their time.

Elias, who appeared at the time of the Transfiguration (Matt. 17:1-4) along with Moses, is John the Baptist (Mark 9:3). A man named Elias apparently lived during the time of Abraham, who committed the dispensation of the gospel of Abraham, to Joseph Smith, and Oliver Cowdery in the Kirtland, Ohio temple (D&C 110:12).

Elizabeth: Mother of John the Baptist, and cousin of Mary the mother of Jesus (Luke 1:5-59). She belonged to the priestly family of Aaron. She obviously was close to Mary which would account for why Mary felt comfortable in staying with her.

Eloi: *My God* (see Eli).

Emmanuel: See Immanuel.

Ephphatha: An Aramaic word, meaning *be opened* (Mark 7:33).

Esaias: The NT Greek name for the OT Hebrew name of *Isaiah* (Luke 4:17).

Espoused: This was the beginning of marriage, and was an agreement made by the parents if the parties were under age 18. It was a formal public proceeding, confirmed by oaths, and presents to the bride. Twelve months were allowed to pass before the marriage ceremony.

The betrothal could only be broken off by a bill of divorcement.

Eternal life: Is to be judged worthy of the highest level in the Celestial kingdom where we will live in God's presence and continue as families (D&C 131:1-4). Like immortality, this blessing is made possible through the Atonement of Jesus Christ. However, it requires obedience to the laws and ordinances of His gospel (Article of Faith 1:3).

Eunuch: A class of emasculated men. They were employed to watch over harems, and also were often given positions as trusted officials. In OT times it was a practice contrary to the law (Deuteronomy 23:1). As used by our Lord (Matthew 19:12) it would appear that he is suggesting castration as a means to be of greater service in his kingdom here upon the earth. However, for him to have been tested and to overcome all trials and temptations himself, he would not have been emasculated. For us to obtain the highest degree of glory, we too must overcome all trials and temptations as did our Lord. For this reason, the principal of emasculation is not a part of the teachings of those seeking eternal life.

Evil Spirits: Disembodied spirits who have chosen to follow Satan.

Ezekias: The NT Greek name for the OT Hebrew name of *Hezekiah* (Matt. 1:3).

| F

Faith: Is the assurance of things hoped for which are not seen, but which are true (Hebrews 11:1; Alma 32:21). To have faith unto salvation is to have confidence in Jesus Christ who has revealed himself and his perfect character, possessing in their fullness all the attributes of love, knowledge, justice, mercy, unchangeableness, power, and every other needful thing, so as to enable the mind of man to place confidence in him without reservation. Faith is a principle of action and power. True faith must be based on truth or it cannot produce the desired results. Faith is a gift from God and must be nourished until it becomes a perfect knowledge. The most complete and systematic exposition on faith are the Lectures on Faith, delivered to the school of the prophets in Kirtland, Ohio.

Farthing: A coin made of copper or bronze and was one quarter of an assarion or equal to two mites (see Money).

Fast: A voluntary abstinence from

food and is a principal of the gospel of Jesus Christ for developing spiritual strength. Our Lord taught the religious value of fasting (Matt. 6:17-18; Luke 4:2). He also taught that we are to wash and dress as usual and not appear unto men as though we are fasting (Matthew 6:18) so that we may be able to receive a blessing from our Heavenly Father. The public fast among the ancient Hebrews as well as modern Arabs was a total abstinence from food for 24 hours. Today this practice is upheld once a month on the first Sunday among Latter-day Saints.

Fear: Care should be taken to distinguish between two different uses of this word. The 'fear of the Lord', also described as 'Godly fear', is equivalent to reverence, awe, or worship. On the other hand, perfect love casteth out all fear (1 John 4:18). As referred to here, fear is in the heart or mind.

Feasts: The law commanded that three times a year all the males of the covenant people appear before the Lord (Exodus 23:14-17) at the (1) *Feast of Unleavened Bread* held in Abib (Hebrew) NT Nissan or April, (2) *The Feast of Harvest* held in Sivan or June, and (3) *The Feast of Ingathering* held in Tishri or October. All three were accompanied by a sacred assembly including the weekly Sabbath. The Passover (which came later) began the *Feast of Unleavened Bread* and was instituted to commemorate the passing over the houses of the Israelites in Egypt when God smote the firstborn of the Egyptians (Ex. 12:27, 13:15). It lasted seven days. The name Pentecost (meaning 50 days after) the *Feast of Harvest* was kept. In NT time the *Feast of Ingathering* was known also as the *Feast of Tabernacles* commemorating Israel's 40 year journey in the wilderness. The *Feast of Tabernacles* was said to be the holiest and greatest of all the feasts and lasted eight days. In addition to these required feasts were the *Feast of Trumpets* (commemorating the New Year) the *Feast of Purim* (called Mordecai's Day) and the *Feast of the Dedication* (known today as Hanukkah) held in Kislev or December, to celebrate the rededicating of the temple 164 B.C. It lasts for eight days. There were other feasts not mentioned here.

First born: In the patriarchal order, the firstborn son is the heir and inherits the leadership of the family upon the death of the father. This is often spoken of in the scriptures as birthright. This birthright included a double portion of his father's possessions which would help in caring for his mother and sisters. Jesus is the firstborn of the

Father, the only begotten of the Father in the flesh, and the first to be resurrected, "that in all things he might have preeminence" (Col. 1:13-18).

Fool: Used to indicate a moral deficiency rather than an intellectual deficiency. One who does not fear God and acts without regard to his laws.

Forgiveness: To cease to feel resentment against an offender or to give claim to requital. The scriptures refer to forgiveness two ways. The Lord commands us to repent of our sins and seek His forgiveness. He also commands us to forgive others (Matt. 6:13).

Frankincense: The fragrant resinous exudation of various spices of Boswellia; it was imported to Judea from Arabia. It was an ingredient in the Holy incense for sacrificial purposes (Ex. 30:34) and was highly valued as a perfume.

Furlong: 220 feet.

| G

Gabriel: Means *man of God*. The angel sent to Daniel (Dan. 8:16; 9:21) to Zacharias (Luke 1:11-19) and to Mary (Luke 1:26-38). He is identified by latter-day revelation as Noah (HC 3:386).

Galilee: The most northern territory of the three divisions into which Palestine west of the Jordan was divided, and included the territories of Issachar, Naphtali, Zebulun, and Asher. During Roman rule it encompassed north of the Kishon River and Mount Gilboa, to Leontes and Hermon, from the Jordan River to the sea. It contained some of the best land and busiest towns of Palestine, and was populated by a hardy warlike people.

Galilee, Sea of: Was also called the *Sea of Chineroth*, the *Lake of Gennesaret*, and the *Sea of Tiberius*. It is a fresh water lake and is pear-shaped, 12½ miles long, and 7½ miles across at its greatest width. It lies 680 feet below sea level. The water in some places is 250 feet deep. The Jordan River runs through it from the north to the south. The basin around it has a scathed, volcanic look. The climate is tropical with palm trees as well as many other kinds of trees, flowers, and vegetables which grow luxuriantly. The beach is pebbly everywhere and is covered with small, twisted shells.

Gall: Generally held to be myrrh that was mingled with wine. However, Joseph changed 'wine' to 'vinegar' and 'myrrh' to 'gall' (JST Mark 15:26) This would be consistent with Psalms 69:21. In Matthew (27:52) the Greek word *oxos* is used; which means sour wine or vinegar and water with flavoring herbs (see Wine).

Genealogy: Pedigree or an account of the descent of one's ancestors. The two genealogies of Jesus, which are constructed on different principals, require careful comparison and study if they are to be understood. Both accounts in Matthew and Luke, are of Joseph's lineage. Some scholars attribute the differences to the Levirate marriage tradition; that if a man die without bearing any sons, his brother would then marry his widow. For this theory to hold up, it would mean that Joseph had both a legal father (Heli), and a biological father (Jacob), through a Levirate marriage. Joseph's grandfathers would have been brothers, both married to the same woman, one after the other. Matthan's son Jacob was Joseph's biological father and Matthat's son Heli was Joseph's legal father. Matthew's genealogy would trace his biological lineage and Luke's, his legal lineage. Although there are other theories, this is one of the more widely accepted.

Gennesaret, Land of: The fertile plain on the western shore of the Sea of Galilee, toward the northern end, one mile wide and 2½ miles long, 500 feet below sea level. In Jesus' day it was considered the best part of Galilee.

Gentile: The word gentile means *nations* and eventually came to be used to mean *all those not of the house of Israel.*

Gergesenes: People of Gergesa (Matt. 8:29) on the east side of the Sea of Galilee.

Gethsemane: Means *oil-press garden* or *wine-press* (Gath, wine). It is a garden, across the Kedron brook, on the slope of the Mount of Olives (Matt. 26:33; Mark 14:36; John 18:1) where Jesus atoned for the sins of mankind. Today it is walled in and has eight very old olive trees, ornamented with beds of flowers. One of the trees is 25 feet in girth. The antiquity of these trees is argued from the tax of one medina for each tree, which rate was fixed for trees that stood at the time of the conquest; all those planted since being taxed one half their produce. This would carry the date back to A.D. 634 when Omar took Jerusalem, or if the tax was decreed after the Turks took the city in A.D. 1087.

Gifts of the Spirit: Gifts given to us from God through the power of the Holy Ghost. God gives at least one gift to every faithful member of his church. They are intended to bless and strengthen us individually and help us to serve others and are given for the benefit of those who love Him and keep all of his commandments, and him that seeketh so to do (D&C 46:8-12). Gifts of the spirit, unlike talents, are given as a temporal or temporary endowment for this life only as indicated by the use of the word *occupy* found in Luke (19:25). None of the gifts of the spirit mentioned in the NT, Book of Mormon, or the D&C would have any importance after the resurrection, whereas individual talents, we will take with us.

God: *Is an immortal exalted and perfected man.* Unlimited in his power, intelligence, goodness, and grace, He has made it his work and his glory to bring to pass the immortality and eternal life of man (Moses 1:39). Of all of His creations both in heaven and on earth, man is his most important creation. He created man in his own image (Moses 2:27) for "As man is, God once was, and as God is, man may become" as revealed through latter-day revelation. For all of God's power, majesty and omnipotence, He has chosen the title of Father above all else. For us as mortals, perhaps the most important service He fulfills is to hear and answer our prayers. Otherwise, without this one great gift and blessing to mankind, His greatness and power would go largely unrecognized without His loving reassurance of His existence through answers to our prayers. We learn to love Him because He loved us first (1 John 4:19). A correct understanding of the roles between God the Father, Jesus Christ, and the Holy Ghost reveals that it is our Father in Heaven to whom we pray and from whom we receive blessings. Although His voice has been heard on several occasions (Matt. 3:45-46, 17:1-7; 3 Ne. 11:7), outside of the Garden of Eden where Adam walked and talked with God prior to the fall of man, the only other known instance where God the Father has been seen since the fall is when He appeared to Joseph Smith in answer to his prayer in the sacred grove (JSH 1:11-20), which makes this occasion very unique.

Godhead: Consists of God the Father, His Son Jesus Christ, and the Holy Ghost (First Article of Faith). They preside over the world and all other creations of our Heavenly Father.

Golgotha: Means a *place of burial* (Matt. 27:35). It is located on the north end of Jerusalem and is where Jesus was crucified. There was a garden or orchard nearby.

Gospel: Means *good news* or *good*

tidings. While there is much that comprises the gospel of Jesus Christ, the "good news of the gospel" is that all of mankind will one day be resurrected to live eternally. Other than coming to earth to gain a body, nothing else is required of us to obtain immortality. But it gets even better. We have been offered the opportunity to become like God through His plan of salvation and the atonement of our Lord and Savior Jesus Christ. This can be obtained through faith and obedience to His commandments and the grace of Jesus Christ, after all that we can do (2 Ne. 25:23).

Gospels: The four canonized gospels of the NT are Matthew, Mark, Luke, and John. **Mark's gospel** is thought to be the first gospel written under Peter's tutelage or perhaps direct supervision. It is the shortest of the four gospels and for this reason may have influenced other gospel writers to write a more lengthy and detailed account of our Lord's life and mission. **Matthew's gospel** was written to persuade the Jews that Jesus is the promised Messiah. To do so, he cites several OT prophecies and speaks repeatedly of Jesus as the Son of David, thus emphasizing his royal lineage. **Luke's gospel** is written to Theophilus (whom he addresses as "most excellent" which may have been a Roman

title since Christians did not use such titles. Nothing else is known of him). It appears to have been written mainly to the gentiles. If the gospel of Mark was written under Peter's direction, Luke would be the only gospel written whose author was not an eye witness of the events of which he wrote. He was inspired to give hope to the poor and down trodden because of the poverty and trials of the early saints. His is the longest of the four gospels even without the book of Acts, which is a continuation of his gospel. All three of these gospels are referred to as the 'synoptic gospels' because they are alike in vocabulary, phraseology, and presentation of events. **John's gospel** appears to be written to members of the church who already had a basic understanding about our Lord. It does not contain much of the fundamental information that the other gospels have but has new information, 92 percent of it being unique to his gospel. It is generally accepted that the gospel of John was written much later than the other three gospels. This may account for why he took the liberty of identifying people by name, assuming that they had already died. The other gospel writers did not use names to protect the individuals they wrote about.

Grace: All have sinned and come

short of the glory of God (Romans 3:23). Regardless of the sin, all sin, both small and great, places us in a position of being subject to the judgment of Jesus Christ (John 5:22) given the right to judge from *the* Father. Through His atoning sacrifice, He will judge all mankind according to our works and our righteous desires. In the end it will be His decision as to who He wants to have in His kingdom of exalted and glorified saints. No one can earn their way into His kingdom by their righteous deeds alone, expecting to nullify their sins by their works. In the final judgment it may be more a matter of who we have become rather than what we have done.

| H

Happiness: Is to serve God, take delight in our existence, well being, and prosperity.

Heaven: The place where God lives and future home of the saints (Matt. 6:10). In the sense of being God's home it is clearly distinguished from paradise, which is the temporary abode of the faithful spirits who have lived and died on this earth. Jesus visited paradise after his death, but after his resurrection he informed Mary that he had not yet been to see *the* Father (John 20:17).

Hell: Signifies the abode of departed spirits also referred to as spirit prison. It denotes a place of torment for the wicked. It is a temporary place for the disobedient that will be taught the gospel and hopefully accept the ordinances performed for them in the temples (D&C 138:30-35). Some will remain there until the last resurrection (D&C 76:84-85). Hell therefore, will have an end when all the captive spirits will have paid the price for their sins and inherit a degree of glory (see Damnation).

Herod: The Herodian families were Idumeans (a term used to represent the world) by birth, but had become converts to the Jewish faith. Their object was to create, under Roman protection, a semi-independent kingdom. By his marriage to Mariamne, Herod the Great allied himself with the family of the Maccabees, who had been, for several generations, the leaders of the patriotic party among the Jews. In order to gain favor with his subjects, with whom he was most unpopular, he rebuilt the temple at immense cost (see Temple of Herod). Out of jealousy, he put to death his wife and also had three of his sons put to death. He was responsible for the massacre of the infants at Bethlehem. Herod died a few months after this incident (Matthew 3:19-25).

Herodians: Were political supporters of Herod and his family. They may have been extended family members of Herod or even his soldiers. They, along with the Pharisees, were opposed to Jesus because they thought he posed a political threat to Herod, while the Pharisees saw Jesus as a threat to their theocracy.

Herodias: A sister of Agrippa I. She first married Herod Philip and they had a daughter named Salome. Later she left Philip for his half brother Herod Antipas. Both she and Antipas were called to repentance by John the Baptist, which was a public humiliation to them. She influenced Antipas to imprison John and eventually was the cause of him being put to death by using her daughter Salome who danced before Antipas at his birthday. Eventually she went with her husband into exile in St. Bertrand de Commingres, in France.

High Priest: Before and during Jesus' ministry, the office of High Priest among the Jewish leaders was the designation of the presiding authority of the Aaronic priesthood. Along with many other things, Jesus restored the Melchizedeck Priesthood during his ministry. As in NT times, today the office of High Priest administers the affairs of the church. A significant difference today is that the office of High Priest administers the keys of sealing, not had among the Jews until after Jesus' ministry.

Holy Ghost: The third member of the Godhead and as the name implies, a personage of spirit, not possessing a body of flesh and bones. The Holy Ghost is manifest to men on earth both as the *power* of the Holy Ghost and as the *gift* of the Holy Ghost. The power can come upon one before baptism, and is the convincing witness that the gospel is true. The gift can only come after proper and authorized baptism, and is conferred by the laying on of hands (Acts 8:12-25). The gift of the Holy Ghost is the right to have, when worthy, the constant companionship of the Holy Ghost. Other names that sometimes refer to the Holy Ghost are: Holy Spirit, Spirit of God, Spirit of the Lord, Comforter, and Spirit.

Holy Place: Jesus, when talking about the future destruction of the Jews and the gentiles, also mentions in a conundrum to "stand in the Holy place" (Matt. 24:12; Mark 13:14) and in "Holy places" (D&C 87:8, 101:22, 64). At the time of the destruction of Jerusalem A.D. 66, the Romans trapped the Jews, attending Passover, inside the temple compound and killed them all. For them, this was not the Holy

Place where they needed to be at that time.

Holy Spirit: See Holy Ghost.

Hosanna: Means *save now.*

Hypocrite: Denotes one who pretends to be righteous when he is not. Jesus condemned hypocrisy (Matt. 23:10-30; Mark 12:45-46; Luke 11:38-45, 20:46-47).

Hyssop: A plant with a slender square stem, free from thorns or spreading branches, ending in a cluster of heads having a pleasant aromatic smell. No plant grown in the holy land is better suited for sprinkling or, in this case, holding moisture. Its leaves are often eaten with bread. Hyssop is thought to be marjoram.

I

Immanuel: Means *God with us* (also spelled Emmanuel). He was the prophesied child of the house of David (Isaiah 7:14). The name Immanuel is specifically identified by Matthew as a prophecy of Jesus' birth (Matt. 2:6).

Incense: A compound of sweet-smelling gums used in acts of worship. Its use was forbidden in private life (Exodus 30:27-32). The mixture was said to have equal parts of stacte, onycha, frankincense, and galbanum. The duty of offering incense in NT times was extended to all priests through the casting of a lot (Luke 1:9).

Israel: Means *one who prevails with God* or *let God prevail.* This name was given to Jacob when he wrestled with an angel at Peniel (Gen. 32:28, 35:10) and applies to his descendants. It has also come to denote true believers in Jesus Christ regardless of their lineage or geographical location. Israel had twelve sons which have become known as the twelve tribes of Israel.

J

James the Apostle: Son of Zebedee and brother of John. He and John were given the name Boanerges (Mark 3:14) meaning *sons of thunder.* He was one of the inner circle of three chosen to be with our Lord on certain occasions (Matt. 17:1, 26:34; Mark 5:29, 9:1, 14:38; Luke 8:51, 9:28). He is the only one of the original apostles whose death is recorded. He was beheaded by Herod Antipas ten years after the crucifixion (Acts 12:2).

2nd James the Apostle: Surname Thaddaeus (Matt. 10:2). Son of Alphaeus. He was one of the original Twelve Apostles known as James the less (Mark 3:14; Luke

6:15). He had a brother named Joses, and a sister named Salome. Neither of the two James mentioned in the four gospels should be confused with James the brother of Jesus Christ, son of Mary, of whom it is generally accepted, wrote the Epistle of James found in the N.T.

Jehovah: Means *unchangeable One.* Jehovah is the pre-mortal Jesus Christ and came to earth being born of Mary (3 Nephi 15:1-5; D&C 110:1-4).

Jerusalem: *City of peace.* First mentioned in Genesis (14:17) as Salem. It is about 2600 feet above sea level and was chosen by David to be the capital. Until then it was a mountain fortress, surrounded by deep valleys on all sides. After the tribes were divided, Jerusalem remained the capital of Judah. It appears that Jerusalem has a series of underground water courses which were alluded to by Josephus and other ancient writers. It has been prophesied that eventually water will come forth from Temple Mount and will flow into the Dead Sea (Ezekiel 47:1) and heal or make pure the water of the Dead Sea. This is believed to be symbolic of the gospel that will flow from the temple, which will heal the people of their sins.

Jesus: The Greek form of the name Joshua or Jeshua, meaning *Savior,* or *God is help.*

Jesus Christ: Means *the anointed Savior.* He is the only begotten of the Father in the flesh. It was the name given by Joseph and Mary (Matt. 2:8) in accordance with the direction of the angel Gabriel (Luke 1:31; Matthew 2:4). He is Jehovah of the OT come in mortality (3 Nephi 15:1-5; D&C 110:1-4). He is the creator of heaven and earth (John 1:3, 10) under the direction of God the Father (Ephesians 3:9). He (rather than God the Father) is the one who was seen as a spirit personage to Moses (Exodus 6:2-3; Moses 1:2), Abraham (Abraham 2:6), the brother of Jared (Ether 3:15) and many others. His followers, known as Christians, believe that Jesus Christ is the promised Messiah and look forward to his second coming while the Jews reject this claim and still wait for the Messiah to come. His mortal mission was to help save mankind rather than to judge it (Luke 9:53-56) as evidenced by His many acts of compassion and through His gospel of love. This was highlighted by His atoning sacrifice in the Garden of Gethsemane and giving His life for mankind in order that we too, might one day live again. "Greater love hath no man than this, that a man lay down his life for his friends" (John 15:13). One of the greatest gifts of the spirit is to know that He is the Son of God and that He was crucified for the sins of the world (D&C 46:13). Also see the declaration of the Twelve Apostles, *The Living Christ.*

Jew: The name of a person from the tribe and kingdom of Judah, as distinguished from the northern tribes of Israel. All Jews are Israelites, but not all Israelites are Jews.

Joanna: (1) Ancestor of Jesus (Luke 3:34). **(2)** Wife of Chusa, steward to Herod Antipas, tetrarch of Galilee; also a follower of Jesus (Luke 8:2-3, 24:9). She appears to be a woman of wealth and position who contributed to Jesus' support and ministry. She also brought spices to put into the tomb where Jesus' body was laid.

John the Apostle: Also know as *John the Beloved.* He was the son of Zebedee and brother of James, and the youngest of the Twelve Apostles. He and James were given the name of Boanerges (Mark 3:14), meaning *sons of thunder.* He was one of the inner circle of three chosen to be with our Lord on certain occasions (Matt: 17:1, 26:34; Mark 5:29, 9:1, 14:38; Luke 8:51, 9:28). He wrote the Gospel of John (see Gospels) and often referred to himself in the third person as 'the

disciple whom Jesus loved' (John 13:23). He also wrote John 1, 2, 3, and the book of Revelation. He is a person of unusual interest. At the time of the trial and crucifixion he 'was known unto the high priest' and spoke to the door keeper to arrange to have Peter let in (John 18:15-16). His family was not poor because they had servants and contributed to Jesus' support. John did not die but has been allowed to remain on the earth as a ministering servant of the Lord (D&C 7). He helped restore the Melchizedeck Priesthood (D&C 27:12) along with Peter and James. He is responsible for the gathering of Israel in the last days and describes this assignment as being sweet as honey in his mouth but bitter in his belly (Rev. 10:9-10), as symbolism for the joyfulness of his calling but realizing that he would also witness the destruction of the wicked.

Jonah or **Jonas:** Father of Peter and Andrew (John 1:42, 21:15-17).

John the Baptist: Son of Zacharias and Elizabeth, being of priestly descent through both parents. This lineage was essential, since John was the embodiment of the Law of Moses, prophesied to prepare the way of the Messiah and make ready a people to receive him. John taught repentance and baptism, as did Jesus, but in stark contrast

so as to leave the Jews without excuse for not accepting the gospel (Matt: 11:17-21). John also appeared to Jesus at the Mount of Transfiguration along with Moses (Mark 9:3). Jesus praised John as a prophet, saying there was "none greater" (Matt. 11:7-11). He was beheaded by Herod Antipas (Matt. 14:2-10). He restored the Aaronic Priesthood to Joseph Smith and Oliver Cowdery on May 15, 1829, as a resurrected being.

Joseph: **(1)** Jesus' stepfather and husband to Mary whose genealogy is found in Matthew (1:1-4) and Luke (3:30-45). Mary had several children by Joseph who would have been half brothers and sisters to Jesus. Among the most notable was his brother James who is considered to have written the book of James in the NT. After he took his family to Jerusalem, at the time Jesus was twelve, there is no further mention of him in the gospels. **(2)** Joseph of Arimathea: A member of the Sanhedrin and also a secret follower of our Lord. After the crucifixion he obtained permission from Pilate to bury Jesus in his own tomb (John 19:38-40). This is significant because it was not Mary (the mother of Jesus) or the apostles, but Joseph (who may have been an uncle to Mary and a granduncle to Jesus). It was Joseph, Nicodemus, and faithful women who followed Jesus and saw to his burial. **(3)** Joseph Smith: (1805-1844) A prophet of God called to usher in the last dispensation by restoring the priesthood, organizing the church, translating the Book of Mormon, and establishing temple work. The truthfulness of The Church of Jesus Christ rests upon the first vision, and the revelations given to Joseph Smith and of the living prophet of the church today. Joseph Smith has done more, save Jesus only, for the salvation of men, than any other man that has ever lived (D&C 135:3).

Joseph Smith Translation (JST): *The revised King James Version of the Bible.* Joseph was told to begin translation on March 7, 1831 (D&C 45:61), but appears to have been called as early as 1830. A study of the JST reveals that more than twice as many verses were changed in the NT than in the OT. Of those changes, the overwhelming majority is in the gospel of Matthew. We find additional insight as to why this translation was so important in D&C section 93. In verses 6-12 our Lord revealed part of John's testimony which we did not have. In verse 19, He adds this important reason for doing so: "that [we] may understand and know how to worship and know what [we] worship". Although the JST restores many plain and precious truths and clarifies what was previously written in the Bible, its primary purpose is to help us to better come to know Jesus Christ. The majority was completed in July 1833. While most scholars feel that it was never finished, they do agree that what was completed is of great worth.

Jot or Tittle: Hebrew meaning *yod*. It is the smallest letter in the Hebrew alphabet, used as a symbol of the least (Matthew 5:28). Tittle is a tiny accent mark to distinguish the Hebrew alphabet.

Jordan River: A major river in Palestine, formed by several springs rising in Mount Hermon. It descends 682 feet below sea level to the north end of the Sea of Galilee and exits the south end. The river continues to descend to 1292 feet below sea level until it reaches the Dead Sea. It is well over 100 miles in length and the width varies from 90 to 100 feet, and is 3 to 12 feet deep. The exact location of our Lord's baptism is not known but is generally believed to have been near Bethabara.

Judas the Apostle: (1) Also known as Lebbaeus Thaddaeus called as one of the original Twelve (Matt. 10:2; Mark 3:14). Known also as Judas (Luke 6:16) the brother of James the 2nd. **(2) Judas Iscariot:**

The only one of the original Twelve Apostles who was not a Galilean (he was Judean). Jesus knew of Judas' character and said, "Have not I chosen you twelve, and one of you is a devil?" (John 6:70-71) in reference to Judas. The scriptures give us an indication as to why Judas betrayed our Lord and states, "he was offended because of His words" (Mark 14:31). Although the Lord told the apostles at the Last Supper that one of them would betray Him, none of the other eleven suspected him. Before His betrayal, Jesus told Judas to "beware of innocent blood" (Mark 14:30) and further stated: "It had been good for that man if he had not been born" (Matt. 26:20). Even before Jesus' crucifixion, Judas "saw that he was condemned" and with the weight of what he had done, hanged himself (Matt. 27:3-6).

| K

Keys of the priesthood: See Priesthood.

Kidron: The stream bed on the east side of Temple Mount between the Mount of Olives; also called Cedron (which is Hebrew) by John (John 18:1). In the original Hebrew it is referred to as a dry water course. It joins at the pool of Siloam and leads to the Dead Sea about twenty miles away. It used to be fed by the Gihon spring before Hezekiah (B.C. 726) diverted it through a series of underground tunnels. There is an occasional flow of water in the winter which goes for a few hundred feet and then disappears.

Kingdom of Heaven or **Kingdom of God:** Generally, the kingdom of God on earth is the church. It is a preparation for the celestial kingdom in heaven (D&C 65). However, kingdom of heaven is sometimes used in scripture to mean the church which is the path to the kingdom of heaven (Matt: 3:28, 4:16, chapter 13, 25:1-12). The church is at present limited to an ecclesiastical kingdom. During the millennium the kingdom of God will be both political and ecclesiastical (Dan 7:18, 22, 27; Revelation 7, 11:15; D&C 65).

Knowledge: Knowledge of the gospel of Jesus Christ is essential for our salvation. Spiritual knowledge then becomes the most important kind of knowledge. The purpose of the gospel is so that we might know how to worship and know what we worship (D&C 93:19). The 'key of knowledge, is the fullness of the scriptures' (Luke 11:53). No one can be saved in ignorance (D&C 131:6). The person who gains gospel knowledge will have "so much the advantage in the world to come" (D&C 130:18-19).

| L

Lamb of God: A name for our Savior used by John the Baptist (John 1:29) and others. It has reference to Jesus being a sacrifice for the sins of mankind (1 Peter 1:19).

Law of Moses: The name assigned to a whole collection of written laws given through Moses to the house of Israel; a lesser law in place of the higher law they failed to obey. The Law of Moses consisted of many ceremonies, rituals, and symbols, to remind the people of their duties and responsibilities.

Lawyer: Unlike the scribes who were teachers of the law, a lawyer was a designated profession based upon the law or commandments.

Laying On of Hands: Those having priesthood authority perform many priesthood ordinances, such as confirmation, ordination, setting apart to serve in callings, administering to the sick, and other priesthood blessings (D&C 42:44, Articles of Faith 1:4-5). It is done by placing their hands upon the head of the person receiving the ordinance or blessing.

Lazarus: Means *helped of God.* He lived in Bethany and was a brother to Martha and Mary and was raised from the dead by Jesus (John 11:1-

44). Not coincidentally, Lazarus is the only proper name our Lord used in His parables (see the rich man and Lazarus, Luke 16:24-36). The parable was directed toward the Pharisees and the Scribes; and could not have gone unnoticed by them when a Lazarus was literally raised from the dead. This event, which leaves them without excuse, fulfills Jesus parable; "neither will they be persuaded, though one should rise from the dead" (Luke 16:36).

Leaven: Has three different meanings as used here; **(1)** it is compared to the growth and the influence of the kingdom of heaven (church) upon the earth. **(2)** Jesus uses leaven as a figure describing the corruption of Scribes and Pharisees. **(3)** The word leaven was used in the parable of the leaven which is like our yeast of today. Leaven was strictly forbidden in all bread sacrifices, as typical of corruption and decay.

Lebbeus the Apostle: Whose surname was Thaddaeus. See Judas the Apostle.

Leper: Anyone having Leprosy. It is caused by the bacteria Mycobacterium leprae and Mycobacterium lepromatosis. Leprosy is primarily a granulomatous disease of the peripheral nerves and mucosa of the upper respiratory tract. Skin sores are the primary external sign. Left untreated, it can cause permanent damage to skin, nerves, limbs and eyes. It is thought to be spread from person to person through respiratory droplets. In NT times it was supposed to be caused by offending deity. Leprosy still plagues the world today and in India alone there are over 1000 leper colonies.

Levites: *Descendants of Levi.* The work of ministering in the sanctuary was assigned to this tribe. They had no inheritance in Canaan (Numbers 18:23-24) but had the tithe (Numbers 18:21) and a claim on the alms of the people at feast times (Deuteronomy 12:18-19). The Levites were themselves offered as a wave offering on behalf of Israel (Numbers 8:11-15) and became God's peculiar property in place of the first born (Numbers 8:16), dedicating their lives to the service of God.

Locust: The swarming phase of the short-horned grasshopper (of the Acrididae family). Moving in large numbers they can destroy all vegetation. John the Baptist ate them for food (Matt. 3:4).

Lord: Refers to Jehovah of the OT and Jesus Christ of the NT (see Jesus Christ).

Love: The two great commandments are to love God and our fellow man as ourselves and upon these two commandments hang all the law and the prophets (Matt: 22:34-39). To help put into perspective how important love is, James says that if we fail to learn to love our fellow man as our self, we are guilty of having broken all the commandments because they teach us how to love our fellow man (James 2:8-10). Our Lord taught us the purest form of love when He said, "greater love hath no man than this, that a man lay down his life for his friends" (John 15:13). In other words, love is to put other's needs ahead of our own.

Luke: The writer of the third gospel and Acts (see Gospels). We know he was born a gentile at Antioch in Syria and that he practiced medicine. The first mention of him is when he joined Paul at Troas (Acts 16:10). He was with Paul during his second Roman imprisonment (2 Tim. 4:11). The JST attributes to Luke a high calling as a 'messenger of Jesus Christ' (Luke 1:1). Some believe he was one of the Seventy. History tells us nothing of Luke's later years but tradition says he died a martyr.

| M

Magi: Called 'wise men' (Matt 3:1). Their knowledge was precise and accurate. Their spirituality is evident; they saw the star and knew the meaning, and brought gifts to the young child: gold, which was symbolic of a king, frankincense, which was symbolic of sacrifice, and myrrh, which is used in preparation for burial. They were warned of God in a dream to return home by another route (Matt. 3:12). We do not know how many there were but tradition speaks of three because there were three gifts. The Roman Church gives their names as Gaspar, Melchoir, and Balthasar. There is a legend that they were later converted to the gospel by Thomas.

Mammon: Aramaic word meaning *riches* (Matt. 6:24). It should be pointed out that our Lord does not expect His followers to take a vow of poverty. Preaching the gospel cannot be done without the means to do it. Food and clothing cannot be given from empty shelves. Mammon, as used in the NT, is excess material wealth which encumbers us.

Mark: Also known as John Mark. He is generally recognized as being the writer of the gospel of Mark under the direction of Peter. He was the cousin or nephew of Barnabas (Col. 4:10). He may not have known Jesus personally unless he is the boy in Jerusalem during the night of Jesus' arrest (Mark 14:57). He is mentioned several times in the NT as traveling companions to Paul, Barnabas, and Peter. It should be kept in mind that Greek was a second language for Mark. He often used a double preposition in his writings such as: 'pre' preordained and 're' repeat which was not translated into English. Knowing this helps us to understand some of the word uses which deviate from the other gospels. Tradition states that after Peter's death, Mark visited Egypt, founded the church of Alexandria, and died a martyr.

Martha: The eldest sister of Lazarus and Mary (Luke 10:39-43; John 11:1-45, 12:2). It appears that they were all children of Simon the leper. Jesus came to visit them at Bethany and as he taught, Mary sat at His feet to listen. Martha asked the Lord to tell her sister Mary to help with serving the dinner to which our Lord commended her for her ability to serve but gently reminded her that Mary had chosen the better part (Luke 10:41-43).

Martyr: From a Greek word meaning *witness* (Acts 22:20).

Mary: (1) The virgin mother of Jesus (Luke 1:30-35). She was a cousin to Elizabeth (Luke 1:36). Her name was revealed a little over a century before her birth (Mosiah 3:8; Alma 7:10). Mary was taught concerning the mission of her son and as events began to unfold she quietly reflected on their meaning (Luke 2:19, 33, 51). We learn a great deal about the hardships associated with being with child during her espousal to Joseph. In the JST, it states: "there was none to give room for them in the inns" (Luke 2:7). This change states that there was more than one inn and we can assume that although there may have been room, they were not given the opportunity to stay there because of their perceived infidelity before marriage. A second insight is found in the fact that Mary had a sister named Mary (John 19:25). It appears to have been a practice to name subsequent children the same name as a previous child who had died. Upon discovering that Mary was with child, she would have been dead to her family. She was entrusted to John's care while Jesus hung upon the cross (John 19:25-26). **(2) Mary Magdalene:** *Mary from Magdala* on the western shore of the Sea of Galilee. Seven devils were cast out of her (Luke 8:2). Because of her faithfulness she was the first mortal to see our resurrected Lord (John 20:11-16). This event has significant meaning. Everything our Lord did had at its heart a purpose. When Mary came to tell the apostles that she had seen the risen Lord it states they "believed not" (Mark 16:10). The apostles did not believe Mary because they did not see her as their equal. To them she was still Mary 'the sinner'. This one act taught them, and the world, that all who are in the kingdom of God are equal. A second reason why our Lord appeared to her and the other 'two disciples', was to teach the apostles a lesson on faith. Soon it would be their turn to teach an unbelieving world about our resurrected Lord. Two valuable lessons as only the Master could teach them. **(3) Mary:** Sister of Lazarus and Martha (Luke 10: 39-43; John 11:1-45). She washed our Lord's feet with her tears and wiped them with her hair and anointed his head with ointment (John 11:2). **(4) Mary:** Wife of Caiphas and sister of Mary, mother of our Lord (John 19:25). **(5) Mary:** Mother of Mark who wrote the second gospel. She had a large house in Jerusalem (Acts 12:12).

Matthew the Apostle: Known before his conversion as Levi, son of Alpheus (Mark 2:11). He was a tax collector at Capernaum on an important caravan route leading to Damascus. His job was to collect the tolls on merchandise that passed through the dominions of Herod Antipas. He belonged to a despised class known as Publicans and was ostracized socially. His humility is seen by reference to him being a 'publican' in his own gospel (Matt. 10:2). None of the other gospel writers included this reference out of respect for him. His call as an apostle was justified because it brought Jesus into contact with a class of people whose spiritual welfare was abandoned by the Jewish leaders. He is also referred to as Levi in Mark and Luke. Matthew was probably a Jew with a wide knowledge of OT scriptures, and able to see our Lord's fulfillment of prophecy. He gave a feast in Jesus' honor in which he invited many of his friends who were also publicans as a farewell upon receiving his calling (Luke 5:27-30). It cost him much to forsake all and to follow Jesus. It is not known how or where he died. Tradition says that he lived in Jerusalem fifteen years after the crucifixion of our Lord and that he died a martyr in Persia.

Mercy: Mercy may seem to conflict with the law of justice, which requires that no unclean thing be permitted to dwell with God (1 Nephi 10:21). But the atonement of Jesus Christ made it possible for God to "be a perfect, just God, and a merciful God also" (Alma 42:15). The glory of an exalted man or woman is to dwell with our resurrected Lord in the next life. It is his kingdom which we seek to build both here on earth and in heaven. All judgment of mankind has been given to Jesus from *the* Father (John 5:22). Jesus gave his life for all of mankind but in the end it will be a matter of His choosing as to whom he wants in His kingdom.

Messiah: Aramaic word meaning *the anointed.* The word in the original Hebrew is found many times, but is translated as *anointed* with the exception of Dan. 9:25-26 and John 1:41, 4:25 as Messias; but was added by Joseph in JST (Matt. 3:2). Anointed has specific reference to that of a king. Samuel anointed Saul and David. In the NT the deliverer is called Christ, which is the Greek equivalent of Messiah. The prophetic use of the title was historic among the Hebrews and well known to Herod. The true messiah was to be an instrument in God's hand to deliver mankind from sin and death. The Jews expected the messiah to deliver them from their political enemies. They still wait for the messiah to come.

Mite: A bronze coin of the smallest denomination. The edges of ancient coins were left unfinished.

Money: The following coins are mentioned in the NT (1) **drachme**, the ordinary silver Greek coin, and the **drachmon** (or double drachme) (2) **stater**, a silver coin equal to four drachmes (3) **lepton** (or mite), the smallest bronze coin used by the Jews equaled one half quadrans (4) **denarius**, a Roman silver coin. The KJV always translates this as penny (5) **assarion** or farthing, a bronze coin in NT times one-sixteenth of a denarius (6) **kodrantes**, (Latin quadrans) translated farthing (Matt: 5:28) and mite (Mark 12:48) equal to one-fourth assarion. The talent and pounds are not coins but sums of money.

Mount of Olives: A limestone hill east of Jerusalem, with the Kidron valley lying between. On its western side lay the Garden of Gethsemane, and on the east, Bethphage and Bethany. It is where the atonement took place (Luke 22:39-44). It will also be prominent in the events of the second coming (Zechariah 14:4-5; D&C 45:48, 133:20).

Mount of Transfiguration: Thought to be Mount Hermon because of it being a 'high mountain' (Matthew 17:1) at 9,232 feet which Mt. Tabor is not, being 1,929 feet. Jesus Christ, Moses, and Elias (John the Baptist, Mark 9:3) gave the keys of the priesthood to Peter, James, and John (HC 3:387). This enabled them to continue the work after

Jesus' death.

Myrrh: Is the gum of the rock rose. It is used in preparation of the holy ointment (Ex. 30:23) in the purification of women (Esther 2:12) as a perfume (Psalms 45:8) and for embalming (John 19:39).

Mystery: As used in the NT are spiritual truths hidden from the unenlightened. They included the doctrine and parables which Jesus taught, such as his death and resurrection, which were not understood by the apostles until they were unveiled by the actual events.

| N

Nathaniel the Apostle: See Bartholomew.

Nazarene: A person from Nazareth, and was said of Jesus (Matthew 3:23). Whether they kept a Nazarite vow is not certain. But that the people of Nazareth were different from the rest of society is attested by the statement made by Nathaniel when he asked "can any good thing come out of Nazareth?" (John 1:46). At the very least, they seem to have been separatists. This may account for why Joseph and Mary chose to live there after returning from Egypt. Luke is the only one to assert that Joseph and Mary lived in Nazareth

before they went to Bethlehem to be taxed. Christians were called the "sect of the Nazarenes" (Acts 24:5). It was used as a name of contempt for Jesus' followers.

Nazareth: A small village built on the north slope of a small ridge. The valley runs nearly east to west and is about a mile long and a quarter mile wide. The hills vary from 100 to 500 feet above the valley floor.

Nazarite: Means *a consecrated man.* A person under a vow to abstain from wine, from cutting of the hair and any contact with the dead (Judges 13:5, 16:17, 17:1; Samuel 1:11; Amos 2:11, 12). For full regulations see Numbers 6. The vow might be lifelong, or for a short definite period. It appears that John the Baptist was a Nazarite (Luke 1:13-15) and that perhaps our Lord was also until His ministry began. After which, he was called a winebibber to which Jesus makes the comment "but wisdom is justified of all her children" (Luke 7:33-35). In light of latter-day revelation to abstain from strong drink, it would be unlikely that Jesus himself had not lived the law of the Nazarite at some point in his life time (see Vows).

Nicodemus: Was a Pharisee and a member of the Sanhedrin. He came to Jesus by night to avoid detection by others in Jewish leadership. However, he uses the word 'we' indicating that he also represented others who believed in Jesus (John 3:2). He defended Jesus at the Sanhedrin (John 7:50-51). Whatever reservations Nicodemus may have had at the time of Jesus' crucifixion, he openly brought spices and attended to Jesus' burial along with Joseph of Arimathea and faithful women.

Nobleman: *A man of high rank.*

| O

Only Begotten: Jesus was the Only Begotten child of God in the flesh. This made him half mortal and half immortal giving him power to voluntarily give his life with power over death to be able to reclaim his body again as the first resurrected mortal of this earth.

Ordinance: A sacred, formal act performed by the authority of the priesthood. Some ordinances are essential to our exaltation. These ordinances are called saving ordinances. They include baptism, confirmation, ordination to the Melchizedek Priesthood (for men), the temple endowment and the marriage sealing. With each of these ordinances, we enter into solemn covenants with the Lord. Other ordinances, such as naming and blessing of children, consecrat-

ing oil, and administering to the sick are also performed by priesthood authority. While they are not essential to our salvation, they are important for our comfort, guidance, and encouragement.

| P

Palsy: A condition marked by an uncontrollable tremor or paralysis by disabling the nerves in a part of the body.

Parable: From the Greek word parabole meaning *comparison.* Our Lord used parables extensively during His ministry (Mark 4:36) and told us the reason for using this method was to veil the meaning (Luke 8:10). The parable conveys to the hearer religious truths exactly in proportion to their faith and intelligence; but to the dull and uninspired, it is merely a story. Our Lord used 35 parables as documented in The Fifth Gospel. He continued to use parables in latter-day church history which are recorded in the D&C.

Paradise: Means a *garden.* It is a condition of happiness and peace reserved for those who have been baptized and remain faithful (Alma 40:12). The JST changed the reply of our Lord to the thief on the cross to "world of spirits" (Luke 23:44). Paradise is that part of the spirit world in which the righteous spirits who have departed this life await the resurrection of their body (Moroni 10:34), see Spirit Prison.

Passover: See Feasts.

Peace: The absence of conflict is not enough to bring peace to our heart. Freedom from oppressive thoughts and emotions comes through living the gospel and understanding the atonement of Jesus Christ.

Peace Offerings: See Sacrifices.

Penny: Was a Roman silver coin called the Denarius. In the King James Version it is interpreted as *penny*. It was a day's wages of a Roman soldier and also the day's wages in Jesus' parable of the laborers in the vineyard.

Peter the Apostle: Originally known as Simon. He was the son of Jonah (Matt. 16:17) and brother of Andrew (Matt. 10:2). His wife's name was Concordia and they lived with his mother-in-law at Capernaum. He was a fisherman from Bethsaida, on the northern coast of the Sea of Galilee. He was called to be a disciple by our Lord (Matt. 4:17-21) and given the Aramaic name of Cephas; Peter is the Greek equivalent (John 1:40-42). He was one of the inner circle of three whom our Lord chose to be with Him on certain occasions (Matt. 17:1, 26:34; Mark 5:29). Peter received the keys of the priesthood on the Mount of Transfiguration and became the chief apostle. He, along with James and John, conferred the Melchizedek Priesthood and its keys upon Joseph Smith and Oliver Cowdery in May or June of 1829 (D&C 27:12-13). Herod put him in prison but he was released by an angel. Whatever weaknesses he possessed in denying knowing our Lord during His trial, he was able to overcome during his lifetime. It is generally believed that Peter was crucified upside down at his own request because he felt unworthy to be crucified in the same manner as Jesus. He was martyred at Rome by Nero in A.D. 64 or 65.

Pharisee: The name means *separated by special works*. Pharisees prided themselves on their strict observance of the Law of Moses and the care with which they avoided contact with the gentiles. They were the largest of the three sects of Judaism (the others being Scribes and Sadducees). They believed in the resurrection and in immortality. The tendency of their teaching was to reduce religion to the observance of a multiplicity of ceremonial rules. Jesus rebuked the Pharisees and their works on more than one occasion (Matt. 23; Mark 7; Luke 11:38-55) with just cause. The Talmud says there were seven kinds of Pharisees; (1) Shechemites; who keep the law for what it will profit them. (2) Tumblers; always hanging their head down and dragging their feet. (3) Bleeders; to avoid women would shut their eyes and would bump their heads. (4) Mortars; who wore caps to cover the eyes to keep from seeing impurities. (5) What-am-I-yet-to-doers; who when one law is kept, ask what is next. (6) Fearers; who keep the law from fear of a judgment. (7) Lovers; who obey Jehovah because they love him with all their heart.

Philip the Apostle: He was chosen by our Lord as one of the original Twelve (Matt. 10:2). Originally from Bethsaida in Galilee, he was a follower of John the Baptist. He asked Jesus to show us *the* Father to which Jesus replied, "have I been so long time with you, and yet thou hast not known me, Philip?" (John 14:8-9) attesting to His divine roll in the hereafter. There is no account of his death. Tradition says that he preached in Phrygia.

Phylactery: The law of Moses written on bits of parchment and put in little cases of leather (metal in our day) and bound on the forehead between the eyes and on the left forearm. The ribbon used

by the Pharisees was made purple and made showy and broad to attract attention. It was like a kind of amulet such as worn by modern Arabs.

Pinnacle of the Temple: (Matt. 4:5; Luke 4:9) It is uncertain what is meant; probably part of the roof or one of the temple porches overlooking the deep Kidron valley. Excavations have revealed the foundation wall to be 150 feet high. The temple was probably an additional 50 to 75 on top of that. The pinnacle of the temple was probably in excess of 200 feet.

Plan of salvation: In the premortal existence, Heavenly Father presented a plan to enable us to become like Him in order to receive a fullness of Joy. The plan of salvation is the fullness of the gospel; it includes the Creation, the fall, the Atonement by Jesus Christ and all the laws, ordinances, and doctrines of the gospel. Moral agency, the ability to choose and act for ourselves, is also essential in Heavenly Father's plan.

Pontius Pilate: The fifth Roman procurator in Judea, A.D. 26-36 (Luke 3:1). He oppressed the Jews and violated Roman law which respected the Jewish religion. His headquarters were in Caesarea, but he was generally in Jerusalem at feast times and stayed at his official residence, Herod's palace. The Sanhedrin did not have the power to carry out a death sentence, therefore Pilate's consent had to be obtained. He saw there was no evidence to support their charge and having received a warning from his wife (Matt. 27:20), he wanted to dismiss the case. It was not until the Jews threatened to send a report to the Emperor Tiberius that he passed a death sentence, knowing it to be unjust. Pilate was removed from office after an appeal from the Samaritans, whom he oppressed, which caused him to be sent to Rome to answer the charges brought against him. Eventually he did end up giving an account to Tiberius of the crucifixion of Jesus, which account is also mentioned by Chrysostom. Eusebius says that Pilate killed himself, being "wearied with misfortunes," and perhaps on account of remorse for his conduct in Jerusalem.

Potter's Field: The name of a field bought with the thirty pieces of silver returned by Judas to the chief priests (Matt. 27:3-10). It was also called Aceldama.

Priesthood: The eternal power and authority of God. Through the priesthood God created and governs the heavens and the earth. Through this power He redeems and exalts His children, bringing to pass "the immortality and eternal life of man" (Moses 1:39). Although the priesthood is bestowed upon all worthy male members of the church twelve years and older, its blessings are available to all. There are two main divisions in the priesthood but both are the same priesthood; **(1)** the Aaronic or Lesser Priesthood, which includes the offices of Deacon, Teacher, Priest, and Bishop, and **(2)** the Melchizedek Priesthood which includes the offices of Elder, Seventy, High Priest, Apostle, and Patriarch.

Prophet: The work of a prophet is to act as God's messenger and make known his will. However, in order to do so, he must first be called of God. In certain dispensations there has been more than one prophet on the earth at a time. This was in part because of people being in various places on the earth making it impractical if not impossible to communicate to everyone. Today there is one prophet who has authority to speak for God.

Proselyte: Means *a stranger*. The law specified that they should be treated with forbearance and kindness (Exodus 22:21). It came to mean one 'who comes over' from one faith to another.

Proverb: A short story or maxim dealing concisely with a thought or an event.

Publican: Man who collected taxes for the Romans. They were disliked by the Jews and any Jew who undertook the work was excommunicated. Many of the tax collectors in Galilee would be in the service of Herod, and not of Rome. In the NT they were regarded as traitors and were classed with sinners and harlots. No money was allowed to be given by them in the alms-box. They were not allowed to sit in judgment or to give testimony. Some of them were the earliest disciples of John the Baptist.

Purification: There are two types: physical and spiritual. Its aim was to remove a defined uncleanness prior to certain activities of worship. It sometimes involved water for actual cleansing and used symbolically for spiritual cleansing. Sometimes it involved animal sacrifices. And it could also require a certain time period. In this instance (Luke 2:22) there was both a time period and an animal sacrifice (Leviticus 12).

| R

Rabbi: Means *master.*

Rabboni: Means *my master.*

Remission of Sins: *Is to release from guilt or penalty of sin.*

Repentance: One of the first principles of the gospel (Articles of Faith 1:4). It is much more than just acknowledging wrongdoings. It is a change of mind and heart that gives us a fresh view about God, about our self, and about the world which includes wrongdoings. It includes turning away from sin and turning to God for forgiveness. It is motivated by love for God and a sincere desire to obey His commandments. It is a blessing based upon the principal of faith rather than of knowledge (Matt. 5:3-4; 3 Nephi 12:1-2).

Resurrection: Because of the fall of Adam and Eve, we are subject to physical death, which is the separation of the spirit from the body. The resurrection is the reuniting of the spirit with the body in a perfect, immortal state, no longer subject to disease or death. Jesus Christ was the first person on this earth to be resurrected. All people will be resurrected (1 Corinthians 15:22) regardless of their works in mortality. This is a fundamental part of the 'good news' of the gospel. Of all the religions in the world, only Christianity has claim as to its founder, Jesus Christ, coming back from the dead. It is because Jesus did rise from the dead that we can have faith in the rest of his gospel.

Roman Empire: During NT time, the Roman Empire was the one great power of the world. It included everything between the Euphrates, the Danube, the Rhine, the Atlantic, and the Sahara desert. Palestine became a client state in B.C. 63, when Pompeius took Jerusalem and at the banishment of Archelaus (A.D. 6), Herod was made the first king under Roman rule by Anthony (B.C. 40). Under Roman rule, taxes paid to Julius Caesar were in the form of one fourth of their agricultural produce in addition to tithes. After A.D. 6, Judea was made a province of Syria at the request of the Jews, who were tired of the cruelties of the Herod's, with the capital in Caesarea. Coponius was the first procurator, and Pilate was the fifth.

| S

Sabbath: *The Lord's Day* set apart each week for rest and worship. In OT times, it was observed on the seventh day of the week. Keeping the Sabbath day holy is the oldest ordinance along with marriage since the creation. The observance of this Holy day indicates prosperity of religion while neglect shows a decay of religion generally. The blessings for keeping the Sabbath

day holy are abundant (D&C 59:16-20). After the resurrection of Jesus Christ, which occurred on the first day of the week, the Lord's disciples began observing the Sabbath on the first day of the week, Sunday (Acts 20:7).

Sabbath Day's Journey: It is the distance that was supposed that the law allowed a man to walk on the Sabbath; 2,000 cubits, being the distance between the ark and the people during the march in the wilderness (Josh. 3:4), and also the distance between the tabernacle and the farthest part of the camp (Acts 1:12). The common cubit was 18 inches and would be 3,000 feet. The sacred cubit of 19.05 inches would be 4,762 feet. A mile is 5,280 feet.

Sabbatical Year: As was the seventh day in every week and the seventh month in every year, so also was every seventh year consecrated to the Lord. It commenced with the Feast of the Tabernacles. During the Sabbatical year there was to be no sowing or reaping. In addition, any Israelite who owed another Israelite was to be forgiven of their debt. It commenced in the seventh month of the year. Understanding this gives insight into scriptures such as John 4:37 in which our Lord acknowledges that the wheat was ready to harvest but the people must wait four months to harvest it. It is also important to note that our Lord started His ministry in "the Lord's acceptable year" (Luke 4:17-21). Just as forgiving a debtor was expected during this year, so also was "unloosing the bands of wickedness, undoing heavy burdens, letting the oppressed go free, and the breaking of every yoke" (Isaiah 58:6) which typified our Lord's ministry.

Sackcloth: A course stiff fabric, of dark color, often made of goats hair and the coarse black hair of the camel. In times of trouble, calamity or penitence, the Jews wore sackcloth. The robe resembled a sack, and was held in place by a girdle of the same material.

Sacrifice: A law first given to Adam and Eve which included offering the firstlings of their flocks in a similitude of the sacrifice that would be made of the Only Begotten Son of God (Moses 5:48). This practice continued until the death of Jesus Christ, which ended the shedding of blood as a gospel ordinance. It has been replaced in the church by the sacrament of bread and water, in remembrance of the offering of Jesus Christ.

Sadducees: One of three religious sects of the Jews who refused to accept that the oral law was revelation from God to the Israelites, and believed exclusively in the written law. They are identified with the priestly aristocracy, whose influence was based on wealth and priestly status. They did not believe in life after death, the resurrection, the final judgment, or heaven and hell. They never had the influence that the Pharisees had, and were somewhat more tolerant. They joined with the Pharisees in getting Jesus crucified but opposed their doctrine otherwise. They disappeared from historical record when the temple was destroyed in A.D. 70.

Saint: From a Greek word, *Nagios,* also rendered *Holy one,* a title by which the disciples of Jesus were known. The idea being that they were consecrated or separated for a sacred purpose. In the NT the saints were those who were baptized into the Christian covenant (Acts 9:13).

Salome: (1) Salome wife of Zebedee mother of James and John. Came to Jesus to see if her sons could sit on the right and left hand of Jesus in His heavenly kingdom (Matt. 20:18-23). She helped see to Jesus' burial (Matt. 27:59). **(2) Salome** was the daughter of Herodias and Philip, Herod's brother, who danced before Herod Antipas, culminating in the death of John the Baptist (Matt. 14:3-11). Her name is not mentioned in the NT but is given to us by Josephus, *Antiquities* XVIII: 5:4.

Salvation: (1) from physical death, and **(2)** from spiritual death. Through the death and resurrection of Jesus Christ all mankind will be resurrected. Through the atonement of Jesus Christ all mankind can be cleansed from sin on conditions of repentance, baptism, and receiving the Holy Ghost (Acts 2:37-38).

Samaria: A district before there was a city named Samaria. It was built by Omri as the capital of the kingdom of Israel, on a hill which he bought (B.C. 925) of Shemer for two talents of silver (1 Kings 16:24). The capital in OT times included all the tribes who accepted Jeroboam as their king. In NT times Samaria was the name of the whole of the central district of Palestine west of Jordan. It lay between Galilee and Judea. There were five conquests of the northern tribes of Israel in which the Israelite people were carried away by their conquerors. The first was the captivity of the tribes of Simeon and Dan. The second, when Pul, king of Assyria B.C. 771 carried away the Reubenites and Gadites, and the half tribe of Manasseh (1 Chronicles 5:26). The third, when

Galilee and Gilead were taken by the Assyrians (2 Kings 15:29). The fourth when Shalmanezer, king of Assyria conquered Samira after a three year siege in B.C. 721 (2 Kings 18:9-19). John Hyreanus conquered it in B.C 109 after a one year siege (Josephus Ant. XIII. 10, 2). Herod the great rebuilt it and called it Sebaste (Augustus, after Emperor Augustus). Today the ancient city has remains of ancient colonnades of Herod's time or older.

Samaritans: The people who inhabited Samaria after the captivity of the northern kingdom or ten tribes of Israel. Eventually some of the people were allowed to return. There was generally a great dislike between the Samaritans and the Jews not only because of blood lines from intermarrying but also because of idolatrous religious beliefs, some of which were introduced before their captivity and some by their captors in Assyria before their return.

Sanctify: In the NT it means *to make holy what was before defiled and sinful.* This is accomplished through repentance, obedience to God's commandments, and the grace of Jesus Christ. It is a gradual cleansing from sin to eventually be presented to God as clean. In the OT it means *to consecrate one's life* *to God.*

Sanhedrin: From the Greek word sunedrion meaning *council.* It was the Jewish senate and the highest native court in both civil and ecclesiastical matters. It consisted of 70 members being made up of chief priests, scribes, and elders. With the chief priest there were a total of 71 members. At the time of our Lord, the Pharisees had the predominating influence on it. It had officers of its own who arrested accused persons and carried out its sentences and decrees. It did not have the right to carry out the death sentence. Its jurisdiction was limited to Judea although its decisions were regarded morally binding all over the Jewish world. Had Jesus remained in Galilee, He would have been beyond its power (John 7:1).

Satan: The enemy of righteousness and those who seek to do the will of God. He was literally a spirit son of God in the pre-mortal life. Known as Lucifer (only mentioned once in the Bible, Isaiah 14:12) meaning *the shining one* or *light bringer* or *son of the morning.* At one time he was an angel of authority in the presence of God. He rebelled against the plan of salvation and persuaded a third of the spirit children of Father to rebel with him and continues to try and persuade

us to rebel in this life. Since the devil and his pre-mortal followers have no physical bodies, they often seek to possess the bodies of mortal beings (Matt. 9:38, 12:22; Mark 1:21, 5:2-9; Luke 8:27-34; Acts 19:15; Mosiah 3:16).

Scribe: Scribes in the O.T. copied sacred writings. In N.T. times they were elevated to the status of teachers of the law and commandments. It was their business to develop the law in detail and apply it to their circumstances. They never taught on their own authority which contrasted our Lord's way of teaching (Matt. 7:37). They were a determined opposition to our Lord mainly because He disregarded the traditions of the elders.

Scripture: The official scriptures of The Church of Jesus Christ of Latter-day Saints, often called the standard works are: the *Bible,* the *Book of Mormon,* the *Doctrine and Covenants,* and the *Pearl of Great Price.* In addition, when holy men of God write or speak by the power of the Holy Ghost, their words "shall be scripture" and "shall be the voice of the Lord, and the power of God unto salvation" (D&C 68:4).

Scourge: Forty lashes of a whip on the bare back.

Seed of Abraham: The heirs of the

promises and covenants made to Abraham, and obtained by obedience to the laws and ordinances of the gospel of Jesus Christ.

Seventy: Designates an office held within the Melchizedek Priesthood. The Lord appointed the Seventy to go before Him (Luke 10:1, 17) and preach the gospel. However, the number seventy is significant. It was the same number as the Sanhedrin. Jesus essentially established a new Sanhedrin which was a symbol of the new covenant. The seventy were given directions much the same as the apostles. But it should be noted that their mission was not limited just to the Israelites while Jesus was still alive. They are still a part of His church today (D&C 107:25).

Sheep: Prominent in NT times, and frequently mentioned, sheep were watched over by shepherds. They went before their sheep and the sheep followed, apparently being attracted to their master's voice which they recognized. Our Lord uses this analogy in his parables of the 'lost sheep' (Matthew 18:12-24); and the parable of 'his sheep know his voice' (John 10:1-16).

Shewbread: On the north side in the holy place of the Tabernacle was a table of acacia wood. Upon it every Sabbath were placed two piles of unleavened bread made of fine flour, which represented the twelve tribes of Israel as an offering. A golden pot filled with incense was placed on top of each pile, and remained until the next Sabbath, when the incense was burned. The loaves were then eaten by the priests in the Sanctuary, and twelve fresh ones laid for an offering. David, in extreme hunger, ate of the shewbread (1 Sam. 21:4-6; Matt. 12:3).

Shiloh: Means *He to whom it belongs*. It is also mentioned in the OT as one of the oldest and most sacred of the Jewish sanctuaries. The Ark of the Covenant was kept there (Joshua 18:1).

Signs of the times: Throughout the history of the world every event of the gospel has been prophesied by prophets prior to its actually happening (Amos 3:7). As used here, Jesus was chastising the Jewish leaders for being able to predict the weather but not being able see the fulfillment of the prophesies concerning his mission.

Simon: (1) Simon Peter the Apostle (see Peter), **(2) Simon** the brother of Jesus (Matt. 13:56) **(3) Simon** the Canaanite, one of the Twelve (Matt. 10:2) also called Zelotes (Luke 6:15), **(4) Simon** of Cyrene (Matt. 27:34) who carried

Jesus' cross, **(5) Simon** the leper and Pharisee in whose house Mary anointed Jesus (Matt. 26:5; Mark 14:4; Luke 7:36-43).

Sin: Is only incurred when we knowingly disobey God's commandments. Only those eight years old and older, of sound mind and who have been taught the commandments, are capable of sin (D&C 68:25; Mormon 8).

Sion: The Greek word for Zion (see Zion).

Solomon: The youngest son of David and Bathsheba (1 Chronicles 3:5). He was educated under the care of Nathan, the prophet, in all that the priests, Levites and prophets had to teach (2 Samuel 12:25). He was acknowledged by the people as heir to the throne only after his brother Absalom's revolt and death. He was anointed king by Nathan at the age of 19 or 20, B.C. 1015. He inherited his father's wealth which was estimated at 100,000 talents of gold, 1,000,000 talents of silver, and of brass and iron without weight, in addition to stone and timber (1 Chronicles 22:14) for the purpose of building a permanent structure for a temple of God. This alone says much about his character and dedication to the Lord. Solomon's true wealth however was in the blessing

of the Lord which he obtained at Gibeon. Because of his humility, he was given great wisdom and an understanding heart (1 Kings 3:5-12). He exceeded all the kings of the earth in riches and wisdom (1 Kings 10:23-25).

Son of God: Although Jesus speaks of himself as being the Son of God, there is not a single passage of scripture in which the sonship of others is spoken of as being the same as His own. He speaks of "*my* Father" and "*your* Father", but never *our* Father (the Lord's Prayer is no exception, as it was intended for the disciples as an example). Jesus Christ is the only begotten Son in the flesh of *His* Father.

Son of Man: A title used by the Lord about 80 times in the gospels to refer to Himself, but never used by anyone else in speaking of Him during His lifetime. Latter-day revelation confirms the sacredness of the title when used as a name for our Savior (D&C 45:39, 49:6, 22, 58:65; Moses 6:57).

Soul: (1) a spirit united with a physical body, whether in mortality or after resurrection (D&C 88:15-16), **(2)** our spirits are sometimes called souls (Matthew 10:25).

Spikenard: A highly perfumed ointment made from a plant from

India, with a strong, pleasant, aromatic odor. It was prized by the ancients and was very costly (John 12:3).

Spirit: Although used in several ways, the most basic use refers to our individual entity that had an existence prior to mortality. Our spirit is in the likeness of our body (Genesis 2:4-65; 1 Nephi 11:11; Ether 3:15-16; Moses 3:4-7).

Spirit Prison: A waiting place for people who have died without having either heard or accepted the gospel (1 Peter 3:18-20). Sometimes called the 'world of spirits' (Luke 23:44). It is where people go who will be given the opportunity to hear and accept the gospel (see Baptism also).

Spiritual Death: *Being separated from God.* The scriptures teach of two causes of spiritual death; **(1)** the fall of Adam and Eve, **(2)** through our own disobedience.

Spiritual Gifts: See Gifts of the Spirit.

Stranger: Denotes a man or woman who was a resident of the Promised Land but of non-Israelite birth.

Synagogue: Means *congregation.* It is a Jewish meeting house for religious purposes, managed by the local council of elders. In smaller towns there was often only one Rabbi. The most important official was the ruler of the synagogue (Luke 13:14) who was generally a scribe. The Sabbath morning service was the most important of the week. Moses was read in the synagogue every Sabbath day, the whole law being read consecutively, so as to be completed in one cycle every three years. The writings of the prophets were second lessons in a corresponding order. They were followed by the Derash, the exposition or sermon of the synagogue (Luke 4:16-28). Times of prayer were in the third, sixth, and ninth hours in the NT. It stood on the highest ground in or near the city in which it was located. They were all built so that worshippers as they entered and prayed faced Jerusalem. At the upper end closest to Jerusalem, stood the ark, a chest which contained the Book of the Law. Here also were the chief seats after which the Pharisees and the Scribes eagerly desired (Matthew 23:4). From these synagogues came the use of fixed forms of prayer.

| T

Tabernacle: Peter wished to prolong the heavenly visitors stay by offering to build them three tabernacles (Matthew 17:3). As used here, a tabernacle is any type of a roofed structure with or without walls such as a booth.

Tares: Denotes darnel grass, a poisonous weed, which until it comes to ear, is similar in appearance to wheat (Matt. 13:22-29). If mixed with bread, it causes dizziness and often vomiting.

Temple: Throughout history the Lord has commanded His people to build temples. Temples are literally houses of the Lord. They are holy places of worship where the Lord may visit.

Temple of Herod: To win popularity with the Jews, Herod proposed to rebuild the temple at Jerusalem (17 B.C.). The Jews did not trust Herod, should he tear down the existing temple and not rebuild a new one. As a show of good faith, Herod gathered the materials before beginning work. The site was inadequate for his design, and to enlarge it he built up a wall from the bottom of the valley, nearly square, each side 600 feet long. The temple itself was built by the priests in a year and six months. The cloisters (outer enclosures) were built in eight years. Other buildings were added from time to time continuing through our Lord's life and were not complete until A.D. 64, only six years before the temple's final destruction in A.D. 70.

Temptation: In looking at the three temptations of Jesus, the temptation of turning the stones to loaves of bread was not about whether eating bread was a sin but rather giving control of his appetites to Satan. The three temptations of Jesus centered on appetite, passion, and greed. Temptation is the act of enticement. All mankind are tempted by Satan and his followers. Giving into temptation is what leads to sin. We need not feel as though we have sinned simply because we have been tempted to do so. Not giving into temptation is what strengthens us and builds character.

Testament: Means *covenant with God*.

Tetrarch: Originally meant the ruler of the fourth part of a country but was also used with some other fraction of the whole. The title is applied to Herod Antipas who was tetrarch of Galilee, Herod Philip who was tetrarch of Iturea and the region of Trachonitis, and Lysanias who was tetrarch of Abilene (Luke 3:1).

Thomas the Apostle: He was chosen as one of the original Twelve (Matt. 10:2; Mark 3:14; Luke 6:15). He was not present when Jesus first appeared to the remaining ten apostles at Jerusalem. When told, he refused to believe until he had seen the resurrected Lord Himself (John 20:24-28) earning him the title of 'doubting Thomas'. He was willing to die for Jesus (John 11:16). The Greek word didymus means *twin*. His twin sister was named Lydia. Tradition says he preached in Parthia, and was a martyr, and was buried in Edessa. The church in Malabar claims him as its founder, and shows a tomb as his.

Tiberias: A large town on the western shore of the Sea of Galilee built by Herod Antipas, who made it his capital and called it after the name of the reigning emperor, Tiberius (note the difference in spelling).

Tiberius: The second emperor of Rome, successor of Augustus, A.D. 14-37. At first he was moderate and just but soon became infamous for his vices and crimes. He died in A.D. 37. He is mentioned several times as Caesar (Luke 20:22-25). His subjects were commanded to worship his image.

Tithe: The word denotes one-tenth of a person's increase annually given for the building of the kingdom of God. It was first recorded when payment was made by Abraham to Melchizedek (Gen. 14:29). It is still a 'duty and test of faith' for members of the church today (D&C 64:23-25, 85:3, 97:11, 119).

Tribute: During the time that Rome occupied Jerusalem there were import taxes levied at harbors, piers, and the gates of cities. In addition to this, there was a poll-tax paid by every Jew. This was most likely the tax that was paid by Jesus and Peter from the coin found in the fish's mouth (Matthew 17:23-26). In addition to these taxes there appears to be a property tax of some kind which was one fourth of what they produced. These taxes did not include tithes and offerings made by the Jewish people nor did it include temple dues. Tribute was any one of these taxes.

| U

Unclean spirit: Those people who have lived on earth and then died and whose spirit remains on earth because they refuse to return to God. They in effect chose to follow Satan rather than to face a partial judgment now and go to spirit prison.

| V

Veil of the Temple: Separated the inner sanctuary, called the 'Holy of Holies', which in the time of the OT contained the Ark of the

Covenant and the mercy seat part of the Ark itself, considered to be God's throne (Ex. 25:22). In NT times a stone was set in the place of the Ark and used as part of the temple ceremony.

Vows: Were of two kinds; **(1)** dedication; some person or thing was given to the Lord (Lev. 27:1-24), **(2)** abstinence; a promise made to abstain from some lawful act of enjoyment (Numbers 6:3). There were certain laws regarding vows. A man might devote to sacred uses possessions or persons, but not the firstborn either of man or beast because they were already the Lord's (Leviticus 27:26). The vows of minors were not binding without the consent of the head of the family (Numbers 30); see Espoused also.

| W

Washing the Hands and the Feet: Knives and forks were not used at the table, therefore washing hands before and after meals was necessary (Matthew 15:2). Because of the eastern climate, washing the feet upon entering a house was an act of respect and of refinement to the traveler (Genesis 18:4). When done by the master of the house it was a mark of respect and honor to the guest.

Watch: Is a division of the night. In NT times there were four watches (Matthew 14:21; Mark 6:50). In OT times there were only three watches.

Weights and Measures: The references in the Bible are few and incomplete. Scholars have supplied lacking information from systems of ancient nations to construct various tables of weights and measures but do not always agree. So far as specific words have been used in The Fifth Gospel, see individual definitions.

Wine: The word wine in the OT has ten different Hebrew words to describe how it was made, if it was a fruit juice or an alcoholic wine, or if it was a wine that had turned to vinegar. Contrasted with the NT which uses only two different Greek words: *Oinon* (translated oinos) in Matthew 9:23, used in the parable of putting new wine into old bottles but not intended to be fermented as this would have burst the bottles or skins in which it was kept; and *Oxos* (phonetic spelling Ozos), *a* sour wine or vinegar mixed with water and herbal flavoring (John 19:29) which the Roman soldiers gave to Jesus while he was on the cross. Some wines of poor quality, due to improper storage, would degrade to vinegar. Because of its antibacterial quality it was mixed with water to make it safe to drink and herbal flavorings to improve the taste. This was also called *Posca* used in ancient Rome and Greece. Since *Oinos* refers to both alcoholic and non-alcoholic wine, it is necessary to read the surrounding Greek words as to the type of wine referred to. The water that was turned into wine (John 2:1-11) uses the Greek word *Mequvw* (translated methou) which means that the men at the marriage feast were drunk. However this does not prove that Jesus made alcoholic wine to make them drunker. Whatever type of wine, it was of superior quality. Mark 15:26 uses the word *Oinos* that was offered to Jesus on the cross but it should be kept in mind that Greek was a second language for Mark and most likely he used the wrong word. This is born out in the fact that Joseph Smith changed the word wine to vinegar.

Wise Men of the East: See Magi.

Worship: To worship God is to give Him our love, reverence, service, and devotion. The main reason for Joseph Smith being commanded to translate the Bible was so that we might "know who to worship and how to worship" (D&C 93:6-19).

| Z

Zacharias: A priest, husband to Elizabeth (Luke 1:5) and father to John the Baptist (Luke 1:58-62). Many of the Greek Fathers have maintained that he was the person referred to by our Lord in Matt. 23:32, who was slain between the altar and the temple. But there can be little doubt that Zachariah, the son of Jehoiada the priest, was the one Jesus referred to (2 Chronicles 24:20-21).

Zebedee: He was the husband of Salome and father of James and John (Matthew 4:21). He was also a fisherman.

Zelotes: A name for Simon (3), one of the Twelve Apostles (Luke 6:15) to distinguish him from Simon Peter (see Simon).

Zion: The most general definition of Zion is "the pure in heart" (D&C 97:21). The word can also refer to a specific geographical location. The city of Enoch was called Zion (Moses 7:18-19), Jerusalem was once referred to as Zion, (2 Samuel 5:6-7), the New Jerusalem which is too be built in Jackson County, Missouri (D&C 45:66-67, 57:1-3; Article of Faith 1:10), will also be Zion.

CONCORDANCE

Preface

English words often have more than one meaning. This concordance shows in Italics the different meanings as used in the text of The Fifth Gospel. References are made to the page and then the verse within the page. Because there may be more than one page with the same verse number you will need to decide which verse is the one you are looking for.

| A

Abased. *Demean, humiliate.*
p98[14] exalteth himself shall be a.

Abba. *Father.*
p149[40] A. take away this cup.

Abide. *Stay, settle, dwell.*
p67[10] inquire who is worthy, a. there.
p107[5] a. at Zacchaeus' house.
p120[46] believeth not shall a. in darkness.
p143[16] Comforter a. with you forever.
p144[4] a. in me, and I in you.
p144[7] my words shall a. in you.
p166[28] a. with us, toward evening.

Abideth. *Abide.*
p79[35] servant a. not in house forever.
p119[24] corn of wheat die, it a. alone.
p119[34] the Christ a. for ever.

Abiding. *Abide.*
p6[8] shepherds a. in the field.
p57[39] have not his word a. in you.

Ability. *Capacity, talent, gift.*
p135[15] according to his several a.

Abode. *Abide.*
p4[55] Mary a. with Elizabeth.
p16[31] Spirit like a dove a. upon him.
p17[39] John, Andrew a. with Jesus
p35[42] a. with Samaritans two days.
p79[44] a. not in the truth.
p112[40] Jesus a. beyond Jordan.
p143[23] make our a. with him.

Abomination. *Impure, detestable.*
p104[15] lightly esteemed is an a. in the sight of God.
p132[33] a. of desolation spoke by Daniel.

Abound. *Plentiful.*
p131[10] because iniquity shall a.
p132[31] because iniquity shall a.

About. *Around, on, upon.*
p7[9] glory of the Lord round a. them.
p11[49] be a. my Father's business.
p12[30] a leathern girdle a. his loins.
p12[31] all the reagon round a. Jordan.
p14[30] to be a. thirty years of age.
p18[14] went out a fame round a.
p24[38] let your loins be girded a.
p38[22] Jesus went a. all Galilee.
p64[25] Jesus looked round a. to see her.
p116[41] cumbered a. much serving.

Above. *On high, higher than.*
p31[32] he who cometh from a.
p49[7] exalted themselves a. another.
p51[2] were sinners a. all Galileans.
p68[21] disciple is not a. his master.
p157[11] it were given thee from a.

Abraham. *O.T. patriarch, prophet.*
p4[54] as he spake to A. and his seed.
p5[72] oath which he sware to A.
p13[36] we are the children of A.
p48[11] shall sit down with A.
p79[39] A. is our father.
p80[53] art thou greater than A.

p80[56] A. rejoiced to see my day.

p80[58] before A. was, I am.

p105[28] in torments and saw A. afar off.

p124[31] I am the God of A.

Abroad. *Outside, far and wide.*

p5[64] these sayings were noised a.

p21[25] not with me scattereth a.

p58[19] kept in secret should go a.

p65[32] the fame of Jesus went a.

Absence. *Not being present.*

p138[12] opportunity to betray Jesus in the a. of the multitude.

Abundance. *Plenty, wealth.*

p22[29] out of the a. of the heart

p29[17] life consisteth not in the a.

p130[50] rich did cast in of their a.

p136[29] who hath other talents, shall have in a.

Abundantly. *Abundance.*

p110[10] I am come that they might have life more a.

Acceptable. *Pleasing.*

p35[19] the a. year of the Lord.

Accepted. *Received.*

p36[24] no prophet is a. in his own country.

Accomplish. *Complete, carry out.*

p87[31] which he should a. at Jerusalem.

Accomplished. *Accomplish.*

p25[59] am I straightened until it be a.!

p103[31] all things written shall be a.

p149[37] this that is written must be a.

p160[28] knowing that all things were now a.

According. *Agreeable to, just as.*

p3[38] be it unto me a. to thy word.

p7[24] offer a sacrifice a. to the law.

p47[31] to be judged a. to their works.

p65[35] a. to your faith be it unto you.

p154[31] judge him a. to your law.

Account. *Report, reckoning.*

p22[31] men to give an a. in the day of judgment.

p93[23] king took a. of his servants.

p103[2] give an a. of thy stewardship.

Accounted. *Recognized.*

p140[24] who should be a. the greatest.

Accusation. *Accuse.*

p154[29] what a. bring ye against this man?

Accuse. *Indictment, charge.*

p13[21] neither a. any falsely.

p27[55] that they might a. him.

p57[46] that I will a. you to the Father.

p153[59] found none that could a. him.

p156[14] found no fault whereof ye a. him.

Accused. *Accuse.*

p154[13] Jesus a. of the chief priest and elders.

p155[10] scribes vehemently a. him.

Accuseth. *Accuse.*

p57[46] there is Moses who a. you.

Act. *Do something, perform.*

p77[4] woman taken in adultery in the very a.

Adam. *First man upon the earth.*

p15[45] A. who was formed of God.

Add. *Give, Increase.*

p45[31] and a. one cubit to his stature.

Added. *Add.*

p45[38] all these things shall be a. unto you.

Adjure. *To charge or command.*

p153[64] I a. thee by the living God.

Adorned. *Decorated, ornamented.*

p130[5] temple a. with goodly stones.

Adulterous. *Adultery.*

p22[34] a. generation seeketh a sign.

p84[4] a. generation seeketh a sign.

p87[41] a. and sinful generation.

Adultery. *Infidelity, disloyalty, betrayal, faithlessness.*

p41[29] thou shalt not commit a.

p41[30] committed a. in his heart.

p41[36] causeth her to commit a.

p77[3] woman taken in a.

p100[9] marry another, committeth a.

p104[23] marry another, committeth a.

Afflicted. *Afflict.*

p55[6] had been now a long time a.

Affrighted. *Afraid.*

p163[4] a. and bowed down their faces.

p166[36] they were terrified and a.

Afoot. *On foot.*

p70[34] people ran a. to see Jesus.

Afraid. *To fear.*

p7[9] angel, and they were sore a.

p10[22] Herod was a.

p27[4] be not a. of those who kill the body.

p28[10] were a. to confess him.

p50[26] is a. to lay down their life.

p65[28] be not a. only believe.

p71[53] be of good cheer, be not a.

p88[5] Mt. of Transfiguration, a.

p136[25] was a. and hid thy talent.

p157[8] Pilate was the more a.

After. *Following.*

p12[28] who, coming a. is preferred.

p50[27] bear his cross, and come a. me.

p68[33] taketh not his cross and follow a. me.

Again. *A second time.*

p29[3] except a man be born a.

p29[7] ye must be born a.

p103[33] and the third day rise a.

p164[9] that he must rise a. from the dead.

Age. *Period of existence.*

p3[36] in her old a.

p8[36] Anna was of great a.

p64[43] about twelve years of a.

p109[21] he is of a. ask him.

Agony. *Anguish, pain, suffering.*

p150[44] being in a. he prayed more earnestly.

Agree. *Concur, consent, approve.*

p40[27] a. with thine adversary.

p93[19] two of you a. on earth.

p102[12] a. with me for a penny.

Alabaster Box. *Stone box.*

p53[37] a. box of ointment.

p137[4] a. box of spikenard.

Alive. *Living.*

p92[24] my son was dead, and is a.

p162[64] deceiver said while he was a.

p165[10] they heard that he was a.

p166[22] angels who said he was a.

Alms. *Kind act, charity, mercy.*

p23[36] sell that ye have and give a.

p26[42] rather give a. of such as ye have.

p42[1] do not your a. before men.

p43[3] doest a. let not the right hand.

Alone. *Only, separate.*

p15[4] man shall not live by bread a.

p77[9] Jesus and the woman left a.

p78[16] for I am not a.

p93[15] tell thy brother, he and thee a.

p137[6] let her a. why trouble ye her.

p147[32] and shall leave me a.

p148[20] neither pray I for these a.

p159[22] what I have written, let it a.

Already. *Now, by this time.*

p30[18] believeth not is condemned a.

p35[37] field is white, a. to harvest.

p41[30] hath committed adultery a.

p88[11] Elias has come a.

Altar. *Raised structure or place.*

p2[11] right side of a. of incense.

p27[51] perished between the a.

p40[26] leave thy gift before the a.

Although. *Even though.*

p133[36] a. the days will come.

Altogether. *In total.*

p83[9] a. ye reject the commandments.

p110[34] thou wast a. born in sins.

Always. *Forever.*

p52[24] Lord shall not a. strive with man.

p78[29] I do a. those things.

p98[1] men ought a. to pray.

p138[7] ye have the poor with you a.

p171[47] lo, I am with you a.

Amazed. *Astonished.*

p20[24] and they were all a.

p88[13] greatly a. and running to him.

p102[31] the apostles were a.

p149[36] disciples sore a. at Gethsemane.

Amen. *Hebrew; truth.*

p171[25] contain all books written. A.

Amiss. *Incorrect, wrong.*

p93[19] that they may not ask a.

p159[42] this man hath done nothing a.

Among. *In the midst of.*

p1[14] the word dwelt a. us.

p12[27] one a. you whom ye know not.

p90[31] who was greatest a. them.

Andrew. *The apostle.*

p19[44] Bethsaida, city of A. and Peter.

p21[26] the house of Simon and A.

p23[14] A. ordained one of the twelve.

p66[2] is sent forth to teach.

p66[2] Simon Peter's brother.

p70[8] barley loaves and small fishes.

p119[22] tells Jesus about the Greeks.

Angel. *Messenger of God.*

p2[13] a. announces John's birth.

p3[26] a. announces Jesus' birth.

p6[3] an a. appears to Joseph.

p7[9] a. appeared to the shepherds.

p9[13] a. appears to Joseph a second time.

p10[19] a. appears to Joseph a third time.

p149[43] a. appears to Jesus at Gethsemane.

Anger. *Annoyance, indignation.*

p81[5] Jesus looked upon them with a.

Angry. *Anger.*

p27[54] scribe and Pharisees were a.

p40[24] whosoever is a. with his brother.

p104[22] being a. for the saying.

p122[48] and they were a. with him.

Anguish. *Pain, suffering.*

p146[21] she remember no more the a.

Anise. *Dill.*

p128[20] pay tithe of a.

Anna. *Prophetess at the temple.*

p8[38] gave thanks for Jesus' birth.

Anoint. *Apply or rub.*

p44[18] when thou fastest, a. thy head.

p138[8] a. my body to the burying.

p162[1] spices to a. his body.

Anointed. *Anoint.*

p54[46] Mary a. Jesus' feet.

Another. *An additional, a different.*

p142[34] love one a. as I have loved you.

p143[16] Father to give a. Comforter.

p144[12] commandment to love one a.

Answer. *Reply.*

p28[13] give no thought what to a.

p124[26] they marveled at his a.

p127[44] no man was able to a. him.

p130[12] before what ye shall a.

p157[9] Jesus gave him no a.

Apiece. *Each.*

p17[6] two or three firkins a.

Apostles. Means *sent forth.*

p23[13] whom also he named a.

p27[50] I will send them a.

p66[2] the names of the twelve a.

p136[34] sit upon his throne, and the twelve a. with him.

Apparel. *Clothing.*

p168[10] two men in white a.

Appear. *Seem, show.*

p26[45] Pharisees as graves which a. not.

p44[18] a. unto men to fast.

p107[11] kingdom of God should a.

p128[21] a. that ye would not commit sin.

p128[24] sepulchers a. beautiful.

p128[25] outwardly a. righteous.

p133[37] then shall a. the sign.

Appoint. *Assign, designate.*

p25[55] a. his portion with unbelievers.

p134[55] a. his portion with hypocrites.

p142[29] a. unto you a kingdom.

Appointed. *Appoint.*

p13[18] exact no more than is a.

p13[19] was a. unto the poor.

p95[1] Lord a. other seventy.

p96[46] is a. to watch over you.

p142[29] my Father hath a. unto me.

p170[15] Jesus a. the apostles.

Arise. *Get up, occur.*

p9[13] a. and flee into Egypt.

p10[20] a. and return to Israel.

p38[8] say to the sick of palsy, a.

p53[14] said to the young man, a.

p65[33] said to the damsel, a.

p88[6] a., be not afraid.

p132[23] shall a. false Christs.

p150[43] a., let us be going.

p166[37] why do thoughts a.

Ariseth. *Arise.*

p61[19] persecution a. because.

p77[52] Galilee a. no prophet.

Ark. *Large ship.*

p133[45] Noah entered into the a.

Arm. *Upper limb.*

p4[50] shown strength with his a.

p119[38] whom hath the a. of the Lord been revealed?

Arrayed. *Dressed.*

p45[33] Solomon not a.

p155[11] a. him in a gorgeous robe.

Ashamed. *Embarrassed, feel guilty.*

p52[17] adversaries were a.

p87[40] be not a. of me.

p87[41] whosoever shall be a. of me.

p103[3] to beg I am a.

Ashes. *Dust, remains.*

p94[23] sackcloth and a.

Ask. *Inquire, solicit.*

p12[20] Jews a. who John is.

p44[10] a. and it shall be given you.

p46[12] a. of God.

p47[20] good things to them that a.

p93[19] a. not amiss.

p96[45] a. in faith.

p120[22] I will also a. you one thing.

p127[44] not a. any more questions.

p143[13] ye shall a. in my name.

p145[16] a. the Father in my name.

p146[19] Jesus knew they wanted to a.

p169[12] none of disciples durst a. him.

Asleep. *Sleep.*

p62[23] Jesus fell a. in the ship.

p150[45] found the apostles a.

Ass. *Donkey.*

p52[15] loose an a. from the stall.

p117[4] sitting upon an a.

Athirst. *Thirsty.*

p137[45] hungered or a.

Austere. *Harsh, rough.*

p108[22] knewest I was an a. man.

Authority. *Privilege, right, power.*

p20[20] taught them as having a.

p20[24] with a. command the spirits.

p48[37] a. from God, and not from the scribes.

p48[8] I also am a man set under a.

p56[27] Jesus given a. to judge.

p106[25] gentiles exercise a.

p120[21] Jesus asked by what a.

p121[25] neither tell I by what a.

Avenge. *Retaliate, vindicate.*

p98[3] a. widow of her enemy.

p98[8] God shall a. his saints.

Awake. *Conscious.*

p88[32] when a., saw his glory.

p113[11] go and a. Lazarus.

Aware. *To know.*

p26[45] graves which men are not a. of.

p134[55] in an hour he is not a. of.

Awoke. *Waked.*

p62[24] a. Jesus and said carest thou not.

Axe. *Blade.*

p13[37] a. laid to the root of the trees.

B

Babe. *Baby, infant.*

p3[41] the b. leaped in her womb.

p7[12] b. wrapped in swaddling clothes.

p7[16] b. lying in a manger.

Backward. *Rearward.*

p150[6] b. and fell to the ground.

Bad. *Evil, wicked.*

p62[48] cast the b. away.

p123[10] wedding furnished with both b. and good.

Bag. *Purse, sack.*

p139[29] Judas held the b.

Band. *Group, garrison.*

p150[3] Judas received a b. of men.

p151[12] b. of the Jews took Jesus.

p156[19] soldiers called together the whole b.

Bank. *Depository.*

p108[23] gavest my money to the b.

Baptism. *Ordinance.*

p5[76] b. for the remission of sins.

p12[33] Pharisees and Sadducees
came to John's b.

p20[18] why will you not receive our b.

p32[29] baptized with the b. of John.

p105[21] I have a b. to be baptized with?

p121[23] b. from heaven or of men.

Baptist. *See John the Baptist.*

Baptized. *Baptism.*

p12[32] many b. of John.

p13[17] publicans came to be b.

p16[41] Jesus came to John to be b.

p16[31] John bear record that Jesus was
b. of him.

p30[23] Jesus b. his followers.

p32[30] Pharisees were not b. of John.

p33[1] Jesus b. more than John.

p105[21] drink the cup I am b. with.

p168[5] b. with the Holy Ghost.

p170[15] he that is b. shall be saved.

Bartholomew. *The apostle.*

p23[14] chosen to be an apostle.

p66[2] ordained one of the twelve.

Barn. *Shelter, outbuilding.*

p59[29] gather the wheat into the b.

Barren. *Infertile, unfruitful.*

p1[7] Elizabeth was b.

p3[36] sixth month who was called b.

p158[29] blessed are the b.

Beam. *Board, large piece of wood.*

p46[8] cast out the b. from thine eye.

Bear. *Accept, contain, produce, support,
testify.*

p12[28] he it is of whom I b. record.

p15[6] angels charge to b. thee up.

p21[17] took our infirmities and b. our
sicknesses.

p46[11] world cannot receive that which
ye are not able to b.

p50[27] who doth not b. his cross.

p56[32] if I b. witness of myself.

p79[43] ye cannot b. my word.

p101[18] thou shalt not b. false witness.

p141[25] b. record of me unto the end.

p144[4] branch cannot b. fruit of itself.

Beat. *Hit, strike, blow.*

p25[54] b. the man servants.

p47[34] rain b. upon the house.

p121[37] husbandmen b. his servants.

Beaten. *Beat.*

p25[56] shall be b. with many stripes.

p25[57] shall be b. with few stripes.

Beautiful. *Pleasing, scenic.*

p128[24] sepulchers appear b. outwardly.

Become. *Turn into, developed into.*

p1[12] power to b. sons of God.

p90[33] b. as little children.

p96[42] if he b. a transgressor.

p122[44] is b. the head of the corner.

Bed. *Cot.*

p38[4] let down the b.

p38[8] take up thy b. and walk.

p55[8] take up thy b. and go thy way.

p55[10] not lawful to carry thy b.

p134[38] one from the b. the other from
the mill.

Beforehand. *In advance.*

p138[8] b. to anoint my body.

Beg. *Ask, seek, entreat.*

p103[3] to b. I am ashamed.

Beginning. *Commencement.*

p1[2] from the b. were eyewitnesses.

p1[1] in the b. was the gospel.

p1[2] was in the b. with God.

p17[11] the b. of miracles.

p99[5] divorce not so from the b.

p131[19] are only the b. of sorrows.

p145[27] you have been with me from
the b.

Begotten. *Brought forth.*

p1[14] Only B. of the Father.

p30[16] Only B son.

p30[18] Only B. son of God.

Beheaded. *Decapitated.*

p69[17] John whom I b.

p69[28] b. him in prison.

Behind. *Back at, back of.*

p11[43] Jesus tarried b. in Jerusalem.

p64[21] press b., and touch his garment.

p86^{24} Peter told to get b. me.

Behold. *See, look.*

p3^{38} b. the handmaid of the Lord.

p22^{35} b., a greater than Jonas is here.

p22^{43} b. my mother and my brethren.

p156^{5} b. your King!

p160^{27} John told b. thy mother!

p166^{38} b. my hands and my feet.

Beholding. *Behold.*

p101^{19} Jesus b. him, loved him.

p160^{49} people b. what was done.

p161^{50} women stood afar off b.

Believe. *Faith, conviction.*

p113^{27} (Martha) I b. thou art the Christ.

p120^{47} hear my words, and b. not.

p126^{26} when ye pray, b.

p132^{22} Lo! here, b. him not.

p141^{19} tell you that, ye may b.

p141^{24} blood is shed for those that b.

p147^{31} do ye now b.?

p171^{16} signs follow them that b.

Belly. *Stomach.*

p22^{34} in the whale's b.

p76^{38} out of his b. rivers of water.

p84^{16} goeth into the b., and is cast.

p92^{16} filled his b. with husks.

Belong. *Appertain, part of.*

p90^{38} ye b. to Christ.

p117^{41} things which b. to thy peace.

Beloved. *Loved dearly.*

p16^{46} this is my b. Son.

p57^{14} my b. in whom my soul is pleased.

p88^{4} my b. Son in whom I am well pleased.

Beside. *Extreme excitement, in addition.*

p23^{16} he is b. himself.

p105^{31} b. all this, there is a great gulf.

Best. *Most excellent.*

p92^{22} bring forth the b. robe.

Bestow. *Put, store.*

p29^{20} there will I b. all my fruits.

Betray. *Deceive, hand over.*

p74^{64} Jesus knew who should b. him.

p131^{8} many offended and shall b. one another.

p138^{12} sought opportunity to b. Jesus.

p139^{21} one of you shall b. me.

p151^{47} b. me with a kiss?

Better. *Preferable.*

p41^{31} b. to deny yourselves.

p41^{41} b. to offer the other cheek.

p45^{29} b. than the fowls of the air.

p81^{10} a man b. than a sheep?

p96^{40} b. to enter life maimed.

p96^{48} b. that thyself be saved.

Between. *Among, involving.*

p31^{26} question b. John's disciples.

p93^{15} fault b. thee and him alone.

p105^{31} b. you and us is a great gulf.

p155^{12} enmity b. themselves.

Beware. *Be careful, watch out.*

p27^{1} b. of leaven of the Pharisees.

p29^{17} b. of covetousness.

p47^{24} b. of false prophets.

p139^{27} b. of innocent blood.

Bid. *Say, invite.*

p49^{12} b. thee again and a recompense.

p99^{61} let me go and b. them farewell.

p123^{9} many b. to the marriage feast.

p127^{2} they b. you observe and do.

Bier. *Stand to carry coffin.*

p53^{14} Jesus touched the b.

Bill. *Writing, invoice.*

p99^{4} write a b. of divorcement.

p103^{6} take thy b. and write.

Bind. *Constrain, oblige.*

p63^{3} no man could b. him.

p86^{20} thou shalt b. on earth.

p93^{18} ye shall b. on earth.

p127^{3} they b. heavy burdens.

Birth. *Nativity, delivery.*

p2^{14} many shall rejoice at his b.

p5^{1} as was written the b. of Jesus.

p108^{1} man blind from his b.

Birthday. *Birth.*

p69^{22} Herod's b. he made a supper.

Bitterly. *Mournfully.*

p153⁶² Peter wept b.

Black. *Opposite of white, dark.*

p41³⁸ one hair white or b.

Blade. *Leaf, plant shoot.*

p59²⁴ the b. sprung up and brought.

p60²² first the b., then the ear.

Blameless. *Without blame.*

p1⁶ Zacharias and Elizabeth b.

p80⁴ priests ye say are b.?

Blasphemy. *Contempt.*

p112³³ Jesus to be stoned for b.

p153⁶⁶ Jesus accused of b.

Blaze. *Tell, spread.*

p37⁴⁰ to b. abroad the matter.

Bless. *Bestow, favor.*

p42⁴⁶ b. them that curse you.

Blessed. *Happy, bless.*

p3²⁸ Mary b. among women.

p4⁴⁷ generations shall call me b.

p8³⁴ Simeon b. Jesus.

p32²³ b. are those who are not offended in Jesus.

p39³ the beatitudes, b. are.

p53³⁶ b. is he who comes in the name of the Lord.

p70⁴³ b., and break the loaves.

p86¹⁸ b. art thou, Simon Barjona.

p100¹⁴ Jesus b. the little children.

p120¹³ Jesus b. the disciples.

p134⁵³ b. is that servant.

p141²⁰ Jesus took bread and b. it.

p158²⁹ b. are the barren.

p166²⁹ he took bread, and b.

p168²⁹ b. are they who have not seen.

p168⁴⁹ lifted up his hands and b.

Blind. *Can't see, closed.*

p32²¹ many b. he gave sight.

p65³³ two b. men followed him.

p84¹³ they be b. leaders of the b.

p85²³ Jesus heals a b. man in stages.

p106³⁵ b. Bartimaeus.

p108¹ a man b. from his birth.

p110⁴¹ b., ye should have no sin.

p128¹³ woe unto you, b. guides.

p128²³ ye b. Pharisees!

Blindfolded. *Cover around eyes.*

p153⁷¹ when they had b. him.

Blood. *Life.*

p27⁵¹ the b. of all the prophets.

p51¹ Galileans whose b. Pilate mingled.

p64²¹ woman who had an issue of b.

p73⁵⁴ eat my flesh and drink my b.

p83¹¹ b. of the prophets shall be upon.

p86¹⁸ flesh and b. hath not revealed.

p129³² from the b. of Able.

p139²⁷ beware of innocent b.

p141²⁴ my b. of the new testament.

p150⁴⁴ sweat great drops of b.

p154⁴ I have betrayed innocent b.

p154⁸ the field of b., unto this day.

p157²⁶ I am innocent of the b.

p158²⁷ his b. come upon us.

p161³⁴ came out b. and water.

Boat. *Water craft.*

p72²² Jesus went not into the b.

Body. *Flesh, group.*

p26²¹ spake of the temple of his b.

p44²² light of the b. is the eye.

p45²⁸ the b. more than raiment?

p58³⁵ light of the b. is the eye.

p64²² felt in her b. she was healed.

p68²⁵ fear not them who kill the b.

p69³⁰ laid John's b. in a tomb.

p133³⁷ where the b. is gathered.

p138⁸ anoint my b. to the burying.

p141²¹ do in remembrance of my b.

p161⁵³ Joseph begged the b. of Jesus.

p162⁴⁰ wound Jesus' b. in linen.

p162⁵⁶ beheld how his b. was laid.

p164¹² where the b. of Jesus had lain.

p166²² they found not his b.

Boisterous. *Strong.*

p71²⁵ Peter saw the wind b.

Bond. *Affliction.*

p52¹⁶ loosed from this b. on the Sabbath day.

Bondage. *Servitude.*

p79³³ never in b. to any man.

Bone. *Body structure.*

p161³⁶ a b. shall not be broken.

Book. *Manuscript.*

p13[5] written in the b. of the prophets.

p35[17] b. of the prophet Esaias.

p126[42] saith in the b. of Psalms.

p171[30] which are not written in this b.

Born. *Brought into existence.*

p1[13] b. not of the will of man.

p6[7] Mary brought forth her first b.

p7[11] for unto you is b. this day.

p8[2] the child that is b., the Messiah.

p9[5] should be b. in Bethlehem.

p29[7] ye must be b. again.

p79[41] Jews be not b. of fornication.

p100[12] eunuchs which were so b.

p108[2] man who was b. blind.

p146[21] joy that a man is b.

p155[37] to this end was I b.

Borrow. *Ask, use.*

p42[44] b. of thee, turn not away.

Bosom. *Abode, home.*

p105[27] beggar carried to Abraham's b.

p139[23] John leaning on Jesus' b.

Bottom. *Lowest level.*

p160[55] veil rent from top to b.

Bowels. *Internal organs.*

p154[6] Judas' b. gushed out.

Bread. *Food.*

p15[3] command stones be made b.

p15[4] shall not live by b. alone.

p43[12] give us, our daily b.

p47[18] if a son ask b., will give him.

p70[7] two hundred pennyworth of b.

p73[48] I am the b. of life.

p82[34] he brake b., and gave to his disciples.

p86[26] take children's b., and cast it to the dogs.

p92[17] servants have b. enough.

p141[18] he that eateth b. with me.

p141[20] Jesus took b. and blessed it.

p166[34] known, by breaking of the b.

p169[9] fish laid thereon, and b.

Break (n). *Rupture, smash.*

p20[23] else the bottles b.

p44[19] where thieves b. through.

p57[16] a bruised reed he shall not b.

p70[43] and b. the loaves.

Break (v). *Violate.*

p40[21] b. one of these least commandments.

Breaking. *Break.*

p166[34] known by the b. of bread.

Breast. *Chest.*

p98[13] publican smote upon his b.

p139[25] John lying on Jesus' b.

Brethren. *Brothers.*

p10[24] Jesus grew up with his b.

p22[40] Jesus' mother and b. stood.

p22[43] Behold my mother and b.!

p42[49] if ye salute your b. only.

p74[3] b. said, go into Judea.

p75[5] neither did his b. believe in him.

p101[28] no man hath left house, or b.

p124[24] seven b. had a wife.

p127[5] and ye are b.

p131[15] betrayed by parents, and b.

p137[41] one of the least of these my b.

p142[32] converted strengthen your b.

Bride. *Woman to be married.*

p31[30] he who hath the b.

Bride chamber. *Nuptial chamber.*

p20[16] can the children of the b.

Bridegroom. *Man to be married.*

p20[16] as long as the b. is with them?

p31[30] he who hath the bride is the b.

p134[1] virgins went to meet the b.

p135[4] b. tarried.

p135[9] b. came and went to marriage.

Brim. *Upper edge.*

p17[7] water pots filled to the b.

Bring. *Convey, take, produce.*

p6[4] she shall b. forth a son.

p7[10] I b. you good tidings.

p9[8] b. me word again.

p13[35] b. forth fruits meet for repentance.

p13[36] power to b. seed.

p40[25] if thou b. thy gift to the altar.

p111[16] other sheep I must b.

p144[2] purgeth it that it b. forth more.

Bringing. *Bring.*

p122⁵³ a nation b. forth the fruits.

Broad. *Wide.*

p47²² b. is the way to death.

p127⁴ make b. their phylacteries.

Broiled. *Grill, cook.*

p167⁴¹ Jesus ate a piece of b. fish.

Broken. *Break.*

p24⁴⁶ not suffered his house to be b.

p38⁴ b. the roof and let down.

p63³ fetters b. in pieces.

p82³⁵ took up the b. meat.

p122⁴⁶ stone shall fall, shall be b.

p161³¹ that their legs might be b.

p161³⁶ a bone of him shall not be b.

p169¹¹ yet was not the net b.

Brook. *Creek.*

p149¹ over the b. Cedron.

Brother. *Family, kinsman.*

p11¹ Herod's b. Philip.

p18⁴⁰ Andrew, Peter's b.

p22⁴⁴ the same is my b., and sister.

p23¹⁴ John the b. of James.

p29¹⁵ Master, speak to my b.

p40²⁴ whosoever is angry with his b.

p40²⁵ thy b. hath aught against thee.

p67¹⁸ b. shall deliver up b.

p93³² thy b. is alive again.

p93¹⁵ if thy b. trespass against thee.

p93²¹ how oft shall I forgive my b.

p96⁴⁰ b. shall be cut off.

p113²¹ my b. had not died.

p124²³ his b. shall marry his wife.

Brow. *Summit.*

p36²⁹ led him unto the b. of a hill.

Bruised. *Injured, beaten.*

p35¹⁸ set at liberty them that are b.

p57¹⁶ a b. reed shall he not break.

Build. *Construct, foster.*

p27⁴⁸ you b. the sepulchers.

p29²⁰ pull down my barns and b.

p45³⁸ seek first to b. the kingdom.

p50²⁹ intending to b. a tower.

p86¹⁹ upon this rock I will b.

p128²⁶ you b. the tombs of the

prophets.

p153⁶⁰ destroy the temple and b.

Building. *Constructing.*

p26²⁰ forty six years was the temple in the b.

Burden. *Load.*

p95³⁰ my b. is light.

p102¹¹ the b. and heat of the day.

Burial. *Entombment.*

p158³⁴ Golgotha, the place of b.

p161⁵⁰ women ministering to his b.

Burn. *Consume by fire, tingle.*

p2⁹ his lot was to b. incense.

p14²⁴ the chaff he will b.

p166³¹ did not our hearts b.

Burning (n). *Burn.*

p24³⁸ have your lights b.

p56³⁶ a b. and a shining light.

Bury. *Lay to rest.*

p99⁵⁹ let me first b. my father.

p99⁶⁰ let the dead b. the dead.

p154⁸ potter's field to b. strangers in.

p162⁴⁰ the manner of the Jews to b.

Burying. *Bury.*

p138⁸ to anoint my body to the b.

Business. *Work.*

p11⁴⁹ I must be about my Father's b.?

Buy. *Purchase.*

p33¹⁰ go to the city to b. meat.

p135⁸ virgins told to b. oil for themselves.

p149³⁶ sell his garment and b. a sword.

By and by. *In due time.*

p23⁸ b. you shall eat.

p61¹⁹ b. he is offended.

p69²⁶ b. the head of John the Baptist.

| C

Caesar. *Title of the Roman emperor.*

p11¹ fifteenth year of Tiberius C.

p124¹⁷ is it lawful to give tribute unto C.?

p154² forbidding to give tribute to C.

p156¹⁵ we have no king but C.

p157¹² whosoever maketh himself a

king speaketh against C.

Caiaphas. *High Priest.*

p115⁴⁹ was high priest that year.

p138³ consulted how to take Jesus by subtlety.

p151¹³ Annas was father-in-law to C.

Calf. *Young cow.*

p92²³ bring the fatted c.

Call. *Identify, invite.*

p2¹³ shalt c. his name John.

p3³¹ c. his name Jesus.

p19¹⁴ I am not come to c. the righteous, but sinners.

p34¹⁸ go, c. thy husband.

p49¹² c. not thy friends.

p91¹¹ c. sinners to repentance.

p102⁹ c. the laborers.

p127⁶ c. no man your creator.

p140¹³ ye c. me Master.

p145¹⁵ I c. you not servants.

p156²⁰ whom ye c. the King of the Jews.

Calling. *Call.*

p31¹⁹ John c. two of his disciples.

p32³² children in the market place c.

p126²³ Peter c. to remembrance.

p161⁴⁸ Pilate c. the centurion.

Calm. *Still.*

p62²⁴ there was a great c.

Camel. *Ruminant mammal.*

p101²⁴ c. to go through the eye.

p128²¹ swallow a c.

Can. *Be able.*

p3³⁴ how c. this be?

p19⁴⁶ c. any good thing come.

Candle. *Lamp, light.*

p40¹⁷ light a c. and put it under.

p58¹⁸ parable of the c.

p58³⁷ bright shining of a c.

p91⁸ light a c. and sweep the house.

Candlestick. *Candle holder.*

p58¹⁸ put a candle on a c.?

Cannot. *Unable.*

p29³ unless born again c. see the kingdom of God.

p44²⁴ c. serve God and mammon.

p50²⁶ c. be my disciple.

p78²¹ whither I go, ye c. come.

p79⁴³ ye c. bear my word.

p84³ ye c. tell the signs of the times.

p112³⁵ the scripture c. be broken.

p144⁴ branch c. bear fruit of itself.

p159⁴⁵ himself he c. save.

Captain. *Chief, leader.*

p151¹² the band and the c.

Captive. *Enslaved.*

p131²³ led away c. into all nations.

Carcass. *Dead body.*

p132²⁸ wheresoever the c. is.

Care. *Concern, burden.*

p44²⁵ c. not for the world will hate you.

p61²⁰ the c. of this world and riches.

p116⁴¹ c. that my sister hath left me.

p125³⁵ took him to an inn and took c.

Carpenter. *Worker of wood.*

p66⁴ is not this the c., the son of Mary.

Carry. *Take.*

p55¹⁰ not lawful to c. thy bed.

p95⁴ c. neither purse nor scrip.

p118¹⁸ no man should c. a vessel.

p170¹⁸ c. thee whither thou wouldest not.

Carried. *Carry.*

p53¹² a dead man c. out.

p105²⁷ beggar c. of the angels.

p168⁵⁰ Jesus c. up into heaven.

Case. *Situation.*

p40²² in no c. enter the kingdom of heaven.

p100¹⁰ if the c. of the man be so.

Cast. *Throw.*

p13³⁷ hewn down and c. into the fire.

p15⁶ Son of God, c. thyself down.

p21³⁰ c. out many devils.

p21²⁰ c. out by Beelzebub.

p27⁵ hath power to c. into hell.

p31¹¹ John was c. into prison.

p36²⁹ might c. him down headlong.

p39¹⁵ salt to be c. out.

p41³² pluck it out and c. it from thee.

p46[10] c. ye your pearls.

p48[12] c. into outer darkness.

p77[7] let him first c. a stone.

p89[25] why could we not c. him out?

p91[39] and were c. into the sea.

p158[24] c. lots for Jesus' coat.

p169[6] c. the net on the right side.

Catch. *Capture or seize.*

p18[10] thou shalt c. men.

p27[55] c. something out of his mouth.

Cattle. *Ruminant mammal.*

p23[7] plowing or feeding c.

p33[14] his children, and his c.?

Cause. *Reason, grounds.*

p41[36] saving for the c. of fornication.

p67[18] c. them to be put to death.

p99[2] put away his wife for every c.?

p99[7] for this c. shall a man leave.

p119[27] for this c. came I to this hour.

p131[15] they c. to be put to death.

p157[22] found no c. of death in him.

Cave. *Cavern.*

p114[38] a c., and a stone lay upon it.

Centurion. *Leader of a hundred men.*

p48[6] c. sent friends unto him.

p160[44] c. who stood over against him.

p161[48] Pilate calling the c.

Chaff. *Husk, straw.*

p14[24] but the c. he will burn.

Chamber. *Designated room.*

p20[16] children of the bride c. mourn.

p139[11] where is the guest c.

Chance. *coincidence, occasion.*

p125[32] by c. there came a priest.

Charge. *Care, control.*

p15[6] angels c. concerning thee.

p22[44] gave them c. concerning her.

p89[22] I c. thee to come out of him.

Charger. *Meat platter.*

p69[29] brought his head in a c.

Cheek. *Jaw.*

p41[41] smite thee on thy c.

Cheer (n). *Courage.*

p71[53] be of good c., it is I.

p147[33] be of good c.; I have overcome

the world.

Cheer (v). *Rejoice.*

p38[5] good c., thy sins are forgiven.

Chief. *Highest, ruler, leader.*

p49[7] Jesus knew how they chose out

the c. rooms.

p106[27] he that will be c. among you.

p106[2] Zacchaeus who was c. among

the publicans.

p127[4] c. seats in the synagogues.

p140[26] who is c., doth serve.

Child. *Infant, youth.*

p6[5] Mary being great with c.

p8[34] this c. is set for the fall.

p8[2] where is the c. born, the messiah.

p9[8] found the c., bring me word.

p11[43] the c. Jesus tarried behind.

p37[51] come before my c. die.

p89[15] for he is mine only c.

p90[33] taken the c. in his arms.

p100[13] receive the kingdom as a c.

p128[12] two fold more the c. of hell.

p131[16] woe unto them that are with c.

p146[21] soon as she is delivered of the c.

Children. *Child, immature person.*

p10[16] Herod slew all the c.

p10[18] weeping for the loss of her c.

p13[36] we are the c. of Abraham.

p21[22] whom do your c. cast out devils?

p32[32] c. sitting in the market place.

p33[35] wisdom is justified of all her c.

p39[11] called the c. of God.

p47[20] give good gifts to your c.

p61[37] good seed are the c. of the king-

dom.

p67[18] c. rise up against their parents.

p86[26] let c. of the kingdom be first.

p90[33] except ye become as little c.

p94[25] tribute of their own c., or of

strangers.

p100[12] suffer the little c. to come to me.

p103[8] c. of this world are wiser.

p118[13] c. in the temple saying Hosanna.

p142[31] that he may sift the c. of the

kingdom.

p158[27] blood be upon us and our c.

p169[5] c. have ye any meat?

Chose. *Desire, select.*

p49[7] how they c. out the chief rooms.

Chosen. *Selected, preferred.*

p3[28] art c. among women.

p57[14] I have c. my beloved.

p74[70] have I not c. you twelve.

p102[15] many called but few are c.

p141[18] I know whom I have c.

p145[16] ye have not c. me.

p145[19] I have c. you out of the world.

Christ. *Means anointed one.*

p5[1] birth of Jesus C.

p7[11] a Savior, who is C. the Lord.

p18[41] we have found the C.

p76[27] when C. cometh, no man knoweth whence he is.

p76[41] shall C. come out of Galilee?

p86[17] thou art the C., the Son of the living God.

p86[21] tell no man that he was Jesus, the C.

p109[22] if any man did confess that he was the C.

p111[24] if thou be the C.

p126[40] C., whose son is he?

p127[5] one is your master, which is C.

p141[19] ye may believe that I am the C.

p147[3] that they might know thee the only true God, and Jesus C.

p153[64] tell us whether thou be the C.

p159[40] if thou be the C., save thyself.

p166[25] ought not C. to have suffered these things.

p171[31] these things are written they ye might believe that Jesus is the C.

Church. *Organization, assembly.*

p86[19] I will build my c., and the gates.

p93[17] tell it unto the c., but if he.

Circumcise. *Cut off foreskin of a male.*

p4[58] c. John the Baptist.

p75[22] ye c. on the Sabbath day.

Citizen. *Resident.*

p92[15] he joined himself with a c.

Citizens. *Subjects.*

p107[14] but his c. hated him.

City. *Town.*

p6[3] everyone in his own c.

p21[21] every c. divided against itself.

p40[16] a c. that is set on a hill.

p67[10] town or c. ye shall enter in.

p117[40] beheld the c., and wept.

p161[52] Arimathea, a c. of the Jews.

p163[57] went into the c. and appeared unto many.

Clay. *Mud.*

p108[6] made a c. of the spittle.

p109[15] he put c. upon mine eyes.

Clean. *Worthy, uncontaminated.*

p26[40] Pharisees make c. the outside.

p37[36] thou canst make me c.

p140[10] save to wash his feet, but is c.

p140[11] ye are not all c.

p144[3] ye are c. through the word.

Cleanse. *Clean.*

p67[7] c. the lepers.

p128[23] c. first the cup and platter.

Cleave. *Hold.*

p99[7] man shall c. to his wife.

Cleopas. *May have been an uncle-in-law to Jesus.*

p165[17] Jesus appears to C.

Cloak. *Outer garment, covering.*

p13[34] for your sins ye have no c.

p42[42] let him have thy c. also.

Closed. *Shut.*

p35[20] Jesus c. the book.

p60[14] their eyes they have c.

Closet(s). *Private, personal space.*

p27[3] spoken in the ear in the c.

p43[6] when thou prayest enter thy c.

Cloth. *Material, textile.*

20[22] new c. on an old garment.

Clothes. *Garment.*

p64[21] if I may touch his c.

p131[15] return back to take his c.

p153[66] high priest rent his c.

p164[6] and seeth the linen c. lie.

Clothing. *Clothes.*

p47²⁴ who come to you in sheep's c.

Cloud. *Mist, fog. haze.*

p87⁴³ in a c. on the right hand.

p88⁴ a light c. overshadowed them.

p168⁵⁰ a c. received him out of their sight.

Coast. *Shore, edge of.*

p36¹² upon the sea c., in the borders of Nephthalim.

p82³⁷ into the c. of Magdala.

Coasts. *coast, border.*

p10¹⁶ Bethlehem, and the c. thereof.

p85²⁰ the c. of Tyre and Sidon.

p86¹⁴ come into the c. of Caesarea.

p89³⁰ the c. of Decapolis.

p99¹ the c. of Judea.

Coat. *Garment, layer.*

p42⁴² take away they c.

p158²³ c. was without seam.

p169⁷ Peter girt his fisher's c.

Cock. *Rooster.*

p142³⁴ c. shall not crow this day.

p152⁶⁰ while he spake the c. crew.

p153⁶¹ before the c. crow.

Cold. *Indifferent, chill.*

p132³¹ love of men shall wax c.

p152¹⁸ it was c. and they warmed.

Colt. *Foal, young horse.*

p116² shall find a c. tied.

p117⁴ sitting upon a c.

p117⁵ why loose ye the c.?

p117⁷ they brought the c. to Jesus.

Come. *Get nearer, arrive.*

p4⁴³ the mother of my Lord c. to me?

p8² and have c. to worship him.

p9⁶ out of Judea shall c. the Messiah.

p19⁴⁶ good thing c. out of Nazareth?

p20²¹ art thou c. to destroy us?

p31¹⁹ art thou he that should c.

p40²⁵ if ye shall c. unto me.

p43¹¹ Thy kingdom c. Thy will be done.

p48¹¹ c. from the east, and the west.

p50²⁶ if any man c. to me.

p50²⁷ bear his cross, and c. after me.

p57⁴⁴ I am c. in my Father's name.

p73⁴⁴ no man can c. unto me.

p76³⁴ where I am, ye cannot c.

p87²⁸ find his life in the world to c.

p110¹⁰ I am c. that they might have life.

p119²³ the hour is c.

p136³² Son of Man shall c.

Coming. *Come.*

p12²⁸ who c. after me is preferred.

p16²⁹ John seeth Jesus c.

p56²⁸ the hour is c. in the which all.

p130⁹ what is the sign of thy c.

p133⁴⁴ so shall it be at the c. of the Son.

p158²⁹ the days are c.

Comfort. *Console.*

p113¹⁹ Jews came to c. Martha and Mary.

Comforter. *Holy Ghost.*

p143²⁶ c. which is the Holy Ghost.

p146⁷ the c. will not come unto you.

Comfortless. *Without hope.*

p143¹⁸ I will not leave you c.

Command. *Direct, order.*

p15³ c. these stones be made bread.

p50²⁸ do the things I c. you.

p63³³ that he would not c. them.

p99⁵⁴ wilt thou that we c. fire.

p99³ what did Moses c. you?

p145¹⁴ if ye do whatsoever I c. you.

p145¹⁷ I c. you to love one another.

Commandment. *Command.*

p41³¹ I give unto you a c.

p83⁹ ye reject the c. of God.

p111¹⁸ this c. I received of my Father.

p116⁵⁷ Pharisees had given a c.

p120⁴⁹ the Father gave me a c.

p125³⁵ which is the great c. in the law?

p142³⁴ a new c. I give unto you.

p162⁵⁷ rested the Sabbath day according to the c.

Commend. *Entrust, give.*

p160⁵⁴ into thy hands I c. my spirit.

Commit. *Do, give.*

p26²⁴ Jesus did not c. himself.

p41²⁹ thou shalt not c. adultery.

p41³⁶ causeth her to c. adultery.

p104[11] who will c. to your trust true riches?

p128[21] would not c. the least sin.

Commonly. *Generally.*

p164[14] saying is c. reported among the Jews.

Communed. *Conversed.*

p15[2] had c. with God.

p165[14] while they c. together.

Communication. *Conversation.*

p41[39] let your c. be yea, yea.

Communications. *Conversations*

p165[16] what manner of c. are these.

Companies. *Groups.*

p70[41] make all sit down by c.

Company. *Group.*

p11[44] supposing him to have been in the c.

p70[5] Jesus saw a great c. come.

p158[27] there followed him a great c.

p165[21] certain women also of our c.

Comparison. *Evaluation, likeness.*

p59[24] what c. of the kingdom of God?

Compass. *Area, extent.*

p118[42] and c. thee around.

p128[12] ye c. sea and land to make one proselyte.

Compassion. *Empathy, concern.*

p37[37] Jesus, moved with c.

p53[13] had c. on the widow.

p70[35] Jesus had c. for the multitude.

p89[19] have c. on us.

p92[20] father had c. for his son.

p93[27] servant was moved with c.

p94[32] shouldest thou not also have c.

p125[34] good Samaritan had c.

Compel. *Require.*

p42[43] who shall c. thee to go a mile.

p42[43] c. thee to go with him twain.

Conceive. *Become pregnant.*

p3[31] thou shalt c. and bring forth.

Concerning. *About, relating to.*

p7[17] told them c. the child.

p60[13] prophecy of Esaias c. them.

p75[12] murmuring among them c. him.

p130[8] c. the destruction of the temple.

p149[37] things c. me have an end.

p165[18] c. Jesus of Nazareth.

p166[26] the scriptures c. himself.

p167[43] the Psalms c. me.

Condemn. *Find guilty.*

p22[35] men of Ninevah shall c.

p22[36] queen of the south shall c.

p30[17] sent not to c. the world.

p77[11] neither do I c. thee.

p104[20] c. whom the Father hath sent.

p121[34] preaching of John shall c. you.

Condemnation. *Condemn.*

p28[11] he speaketh to our c.

p30[19] c. is that the light is come.

p56[24] shall not come into c.

p159[41] seeing thou art in the same c.?

Confess. *Admit, profess.*

p28[8] whoso shall c. me before men.

p28[10] apostles afraid to c. Jesus.

p68[28] him will I c. before the Father.

p96[40] brother offend thee and c. not.

p109[22] any man c. that Jesus was the Christ.

p120[42] they did not c. him.

Confirming. *Establish.*

p171[21] c. the word with signs.

Conscience. *Sense of right and wrong.*

p77[9] convicted by their own c.

Consented. *Agreed.*

p161[52] had not c. with the counsel.

Consider. *Think about, bear in mind.*

p45[32] c. the lilies of the field.

p46[4] c. not the beam.

p115[50] nor c. that it is expedient.

Consisteth. *Exist.*

p29[17] c. not in the abundance of things.

Constrained. *Compel, pressure.*

p71[47] c. them to get into the ship.

166[28] they c. Jesus to abide.

Consulted. *Confer, seek advice.*

p50[32] c. whether he be able.

p116[10] c. that they might put Lazarus.

p138[3] c. that they might take Jesus.

Consume. *Destroy.*

p99[54] command fire to c. them.

Content. *Satisfied.*

p13[21] be c. with your wages.

p158[18] Pilate, willing to c. the people.

Continually. *Constantly.*

p168[52] were c. in the temple.

Continue. *Persist, remain.*

p50[31] not follow unless able to c.

p58[20] c. to receive, more be given.

p78[31] if ye c. in my word.

p82[30] they c. with me three days.

p144[9] c. ye in my love.

Continued. *Continue.*

p77[7] Pharisee c. asking Jesus.

p115[54] c. with his disciples.

p141[28] c. with me in my temptations.

Contrary. *Opposing.*

p71[49] the wind was c. to them.

Converted. *Changed, new.*

p60[14] with their hearts, and be c.

p90[33] except ye be c. and become as little children.

p142[32] when thou art c. strengthen.

Conveyed. *Moved.*

p55[13] Jesus had c. himself away.

Convicted. *Awakened to wrong doing.*

p77[9] being c. by their own conscience.

Convince. *Persuade.*

p14[9] to c. all the ungodly.

p79[46] which of you c. me of sin?

Cool. *Cold.*

p105[29] and c. my tongue.

Corban. *Offering, or gift.*

p83[13] say to father or mother, c.

Corn. *Vegetable, or grain.*

p45[33] the ox treadeth out the c.

p60[22] the full c. in the ear.

p80[1] he went through the c. field.

p119[24] except a c. of wheat fall into the ground.

Corner. *Strong point of a building.*

p122[44] stone which was rejected became the head of the c.

p122[52] I am the head of the c.

Corrupt (a). *Bad*

p22[28] make the tree c. and his fruit.

p47[26] a c. tree bringeth forth evil fruit.

Corrupt (v). *Damage, destroy.*

p44[19] where moth and rust doth c.

Cost. *Expense.*

p50[29] first counteth the c.

Council(s). *Assembly, Sanhedrin.*

p40[24] shall be in danger of the c.

p67[15] shall deliver you up to the c.

p114[47] Pharisees gathered a c.

p153[58] the c., sought false witness.

Countenance. *Face, expression.*

p44[17] as the hypocrites of a sad c.

p163[3] their c. was like lightning.

Country. *Rural area, territory.*

p3[39] Mary went into the hill c.

p6[8] were in the same c., shepherds.

p9[12] wise men departed into their own c.

p36[23] do also here in thy c.

p36[24] no prophet accepted in his own c.

p66[1] Jesus came to his own c.

p66[6] save in his own c.

p115[54] Jesus went into a c.

Course. *Division.*

p1[5] being of the c. of Abia.

Cousin. *Kinswoman.*

p3[36] Mary's c. Elizabeth.

Covenant. *Agreement, contract.*

p5[71] remember his Holy c.

p132[23] elect according to the c.

Covetous. *Envious, Jealous.*

p104[14] Pharisees who were c.

Covetousness. *Greedy.*

p29[17] beware of c.

Creation. *Making.*

p99[6] beginning of c. God made.

Creditor. *Lender.*

p54[41] c. who had two debtors.

Crooked. *Twisted, uneven.*

p14[10] the c. shall be made straight.

Cross. *Structure for crucifixion, trial or affliction.*

p50[27] whosoever doth not bear his c.

p68[33] he who taketh not his c.

p87[25] take up his c. and follow me.

p158²⁴ Simon, to bear his c.
p159⁴⁴ come down from the c.
p159¹⁹ Pilate put a title upon the c.
p159²⁵ there stood by the c.
p161³¹ bodies should not remain on c.

Crow. *Sound, sing.*
p142³⁴ the cock shall not c.
p153⁶¹ before the cock c.

Crown. *Coronet, tiara.*
p156²⁰ platted a c. of thorns.
p156⁵ Jesus wearing the c. of thorns.

Crucify. *Death on a cross.*
p129³¹ and of them you shall c.
p156¹⁵ shall I c. your King?
p157¹⁵ away with him. c. him.
p157¹⁰ I have power to c. thee.
p158²³ led him out to c. him.

Crumbs. *scraps, fragments.*
p86²⁶ yet the dogs eat the c.
p105²⁶ desiring to be fed with the c.

Cry. *Call upon, groan.*
p57¹⁵ he shall not strive nor c.
p98⁷ elect who c. day and night.
p118³⁹ stones would c. out.
p135⁵ at midnight there was a c.

Crying. *Cry.*
p11²⁹ voice c. in the wilderness.
p12²⁴ I am the voice c.
p63⁴ in the tombs, c.
p118¹³ children of the kingdom c.

Cubit(s). *Measure, forearm.*
p45³¹ can add one c. to stature.
p169⁸ two hundred c. dragging the net.

Cumbered. *Troubled.*
p116⁴¹ Martha was c. about.

Cumbereth. *Burden.*
p51⁷ why c. it the ground.

Cumi. *Arise.*
p65³³ Talitha c.; which is interpreted.

Cummin. *Fennel, used as a septic after circumcision.*
p128²⁰ pay tithe of c.

Cup(s). *Glass, mug.*
p26⁴⁰ clean the outside of the c.
p68³⁸ little ones, a c. of water.

p83⁵ traditions such as washing of c.
p90³⁸ whoever shall give you a c.
p105²¹ are you able to drink of the c.
p128²³ cleanse first the c.
p141²² and he took the c.
p149⁴⁰ take away this c.
p151⁵² the c. which my Father.

Cured. *Healed.*
p32²¹ he c. many infirmities.
p55¹⁰ who was c. on the Sabbath.

Cures. *Healings.*
p52³² and do c. today and tomorrow.

Curse (n). *Execration.*
p42⁴⁶ bless them that c. you.

Curse (v). *Swear.*
p152⁶⁰ Peter began to c.

Cursed. *An evil in response to.*
p77⁴⁹ knoweth not the law are c.
p137⁴² depart from me ye c.

Curseth. *Curse.*
p83¹² whoso c. father or mother.
p126²³ fig tree which thou c.

Custom. *Tradition, tribute.*
p10⁴² after the c. of the feast.
p13¹⁹ according to the c. of their law.
p35¹⁶ as his c. was he went into the synagogue.
p94²⁵ kings take c. or tribute?
p140¹⁰ this was the c. of the Jews.
p156³⁹ a c., that I should release.

Cut. *Sever.*
p25⁵⁵ Lord of the servant will c.
p51⁷ c. down the fig tree.
p96⁴⁰ right hand offend thee, c. it off.
p117⁶ others c. down branches.
p134⁵⁵ shall c. him asunder.
p134⁵⁶ c. off from among the people.
p151¹⁰ c. off his right ear.

| D

Daily. *Each day.*
p43¹² give us our d. bread.
p151⁵³ sat d. with you in the temple.

Damnation. *Punishment.*
p129³⁰ how can you escape the d.

Damned. *Punished.*
p170[15] believeth not shall be d.

Damsel. *Girl, lass.*
p65[31] the d. is not dead.
p65[33] d., I say unto thee, arise.
p69[23] Herod said unto the d.
p152[56] the d. that kept the door.

Danced. *Rhythmic pattern.*
p32[32] piped and ye have not d.
p69[23] d. before Herod.

Danger. *Jeopardy.*
p40[23] in d. of judgment.
p40[24] in d. of hell fire.
p62[23] the boat was in d.

Daniel. *O.T. prophet.*
p131[12] abominations of desolation, spoken of by D.
p132[33] abominations of desolation, spoken by D.

Dark. *Evil.*
p58[37] body full of light, having no d.

Darkness (a). *Evil, shadowy.*
p27[3] what ye have spoken in d.
p30[19] men love d. rather than light.
p44[23] if an eye be evil, thy whole body shall be full of d.
p68[24] tell you in d., preach in the light.
p144[30] prince of d., cometh.

Darkness (n). *Ignorance, obscurity, night.*
p5[78] give light to them who sit in d.
p36[15] the people which sat in d.
p48[12] cast out into outer d.
p78[12] follow me shall not walk in d.
p119[35] he that walketh in d. knoweth not whither he goeth.
p160[45] there was d. over all the earth.

Daughter. *Female child.*
p52[16] being a d. of Abraham.
p64[43] an only d., about twelve.
p65[27] Jairus told his d. is dead.
p68[32] loveth son or d. more than me.
p86[27] heals Canaanite woman's d.
p117[4] tell ye the d. of Zion.

David. *Second king of Israel.*

p5[68] raised up a horn of salvation, in the house of D.
p6[4] city of D., which is called Bethlehem.
p76[42] Christ cometh of the seed of D.
p80[4] D. ate the shewbread.
p117[7] Hosanna to the Son of D.
p127[43] if D. call him Lord.

Day. *Time, period, sun light.*
p4[58] the eighth d. they came to circumcise the child.
p7[11] unto you is born this d.
p16[29] next d. John seeth Jesus.
p22[31] an account in the d. of judgment.
p23[31] a great while before d.
p35[21] this d. is this scripture fulfilled.
p43[12] give us this d., our daily bread.
p45[39] sufficient unto the d. shall be.
p52[32] the third d. I shall be perfected.
p80[56] Abraham rejoiced to see my d.
p80[26] Sabbath given as a d. of rest.
p113[9] walk in the d., he stumbleth not.
p166[19] the same d. at evening.
p167[45] rise from the dead the third d.

Dead. *Lifeless.*
p10[20] they are d. who sought the child's life.
p32[22] the d. are raised.
p53[15] he who was d., sat up.
p65[31] damsel is not d., but sleepeth.
p69[15] John the Baptist risen from the d.
p88[8] what the raising of the d. should mean.
p92[24] my son was d., and is alive.
p99[60] let the d. bury the d.
p105[36] persuaded, though one should rise from the d.
p113[25] though he were d., yet shall he live.
p124[31] God is not the God of the d.
p161[33] saw Jesus was d. already.
p161[48] if he had been any while d.
p162[65] his disciples say he is risen from the d.
p163[4] why seek ye the living among

the d.?

p167⁴⁵ rise from the d. the third day.

Deadly. *Dead.*

p171¹⁸ drink any d. thing.

Deaf. *Unable to hear.*

p32²² the d. hear.

p89²³ the dumb and d. spirit.

p90³¹ heals a d. and dumb man.

Dealings. *Transactions.*

p33¹¹ Jews have no d. with the Samaritans.

Dealt. *To give portion, administer.*

p3²⁵ thus hath the Lord d. with me.

p11⁴⁸ why hast thou thus d. with us?

Dear. *Beloved.*

p48² who was d. unto him.

Death. *Dead.*

p5⁷⁸ who sit in the shadow of d.

p8²⁶ Simeon should not see d.

p10¹⁵ there until the d. of Herod.

p33² sought to put him to d.

p53³⁴ he spake, signifying his d.

p79⁵¹ shall never see d.

p112⁴ this sickness is not unto d.

p113¹³ Jesus spake of his d.

p115⁵³ took counsel to put him to d.

p116¹⁰ put Lazarus to d.

p119³³ signifying what d. he should die.

p131¹⁵ some of you will be put to d.

p142³³ both to prison, and unto d.

p153⁶⁷ he is guilty, and worthy of d.

p154³¹ not lawful for us to put to d.

p156¹⁵ nothing worthy of d.

p165¹⁹ him to be condemned to d.

Debt. *Obligation, balance due.*

p93²⁷ had compassion, forgave the d.

p94³⁰ in prison, until he pay the d.

p94³² I forgave thee all the d.

Debtor. *Owes debt.*

p128¹³ committeth sin and is a d.

Deceased. *Dead.*

p124²⁴ when he had married a wife, d.

Deceitfulness. *Falseness.*

p61²⁰ and the d. of riches.

Deceive. *Mislead, delude.*

p130⁵ take heed that no man d. you.

p130⁶ and shall d. many.

p132²³ they shall d. the very elect.

Deceived. *Deceive.*

p77⁴⁷ are ye also d.?

p133³⁹ my words,sd shall not be d.

Deceiver. *One who deceives.*

p162⁶⁴ we remember the d. said.

Declaration. *Statement.*

p1¹ d. of those things believed among us.

Declare. *Make known.*

p61³⁵ d. unto us the parable.

p63⁶ d. thy name.

p84¹⁴ d. unto us the parable.

Declared. *Proclaim.*

p149²⁶ d. unto them thy name.

Decrease. *Diminish.*

p31³¹ he must increase, but I must d.

Decree. *Dictate.*

p6¹ went out a d. from Caesar.

Deed. *Action.*

p161⁵² consented to the counsel and d.

p165¹⁸ prophet mighty in d.

Deeds. *Deed.*

p14⁹ convince of their ungodly d.

p27⁴⁹ allow the d. of your fathers.

p30¹⁹ because their d. are evil.

p30²¹ his d. may be manifest.

p79⁴¹ ye do the d. of your father.

p159⁴² receive the reward of our d.

Deep. *Far down.*

p18⁴ launch out into the d.

p33¹³ and the well is d.

p63³³ go out into the d.

p132²⁵ troubled the waters of the d.

Deeply. *Intensely.*

p84¹¹ he sighed d. in spirit.

Defile. *Pollute, unclean.*

p83¹⁵ nothing entering into can d.

p84¹⁷ proceed out of the mouth, can d.

Defiled. *Defile.*

p83² eat bread with d. hands.

p154²⁸ went not into lest they be d.

Degree. *Meek, humble.*

p4[51] exalted them of low d.

Delayeth. *Defer, postpone.*

p25[54] my Lord d. his coming.

p134[55] my Lord d. his coming.

Delicately. *Luxuriously.*

p32[25] live d., are in king's courts.

Deliver. *Give, hand over, save.*

p40[27] adversary d. to the judge.

p43[14] but d. us from evil.

p67[15] they will d. you to the councils.

p67[18] brother shall d. brother.

p138[11] what will ye give me that I d.

p157[15] d. him unto us.

p159[46] trusted in God, let him d.

Delivered. *Deliver.*

p1[2] even as they d. them unto us.

p5[73] we being d. out of the hand.

p6[6] days accomplished that she should be d.

p14[8] keys of the kingdom d. up.

p35[17] d. unto him, the book of Esaias.

p95[28] d. unto me of my Father.

p146[21] a woman as soon as she is d.

p153[2] d. him to Pilate.

p156[12] chief priest d. him for envy.

p163[6] Son of man must be d.

Deliverance. *Deliver.*

p35[18] to preach d. to the captives.

Demanded. *Asked, questioned.*

p9[4] Herod d. of them where Christ should be born.

p13[21] soldiers likewise d. of him.

p97[20] d. of him when the kingdom of God should come.

Den. *Refuge.*

p118[19] made the temple a d. of thieves.

Deny. *Renounce, give up, reject.*

p41[31] better ye d. yourselves.

p68[29] whosoever shall d. me.

p87[26] for a man to d. himself.

p104[20] teach ye the law and d.

p142[34] thrice d. that you know me.

p142[32] I will not d. thee.

Denied. *Deny.*

p12[21] John d. not that he was Elias.

p28[9] be d. before the angels of God.

p152[57] Peter d. him.

p152[72] again Peter d. with an oath.

Depart. *Leave, go away.*

p8[29] let thy servant d. in peace.

p18[8] d. from me; I am a sinful man.

p47[33] d. from me ye that work iniquity.

p52[31] d. hence; Herod will kill thee.

p63[38] Gadarenes asked Jesus to d.

p137[42] d. from me, ye cursed.

p168[4] should not d. from Jerusalem.

Departed. *Depart.*

p8[37] Anna d. not from the temple.

p9[9] when they heard the king, they d.

p16[12] d. from him for a season.

p23[31] d. into a solitary place.

p70[33] d. into a solitary place.

p71[48] d. into a mountain.

p163[6] they d. quickly from the sepulcher.

Depth. *Deepness, strength.*

p39[4] come down in the d. of humility.

p58[5] had no d. of earth.

Derided. *Scoff, ridicule.*

p104[14] Pharisees d. Jesus.

Descend. *Come down.*

p123[56] Lord should d. out of heaven.

Descended. *Descend.*

p47[34] the rains d.

p163[2] two angels d. from heaven.

Descending. *Descend.*

p16[45] spirit of God d. like a dove.

p16[32] d. and remaining on him.

p19[51] angels d. upon the Son of Man.

p134[38] angels d. and gathering.

Desert. *Waste places, wilderness.*

p72[31] fathers did eat manna in the d.

p132[26] behold he is in the d., go not.

Deserts. *Desert.*

p5[79] John was in the d. until the day of his showing.

Desire. *Want, long for.*

p40[25] d. to come unto me.

p72[26] not because ye d. to keep my sayings.

p90^{32} any man d. to be first.

p97^{22} d. to see one of the days.

p126^{26} whatsoever things ye d.

p139^{15} he said unto them, with d.

Desired. *Desire.*

p60^{16} prophets have d. to see.

p115^{25} prophets and kings have d.

p125^{33} d. in their hearts not to be known.

p139^{15} have d. to eat this Passover.

p142^{31} Satan hath d. to have you.

Desirous. *Desire.*

p146^{19} they were d. to ask him.

p155^{8} Herod d. to see Jesus.

Desolate. *Barren.*

p53^{36} house is left unto you d.

p129^{38} house is left unto you d.!

p130^{3} left unto the Jews d.

Desolation. *Desolate, uninhabited.*

p21^{21} kingdom divided brought to d.

p131^{12} the abomination of d.

p132^{33} the abomination of d.

p158^{32} the d. of the heathen.

Despise. *Loathe, hate.*

p44^{24} hold to the one and d. the other.

p91^{10} d. not one of these little ones.

p104^{13} hold to the one and d. the other.

Despised. *Despise.*

p98^{9} trusted they were righteous and d. others.

Despitefully. *Malice, hate.*

p42^{46} pray for them which d. use you.

Destroy. *End, kill, permanently alter*

p9^{13} seek the young child to d. him.

p20^{21} art thou come to d. us?

p25^{19} d. this temple, and in three days.

p40^{19} I am not come to d. the law.

p68^{25} d. both soul and body.

p81^{9} to save life or to d.?

p81^{7} how they might d. him.

p99^{56} not come to d. men's lives.

p104^{21} seek to d. the kingdom.

p118^{20} sought how they might d. him.

p153^{60} I am able to d. the temple.

Destroyed. *Destroy.*

p123^{56} gentiles should be d.

p123^{7} d. those murderers.

Devil. *Satan.*

p15^{2} left to be tempted of the d.

p16^{12} when the d. had ended.

p33^{33} ye say he hath a d.

p61^{38} enemy that sowed them is the d.

p65^{38} a dumb man with a d.

p74^{70} and one of you is a d.?

p79^{44} ye are of your father the d.

p79^{48} art a Samaritan and hast a d.?

p80^{52} we know thou hast a d.

p85^{21} daughter vexed with a d.

p111^{21} these are not the words of him that hath a d.

p137^{42} prepared of the d. and his angels.

p140^{2} the d. having put into his heart.

Devour. *Consume, dispose of.*

p127^{11} ye d. widow's houses.

Devout. *Sincere, devoted.*

p8^{25} Simeon was just and d.

Die. *Stop living.*

p37^{51} sir, come before my child d.

p73^{49} eat thereof and not d.

p83^{12} let him d. the death of the transgressor.

p113^{16} let us also go, that we may d. with him.

p113^{26} believeth in me shall never d.

p115^{50} one man should d. for the people.

p119^{24} corn of wheat should d.

p119^{33} signifying what death he should d.

p142^{32} though I should d. with thee.

p157^{7} by our law he ought to d.

p170^{23} this disciple should not d.

Died. *Die.*

p113^{21} my brother had not d.

p154^{6} bowels gushed out and he d.

Dig. *Excavate.*

p51^{8} d. about and dung it.

p103^{3} I cannot d.; to beg I am ashamed.

Diligently. *Carefully, attentively.*
p9[7] Herod inquired of them d.
p9[8] go and search d.
p33[2] they sought more d.
p91[8] seek d. until she find it?

Dine. *Eat.*
p26[38] Pharisee asked Jesus to d.
p169[12] Jesus saith come and d.

Dined. *Eaten.*
p169[15] so when they had d.

Dinner. *Banquet, feast.*
p26[39] he had not washed before d.
p49[12] makest a d., call not thy friends.
p123[4] d. is ready and all thing are prepared.

Dip. *Immerse.*
p105[29] he may d. the tip of his finger.

Discern. *Distinguish.*
p84[3] ye can d. the face of the sky.

Disciple. *Follower, apostle.*
p50[26] afraid to lay down their life for my sake cannot be my d.
p50[34] forsaketh not all he hath cannot be my d.
p68[21] d. is not above the master.
p152[15] that d. was known unto the high priest.
p171[24] this is that d. which testifieth.

Disciples. *Disciple.*
p16[35] John stood with two of his d.
p17[2] his d. called to the marriage feast.
p17[11] faith in his d. was strengthened.
p23[36] Jesus instructs his d.
p31[19] John calling two of his d.
p33[1] Jesus baptized more d. than John.
p39[1] his d. came unto him.
p42[1] as Jesus taught his d.
p46[1] Jesus taught his d.
p66[1] gave d. power over spirits
p86[14] Jesus asked his d. whom do men.
p88[5] d. heard the voice.
p142[35] ye are my d., if ye have love.

p151[55] all the d. forsook him.
p163[12] say ye, his d. came by night.
p167[20] then were the d. glad.

Discreetly. *Understandingly.*
p126[39] Jesus saw that he answered d.

Disease. *Sickness, weakness.*
p55[4] made whole of d. he had.
p66[41] every sickness and d.
p66[1] heal all manner of d.

Diseased. *Disease.*
p21[29] brought unto him all that were d.

Disfigure. *Make pretense.*
p44[17] d. their faces, that they appear.

Disobedient. *Defiant, rebellious.*
p2[17] turn the hearts of the d.

Displeased. *Unhappy.*
p100[12] Jesus was much d.
p118[13] high priests were sore d.

Disputed. *Argue.*
p90[30] why was it that ye d.
p90[31] they had d. among themselves.

Distress (n). *Suffering, misery.*
p131[16] shall be great d. in the land.

Distress (v). *Trouble, upset.*
p132[25] upon the earth d. of nations.

Ditch. *Trench, channel.*
p84[13] both shall fall into the d.

Diverse. *Different.*
p38[23] people taken in d. diseases.
p132[30] earthquakes in d. places.

Divide. *Share.*
p29[15] d. his inheritance with me.

Divided. *Split, division.*
p21[21] every kingdom d.
p70[43] two fishes he d.
p91[12] d. unto them his living.

Division. *Disagreement.*
p76[43] there was a d. among the people.
p109[16] a d. among them.
p111[19] d. among the Jews.

Divorced. *Separate, annulment.*
p41[36] marry her that is d. committeth adultery.

Divorcement. *Divorce.*

p41[35] give her a writing of d.

p99[4] Moses suffered a bill of d.

Do. *Perform, accomplish.*

p13[15] what shall we d. then?

p20[21] what have we to d. with thee.

p22[44] whosoever shall d. the will of my Father.

p30[11] we speak that we d. know.

p35[36] d. the will of him who sent me.

p40[21] whosoever shall d. and teach.

p42[32] men should d. to you.

p42[46] d. good to them that hate you.

p55[19] Son can d. nothing of himself.

p78[28] I d. nothing of myself.

p110[33] if this man were not of God he could d. nothing.

p125[29] this d. and thou shalt live.

p125[38] go, and d. likewise.

p139[27] what thou doest, d. quickly.

p141[17] happy are ye if ye d. them.

p141[21] d. in remembrance of my body.

p141[25] d. the things which ye have seen me d.

p159[35] they know not what they d.

Doing. *Do.*

p24[42] that he shall find so d.

p134[53] that he shall find so d.

Doctrine. *Teachings, principles.*

p20[20] they were astonished at his d.

p20[24] what new d. is this?

p75[16] my d. is not mine but his.

p75[17] shall know of the d. whether.

p151[19] high priest asked Jesus of his d.

Dogs. *Canine, domestic mammal.*

p46[10] give that which is holy to the d.

p86[26] bread and cast it to the d.

p105[26] d. licked his sores.

Dominion. *Authority.*

p106[25] gentiles exercise d. over.

Door. *Entrance, access.*

p21[29] city was gathered at the d.

p44[8] the d. is now shut.

p52[25] shut the d. of the kingdom.

p110[1] he that enter not by the d.

p110[7] I am the d. of the sheepfold.

p110[9] I am the d.

p152[16] spake unto her that kept the d.

p162[2] rolled back the stone from the d.

Doors. *Door.*

p133[42] near, even at the d.

p166[19] when the d. were shut.

p167[26] then came Jesus when the d.

Doubt. *Disbelief.*

p71[26] wherefore didst thou d.?

p111[24] how long make us to d.?

p126[6] shall not d. in his heart.

Doubted. *Doubt.*

p170[16] they worshipped him but some d.

Doubtful. *Doubt.*

p45[35] neither be of d. mind.

Doubting. *Doubt.*

p139[22] disciples looked one on another, d. of whom he spake.

Dove. *Fowl, pigeon.*

p16[45] descending like a d.

Doves. *Dove.*

p25[14] those who sold d.

p67[14] harmless as d.

p118[17] seats of those who sold d.

Down. *From above, low.*

p13[37] hewn d., and cast into the fire.

p15[6] if thou be the Son of God, cast thyself d.

p16[44] d. into the water.

p18[4] let d. your net.

p30[13] he who came d. from heaven.

p35[20] closed the book, and he sat d.

p38[4] they let d. the bed.

p50[26] afraid to lay d. their life.

p72[38] I came d. from heaven.

p77[2] he sat d., and taught them.

p77[6] Jesus stooped d., and with his finger wrote on the ground.

p87[43] layeth d. his life for my sake.

p107[5] make haste, and come d.

p111[18] power to lay d. my life.

p130[6] temple stones to be thrown d.

p131[23] Jerusalem shall be trodden d.

p159[44] come d. from the cross.

p164⁵ stooping d., and looking in.

Draught. *Catch, haul, waste.*

p18⁴ let down your net for a d.

p18⁹ astonished at the d. of fishes.

p84¹⁶ is cast into the d.?

Draw. *Obtain, pull, sketch.*

p17⁸ d. out now, and bear to the governor.

p33⁹ woman of Samaria to d. water.

p34¹⁷ neither come hither to d.

p119³² will d. all men unto me.

p169⁶ not able to d. for the multitude.

Drink (n). *Beverage, liquid.*

p2¹⁵ neither wine nor strong d.

p29²¹ eat, d., and be merry.

p33⁹ Jesus said unto her, give me to d.

p33¹⁵ whosoever shall d. of this well.

p45²⁸ or what ye shall d.

p68³⁸ give to d. unto one of these.

p136³⁶ and ye gave me d.

p141²⁶ I will not d. henceforth.

p160²⁹ Jesus would not d.

p171¹⁸ if they d. any deadly thing.

Drink (v). *Endure, go through, symbolism.*

p73⁵³ drink of his blood.

p76³⁷ let him come unto me, and d.

p105²¹ are ye able to d. of the cup.

p151⁵² shall I not d. it?

Drops. *Bead, spherical mass.*

p150⁴⁴ Jesus sweat great d. of blood.

Dropsy. *Edema.*

p49² Jesus heals a man with d.

Drunk (n). *Drink.*

p17¹⁰ the men have well d.

p52²⁶ we have eaten and d.

Drunken (n). *Drink, inebriated.*

p23⁸ I have eaten and d.

p25⁵⁴ drink and to be d.

p134⁵⁵ eat and drink with the d.

Dry. *Uninviting, barren.*

p28³⁸ spirit walketh through d. places.

p158³¹ what shall be done in the d. tree?

Due. *Proper, correct.*

p24⁴⁹ portion of meat in d. season.

p58¹⁹ manifested in d. time.

p159⁴² we received the d. reward.

Dull. *Slothful, unresponsive.*

p60¹⁴ ears are d. of hearing.

Dumb. *Unable to speak.*

p2²⁰ Zacharias struck dumb.

p65³⁸ a d. man possessed with a devil.

p82²⁹ when they saw the d. speak.

p89¹⁵ child who hath a d. spirit.

p90³⁶ and the d. to speak.

Dung. *Manure, fertilizer.*

p51⁸ dig about and d. it.

Dung hill. *Compost pile.*

p51³⁸ neither fit for the d.

Dust. *Fine dirt.*

p67¹² shake off the d. of your feet.

p96¹¹ even the very d. of your city.

Duty. *Responsibility.*

p24¹⁰ was no more than our d.

Dwell. *Reside.*

p13⁷ d. on the right hand of the Father.

p28³⁹ unclean sprit enter in and d.

Dwellest. *Dwell.*

p17³⁸ Master, where d. thou?

Dwelleth. *Dwell.*

p31³⁴ for he d. in him.

p73⁵⁶ drinketh my blood, d. in me.

p128¹⁸ sweareth by him who d. therein.

p134³⁹ wherein d. righteousness.

p143¹⁰ the Father d. in me.

p143¹⁷ spirit of truth; d. in you.

| E

Each. *Every.*

p52¹⁵ e. one of you on the Sabbath.

Eagles. *Carnivorous fowl.*

p132²⁸ there will the e. be gathered.

p133³⁷ thither will the e. be gathered.

Ear. *Organ to hear, fruit of corn.*

p27³ that which is spoken in the e.

p60²² first the blade then the e.

p68²⁴ what ye hear in the e., preach.

p151¹⁰ cut off his right e.

p152²⁶ kinsman whose e. Peter cut off.

Earnestly. *Intently.*

p150[44] Jesus prayed more e.

p152[56] damsel e. looked upon him.

Earth. *World, soil.*

p7[14] and on e. peace; goodwill.

p13[7] light to the uttermost parts of e.

p22[34] three days in the heart of the e.

p25[58] come to send fire on the e.

p38[8] Son of Man has power on e.

p39[7] meek shall inherit the e.

p39[15] to be the salt of the e.

p40[20] heaven and e. must pass away.

p43[11] thy will be done on e.

p44[19] lay not up treasures upon the e.

p58[5] the seed had not much e.

p60[22] e. brings forth fruit of herself.

p86[20] thou shalt bind on e.

p123[56] his vineyard, which is the e.

p129[41] come again upon the e.

p132[28] from the four quarters of the e.

p132[25] the whole e. shall be troubled.

p134[39] shall be a new e.

p134[56] end of the e. is not yet.

p160[45] darkness over all the e.

p160[55] the e. did quake.

p168[8] witnesses to the uttermost part of the e.

Earthquake. *Seismic activity.*

p160[44] watching Jesus, heard the e.

p162[2] there had been a great e.

Earthquakes. *Earthquake.*

p132[30] e. in diverse places.

Ease. *Comfort.*

p29[21] take thine e., eat, drink.

East. *Sun rises from.*

p8[1] wise men from the e.

p8[2] we have seen his star in the e.

p48[11] many shall come from the e.

p132[27] light cometh from the e.

Eat. *Consume food.*

p23[15] could not so much as e.

p29[21] e., drink, and be merry.

p45[28] no thought what ye shall e.

p53[36] desired Jesus to e. with him.

p70[32] no leisure, not so much as to e.

p70[36] people have nothing to e.

p72[26] because ye did e. of the loaves.

p73[53] except ye e. of the flesh.

p83[2] e. bread with defiled hands.

p86[26] dogs e. the crumbs.

p95[8] e. such things as are set before.

p139[15] desired to e. this Passover.

p167[42] and did e. before them.

Eating. *Eat.*

p33[33] John came neither e.

p33[34] the Son of Man is come e.

p95[7] e. and drinking such things.

p133[45] e. and drinking, marrying.

Effect. *Validity, no result.*

p83[13] word of God of none e.

Elder. *Older.*

p92[25] his e. son was in the field.

Elders. *Jewish leader.*

p48[3] centurion sent the e.

p83[3] holding the traditions of the e.

p86[22] suffer many things of the e.

p127[44] e. were offended at him.

p153[1] chief priest and e. took counsel.

p163[11] e. gave money to the soldiers.

Eldest. *Oldest.*

p77[9] convicted beginning at the e.

Elect. *Chosen, choice.*

p98[7] God to avenge his e.

p132[23] deceive the very e.

p132[28] mine e. shall be gathered.

p133[42] mine e., when they shall see.

Elias. *Greek name for Elijah.*

p2[17] spirit of E. to turn the hearts of the fathers to the children.

p12[21] John denied not that he was E.

p36[25] many widows in the days of E.

p86[15] some say E. and others Jeremias.

p88[9] why do the scribes say E. must first come?

p88[13] Who is E.?

p160[40] behold he calleth E.

Elizabeth. *Mother of John the Baptist.*

p1[5] being of the daughters of Aaron.

p1[7] was barren, stricken in years.

p2[24] conceived, and hid herself.

p3[25] take away my reproach.

p4[42] was filled with the Holy Ghost.

p4[43] the babe leaped in my womb.

Eloi. *My God.*

p160[39] E., E., lama sabachthani.

End (n). *Outcome, result..*

p28[39] the e. of the man is worse.

p67[19] he that endureth to the e.

p155[37] to this e. was I born.

End (v). *Stop, finish.*

p3[33] his kingdom there shall be no e.

p61[39] harvest is the e. of the world.

p132[25] but the e. is not yet.

p132[32] gospel to be preached to all nations, then shall the e. come.

p141[25] bear record of me to the e.

p171[47] with you always, unto the e.

Enemy. *Adversary, foe.*

p42[30] suffer thine e. to take these.

p59[23] his e. came and sowed.

p59[26] an e. hath done this.

p115[20] I give you power over the e.

Enemies. *Enemy.*

p5[73] delivered from our e.

p42[35] love your e.

p126[42] make thy e. thy footstool?

Enlarge. *Make bigger.*

p127[4] e. the boarders of their garments.

Enough. *Sufficient.*

p68[21] is e. the disciple be as his master.

p92[17] bread e. and to spare.

p135[8] not e. for us and you.

p149[38] Jesus said unto them, it is e.

p150[46] take rest, it is e.

Entangle. *Ensnare, trap.*

p123[15] they might e. him in his talk.

Enter. *Go in to, go through.*

p27[53] ye e. not in yourselves.

p29[4] e. his mother's womb.

p29[5] cannot e. the kingdom.

p41[31] these things to e. into your heart.

p43[6] prayest, e. into thy closet.

p47[22] e. ye in at the strait gate.

p135[21] e. into the joy of the Lord.

p150[42] watch, lest ye e. into temptation.

Entreated. *Plead, request.*

p92[28] came his father out and e. him.

p103[32] spitefully e., and spitted on.

p123[6] servants, and e. them spitefully.

Envy. *Jealousy.*

p156[12] priest delivered him for e.

Equal. *The same.*

p55[18] making himself e. with God.

p102[11] hast made them e. unto us.

p124[29] they are e. unto the angels.

Err. *Go astray.*

p124[31] ye do greatly e.

Escape. *Avoid, evade.*

p129[30] how can ye e. hell?

p134[36] may be counted worthy to e.

Esaias. *Isaiah in the O.T.*

p11[29] I am he who was spoken of by the prophet E.

p12[24] make straight the way of the Lord as said the prophet E.

p21[17] that it might be fulfilled which was spoken by E.

p35[17] delivered unto him the book of E.

p36[13] that it might be fulfilled which was spoken by E.

p57[14] that it might be fulfilled which was spoken by E.

p60[13] fulfilled the prophecy of E.

p119[38] the saying of E. might be fulfilled.

p120[41] these things said E.

Espoused. *Betroth, marry.*

p3[27] Mary e. to Joseph.

Establish. *Set up.*

p45[38] to e. his righteousness.

Established. *Establish.*

p93[16] every word may be e.

Estate. *Worth.*

p4[47] the low e. of his handmaiden.

Esteemed. *Valued.*

p104[15] lightly e. among men.

Eternal. *Everlasting.*

p30[15] not perish, but have e. life.

p57[40] search scriptures, in them ye think ye have e. life.

p74[68] thou hast the words of e. life.

p100¹⁵ that I may inherit e. life?

p101²⁹ in the world to come e. life.

p111²⁸ I give unto them e. life.

p147³ this is life e. that they might.

Eunuchs. *Castrated men.*

p100¹² some e. were so born.

Evening. *Sundown.*

p84² when it is e. ye say the weather.

p139¹⁶ when the e. was come.

p166²⁸ abide with us, it is toward e.

p166¹⁹ the same day at e.

Ever. *Always.*

p5⁶⁹ his holy prophets e. since the world began.

p79³⁵ the servant abideth not for e.

p119³⁴ the Christ abideth for e.

p151²⁰ I e. taught in the synagogue.

Everlasting. *Eternity.*

p30¹⁶ believeth on him have e. life.

p31³⁶ the Son hath e. life.

p120⁵⁰ his commandment is life e.

p137⁴² depart ye cursed into e. fire.

p137⁴⁷ go away to e. punishment.

Evermore. *Always.*

p72³⁴ e. give us this bread.

Evil. *Sinful, wicked.*

p22²⁹ how can he being e., speak good.

p22³⁴ an e. and adulterous generation seek after a sign.

p39¹³ say all manner of e.

p41³⁹ more than these cometh of e.

p41⁴¹ that ye resist not e.

p42⁴⁷ the sun to rise on the e. and the good.

p43¹⁴ deliver us from e.

p44²³ if thine eye be e.

p45³⁹ sufficient unto the day shall be the e. thereof.

p47²⁰ if ye then being e., know how to.

p84¹⁸ for out of the heart proceed e. thoughts.

p157²² why, what e. hath he done?

Exact. *Compel, require.*

p13¹⁸ e. no more than appointed.

p13²⁰ e. no more than appointed.

Exalt. *Make high, lift up.*

p127⁹ whosoever shall e. himself.

Exalted. *Exalt.*

p4⁵¹ and e. them of low degree.

p49¹¹ humbleth himself shall be e.

p127⁹ shall be e. of him.

Examined. *Investigate, try.*

p156¹⁴ I having e. him before you.

Example. *Case in point, model.*

p6² not willing to make a public e.

p33⁴ an e., preferring one another.

p141¹⁵ I have given you an e.

Exceeding. *Greatly, more than.*

p9¹⁰ rejoiced with e. great joy.

p10¹⁶ Herod was e. wroth.

p149³⁸ my soul is e. sorrowful.

p155⁸ Herod saw Jesus, he was e. glad.

Exchange. *Trade, swap.*

p87²⁹ give in e. for his soul?

Exchangers. *Who exchange money.*

p136²⁷ put my money to the e.

Execute. *Do.*

p56²⁷ authority to e. judgment.

Executed. *Execute.*

p1⁸ while he e. the priest office.

Executioner. *Killer, slayer.*

p69²⁸ the king sent an e.

Exhortation. *To give warning.*

p14²⁵ many other things, in his e.

Expectation. *Hope, looking for.*

p14²² as the people were in e.

Expedient. *Necessary.*

p115⁵⁰ e. that one man should die.

p146⁷ it is e. that I go away.

p152¹⁴ e. that one man should die.

Extortioners. *Force, use of illegal power.*

p98¹¹ I am not as other men, e.

Eye (n). *Organ of vision.*

p41⁴⁰ an e. for an e.

p44²² light of the body is the e.

p46⁴ mote in thy brother's e.

Eye (v). *Judgment, perception.*

p41³² e. offend thee, pluck it out.

p41⁹ man's e., are his own household.

p44²² e. be single to the glory of God.

p102[14] e. evil, because I am good?

Eyes. *Eye.*

p8[30] mine e. have seen thy salvation.

p35[21] and the e. of all those.

p60[14] their e. they have closed.

p98[13] would not lift up his e.

p114[41] Jesus lifted up his e.

p115[24] blessed are the e. which see.

p117[41] but now are hid from thine e.

p119[40] he hath blinded their e.

p150[45] their e. were heavy.

p166[30] their e. were open.

Eyewitnesses. *One who sees an occurrence.*

p1[2] from the beginning were e.

| F

Face (n). *Features, surface.*

p84[3] ye can discern the f. of the sky.

p87[1] Jesus' f. did shine.

p91[10] angels behold the f. of my Father.

p114[44] Lazarus' f. was bound.

p153[71] Jesus was struck on the f.

Face (v). *Mission, preparatory work.*

p5[75] go before the f. of the Lord.

p32[27] I send my messenger before thy f.

p98[51] set his f. towards Jerusalem.

p98[52] sent messengers before his f.

Faint. *Weak, wobbly.*

p82[30] not send them away lest they f.

p98[1] always pray and not f.

Fainted. *Faint.*

p66[42] had compassion because they f.

Fair. *Reasonably good.*

p84[2] the weather is f. for the sky.

Faith. *Belief, conviction.*

p17[11] f. of his disciples strengthened.

p45[34] if ye are not of little f.

p48[9] have not found so great f.

p54[50] thy f. hath saved thee.

p64[26] thy f. hath made thee whole.

p65[35] according to your f., be it unto.

p86[27] O woman, great is thy f.

p89[20] f. as a grain of mustard seed.

p96[45] if ye ask in f., believing.

p98[8] shall he find f. on earth?

p126[5] Lord, increase our f.

p128[20] judgment, mercy, and f.

p142[32] prayed that your f. fail not.

Faithful. *Dedication, loyalty.*

p24[50] who is a f. and wise servant?

p103[10] who is f. in that which is least.

p104[12] not f. which is another man's.

p107[17] f. in little, have authority over.

p135[21] well done, good and f. servant.

Faithless. *Lack of faith.*

p89[16] O f. generation!

p167[27] be not f., but believing.

Fall (n). *Accident, tumble.*

p68[26] sparrow shall not f.

p81[9] sheep f. into the pit.

p84[13] blind shall f. into the ditch.

p86[26] crumbs f. from the master's table.

Fall (v). *Collapse, kneel down.*

p8[34] this child is set for the f.

p15[9] f. down and worship me.

p96[44] let every man stand or f.

p122[46] on whom the stone shall f.

p122[52] the Jews shall f. upon me.

p132[34] stars shall f. from heaven.

p158[30] say to the mountains, f.

Falling. *Fall.*

p115[19] I beheld Satan also f.

p150[44] great drops of blood f.

False. *Fake, pretend, untrue.*

p47[24] beware of f. prophets.

p101[18] shalt not bear f. witness.

p131[9] many f. prophets shall arise.

p132[23] shall arise f. Christs.

p153[58] chief priests, sought f. witness.

p153[60] at last came two f. witnesses.

Falsely. *False.*

p13[21] neither accuse any man f.

p39[13] shall say evil against you f.

Fame. *Notoriety.*

p18[14] went out a f. of Jesus through all the region.

p21[25] his f. spread abroad.

p65[37] his f. in all that country.

Famine. *Food shortage.*

p36²⁵ great f. throughout the land.

p92¹⁴ there arose a mighty f.

p132³⁰ f. and pestilences.

Far. *Distant.*

p83⁷ their heart is f. from me.

p91¹³ journey into a f. country.

p126³⁹ not f. from the kingdom of God.

Farewell. *Say goodbye.*

p99⁶¹ let me first bid f. to my house.

Farm. *Ranch, work.*

p123⁵ one to his f., another to his merchandise.

Farthing. *Tenth of a denarius.*

p68²⁶ two sparrows sold for a f?

p129⁴⁸ two mites, which make a f.

Farther. *Other side.*

p99¹ by the f. side of Jordan.

Fast (n). *Obstain from food or drink other than water.*

p20¹⁵ why do thy disciples f. not?

p44¹⁷ when ye f. be not as the hypocrites.

Fast (v). *Hold, secure.*

p150⁴⁵ hold him f.

Fasted. *See fast (n).*

p15² when he had f. forty days.

Fasting. *See fast (n).*

p82³⁰ I will not send them away f.

p89²¹ goeth not out but by prayer and f.

Father (my). *Jesus' Father.*

p22⁴⁴ my F. hath sent me.

p47³⁰ doeth the will of my F.

p55¹⁷ my F. worketh hitherto.

p68²⁸ confess also before my F.

p68²⁹ also deny before my F.

p72³² my F. giveth the true bread.

p74⁶⁵ my F. who hath sent me.

p78¹⁹ know me, nor my F.

p78²⁸ as my F. hath taught me.

p79³⁸ which I have seen with my F.

p80⁵⁴ my F. honoreth me.

p84¹² every plant which my F.

p92¹⁸ will rise and go to my F.

p93¹⁹ of my F. who is in heaven.

p94³⁴ my heavenly F. do also unto.

p95²⁸ all things delivered of my F.

p96⁴⁵ seek unto my F.

p111¹⁷ therefore doth my F. love me.

p112²⁹ my F. which gave them me.

p112³⁰ I and my F. are one.

p115²³ all things delivered to me of my F.

p119²⁶ him will my F. honor.

p133⁴³ no one knoweth; but my F.

p136³⁵ come ye blessed of my F.

p138⁹ obtained a blessing of my F.

p142²⁹ as my F. hath appointed.

p142⁷ if ye should have known my F.

p143¹² because I go unto my F.

p144⁸ herein is my F. glorified.

p151⁵² the cup which my F. hath given.

p165¹⁷ I am not yet ascended to my F.

p165¹⁷ I ascend unto my F. and your F.

p168⁴⁸ I send the promise of my F.

Father (the). *Elohim (plural, denoting Gods or the Father, meaning collectively).*

p13⁷ on the right hand of the F.

p14⁸ kingdom delivered unto the F.

p34²⁵ worship the F. in spirit and truth.

p55²⁰ for the F. loveth the Son.

p56²² the F. judgeth no man.

p56²³ honoreth not the F.

p56³¹ the F. who hath sent me.

p56³⁷ the works which the F. hath given me to finish.

p57⁴⁶ I will accuse you to the F.

p72²⁷ him hath the F. sealed.

p73⁴⁵ every man that hath learned of the F., commeth unto me.

p95²⁸ no man knoweth the F.

p111¹⁵ as the F. knoweth me.

p112³⁸ the F. is in me.

p115²³ the Son is the F.

p120⁵⁰ the F. said unto me.

p142⁶ no man cometh unto the F.

p143⁸ Philip saith, show us the F.

p143⁹ he hath seen me hath seen the F.

p143¹⁰ I am in the F.

p143¹³ the F. may be glorified.

p143^{16} I pray the F. shall give you the comforter.

p144^{28} I go unto the F.

p145^{16} ask of the F. in my name.

p146^{15} all things that the F. hath.

p147^{25} show you plainly of the F.

p147^{32} because the F. is with me.

p168^{4} wait for the promise of the F.

p170^{15} in the name of the F.

Father (our). *Used as an example.*

p43^{10} our F. who art in heaven.

Father (your). *Different than Jesus' Father.*

p40^{18} glorify your F. who is in heaven.

p42^{30} your heavenly F. who seeth.

p42^{47} children of your F. who is in heaven.

p42^{50} perfect even as your F.

p42^{1} have no reward of your F.

p43^{8} your F. knoweth what things.

p43^{16} your F. will also forgive you.

p43^{5} your F. will not fail to give.

p45^{37} your F. knoweth ye have need.

p67^{17} the Spirit of your F.

p68^{26} without your F. knoweth it.

p91^{14} is not the will of your F.

p165^{17} I ascend unto your F.

Feast. *Festival, banquet.*

p10^{41} his parents went every year to the F. of the Passover.

p10^{42} when he was twelve they went to the f.

p17^{8} draw out and bear unto the governor of the f.

p26^{23} when he was at Jerusalem on the f. day.

p36^{47} Galileans received him because of what he did at the f.

p49^{13} when thou makest a f.

p70^{4} Passover, a f. of the Jews.

p75^{10} he went not openly unto the f.

p76^{37} the last day, that great day of the f.

p111^{22} at the f. of dedication.

p116^{56} will he not come to the f.?

p118^{20} Greeks came to worship at the f.

p138^{4} do not take him on the f. day.

p138^{13} first day of the f. of unleavened bread.

p156^{8} common at the f., to release.

Female. *Feminine, womanly.*

p99^{6} made them male and f.

Fetters. *Bonds, chains.*

p63^{3} often bound with f.

Fever. *Above normal body temperature.*

p21^{27} Simon's wife's mother sick with f.

p37^{54} seventh hour the f. left him.

Few. *Small amount.*

p25^{57} beaten with f. stripes.

p31^{32} f. men receive his testimony.

p47^{23} f. there be that find it.

p52^{23} are there f. that be saved?

p66^{7} laid his hands upon a f. sick folks.

p66^{43} but the laborers are f.

p102^{15} many called, but f. are chosen.

Field. *Meadow.*

p6^{8} abiding in the f., keeping watch.

p45^{32} consider the lilies of the f.

p59^{30} a man took and sowed in his f.

p62^{46} treasure hid in a f.

p133^{47} two shall be in the f.

p154^{8} bought the potter's f.

Fields. *Field.*

p35^{37} f.; are white already to harvest.

p92^{15} sent him to the f. to feed swine.

Fierce. *Violent, strong.*

p63^{29} exceeding f., so that no man could bind him.

p155^{5} Jews were the more f.

Fifteen. *Ten and five.*

p113^{18} about f. furlongs off.

Fifties. *Groups of fifty.*

p70^{42} sat down by ranks of f.

Fifty. *Ten times five.*

p54^{41} debtor owed f. pence.

p80^{57} thou art not yet f. years old.

p103^{6} sit down and quickly write f.

p169^{11} an hundred and f. three fish.

Fig. *Pear shaped fruit.*

p19^{48} under the f. tree.

p51^{6} f. tree planted in his vineyard.

p120¹⁴ Jesus seeing a f. tree.

p126²² f. tree had dried up.

p133⁴¹ parable of the f. tree.

Fight. *Wage war.*

p155³⁶ then would my servants f.

Fill. *Make full, satisfy.*

p12²⁸ whose place I am not able to f.

p17⁷ f. the water pots with water.

p82³¹ so as to f. so great a multitude.

p129²⁹ f. up the measure of your fathers.

Filled. *To fill.*

p2¹⁵ shall be f. with the Holy Ghost.

p4⁵² he hath f. the hungry.

p14¹⁰ every valley shall be f.

p18⁷ they f. both the ships.

p36²⁸ they were f. with wrath.

p82³⁵ they did eat, and were f.

p86²⁶ children of the kingdom must first be f.

p92¹⁶ have f. his belly with the husks.

p146⁶ sorrow hath f. your heart.

p160²⁹ they f. a sponge.

Find. *Discover, retrieve, uncover.*

p7¹² the way you shall f. the babe.

p24⁴⁰ blessed are the servants, he shall f. watching.

p44¹⁰ seek and ye shall f.

p47²³ few there be that f. it.

p68³⁴ loseth his life shall f. it.

p76³⁴ seek, and shall not f. me.

p81⁷ they might f. an accusation.

p91¹² until he f. the lost sheep.

p91⁸ seek diligently till she f. lost coin.

p155³⁸ I f. in him no fault at all.

Fine. *Superior, good quality.*

p104²⁴ clothed in purple and f. linen.

Finger. *Digit, point, touch.*

p77⁶ with his f. wrote on the ground.

p92²² put a ring on his f.

p105²⁹ dip the tip of his f. in water.

p151⁵⁰ put forth his f. and healed.

p167²⁷ reach hither thy f.

Fire (n). *flames, hell.*

p13³⁷ hewn down, and cast into the f.

p14²⁴ chaff he will burn with f.

p25⁵⁸ I am come to send f.

p40²⁴ shall be in danger of hell f.

p61⁴⁴ world shall be burned with f.

p96⁴¹ f. that is not quenched.

p99⁵⁴ command f. to come down.

p137⁴² everlasting f., prepared for the devil.

p152⁵⁶ Peter stood by the f.

p169⁹ a f. of coals, and fish laid thereon.

Fire (v). *Inspire, excite,*

p12²⁸ baptize with f., and the Holy Ghost.

p96⁴⁹ everyone shall be salted with f.

First. *Primary, initial.*

p15⁴⁵ Adam f. man upon the earth.

p28³⁹ end of man is worse than the f.

p40²⁶ f. be reconciled to thy brother.

p45³⁸ seek ye f. to build up kingdom.

p52³⁰ f. which shall be last.

p60²² f. the blade, then the ear.

p77⁷ let him f. cast a stone at her.

p90³² if any man desire to be f.

p102³⁰ many who make themselves f.

p138¹³ on the f. day of the feast.

p162⁶⁵ last imposture worse than the f.

p162² early the f. day of the week.

p166¹⁹ being the f. day of the week.

First born. *First child.*

p6⁸ knew her not until her f.

p6⁷ brought forth her f. son.

Fish. *Aquatic animal.*

p47¹⁹ ask a f., will give him a serpent?

p94²⁶ the first f., that cometh up.

p167⁴¹ a piece of broiled f.

p169⁹ coals, and f. laid thereon.

Fishers. *Fishermen.*

p18¹⁸ I will make you f. of men.

Fishes. *Fish.*

p18⁶ great multitude of f.

p70⁹ loaves, and two small f.

p82³² and a few little f.

p169⁶ for the multitude of f.

Fishermen. *One who fishes.*

p18² f. were gone out of the ships.

Fishing. *Fish.*

p169[3] Peter saith, I go a f.

Fit. *Appropriate, adequate.*

p51[38] salt, neither f. for the land.

p99[62] looking back, is f. for the kingdom.

Fixed. *Set, permanent.*

p105[31] there is a great gulf f.

Flee. *Escape.*

p9[13] f. into Egypt.

p12[33] who hath warned you to f.

p67[20] when they persecute you, f.

p131[13] f. unto the mountains.

p131[14] who is on the housetop, f.

Flesh. *Mankind, mortality.*

p1[14] the Word was made f.

p14[11] all f. shall see the salvation.

p73[51] the bread I will give is my f.

p73[54] whoso eateth my f.

p74[63] the f. profiteth nothing.

p86[18] f. and blood hath not revealed.

p99[7] they two shall be one f.

p131[19] none of their f. be saved.

p150[43] spirit ready, but the f. is weak.

p166[38] a spirit hath not f. and bones.

Flight. *Flee.*

p131[17] that your f. be not in winter.

Flood. *Deluge.*

p133[45] in the days before the f.

Floor. *Earth.*

p14[24] he will thoroughly purge his f.

Flow. *Emanate, emerge.*

p76[38] out of his belly shall f. rivers.

Foes. *Enemy, oppressor.*

p68[31] a man's f. are they of his own household.

Fold (n). *Fenced place, pen.*

p111[16] sheep which are not of this f.

p111[16] there shall be one f.

Fold (v). *Doubled, multiplied.*

p58[7] some thirty f., and some sixty.

p61[21] some an hundred f.

p101[29] shall receive an hundred f.

p128[12] make him two f. the child of.

Folk. *People.*

p55[3] in these porches lay many impotent f.

Follow. *Go after, pursue.*

p18[18] f. me, and I will make you fishers of men.

p50[31] no man to f. unless they are able to continue.

p65[29] suffered no man to f. him.

p87[25] take up his cross and f. me.

p119[26] any man serve me let him f.

p142[36] thou canst not f. me now.

p151[49] when they saw what would f.

p171[16] signs f. them that believe.

Following. *Follow.*

p17[38] Jesus turned, and saw them f.

p171[21] confirming the word with signs f.

Fool. *Moral deficiency.*

p29[22] God said unto him, thou f.!

p40[24] say thou f. shall be in danger.

Foolish. *Imprudent.*

p48[35] likened unto a f. man.

p135[2] five virgins were f.

Foot. *Terminal part of the leg.*

p15[6] dash thy f. against a stone.

p39[15] trodden under f. of men.

p96[42] if thy f. offend thee.

p114[44] Lazarus bound hand and f.

p123[13] bind him hand and f.

Footstool. *Symbolic of dominion.*

p41[38] earth is God's f.

p126[42] make thine enemies thy f.?

p134[40] the f. remaineth sanctified.

Forbid. *Prohibit.*

p90[37] Jesus said, f. him not.

p100[12] f. not the children to come.

Force (n). *Strength, power.*

p32[12] violent taketh it by f.

p104[21] take the children of the kingdom by f.

Force (v). *Compel.*

p71[15] by f., to make him a king.

Forewarn. *Warn.*

p27[5] I will f. you whom ye shall fear.

Forgive. *Absolve, excuse.*

p38[6] who can f. sins but God only.

p38²³ does it take more power to f.

p43¹³ and f. us our trespasses.

p43¹⁶ if ye f. men their trespasses.

p93²¹ how oft shall I f. my brother?

p126²⁷ when praying f. if ye have aught against any.

p159³⁵ f. them for they know not.

Forgiven. *Forgive.*

p28¹¹ and we shall not be f.

p28³⁷ sin against the Holy Ghost shall not be f.

p38⁵ palsy, thy sins be f. thee.

p54⁴⁷ Mary, told her sins are f.

Fornication (s). *Illicit sexual intercourse between unmarried people.*

p41³⁶ should not divorce saving for the cause of f.

p79⁴¹ we be not born of f.

p84¹⁸ out of the heart proceed f.

Forsake. *Renounce, abandon.*

p87²⁹ f. the world and save your souls.

p96⁴⁰ if thy brother f. not.

Forsaken. *Forsake.*

p160³⁹ why hast thou f. me.

Forsaketh. *Forsake.*

p50³⁴ f. not all that he hath, cannot.

Forth. *Onward, into the world.*

p6⁸ Mary brought f. her first born.

p13³⁵ bring f. fruits meet for repentance.

p67³ Jesus sent them f. two by two.

Forty. *Four times ten.*

p15² Jesus fasted f. days and nights.

p26²⁰ f. and six years was the building of the temple.

Foul. *Disagreeable, unclean.*

p84² the weather is f. today.

p89²² he rebuked the f. spirit.

Found. *Find.*

p9⁸ when ye have f. the child.

p18⁴¹ we have f. the Messias.

p92²⁴ he was lost and is f.

Foundation. *Building built upon, organization.*

p50³⁰ laid the f. and not able to finish.

p59³⁴ kept secret from the f. of earth.

p136³⁵ inherit the kingdom prepared for you from the f. of the world.

Fountain. *Source.*

p64²² the f. of her blood was dried up.

Four. *One more than three.*

p82³⁶ all that did eat were f. thousand.

p85¹¹ the seven loaves and the f. thousand.

p113¹⁷ Lazarus in the grave f. days.

p132²⁸ gathered from the f. quarters.

p158²³ garments and made f. parts.

Fourfold. *Four times.*

p107⁸ unjust means I restore f.

Fullness. *Complete.*

p27⁵³ key of knowledge, f. of the scriptures.

p31³⁶ he who believeth shall receive of his f.

| G

Gabriel. *Man (angel) of God.*

p3²⁶ appeared to Mary.

Gain. *Acquire.*

p87²⁹ what is a man profited if he g.

Garden. *Orchard, plants, flowers.*

p149³⁶ Gethsemane which was a g.

p152²⁶ did not I see thee in the g.

p162⁴¹ in the g. a new sepulcher.

Gardener. *Caretaker.*

p164¹⁵ supposing him to be the g.

Garment. *Item of clothing.*

p20²² new cloth on an old g.

p64²¹ woman touched Jesus' g.

p123¹¹ had not on a wedding g.

p134⁴⁰ earth to be come as a g.

p149³⁶ sell his g. to buy a sword.

Garnish. *Beautify.*

p128²⁶ g. the sepulchers.

Gate. *Entrance, door.*

p47²² enter ye in at the strait g.

p52²⁴ enter ye into the strait g.

p53¹² nigh to the g. of the city.

Gather. *Collect, bring together.*

p13^5 g. together those who are lost.
p45^{29} neither do they reap, nor g.
p47^{25} do men g. grapes of thorns.
p61^{43} g. all things that offend.
p71^{12} disciples g. up the fragments.
p115^{52} g. together in one the children.
p133^{40} g. the remainder of his elect.
Generation. *Period from birth to death.*
p12^{33} O g. of vipers!
p22^{34} an evil and adulterous g.
p22^{35} rise up in judgment with this g.
p27^{51} blood may be required of this g.
p84^{11} adulterous g. seek after a sign?
p89^{16} O faithless g.! how long shall I be.
p97^{25} must be rejected of this g.
p103^8 children of this world are wiser
in their g.
p133^{35} this g. in which these things
are shown.
Gentiles. *Not of the house of Israel*
p8^{32} a light to lighten the g.
p123^{56} g. should be destroyed also.
Get. *Go, obtain.*
p15^{10} g. thee hence, Satan.
p52^{31} Pharisees warn Jesus to g.
thee out.
p71^{47} disciples to g. into the ship.
p86^{24} Peter told, g. thee behind me.
Ghost. *Spirit.*
p160^{54} bowed his head and gave up
the g.
Gift. *Offering, grace.*
p33^{12} if thou knewest the g. of God.
p40^{26}leave thy g. before the altar.
p83^{13} Corban, that is to say, a g.
p128^{16} which is greatest the g. or altar.
Gird. *Bind up.*
p24^{40} for he shall g. himself.
p170^{18} another shall g. thee.
Girdle. *Strap, belt.*
p12^{30} a leathern g. about his loins.
Gave. *Give.*
p30^{16} God so loved the world he g.
p35^{20} closed the book and g. it again.
p82^{34} took the loaves and g. thanks.

p112^{29} my father which g. them me.
p136^{36} hungered and ye g. me meat.
p141^{22} given thanks, he g. it to them.
Glad. *Happy, joyful.*
p2^{19} show you these g. tidings.
p39^{14} great joy and be exceeding g.
p80^{56} Abraham rejoiced and was g.
p82^1 preaching g. tidings of the
kingdom.
p113^{15} I am g. for your sakes.
p167^{20} disciples g. when they saw
the Lord.
Glorify. *Worship, praise.*
p40^{18} see your good works, and g.
p80^{26} Sabbath given for men to g. God.
p119^{28} Father, g. thy name.
p147^1 the hour is come; g. thy son.
p170^{19} by what death he should g. God.
Glorifying. *Glorify.*
p7^{20} shepherds returned g. God.
p106^{43} received his sight and
followed him, g. God.
Glorious. *Wonderful.*
p52^{17} rejoiced for the g. things
which were done by him.
Glory. *Magnificence, praise.*
p1^{14} g. as the Only Begotten.
p7^9 g. of the Lord shone round about.
p7^{14} g. to God in the highest.
p43^2 that they may have g. of men.
p43^{15} kingdom, power, and g. forever.
p44^{22} eye be single to the g. of God.
p45^{33} Solomon in all his g.
p75^{18} he that speaketh of himself
seeketh his own g.
p87^{43} clothed with his g. in the cloud.
p97^{18} returned to give g. to God.
p133^{38} with power and great g.
p136^{32} Son of Man shall come in his g.
p147^5 g. which I had before the world.
Gluttonous. *Excessive.*
p33^{34} behold a g. man and a wine
bibber.
Gnashing. *Clench, grind.*
p48^{12} weeping and g. of teeth.

p52^{28} weeping and g. of teeth.

p61^{43} wailing and g. of teeth.

p123^{13} weeping and g. of teeth.

p134^{55} weeping and g. of teeth.

p136^{31} weeping and g. of teeth.

Gnat. *Small fly.*

p128^{21} strain at a g. and swallow a camel.

Go. *Leave, proceed.*

p2^{17} he shall g. before the Lord.

p19^{14} g. and learn what this meaneth.

p34^{18} g., call thy husband.

p38^{5} g. thy way and sin no more.

p42^{43} compel thee to g. a mile.

p45^{26} I will g. before you.

p46^{9} g. ye into the world.

p48^{8} I say unto one, g. and he goeth.

p54^{50} faith hath saved thee; g. in peace.

p74^{67} will ye also g. away?

p76^{33} I g. unto him that sent me.

p77^{11} g., and sin no more.

p97^{23} g. not after them.

p113^{16} let us also g., that we may die.

p132^{26} he is in the desert; g. not forth.

Gone. *Go.*

p7^{15} when the angels were g.

p18^{2} fishermen were g. out of them.

p28^{38} unclean spirit is g. out of a man.

p46^{6} all have g. out of the way.

p64^{23} virtue had g. out of him.

p117^{19} the world has g. after him.

p166^{27} made as though he would have g. farther.

Goats. *Hollow-horned ruminant mammal.*

p136^{33} divideth sheep from the g.

God. *Heavenly Father.*

p1^{1} the Son was with G.

p3^{30} Mary, found favor with G.

p6^{6} Emmanuel, meaning G. with us.

p7^{14} glory to G. in the highest.

p11^{52} favor with G. and man.

p15^{2} and had communed with G.

p16^{45} he saw the spirit of G.

p30^{16} for G. so loved the world.

p38^{6} forgive sins but G. only?

p39^{10} pure in heart; shall see G.

p44^{24} cannot serve G. and mammon.

p45^{38} first build up the kingdom of G.

p46^{12} ask of G.; and it shall be given.

p55^{18} he said G. was his father.

p57^{45} seek not the honor which comes of G. only?

p57^{10} thou art the Son of G.

p71^{28} thou art the Son of G.

p75^{17} whether it be of G., or whether I speak of myself.

p79^{47} he that is of G. receiveth God's words.

p86^{17} thou art the Son of the living G.

p99^{6} G. made them male and female.

p112^{33} thou makest thyself G.

p124^{31} I am the G. of Abraham.

p125^{28} thou shalt love the Lord thy G.

p147^{3} this is life eternal, that they might know thee the only true G.

p160^{39} My G., My G.

p165^{17} I ascend to my G.

p168^{28} my Lord and my G.

p171^{20} sat on the right hand of G.

Good (a). *Better, best.*

p47^{20} ye being evil give g. gifts.

p88^{3} it is g. for us to be here.

p105^{30} thou receivedest thy g. things.

p147^{33} be of g. cheer.

Good (n). *Moral order, praiseworthy.*

p7^{10} I bring you g. tidings.

p19^{46} can any g. thing come out of Nazareth?

p22^{29} being evil, speak g. things?

p22^{30} g. man, out of his heart.

p42^{35} love your enemies, and do g.

p75^{12} some said, he is a g. man.

p100^{16} why callest thou me g.?

p102^{14} eye evil, because I am g.?

p107^{17} well done, thou g. servant.

p111^{11} I am the g. shepherd.

p112^{33} a g. work we stone thee not.

p116^{43} Mary hath chosen that g. part.

p125^{31} parable of the g. Samaritan.

p137[6] wrought a g. work on me.

Goodly. *Beautiful.*

p62[47] merchantman, seeking g. pearls.

p130[5] adorned with g. stones.

Goods. *Property, money.*

p21[24] bind the strong man and spoil his g.

p29[20] there I will bestow my g.

p107[8] half of my g. I give to the poor.

p134[54] make him ruler over his g.

p135[14] delivered unto them his g.

Gorgeously. *Beautifully.*

p32[25] g. appareled, live in kings courts.

Gospel. *Good news.*

p1[1] g. preached through the Son.

p1[1] g. was the word.

p1[4] the g. was the light and life.

p13[6] preach g. unto the Gentiles.

p32[22] unto the poor the g. is preached.

p38[22] went about preaching the g.

p138[8] wheresoever my g. is preached.

p170[14] preach the g. to every creature.

Governor. *Administrator, head.*

p6[2] Cyrenius g. of Syria.

p11[1] Pontius Pilate g. of Judea.

p17[8] bear unto the g. of the feast.

p155[15] g. marveled greatly.

Governors. *Governor.*

p67[16] brought before g. and kings.

p163[13] if this comes to the g. ears.

Grace. *Clemency, mercy.*

p1[14] full of g. and truth.

Gracious. *Godly, marked by tact, courtesy, and kindness.*

p35[22] wondered at the g. words.

Grain. *Granule, kernel.*

p59[30] kingdom like a g. of mustard.

p89[20] have faith as a g. of mustard.

p126[6] faith as a g. of mustard.

Grant. *Allow, give.*

p5[73] g. unto us, deliverance.

p105[20] g. that my two sons may sit.

Grapes. *Small berries, fruit.*

p47[25] do men gather g. of thorns.

Grass. *Meadow, pasture.*

p45[34] God so clothed the g.

p70[41] sit in companies upon the g.

Grave. *Burial place.*

p113[17] Lazarus in the g. four days.

p114[31] she goeth to the g. to weep.

p114[43] called Lazarus out of the g.

Graves. *Grave.*

p26[45] ye are as g. which appear not.

p56[28] all who are in their g. shall hear his voice.

p124[31] he riseth them up out of their g.

p163[56] and the g. were opened.

Great. *Noble, immense, large.*

p2[15] John g. in the sight of the Lord.

p3[32] he shall be g., and called the Son of the Highest.

p4[48] who is mighty hath done g. things.

p6[5] Mary being g. with child.

p7[10] bring tidings of g. joy.

p39[14] g. shall be your reward.

p40[21] whosoever shall teach the commandments shall be called g.

p48[9] I have not found so g. faith.

p62[47] one pearl of g. price.

p86[27] O woman, g. is thy faith.

p106[26] whosoever will be g. among you.

p125[35] which is the g. commandment?

p131[18] g. tribulations upon the Jews.

p150[44] sweat g. drops of blood.

p163[6] departed the sepulcher, with fear and g. joy.

Greater. *Great.*

p19[50] thou shalt see g. things than these.

p22[35] a g. than Jonas is here.

p22[36] a g. than Solomon is here.

p32[28] not a g. prophet than John.

p33[14] art thou g. than our father Jacob.

p56[37] I have a g. witness than John.

p80[53] art thou g. than Abraham.

p80[5] is one g. than the temple.

p112²⁹ my Father is g. than all.

p141¹⁶ servant not g. than his Lord.

p145¹³ g. love hath no man.

Greatest. *Great.*

p59³¹ is the g. among herbs.

p90³¹ who is g. among them.

p128¹⁶ which is g., the gift, or the altar.

p140²⁴ who should be accounted the g.

Greatly. *Great.*

p124³¹ ye therefore do g. err.

p155¹⁵ the governor marveled g.

p160⁴⁴ soldiers feared g.

Greek. *Language of Greece.*

p159²⁰ title written in Hebrew, G. and Latin.

Greeks. *People from Greece.*

p118²⁰ G. asked to see Jesus.

Grieved. *Saddened, lament.*

p81⁵ being g. for the hardness of their hearts.

p101²¹ rich man g. at the saying.

p141²⁶ disciples g. and wept over him.

p170¹⁷ Peter was g.

Grievous. *Heinous, severe.*

p26⁴⁷ burdens g. to be borne.

p127³ burdens g. to be borne.

Grievously. *Seriously.*

p85²¹ daughter g. vexed with a devil.

Grind. *Crush.*

p122⁴⁶ stone will g. him to powder.

Grinding. *Mill.*

p133⁴⁸ two shall be g. at the mill.

Groaned. *Moan.*

p114³³ Jesus g. in the spirit.

Gross. *Indifferent.*

p60¹⁴ people's heart waxed g.

Ground. *Soil, land.*

p58⁵ seed fell on stony g.

p68²⁶ sparrow shall not fall to the g.

p77⁶ Jesus wrote upon the g.

p82³³ multitude to sit upon the g.

p108⁶ Jesus spat on the g.

p118⁴³ shall lay thee even with the g.

p119²⁴ corn of wheat fall to the g.

p150⁶ they went backward, and fell

to the g.

Grow. *Mature, increase.*

p45³² the lilies of the field, how they g.

p59²⁹ let both g. together until harvest.

p60²¹ the seed should spring and g.

Guest. *Visitor.*

p107⁷ g. with a man who is a sinner.

p139¹¹ where is the g. chamber.

Guests.

p123¹⁰ wedding was furnished with g.

Guide. *Direct.*

p5⁷⁸ g. our feet into the way of peace.

p146¹³ Spirit will g. you into all truth.

Guides. *Leader.*

p128¹³ woe unto you blind g.

p128²¹ g. who strain at a gnat.

Guile. *Deceit.*

p19⁴⁷ Nathanael in whom there is no g.!

Guilty. *In the wrong, at fault.*

p128¹⁵ sweareth by the gift is g.

p153⁶⁷ he is g. and worthy of death.

Gulf. *Abyss.*

p105³¹ between us there is a great g.

| H

Habitations. *Dwelling, living arrangement.*

p103⁹ receive you into everlasting h.

Hail. *Greet, acknowledge.*

p3²⁸ h. thou virgin, who art highly favored.

p151⁴⁶ h. Master! and kissed him.

p156²¹ h., king of the Jews.

Hair. *Threadlike out growth.*

p12³⁰ John's raiment of camels h.

p41³⁸ not make one h. white or black.

p112² wiped his feet with her h.

p131¹⁷ not a h. of your head perish.

Hairs. *Hair.*

p27⁷ the very h. of your head are numbered.

p54³⁸ wiped his feet with the h. of her head.

Half. *One of two equal parts.*

p69²⁴ the h. of my kingdom.

p107⁸ h. of my goods I give to the poor.

p125³¹ leaving him h. dead.

Hall. *Large public building.*

p154²⁸ into the h. of judgment.

p155³³ Pilate entered the judgment h.

p156¹⁹ h., called Praetorium.

Halt. *Lame, crippled.*

p55³ in these porches were many who were h.

p96⁴³ better to enter h. into life.

Hand. *Terminal part of the arm.*

p5⁶⁵ h. of the Lord was in it.

p57³ deliver us out of the h.

p11²⁸ kingdom of heaven is at h.

p41³³ if thy h. offend thee.

p41⁹ a man's h. is his friend.

p43³ left h. not know what thy right h.

p81⁶ man whose h. was withered.

p85²⁴ took the blind man by the h.

p99⁶² having put his h. to the plough.

p105²⁰ my sons sit on thy right h.

p111²⁸ neither shall any man pluck them out of my h.

p126⁴² sit thou on my right h.

p129⁴¹ crowned on the right h. of God.

p136³³ sheep on his right h.

p167²⁷ thrust thy h. into my side.

p171²⁰ Jesus received up on the right h. of God.

Handle. *Touch.*

p166³⁸ it is I, h. me, and see.

Handmaid. *Female servant.*

p3³⁸ behold the h. of the Lord.

Hang. *Fasten tie to, based on.*

p125³⁹ on these two commandments h. all the law.

Happy. *Joyful, content.*

p141¹⁷ h. are ye if ye do them.

Hard. *Firm, rigid.*

p74⁶⁰ this is an h. saying.

p101²³ h. for them who trust in riches.

p136²⁴ thou art an h. man.

Hardened. *Stubborn, not teachable.*

p119⁴⁰ blinded their eyes and h. their

heart.

Hardly. *With difficulty, scarcely.*

p101²² h. they that have riches enter.

Hardness. *Hardened.*

p81⁵ grieved for the h. of their hearts.

p99⁵ because of the h. of your hearts.

p167¹³ unbelief and h. of heart.

Harlots. *Prostitute.*

p92³⁰ devoured thy living with h.

p121³¹ h. shall go into the kingdom before you.

p121³² publicans and h. believed on him.

Harmless. *Lacking intent to injure.*

p67¹⁴ servants to be h. as doves.

Harvest. *Season of gathering.*

p35³⁷ fields are white already to h.

p59²⁹ let both grow together until the h.

p61³⁹ the h. is the end of the world.

p95² h. is great but the laborers are few.

Haste. *Speed, swiftness.*

p3³⁹ into the hill country with h.

p7¹⁶ shepherds came with h.

p69²⁶ Salome came with h. to Herod.

p107⁵ Zacchaeus make h. and come.

Hastily. *Haste.*

p114³¹ Mary rose up h. and went out.

Hate (n). *Detest, loathe.*

p42⁴⁵ love thy neighbor, and h. thine enemy.

p44²⁴ either he will h. the one and love the other.

Hate (v). *Enmity, dislike.*

p50²⁶ if any man h. not his father.

p145¹⁸ if the world h. you.

Hated. *Disliked.*

p67¹⁹ ye shall be h. of all the world.

p107¹⁴ but his citizens h. him.

p145¹⁸ h. me before it h. you.

p145²⁵ they h. me without a cause.

Hateth. *Dislikes.*

p30²⁰ who doeth evil h. the light.

p75⁷ me it h., because I testify of it.

p119²⁵ he that h. his life shall keep it.

p145¹⁹ therefore the world h. you.

p145²³ h. me h. my Father also.

Head (n). *Upper part of the body.*

p27⁷ hairs of your h. are numbered.

p69²⁵ the h. of John the Baptist.

p99⁵⁸ Son of Man hath not where to lay his h.

p137⁴ poured ointment on his h.

p156²² smote him on the h.

p160⁵⁴ bowed his h. and gave up the ghost.

p164⁷ napkin about his h.

Head (v). *Foremost, precedence.*

p122⁴⁴ the stone which was rejected become the h. of the corner.

p122⁵² I am the h. of the corner.

p164¹² angel sitting at the h.

Heal. *Made well or whole.*

p23¹³ twelve given power to h.

p35¹⁸ to h. the broken hearted.

p36²³ physician h. thyself.

p49³ lawful to h. on the Sabbath day?

p60¹⁴ be converted and h. them.

p66¹ h. all manner of sickness.

p81⁷ if he would h. on the Sabbath.

Healed. *Heal.*

p21³⁰ he h. many that were sick.

p37⁵⁵ father knew his son was h.

p51¹⁴ Jesus had h. on the Sabbath.

p97¹⁵ saw he was h., turned back.

Healing. *Heal.*

p38²² preaching the gospel and h. all manner of sickness.

p66⁴¹ h. every sickness and disease.

Hear. *Listen, perceive, understand.*

p16⁴⁶ this is my beloved Son, h. ye him.

p32²² the deaf h., the dead are raised.

p32¹⁶ he that hath ears to h., let him h.

p56²⁵ the dead shall h. the voice of the Son of God.

p56²⁸ who are in their graves shall h.

p58²⁰ take heed what you h.

p60¹³ shall h. and not understand.

p68²⁴ h. in the ear, preach upon the housetops.

p77⁵¹ doth our law judge a man before

it h. him.

p88⁴ this is my beloved Son, h. ye him.

p105³⁶ if they h. not Moses and the prophets.

p111¹⁶ other sheep shall h. my voice.

p111²⁷ my sheep h. my voice.

p115²⁵ prophets and kings desired to h. those things which ye h.

p120⁴⁷ if any man h. my words.

p132²⁵ you shall h. of wars.

p143²⁴ word which ye h. is not mine.

Hearing. *Hear.*

p11⁴⁶ doctors, were h. him and asking him questions.

p60¹² h., they hear not.

p60¹⁴ ears are dull of h.

p106³⁶ h. the multitude pass by.

Heart. *Mind, soul.*

p7¹⁹ Mary pondered them in her h.

p11⁵¹ kept all these sayings in her h.

p23³⁷ there will your h. be also.

p39¹⁰ the pure in h. shall see God.

p41³⁰ committed adultery in his h.

p83⁷ but their h. is far from me.

p84¹⁷ proceed out of the mouth, come from the h.

p95³⁰ I am meek and lowly in h.

p119⁴⁰ understand with their h. and be converted.

p125²⁸ love the Lord with all thy h.

p144²⁷ let not your h. be troubled.

p147²² your h. shall rejoice.

Heat. *High temperature.*

p102¹¹ borne the burden and h. of day.

Heathen. *Gentile.*

p13⁵ bring salvation to the h. nations.

p93¹⁷ neglect to hear them, be as a h.

p158³² the desolation of the h.

Heaven. *God's abode.*

p11²⁸ kingdom of h. is at hand.

p16⁴⁶ he heard a voice from h.

p19⁵¹ ye shall see h. open, and angels.

p22⁴⁴ my Father which is in h.

p39⁵ persecuted for theirs is the kingdom of h.

p43[10] our Father who art in h.

p44[20] lay up treasure in h.

p72[38] I came down from h.

p86[20] shall be bound in h.

p91[10] in h. their angels.

p95[27] came a voice out of h.

p104[19] easier for h. and earth to pass away.

p115[21] your names are written in h.

p119[28] there came a voice from h.

p132[34] stars shall fall from h.

p133[36] h. and earth shall pass away.

p168[50] Jesus carried up into h.

p171[20] he was received up into h.

Heavenly. *Pertaining to God.*

p7[13] h. host, praising God.

p30[12] believe if I tell you of h. things?

p127[6] your creator and h. Father.

Heavens. *Pertaining to God.*

p16[45] the h. were opened.

p23[36] provide a treasure in the h.

p133[37] powers of the h. shall be shaken.

p134[39] there shall be new h., and a new earth.

Heavy. *Burdensome, tired.*

p88[32] were with him were h. with sleep.

p127[3] bind h. burdens on men's shoulders.

p149[36] sore amazed, and to be h.

p150[45] eyes were h.

Heed. *Attention, notice, care.*

p29[17] take h. and beware of covetousness.

p42[1] take h. do not your alms.

p58[36] take h. that light in you be not darkness.

p58[20] take h. what you hear.

p85[7] take h. of leaven of the Pharisees.

p91[10] take h. despise not one.

p130[5] take h. that no man deceive you.

Hell. *State of anguish, misery.*

p27[5] fear him who hath power to cast into h.

p41[31] take up your cross than that ye

should be cast into h.

p68[25] both soul and body in h.

p86[19] gates of h. shall not prevail.

p96[41] thee and thy brother cast into h.

p105[28] in h. lifted up his eyes.

p128[12] two fold more the child of h.

p129[30] how can ye escape the damnation of h.?

Help. *Assist, aid.*

p18[7] beckoned they would come h.

p86[24] Lord, h. me.

p89[21] h. thou mine unbelief.

p116[41] bid her that she h. me.

Hen. *Female chicken.*

p53[35] together, as a h. her brood.

p129[37] a h. gathers her chickens.

Hence. *From this place.*

p15[10] get thee h. Satan.

p52[31] depart h. for Herod will kill thee.

p105[31] they who would pass h. to you.

p155[36] my kingdom not from h.

p164[15] if thou hast borne him h.

Henceforth. *From this point on.*

p4[47] h. all generations shall call me blessed.

p18[10] from h. thou shalt catch men.

p129[39] thou shalt not see me h.

p141[26] I will not drink h.

p142[7] from h. ye shall know him.

p145[15] h. I call you not servants.

Herbs. *Plant with aromatic, savory, or medicinal properties.*

p26[43] tithe all manner of h.

p59[31] mustard seed, when it is grown is greatest among h.

Herd. *Flock, group.*

p63[31] a h. of many swine.

p63[34] the h. of swine ran violently.

Here. *This place.*

p22[35] greater than Jonas is h.

p22[36] greater than Solomon is h.

p66[5] are not his sisters h. with us?

p88[3] it is good for us to be h.

p97[21] shall they say lo h.! or, lo there!

p113[21] if thou hadst been h.

p132²² any man shall say lo, h. is Christ.

p163⁵ he is not h.; he is risen.

Hereafter. *Future.*

p19⁵¹ h. see the heavens open.

p120¹⁶ no man eat fruit of thee h.

p140⁷ but thou shalt know h.

p144³⁰ h. I will not talk much with you.

p153⁶⁵ h. shall ye see the Son of Man.

Herein. *In this.*

p35³⁹ h. is the saying true.

p109³⁰ h. is a marvelous thing.

p144⁸ h. is my Father glorified.

Herod. *Tetrarch of Judea.*

p1⁵ there was in the days of H.

p9³ when H. heard of the child.

p9⁷ H. called the wise men.

p9¹³ H. will seek to destroy the child.

p10¹⁵ there until the death of H.

p10¹⁶ H. when he saw he was mocked.

p31²⁶ H. reproved of John.

p52³¹ depart hence for H. will kill thee.

p52³² go and tell H.

p69¹⁵ H. heard of Jesus.

p69²¹ H. feared John.

p69²³ danced, and pleased H.

p155⁷ Jesus was sent to H.

p155¹² Pilate and H. were made friends.

Hewn. *Cut.*

p13³⁷ h. down and cast into the fire.

p41³⁴ h. down and cast into the fire.

High. *Pre-eminent, lofty, above, tall.*

p4⁵¹ mighty from their h. seats.

p15⁸ an exceeding h. mountain.

p69²² made a supper for his h. captains.

p115⁴⁹ being the h. priest that year.

p161³¹ Sabbath was a h. day.

p168⁴⁸ endued with power from on h.

Highest. *Most high, uppermost.*

p3³² Jesus called Son of the H.

p5⁷⁵ John called prophet of the H.

p7¹⁴ glory to God in the h.

p42³⁵ shall be children of the H.

p49⁸ sit not down in the h. room.

p117⁷ Hosanna in the h.!

Highly. *Extremely.*

p3²⁸ Mary h. favored of the Lord.

Hill. *Knoll, lower than a mountain.*

p14¹⁰ every mountain and h. shall be made low.

p36²⁹ led him to the brow of the h.

p40¹⁶ city that is set on a h.

p51³⁸ not fit for the dung h.

Hill country. *Mountainous.*

p3³⁹ Mary went into the h.

p5⁶⁴ noised throughout the h.

Himself. *Referring to oneself.*

p26²⁴ Jesus would not commit h. unto them.

p49¹¹ whosoever exalteth h.

p55¹³ Jesus conveyed h. away.

p55¹⁸ making h. equal with God.

p55¹⁹ the Son can do nothing of h.

p56²⁶ the Father hath life in H.

p95²⁸ they to whom the Son shall reveal h.

p96⁴⁴ let every man stand or fall, by h.

p109²¹ he shall speak for h.

p157⁷ because he made h. the Son of God.

p159⁴⁵ h. he cannot save.

p166²⁶ expounded the scriptures concerning h.

p169¹ Jesus showed h. again.

Hinder. *Rear, stern, back part.*

p62²³ in the h. part of the ship.

Hire. *Payment, wages.*

p45³³ laborer is worthy of his h.

p95⁷ laborer is worthy of his h.

p102¹ went early in the morning to h. laborers.

p102⁹ give them their h.

Hired. *Hire.*

p92¹⁷ how many h. servants.

p92¹⁹ make me as one of thy h. servants.

p102⁷ no man hath h. us.

Hither. *To this place.*

p34¹⁷ neither come h. to draw.

p63[30] art thou come h. to torment us.

p72[25] Rabbi how camest thou h.?

p167[27] reach h. thy finger.

Hitherto. *Until now.*

p55[17] my Father worketh h.

p147[24] h. have ye asked nothing in my name.

Hold. *Keep, impose restraint.*

p23[16] they went to lay h. on him.

p44[24] h. to one and despise the other.

p69[18] laid h. upon John.

p83[8] ye h. the tradition of men.

p106[39] telling him to h. his peace.

p118[39] if these should h. their peace.

p124[26] could not take h. of his words.

p165[17] h. me not.

Holden. *Withheld.*

p165[15] their eyes were h.

Holiness. *Sanctification.*

p5[74] serve him in h.

Holy. *Set apart, sacred.*

p3[35] that h. child that shall be born.

p4[48] will magnify his h. name.

p5[69] spake by the mouth of his h. prophets.

p5[71] to remember his h. covenant.

p7[23] openeth the womb shall be called h. unto the Lord.

p46[10] give that which is h. unto the dogs.

Holy Ghost. *Holy spirit, comforter.*

p4[42] Elizabeth filled with the H.

p5[66] Zacharias filled with the H.

p5[1] Mary found with child of the H.

p8[25] H. was upon Simeon.

p12[28] baptized with fire, and the H.

p28[12] blasphemeth against the H.

p28[14] H. shall teach you.

p28[37] speaketh against the H.

p39[4] visited with fire and the H.

p76[39] H. promised to them that believe.

p143[26] comforter, which is the H.

p167[22] receive ye the H.

p170[15] baptized in the name of the

Father, Son, and H.

Home. *House, abode.*

p77[53] every man went h. to his own house.

p91[6] cometh h., he calleth his friends.

p160[27] took her unto his own h.

Honey comb. *Bee cells with honey.*

p167[41] broiled fish and h.

Honor (n). *Respect, reputation, admiration.*

p49[10] then shalt thou have h. of God.

p57[42] I receive not h. from men.

p57[45] how can ye believe who seek h.

p66[6] a prophet is not without h.

p119[26] him will my Father h.

Honor (v). *Reverence, keep, esteem, glorify.*

p56[23] men should h. the Son.

p57[41] lest ye should h. me.

p79[49] but h. my Father.

p80[54] if I h. myself.

p83[12] h. thy father and thy mother.

p101[19] h. thy father and mother.

Hook. *Used to catch fish.*

p94[26] cast a h. and take up the first fish.

Hope. *Expect.*

p42[34] lend to them whom ye h. to receive.

Hoped. *Hope.*

p155[8] h. to have seen some miracle.

Horn. *Authority, power.*

p5[68] hath raised up an h. of salvation.

Hosanna. *Save now.*

p117[7] H. in the highest.

p118[13] H. to the Son of David.

Host. *Multitude, proprietor.*

p7[13] heavenly h., praising God.

p125[36] gave money to the h.

Hour. *Time.*

p11[26] the h. of his ministry drew nigh.

p17[4] mine h. is not yet come.

p28[14] Holy Ghost shall teach you in the same h.

p37[54] inquired of them the h. when he

began to mend.

p56[28] the h. is coming in which all who are in their graves shall hear.

p67[17] given you in the same h.

p102[6] eleventh h. he went out.

p119[23] the h. is come, that the Son.

p119[27] for this cause I came unto this h.

p133[43] day and h. no one knoweth.

p150[41] couldest not watch one h.?

p158[28] it was about the third h.

p160[45] sixth h., there was darkness.

House. *Structure, household, family, tribe.*

p3[33] Jesus to reign over the h. of Jacob.

p5[68] salvation for the h. of David.

p6[4] Jesus was of the h. of David.

p21[26] entered into the h. of Simon.

p21[21] a h. divided shall not stand.

p21[24] enter into a strong man's h.

p25[16] a h. of merchandise.

p25[17] the zeal of thy h.

p27[3] proclaim from the h. tops.

p45[26] go forth from h. to h.

p47[34] who built his h. upon a rock.

p53[36] your h. is left desolate.

p66[6] without honor in his own h.

p67[5] lost sheep of the h. of Israel.

p95[5] peace to this h.

p101[28] hath left h., or brethren.

p118[19] called of all nations h. of prayer?

p142[2] in my Father's h. are many mansions.

Houses. *Structure, home.*

p101[29] receive h. and brethren.

p103[4] receive me into their h.

p127[11] devour widow's h.

Household. *Family.*

p24[49] make rulers over his h.

p41[9] man's eye, are they of his own h.

p68[31] foes are they of his own h.

p134[52] servant made ruler of his h.

Householder. *House ruler.*

p121[35] h. who planted a vineyard.

Housetop. *Roof.*

p131[14] let him who is on the h. flee.

How. *In what way.*

p93[21] h. oft shall I forgive my brother.

p126[42] h. then doth David call him Lord.

p129[37] h. oft would I have gathered.

p142[5] h. can we know the way?

p151[52] h. shall the scriptures be fulfilled.

Howbeit. *Be it as it may.*

p76[27] h. we know this man.

p83[7] h. in vain do they worship me.

p89[21] h. this kind goeth not out.

p113[13] h. Jesus spake of his death.

Humble. *Not proud or arrogant.*

p90[34] whosoever shall h. himself.

p127[9] he that shall h. himself.

Humbleth. *Humble.*

p49[11] he who h. himself shall be exalted.

Hundred. *Ten times ten.*

p58[7] some thirty, some sixty, and some an h.

p91[12] if a man have an h. sheep.

p101[29] receive an h. fold now.

Hundreds. *Multiple of hundred.*

p70[42] sat down in ranks by h.

Hunger (n). *Lack of food.*

p92[17] I perish with h.!

Hunger (v). *Desire, thirst for.*

p39[8] blessed are they that do h.

p72[35] cometh unto me shall never h.

Hungered. *Hunger.*

p15[2] he was afterwards an h.

p136[36] for I was an h.

p137[45] when saw we thee an h.

Hungry. *Hunger.*

p4[52] he hath filled the h.

p120[14] he was h. and seeing a fig tree.

Hurt. *Harm.*

p115[20] nothing shall h. the seventy.

p171[18] drink any deadly thing shall not h. them.

Husband. *Married man.*

p6[2] her h. being a just man.

p8[36] lived with a h. seven years.

p34[18] go call thy h.
p34[19] I have no h.
p100[10] if a woman put away her h.
p104[23] marrieth her who is put away from her h., committeth adultery.

Husbandman. *Cultivator, farmer.*
p51[6] h. had a fig tree.
p144[1] my Father is the h.

Husks. *Outer covering.*
p92[16] filled his belly with the h.

Hymn. *Song of praise.*
p149[27] when they had sung a h.

Hypocrite. *Professes virtues he does not have.*
p52[15] Lord said unto him, O h.

Hypocrites. *Hypocrite.*
p26[45] scribes and Pharisees, h.!
p43[2] doest alms as the h.
p43[5] pray as the h.
p44[17] h. of a sad countenance.
p83[7] Isaiah prophesied of you h.
p134[55] appoint his portion with the h.

Hyssop. *Possibly marjoram.*
p160[29] sponge put upon a h.

I

Idle (a). *Useless, lacking worth.*
p22[31] every i. word men shall speak.
p164[10] words seemed to them as i. tales.

Idle (v). *Doing nothing.*
p102[3] found others standing i.

If. *In the event, on condition.*
p15[3] i. thou be the Son of God.
p54[39] i. he were a prophet, he would have known.
p71[24] Lord, i. it be thou, bid me.
p75[17] i. any man will do his will.
p78[19] i. ye had known me.
p78[31] i. ye continue in my word.
p87[25] i. any man will come after me.
p105[35] i. one went unto them from the dead.
p111[24] i. thou be the Christ, tell us.
p143[15] i. ye love me, keep my.
p149[36] i. this be the Messiah.

p159[44] i. thou be the Son of God.
p159[40] i. thou be the Christ, save.

Image. *Impression, likeness.*
p124[20] whose i. is this and superscription.

Impart. *Give.*
p13[16] hath two coats, let him i.
p24[51] to i. his portion of meat.

Impediment. *Obstruction.*
p90[31] had an i. in his speech.

Importunity. *Troublesome persistence.*
p44[9] because of i. he will rise up and give him as many as he needeth.

Impossible. *Not possible.*
p3[37] with God nothing can be i.
p89[20] nothing shall be i. unto you.
p101[26] men that trust in riches, it is i.

Imposture. *A counterfeit action passed off as genuine.*
p162[65] last i. will be worse than first.

In. *Within, here.*
p1[1] i. the beginning.
p1[4] i. him was the gospel.

Incense. *Pleasing scent.*
p2[9] his lot was to burn i.
p2[10] at the time of i.
p2[11] right side of the alter of i.

Increase (n). *Grow, spread.*
p31[31] he must i., but I must decrease.

Increase (v). *Add to, expand.*
p126[5] Lord, i. our faith.

Indeed. *Surely, truly.*
p19[47] an Israelite i. in whom is no guile!
p35[44] this is i. the Christ.
p75[26] do the rulers know i. this is the very Christ?

Infirmity. *Disease.*
p51[11] a woman who had a spirit of i.
p55[5] a man who had an i. thirty eight years.

Inherit. *Come into possession, receive.*
p39[7] meek shall i. the earth.
p100[15] what shall I do to i. eternal life?
p136[35] i. the kingdom prepared for you.

Inheritance. *Inherit.*

p29[15] he divide the i. with me.

p122[40] let us seize on his i.

Iniquity. *Gross injustice, wickedness.*

p47[33] depart ye that work i.

p61[43] them which do i.

p128[25] full of hypocrisy and i.

p131[10] because i. shall abound.

Inn. *Lodging place.*

p125[35] brought him to an i.

Inns. *Inn.*

p6[7] none to give them room at the i.

Innocent. *Guiltless, sinless.*

p139[27] beware of i. blood.

p154[4] I have betrayed the i. blood.

p157[26] I am i. of the blood.

Insomuch. *So that.*

p20[24] amazed, i. they questioned among themselves.

p82[29] i. that the multitude wondered.

p155[15] i. the governor marveled.

Instant. *Immediate.*

p8[38] coming in that i. gave thanks.

p157[23] they were i. in loud voices.

Instantly. *Instant.*

p48[4] they besought him i.

Instructed. *Taught.*

p62[53] every scribe well i. in the things of the kingdom.

Intending. *Planning.*

p50[29] which of you i. to build a tower.

Intent. *Intention, purpose.*

p50[36] for this i. they were written.

p113[15] to the i. ye may believe.

p139[28] for what i. he spake to Judas.

Interpreted. *Explain, clarify.*

p6[6] being i. is, God with us.

p17[38] rabbi, being i., Master.

p18[41] Messias, being i., is the Christ.

p65[33] being i., damsel I say unto thee.

p158[34] Golgotha, being i.

p160[39] being i., my God, my God.

Interpretation. *Interpreted.*

p108[7] which by i. means sent.

Inward. *Within.*

p26[40] i. parts be full of ravening.

p26[42] i. parts be clean also.

Inwardly. *Inward.*

p47[24] i. they are ravening wolves.

Isaiah. *O.T. prophet.*

p83[7] well hath I. prophesied of you.

Israel. *Jacob of the O.T., nation of.*

p2[16] children of I. shall he turn to God.

p5[67] blessed be the Lord God of I.

p8[32] the glory of thy people I.

p9[6] who shall save my people I.

p10[20] Joseph told to go into land of I.

p13[5] who are of the sheepfold of I.

p16[30] should be made manifest to I.

p48[9] not found so great faith, in I.

p67[5] go to the lost sheep of house of I.

p82[29] glorified the God of I.

p101[28] judging the twelve tribes of I.

p131[18] was not sent before upon I.

p158[32] signifying the scattering of I.

p159[45] if he be the King of I.

p168[6] restore again the kingdom to I.?

Issue. *Flow, flowing, children.*

p64[21] woman had an i. of blood.

p124[24] having no i., left his wife to his brother.

Itself. *The same.*

p21[21] kingdom divided against i.

p45[39] morrow shall take thought of i.

p144[4] branch cannot bear fruit of i.

p171[25] world i. could not contain.

| J

James. *The apostle, brother of John.*

p18[10] a partner with John and Peter.

p23[14] chosen to be an apostle.

p65[29] the brother of John.

p87[1] went up to the Mt. of Transfiguration with Jesus.

p99[54] wanted to call fire down upon the Samaritans.

p149[38] at Gethsemane during the atonement.

James. *The apostle, son of Alpheus.*

p23[14] chosen to be an apostle.

Jeremiah / Jeremy. *O.T. prophet.*

p10[17] spoken of by J. the prophet.

p154[9] fulfilled that which was spoken by J. the prophet.

Jesus. *Son of God, Messiah.*

p5[1] birth of J. was on this wise.

p6[8] called his name J.

p11[52] J. increased in wisdom and stature.

p15[1] J. led into the wilderness.

p16[41] then cometh J. to be baptized.

p17[7] J. turns water into wine.

p19[45] J. of whom the prophets, did write.

p25[15] J. cleanses the temple.

p71[50] J. walks upon the sea.

p74[64] J. knew who should betray him.

p78[12] J. bares testimony of himself.

p86[22] J. foretells his crucifixion.

p87[1] J. is transfigured.

p116[1] J. triumphal entry.

p118[17] second cleansing of the temple.

p130[6] J. prophesies of the destruction of the temple.

p139[16] J. eats the Passover supper.

p149[36] J. atonement at Gethsemane.

p151[46] Judas betrays J. with a kiss.

p151[12] J. brought before Annas.

p152[56] J. brought before Ciaphas.

p154[28] J. brought before Pilate.

p155[8] J. brought before Herod.

p157[13] J. is crucified.

p164[11] J. appears to Mary Magdalene.

p165[12] J. appears to Cleopas.

p166[19] J. appears to ten of the apostles.

p167[26] J. appears to Thomas

p168[50] J. first ascension.

p171[20] J. final ascension.

Jews. *Israelite tribe of Judah.*

p8[2] where is the child the Messiah of the J.?

p33[11] the J. have no dealings with the Samaritans.

p34[24] salvation is of the J.

p78[31] then said Jesus to those J. which believed on him.

p107[11] J. taught that the kingdom of God should immediately appear.

p111[19] a division among the J. for these sayings.

p112[8] J. as of late sought to stone thee.

p115[54] Jesus walked no more openly among the J.

p130[3] temple of the J. left unto them desolate.

p131[18] shall be tribulations on the J.

p155[33] art thou the king of the J.?

p156[21] hail, King of the J.

p159[19] JESUS OF NAZARETH THE KING OF THE J.

p164[14] reported among the J. until this day.

p166[19] disciples were assembled for fear of the J.

John. *The apostle.*

p65[29] J. the brother of James.

p99[54] J. wanted to call down fire from heaven.

p138[8] J. sent to prepare Passover.

p164[4] Peter and J. ran to the sepulcher.

p170[23] J. will tarry until Jesus returns.

John. *The Baptist.*

p2[13] thou shalt call his name J.

p2[14] many shall rejoice at his birth.

p2[15] he shall drink neither wine nor strong drink.

p2[17] he shall go before the Lord.

p5[76] J. to give knowledge of salvation.

p11[27] preaching in the wilderness.

p12[30] had raiment of camels hair.

p16[44] J. baptizes Jesus.

p16[30] J. bears record of Jesus.

p31[27] Herod shut up J. in prison.

p33[33] J. came neither eating nor drinking.

p69[28] J. is beheaded.

p121[34] preaching of J. shall condemn.

Joined. *United.*

p92[15] j. himself with a citizen.

p99[7] what God hath j. together.

Jonas. *O.T. prophet.*

p22[34] for as J. was three days and nights in the whale's belly.

p84[4] but the sign of the prophet J.

Joseph. *Husband of Mary.*

p6[3] fear not to take Mary as thy wife.

p6[4] went to Bethlehem to be taxed.

p8[33] J. and Mary marveled at the things which were said of the child.

p9[13] warned to flee to Egypt.

p10[20] was told to go back to Israel.

p14[30] genealogy of J.

p73[42] is this not Jesus, the son of J.

Joseph. *Of Arimathea.*

p161[49] Pilate gave the body of Jesus to J.

Jot. *Smallest letter in Hebrew alphabet.*

p40[20] one j. shall in no wise pass from the law.

Journey. *Travel.*

p11[44] went a day's j. and sought Jesus.

p33[8] Jesus weary with the j.

p67[9] nor script for your j.

Joy. *Delight, happiness.*

p4[43] babe leaped in womb for j.

p7[10] bring tidings of great j.

p9[10] wise men rejoiced with exceeding great j.

p39[14] for you shall have great j.

p91[10] j. in the presence of angels over one repentant sinner.

p135[21] enter into the j. of thy Lord.

p146[20] sorrow shall be turned into j.

p147[22] your j. no man taketh.

p167[40] apostles believed not for j.

Joyfully. *Joy.*

p107[6] Zacchaeus received Jesus j.

Judas. *The apostle.*

p143[22] asks Jesus how he will manifest himself to the twelve.

Judas. *Iscariort, the apostle.*

p23[14] ordained one of the twelve apostles.

p74[70] Jesus refers to him as a devil.

p138[11] meets with the high priests.

p139[26] Jesus gives him the sop.

p139[29] held the bag (or money).

p151[46] betrays Jesus with a kiss.

p154[6] hanged himself.

Judge (n). *Magistrate, authority.*

p29[16] who made me a j. over you?

p40[27] adversary deliver thee to the j.

p98[2] parable of the widow and the j.

p104[16] maketh himself a j. over us.

p120[47] I came not to j. the world.

p154[31] j. him according to your law.

Judge (v). *Discern, decide.*

p46[2] j. not unrighteously.

p56[30] as I hear, I j.

p75[24] j. not according to your traditions.

p77[51] doth our law j. any man.

p78[15] ye j. after the flesh.

p120[48] my words shall j. him in the last day.

Judgment. *Judge.*

p40[23] in danger of the j. of God.

p46[3] with what j. ye judge, ye shall be judged.

p56[22] committed all j. unto the Son.

Just. *Upright, righteous.*

p2[17] to the wisdom of the j.

p6[2] Joseph being a j. man.

p42[47] rain on the j. and the unjust.

p50[14] resurrection of the j.

p53[36] a j. recompense for your sins.

p56[30] my judgment is j.

p69[21] John was a j. man.

p157[20] have thou nothing to do with that j. man.

p157[26] I am innocent of the blood of this j. person.

Justified. *Made right, vindicate.*

p22[32] by thy words thou shalt be j.

p32[29] publicans, j. God.

p33[35] wisdom is j. of all her children.

p98[14] publican went to his house j.

Justify. *Excuse, give reason.*

p104[15] ye are they who j. yourselves.

p125[30] but he willing to j. himself.

| K

Keep (n). *Guard, maintain.*
p46[10] mysteries ye shall k. within.
p118[42] compass thee and k. thee in.
p148[11] Father, k. those whom thou hast given me.
p148[15] k. them from evil.

Keep (v). *Observe.*
p20[19] ye k. not the law.
p80[52] if a man shall k. my saying.
p143[15] if ye love me, k. my commandments.

Keepers. *Soldiers, guards.*
p163[3] k. did shake, and became as though they were dead.

Keeping. *Keep.*
p6[8] k. watch over their flocks by night.

Key. *Fundamental, basic principal.*
p27[53] ye have taken away the k. of knowledge.

Keys. *Authority within the priesthood.*
p14[8] k. of the kingdom delivered up.
p86[20] give unto thee the k. of the kingdom of heaven.

Kid. *Young goat.*
p92[29] never gavest me a k.

Kill. *Slay, destroy, murder.*
p40[23] thou shalt not k.
p55[18] Jews sought to k. Jesus.
p68[25] be not afraid of them who k. the body.
p75[19] why go ye about to k. me?
p75[25] is this he whom they seek to k.?
p78[22] will he k. himself?
p129[29] ye k. the prophets.
p138[3] take Jesus by subtlety and k. him.

Kin. *Family.*
p66[6] a prophet is not without honor save with his own k.

Kind. *Caring, type.*
p42[35] God is k. to the unthankful.
p62[48] net gathered of every k.
p89[21] this k. goeth not out but by.

Kindred. *Kin.*

p4[60] none of thy k. is called by this name.
p11[44] they sought him among his k.

King. *Sovereign, ruler.*
p1[5] Herod, k. of Judea.
p19[49] thou art the K. of Israel.
p50[32] parable of k. who went to war.
p71[15] take Jesus to make him k.
p117[4] behold thy k. sitting upon an ass.
p155[33] art thou the k. of the Jews?
p155[37] I am a k.
p156[21] Hail, K. of the Jews.
p156[5] behold your K.!
p156[15] we have no k. but Caesar.
p159[45] if he be the K. of Israel.
p159[19] JESUS OF NAZARETH K. OF THE JEWS.

Kingdom. *God's realm.*
p3[33] there shall be no end to his k.
p11[28] repent for the k. of heaven is at hand.
p14[8] keys of the k. shall be delivered.
p21[21] every k. divided against itself.
p21[23] k. of God is come unto you.
p32[28] he who is least in the k. of God.
p32[12] k. of heaven suffereth violence.
p39[5] for theirs is the k. of heaven.
p43[11] thy k. come.
p45[38] seek ye first to build up the k.
p46[10] mysteries of the k. ye shall keep with yourselves.
p47[30] Lord, Lord, shall enter the k.
p59[30] k. like unto a mustard seed.
p59[32] k. like unto leaven.
p60[9] given you to know the mysteries of the k.
p62[46] k. like unto a treasure.
p62[47] k. like unto a merchantman.
p62[48] k. like unto a net.
p62[53] every scribe well instructed in the things of the k. of heaven.
p69[24] give unto the half of my k.
p82[1] show glad tidings of the k.
p86[26] let the children of the k. first be filled.

p86²⁰ give unto thee the keys of the k.

p93²³ k. like unto a certain king.

p97²⁰ Pharisees ask when the k. of God should come.

p97²¹ k. of God has already come.

p99⁶² looking back, is fit for the k.

p100¹² for of such is the k. of God.

p102¹ k. is like unto a householder.

p122⁴⁵ k. shall be taken from you.

p123² k. like unto a certain king.

p126³⁹ thou art not far from the k.

p134¹ k. like unto ten virgins.

p155³⁶ my k. is not of this world.

Kinsmen. *Kin.*

p49¹² make a dinner, call not thy k.

Kiss. *Sign of affection.*

p54⁴⁵ thou gavest me no k.

p151⁴⁷ betray me with a k.?

Knock. *Ask to enter.*

p44¹⁰ k. and it shall be opened.

p52²⁵ ye shall stand without and k.

Know. *Understand.*

p11⁴⁹ k. ye I must be about my Father's business.

p12²⁷ standeth one among you whom ye k. not.

p20²¹ I k. thee, whom thou art.

p29² we k. thou art a teacher from God.

p30¹¹ we speak that we do k.

p47²⁵ k. them by their fruits.

p60⁹ given unto you to k. the mysteries.

p75¹⁷ he shall k. of the doctrine.

p78¹⁹ neither k. me, nor my Father.

p78²⁸ then shall ye k. that I am he.

p79³² ye shall k. the truth.

p110⁴ sheep k. his voice.

p142³⁵ by this shall all men k. that ye are my disciples.

p147³ this is life eternal, that they might k. thee.

p152⁵⁷ I k. him not.

p159³⁵ they k. not what they do.

p168⁷ not for you to k. the times.

p171²⁴ we k. that his testimony is true.

Knowing. *Know.*

p1¹ k. that many have taken in hand.

p140³ k. the Father had given all things.

p149³⁷ Jesus k. their hearts.

p150⁴ k. all things that should come upon him.

p169¹² John, k. it was the Lord.

Knowledge. *Understanding.*

p5⁷⁶ to give k. of salvation to his people.

p27⁵³ the key of k., is the fullness of the scriptures.

Known. *Understood, recognized.*

p22²⁸ tree is k. by its fruit.

p54³⁹ this man, if he were a prophet, would have k.

p57¹³ should not make him k.

p78¹⁹ if ye had k. me ye would have k. my Father also.

p111¹³ I am k. of mine.

p143⁹ thou hast not k. me, Philip?

p145¹⁵ all things that I have heard of my Father I have made k.

p145³ they have not k. the Father, nor me.

p152¹⁵ that disciple was k. unto the high priest.

L

Labor. *Work, effort.*

p35⁴⁰ reap that ye bestow no l.

p72²⁷ l. not for the meat which perish.

p95²⁹ come unto me all ye that l.

Laborer. *Worker, servant.*

p45³³ l. is worthy of his hire.

Laborers. *Laborer.*

p66⁴³ but the l. are few.

p95² but the l. are few.

p102² agreed with the l. for a penny.

Lack. *Need, want.*

p101²⁰ all these things have I kept; what l. I yet?

Lacked. *Lack.*

p149³⁵ without purse, l. ye anything?

Lade. *Load, put on.*

p26[47] ye l. men with burdens.

Lake. *Body of fresh water.*

p18[1] stood by the l. of Gennesaret.

p18[2] saw two ships on the l.

p62[23] a storm of wind on the l.

p63[34] swine ran into the l.

Lamb of God. *Jesus Christ.*

p16[29] behold the L. who taketh away the sin of the world!

p17[36] behold the L. of God!

Lambs. *Young sheep.*

p95[3] I send you forth as l. among wolves.

p169[15] feed my l.

Lament. *Mourn, grieve.*

p146[20] ye shall l. but the world shall rejoice.

Lamentation. *Lament.*

p10[18] in Ramah, l. and weeping.

Lamps. *Lantern.*

p134[1] ten virgins who took their l.

p135[7] oil in our l. is gone out.

Land. *Country, ground.*

p18[3] he thrust out a little from the l.

p58[1] multitude by the sea on the l.

p128[12] ye compass sea and l. to make one proselyte.

p131[16] there shall be great distress in the l.

Large. *Big, great.*

p139[12] a l. upper room furnished.

p163[11] gave l. money unto the soldiers.

Last. *Following the rest, conclusion.*

p28[39] l. end of the man is worse than the first.

p52[30] l. shall be first, and the first shall be l.

p90[32] any man desire to be first, he shall be l.

p102[30] who make themselves first shall be l.

p102[9] beginning from the l. to the first.

p122[39] l. of all he sent his son.

Latchet. *Shoe strings.*

p12[28] whose shoe's l. I am not worthy to unloose.

Late. *Recent.*

p112[8] Jews as of l. sought to stone thee.

Latin. *Roman language.*

p159[20] written in Hebrew, Greek, and L.

Launch. *Go forth.*

p18[4] l. out into the deep.

Law. *Torah, scriptures.*

p20[18] seeing we keep the whole l.?

p32[13] prophets and the l. prophesied.

p40[19] I am not come to destroy the l.

p42[42] if any man sue thee at the l.

p46[7] why teach ye men the l. when ye.

p46[15] we have the l. for our salvation.

p47[21] this is the l. and the prophets.

p77[49] knoweth not the l. are cursed.

p77[51] doth our l. judge any man.

p104[17] l. and the prophets testify of me.

p104[19] easier for heaven to pass than one tittle of the l. to fail.

p112[34] is it not written in your l., ye are Gods?

p125[35] which is the great commandment in the l.?

p125[39] on these two commandments hang all the l.

p154[31] judge him according to your l.

Lawful. *Legal.*

p69[19] not l. to have thy brothers wife.

p80[2] why do ye that which is not l.

p102[13] is it not l. for me to do what I want with my own?

p124[17] is it l. to give tribute to Caesar.

p154[31] not l. for us to put any man to death.

Lawyer. *A designated profession.*

p125[34] one of them a l. tempting him.

Lawyers. *Scribe, keepers of the law.*

p26[46] one of the l. saying, thou reproachest us also.

p27[53] l. have taken away the key of knowledge.

Lay. *Put down, place.*

p44[19] l. not up treasures upon the earth.

p50[26] is afraid to l. down their life.

p87[37] save his life shall be willing to l. it down.

p99[58] Son of Man hath no where to l. his head.

p111[15] I l. down my life for the sheep.

p163[5] see the place where the Lord l.

p171[19] shall l. hands on the sick.

Lead. *Guide.*

p52[15] l. an ox to watering.

p84[13] blind l. the blind.

Leaning. *Laying on.*

p139[23] John l. on Jesus' bosom.

Learn. *Get knowledge, instructed.*

p19[14] go ye and l. what this meaneth.

p95[30] take my yoke and l. of me.

Learned. *Knowing, instructed.*

p73[45] every man that hath l. of the Father, commeth unto me.

p75[15] how knoweth this man letters, having never l.?

p122[49] they l. that the multitude took him for a prophet.

Least. *Smallest.*

p9[6] Bethlehem l. among Judea.

p32[28] he that is l. in the kingdom of God.

p40[21] shall break one of these l. commandments.

p103[10] he who is faithful in the l.

p128[21] ye would not commit the l. sin.

p137[41] have done it unto the l. of these thy brethren.

Leathern. *Made of leather.*

p12[30] John wore a l. girdle.

Leave. *Go away, set aside.*

p40[26] l. thou thy gift before the altar.

p91[12] l. the ninety and nine.

p99[7] shall a man l. his father and mother.

p118[43] not l. one stone upon another.

p143[18] I will not l. you comfortless.

p144[27] peace I l. with you.

p147[28] I l. the world and go to the Father.

Leaven. *Doctrine, teachings.*

p27[1] beware of the l. of the Pharisees.

p85[12] beware of the l. of the Pharisees and Sadducees.

Leavened. *Raised with yeast.*

p59[32] three measures of meal, till the whole was l.

Lebbeus. *The apostle.*

p66[2] surname was Thaddaeus.

Legion. *Multitude.*

p63[6] my name is L.; for we are many.

Leisure. *Time to one self.*

p70[32] they had no l., so much as to eat.

Lend. *Loan, let use.*

p42[34] if ye l. to them ye hope to receive.

p42[35] l., hoping for nothing again.

p44[6] l. me three loaves.

Leper. *One who has leprosy.*

p137[4] in the house of Simon the l.

Lepers. *Leper.*

p32[22] the l. were cleansed.

p36[27] many l. were in Israel.

p67[7] cleanse the l.; raise the dead.

p97[12] ten men who were l.

Leprosy. *Bacterial disease.*

p37[38] immediately the l. departed.

Let. *Allow.*

p20[21] spirit cried out, l. us alone.

p32[16] ears to hear, l. him hear.

p40[18] l. your light so shine.

p99[60] l. the dead bury their dead.

p99[7] l. not man put asunder.

p142[1] l. not your heart be troubled.

p150[8] l. these go their way.

p157[22] chastise him, and l. him go.

p159[46] l. him save him.

Liar. *Deceiver.*

p79[44] devil is a l.

p80[55] I should be a l. like unto you.

Liberty. *Freedom.*

p35[18] to set at l. them that are bruised.

Licked. *To lick with tongue.*

p105[26] dogs l. his sores.

Lie (n). *Untruth.*
p79[44] speaketh a l., he speaketh of
his own.

Lie (v). *Stretch out, lay.*
p55[6] Jesus saw him l. and knew he
had been a long time afflicted.
p164[6] seeth the linen cloths l.

Life. *Spiritual and physical existence.*
p1[4] gospel was the l., and light of men.
p10[20] sought the young child's l.
p29[17] man's l. not in the abundance of
things.
p30[15] whosoever believeth shall have
eternal l.
p31[36] believeth on the Son hath
everlasting l.
p45[28] take no thought for your l.
p47[23] strait is the gate that leadeth unto
l.
p50[26] if any man is afraid to lay
down his l.
p56[26] Son hath l. in himself.
p68[34] loseth his l. for my sake shall
find it.
p72[35] I am the bread of l.
p100[16] enter into l., keep the
commandments.
p106[28] gave his l. a ransom for many.
p110[10] I am come that they might
have l.
p111[17] I lay down my l.
p113[25] I am the resurrection, and the l.
p145[13] that a man lay down his l. for
his friends.
p147[3] and this is l. eternal.

Lifetime. *Mortal existence.*
p105[30] in thy l. receivedst good things.

Lift. *Raise, pick up.*
p81[9] l. a sheep out of the pit on the
Sabbath.
p98[13] would not so much as l. his eyes
unto heaven.

Light (n). *Not heavy or burdensome.*
p95[30] my yoke is easy and my burden
is l.

Light (v). *Illumination, understanding.*
p1[5] l. shineth in the world, and the
world perceiveth it not.
p5[78] to give l. unto them who sit in
darkness.
p30[19] men love darkness rather than l.
p30[21] he who loveth the truth, cometh
to the l.
p40[16] I give you to be the l. of the
world.
p40[18] let your l. so shine before this
world.
p44[22] l. of the body is the eye.
p58[36] take heed that the l. which is in
thee be not darkness.
p87[1] his raiment was white as the l.
p103[8] wiser than the children of l.
p108[5] I am the l. of the world.
p119[36] while ye have l., believe in the l.
p132[27] l. of the morning cometh out
of the east.

Lighten. *Enlighten.*
p8[32] a light to l. the gentiles.

Lightning. *Produced from a thunder
cloud, illuminate.*
p115[19] Satan falling from heaven as l.
p163[3] countenance was like l.

Like (a). *Compare, similar to.*
p16[45] spirit of God descending l. a
dove.
p43[8] be ye not l. unto them.
p168[11] Jesus shall come in l. manner.

Like (v). *Prefer, chose.*
p77[46] never spake man l. this man.

Liken. *Like.*
p32[31] then shall I l. the men of this
generation?
p47[34] I will l. him unto a wise man.
p50[36] I will l. it unto salt.
p104[23] Pharisees l. unto a rich man.

Likewise. *In like manner.*
p42[32] do ye also to them l.
p51[3] ye shall all l. perish.
p55[19] these also doeth the Son l.
p125[38] go, and do l.

Lilies. *Perennial flower.*
  p45³² consider the l. of the field.
Lineage. *Ancestry, family.*
  p6⁴ Joseph of the l. of David.
Little. *Small.*
  p45³⁵ fear not l. flock.
  p54⁴⁷ to whom l. is forgiven.
  p68³⁸ give drink to one of these l. ones.
  p71²⁶ O thou of l. faith.
  p76³³ yet a l. while I am with you.
  p90³³ except ye become as l. children.
  p100¹² suffer the l. children.
  p100¹³ receive the kingdom of God as a l. child.
  p106³ Zacchaeus was l. of stature.
  p107¹⁷ thou hast been faithful in a very l.
Live. *Be alive.*
  p15⁴ man shall not l. by bread alone.
  p32²⁵ gorgeously appareled, l. in king's courts.
  56²⁵ they who hear shall l.
  p73⁵¹ eat this bread, shall l. forever.
  p74⁵⁷ I l. by the Father.
  p113²⁵ though he were dead, yet shall he l.
  p125²⁹ do this and thou shalt l.
  p143¹⁹ because I l. ye shall l. also.
Living (a). *Live.*
  p33¹² have given thee l. water.
  p73⁵¹ I am the l. bread.
  p74⁵⁷ as the l. Father hath sent me.
  p74⁶⁹ the Son of the l. God.
  p91¹² divided unto them his l.
  p91¹³ wasted his substance with riotous l.
  p124³¹ not the God of the dead, but of the l.
  p153⁶⁴ I adjure thee by the l. God.
  p163⁴ why seek ye the l. among the dead?
Living (n). *Livelihood, income.*
  p130⁵⁰ she did cast in all her l.
Lo. *Behold.*
  p7⁹ l., an angel of the Lord appeared.

p9⁹ l., the star which they saw in the east.
p97²¹ neither shall they say l., here! or, l., there!
Locusts. *Short-horned grasshopper*
  p12³⁰ John ate l. and wild honey.
Lodge. *Temporarily settle.*
  p59³¹ birds l. in the branches.
Loins. *Lower part of the abdomen.*
  p12³⁰ John wore a leathern girdle about his l.
  p14³⁰ Joseph, from the l. of Heli.
  p24³⁸ let your l. be girded about.
Long (a). *Extended, lengthy.*
  p94²³ they would have repented l. since.
  p127¹¹ for a pretense make l. prayers
  p143⁹ have I been so l. with you, yet hast thou not known me.
  p163² clothed in l. white garments.
Long (n). *Strive with, desire for.*
  p89¹⁶ how l. shall I be with you?
  p98⁷ though he bear l. with men?
  p108⁵ as l. as I am in the world.
  p111²⁴ how l. dost thou make us doubt?
Longer. *Continue as.*
  p103² thou mayest no l. be steward.
Look (n). *Vision, sight.*
  p35³⁷ cast your eyes and l. on the fields.
  p85²⁶ put his hands on his eyes and made him l. up.
  p161³⁷ l. upon him whom they pierced.
Look (v). *Expect, search.*
  p31¹⁹ art thou he, or l. we for another?
  p77⁵² l.; for out of Galilee ariseth no prophet.
Looked. *Look.*
  p8³⁸ all those who l. for redemption.
  p81⁵ l. round about with anger.
  p107⁵ he l. up and saw Zacchaeus.
  p120¹³ when he l. round about.
  p139²² disciples l. one on another.
  p153⁶¹ the Lord l. upon Peter.
  p164¹¹ she l. into the sepulcher.
  p168¹⁰ they l. steadfastly toward heaven.
Loose. *Release, let go.*

p52[15] on the Sabbath l. an ox.

p86[20] thou shalt l. on earth.

p114[44] l. him and let him go.

p117[5] why l. ye the colt?

Lord. *Having power and authority.*

p4[45] my soul doth magnify the L.

p5[65] the hand of the L. was with it.

p7[9] the glory of the L. shone round about them.

p7[11] a Savior, who is Christ the L.

p11[29] prepare ye the way of the L.

p15[7] thou shalt not tempt the L. thy God.

p35[18] the spirit of the L. is upon me.

p47[30] not everyone that saith unto me, L., L.

p52[24] the L. shall not always strive with man.

p53[36] blessed is he who cometh in the name of the L.

p74[68] L., to whom shall we go?

p95[27] O Father, L. of heaven and earth.

p125[28] thou shalt love the L. thy God.

p127[43] if David called him L., how is he his son?

p136[23] enter into the joy of thy l.

p140[13] ye call me master and L.

p141[16] servant not greater than his L.

p168[28] my L. and my God.

Lordship. *Lord.*

p140[25] gentiles exercise l. over them.

Lose. *Lost, part with, fail, give up.*

p39[15] if the salt shall l. its savor.

p68[38] he shall in no wise l. his reward

p87[37] will save his life shall l. it.

p87[29] gain the world and l. his soul?

p119[25] he that loveth his life shall l. it.

Lost. *Gone astray, missing, gone.*

p13[5] gather those who are l.

p51[37] if the salt hath l. its savor.

p67[5] go to the l. sheep of Israel.

p71[12] gather up the fragments that nothing be l.

p85[23] I am sent to the l. sheep of Israel.

p91[13] rejoice over that which was l.

p93[32] he was l., and is found.

p107[10] to save that which is l.

p150[9] thou gavest me have I l. none.

Lot. *Assignment, good fortune.*

p2[9] his l. was to burn incense.

Loud. *Intensity, volume.*

p20[23] unclean spirit spake with a l. voice.

p97[15] with a l. voice glorified God.

p114[43] cried with a l. voice, Lazarus.

p157[23] they were instant in l. voices.

p160[39] with a l. voice saying, Eloi.

p160[54] l. voice saying, Father it is finished.

Love. *Care for, worship, serve.*

p42[35] l. your enemies.

p44[24] hate the one and l. the other.

p54[42] which will l. him most?

p101[19] l. thy neighbor as thyself.

p125[28] thou shalt l. the Lord thy God.

p131[10] l. of many shall wax cold.

p142[34] a new commandment I give unto you, that ye l. one another.

p143[15] if ye l. me, keep my commandments.

p145[13] greater l. hath no man than this.

Low. *Humble, down.*

p4[47] the l. estate of his handmaiden.

p4[51] exalted them of l. degree.

p14[10] mountain to be brought l.

Lowest. *Farthest down.*

p49[9] with shame to take the l. room.

Lowly. *Humble.*

p95[30] I am meek and l. in heart.

Lust. *Desire.*

p41[30] look on a woman to l. after her.

p87[26] and every worldly l.

| M

Mad. *Crazy.*

p111[20] he hath a devil, and is m.

Made. *Created, compelled, produced.*

p1[3] all things were m. by him.

p26[41] he who m. that which is without.

p99[6] God m. them male and female.

p148²³ that they may be m. perfect.

p157⁷ because he m. himself the Son of God.

Magnify. *Make great, exalt.*

p4⁴⁵ my soul doth m. the Lord.

p4⁴⁸ will m. his holy name.

Maidens. *Young woman, damsel.*

p25⁵⁴ to beat the man servants and m.

Maimed. *Injured, crippled.*

p49¹³ call the poor, the m., the lame.

p82²⁹ multitudes came unto him, the blind, dumb, m.

p96⁴⁰ better to enter life m.

Make. *Create, produce, compel.*

p11²⁹ m. his paths straight.

p18¹⁸ I will m. you fishers of men.

p22²⁸ either m. the tree good.

p128²¹ m. yourselves appear unto men.

p162⁶⁶ m. it as sure as you can.

Male. *Man, boy.*

p7²³ every m. which openeth the womb. (woman's firstborn)

p99⁶ God made them m. and female.

Malefactor. *Evil doer, law breaker.*

p154³⁰ if he were not a m.

Malefactors. *Malefactor.*

p158³³ there were also two other m.

p158³⁴ m.; one on the right hand.

p159⁴⁰ one of the m. railed on him.

Mammon. *Riches, wealth.*

p44²⁴ ye cannot serve God and m.

p103⁹ make to yourselves friends, of the m.

p104¹¹ ye have not been faithful in unrighteous m.

Man. *Human being, often used with reference to both sexes.*

p1¹³ not of the will of m., but of God.

p15⁴ m. shall not live by bread alone.

p22³⁰ a good m., out of the treasure of his heart.

p26²⁵ needed not that any should testify of m.

p28³⁹ the last end of the m. is worse

than the first.

p31²⁸ a m. can receive nothing, except.

p44²⁴ no m. can serve two masters.

p48⁸ I also am a m. set under authority.

p52²⁴ Lord will not always strive with m.

p56²² the Father judgeth no m.

p56³⁵ he received not his testimony of m., but of God.

p58¹⁹ if any m. have ears to hear.

p62²⁵ what manner of m. is this?

p73⁴⁴ no m. can come unto me, except.

p75¹² some said, he is a good m.

p75¹⁷ if any m. will do his will.

p77⁴⁶ never m. spake like this man.

p77¹⁰ hath no m. condemned thee?

p81¹⁰ is a m. better than a sheep?

p84¹⁷ things which proceed forth from the mouth, defile the m.

p87²⁵ if any m. will come after me.

p87²⁹ what will a m. give in exchange for his soul?

p87⁴¹ reward every m. according to his works.

p96⁴⁴ let every m. stand or fall.

p99⁶² no man having put his hand to the plough.

p99⁷ shall a m. leave his father, and mother, and cleave to his wife.

p101²⁸ no m. hath left house, or brethren.

p104¹⁸ every m. who seeketh truth.

p112³³ being a m., makest thyself God.

p115²³ no m. knoweth that the Son is the Father.

p119²⁶ if any m. serve me.

p127⁴⁴ no m. was able to answer him.

p130⁵ take heed that no m. deceive you.

p142⁶ no m. cometh unto the Father, but by me.

p145¹³ greater love hath no m.

p152¹⁴ one m. should die for the people.

p157²⁰ have nothing to do with this just m.

Manger. *Feeding trough.*

p6⁷ laid him in a m.

p7[16] found the babe lying in a m.

Manifest. *Made known, evident.*

p16[30] he should be m. to Israel.

p30[21] that his deeds may be m.

p108[3] works of God should be m.

p143[21] I will m. myself to him.

Manifested. *Manifest.*

p17[11] Jesus m. forth his glory.

p58[19] nothing hid which shall not be m.

p147[6] I have m. thy name.

Manna. *Food from heaven.*

p72[31] our fathers did eat m.

Manner. *Custom, sort, kind.*

p3[29] what m. of salutation.

p5[65] what m. of child shall this be?

p38[9] the power of God after this m.

p38[22] healing all m. of sickness.

p43[9] after this m. shall ye pray.

p54[39] would know what m. of woman.

p62[25] what m. of man is this?

p162[40] as the m. of the Jews is to bury.

p165[16] what m. of communications.

p168[11] shall so come in like m.

Mansions. *House, manor.*

p142[2] in my Father's house are many m.

Many. *Numerous.*

p2[14] m. shall rejoice at his birth.

p47[32] m. shall say unto me, Lord, Lord.

p78[30] m. believed on him.

p102[15] m. are called but few are chosen.

p106[28] gave his life a ransom for m.

p112[32] m. good works have I showed.

p115[25] m. prophets and kings have desired to see those things.

p116[42] Martha troubled about m. things.

p130[6] for m. shall come in my name.

p141[24] blood shed for as m. as believe.

p142[2] in my Father's house are m. mansions.

p163[56] m. came out of their graves.

Market. *Place of merchandise.*

p32[32] like unto children sitting in the m. place.

p54[2] by the sheep m., a pool.

p83[4] when they come from the m. except they wash.

Marriage. *Wedding, united.*

p17[1] m. in Cana of Galilee.

p123[2] parable of the m. of the King's son.

p124[29] neither marry nor are given in m.

p133[45] eating, drinking, giving in m.

p135[9] virgins went with him into the m.

Married. *Marriage.*

p8[36] Anna m. only seven years.

p69[18] Herodias previously m. to Philip.

p100[10] if a woman be m. to another.

p124[24] seven brothers m. to the same wife.

Marry. *Marriage.*

p41[36] whosoever shall m. her that is divorced.

p100[9] and m. another committeth adultery.

p100[10] it is not good to m.

p124[23] his brother shall m. his wife.

p124[29] neither m. nor are given in marriage.

Martha. *Sister of Mary and Lazarus.*

p116[41] cumbered about much serving.

Marvel. *To wonder.*

p29[7] m. not that ye must be born again.

p55[20] greater works that ye may m.

p56[28] m. not at this, for the hour is coming.

p64[17] and all that heard him did m.

p75[21] I have done one work, and ye all m.

Marvelous. *Marvel.*

p109[30] why herein is a m. thing.

p122[44] the Lord's doings, and it is m. in our eyes?

Mary. *Jesus' mother.*

p3[28] chosen and blessed among women.

p3[38] behold the handmaid of the Lord.

p3[39] visits Elizabeth.

p4[45] my soul doth magnify the Lord.

p4[47] generations shall call me blessed.

p4^{55} abode with Elizabeth three months.

p5^1 espoused to Joseph.

p6^4 goes to Bethlehem.

p6^7 gives birth to Jesus.

p7^{19} kept these things in her heart.

p8^{33} marveled at those things spoken of the child.

p159^{25} Mary's sister, M. the wife of Cleophas.

Mary. *Magdalene.*

p82^2 had seven devils cast out.

p159^{25} stood by the cross of Jesus.

p162^{63} sitting against the sepulcher.

p162^1 brought spices to anoint Jesus' body.

p165^{16} first to see the resurrected Lord.

p165^{18} tells the apostles she has seen the Lord.

Mary. *Sister of Martha and Lazarus.*

p54^{38} washes Jesus' feet with her tears.

p114^{29} arose quickly to meet Jesus.

p116^{40} sat at Jesus' feet to hear his words.

p116^{43} M. hath chosen that good part

p137^4 anoints Jesus' head.

Mary. *Mother of James and John.*

p105^{18} asks Jesus a question.

p162^1 brought spices to anoint Jesus' body.

p164^9 told the apostles that Jesus had risen.

Master. *Teacher, Lord.*

p17^{38} Rabbi, which means m.

p19^{12} why eateth your m. with publicans and sinners?

p30^{10} art thou a m. of Israel.

p62^{24} m., carest thou not that we perish?

p65^{27} why troublest thou the m.

p68^{21} disciple is not above his m.

p100^{15} good m. what shall I do.

p113^{28} the m. calleth for thee.

p126^{37} thou hast said well, m.

p127^5 one is your m., which is Christ.

p127^7 neither be ye called m.

p140^{13} ye call me m. and Lord.

p151^{46} hail, m.! and kissed him.

Matthew. *The apostle.*

p19^{10} Jesus said unto him, follow me.

p23^{14} ordained one of the twelve apostles.

p66^2 identified as a publican.

Matter. *Subject, issue.*

p37^{40} to blaze abroad the m.

p100^8 asked him again of the same m.

May. *Might, be able, can.*

p8^{35} many hearts m. be revealed.

p9^8 that I m. come and worship him also.

p30^{21} deeds m. be manifest.

p38^8 that ye m. know.

p43^5 that they m. be seen of men.

p73^{40} m. have everlasting life.

p93^{16} every word m. be established.

p112^{38} that ye m. know, and believe.

p113^{16} let us go, that we m. die with him.

p143^{13} the Father m. be glorified in the Son.

p147^{24} that your joy m. be full.

p148^{11} that they m. be one.

Meal. *Flour.*

p59^{32} hid in three measures of m.

Mean. *Intend, signify.*

p88^8 what the rising of the dead should m.

Means. *Way, method.*

p33^2 sought m. to put him to death.

p40^{28} by no m. come out thence.

p107^8 taken anything by unjust m.

p109^{21} by what m. he now seeth.

p115^{20} nothing by any m. shall hurt you.

Measure. *Amount, degree.*

p31^{34} giveth him not the spirit by m.

p46^3 with what m. ye mete.

p90^{36} astonished beyond m.

p101^{25} astonished out of m.

p129^{29} and will fill up the m.

Meat. *Food, instruction.*

p13[16] he that hath m., give to him that hath none.

p24[49] their portion of m. in due season.

p33[10] into the city to buy m.

p35[36] m. is to do the will of him who sent me.

p45[28] life is more than m.

p67[9] workman is worthy of his m.

p72[27] labor not for the m. which perishes.

p73[55] my flesh is m. indeed.

p136[36] was an hungered and ye gave me m.

p140[27] who is greater, he who sitteth at m., or he who serveth?

p167[40] have ye here any m.?

p169[5] children, have ye any m.?

Meek. *Humble.*

p39[7] blessed are the m.

p95[30] I am m. and lowly.

p104[21] Pharisees persecute the m.

p117[4] he is m. sitting upon an ass.

Meet (a). *Worthy, fit*

p13[35] bring forth fruits m. for repentance.

p46[10] not m. to give that which is holy to the dogs.

p86[26] not m. to cast the children's bread unto the dogs.

Meet (v). *Assemble, encounter.*

p50[32] m. him with his twenty thousand.

p134[1] went forth to m. the bridegroom.

p138[10] there shall a man m. you.

Memorial. *Remembrance.*

p138[9] what she hath done shall be a m. of her.

Mend. *Heal.*

p37[54] from that very hour he began to m.

Merchandise. *Trade, goods, stock.*

p25[16] make not my Father's house a house of m.

p123[5] went their ways; another to his m.

Merchantman. *Buyer or seller of goods.*

p62[47] kingdom of heaven like unto a m.

Merciful. *Mercy.*

p39[9] blessed are the m.

p98[13] God be m. to me a sinner.

Mercy. *Loving kindness.*

p4[49] his m. on those who fear him.

p5[71] perform the m. promised to our fathers.

p19[14] I will have m. and not sacrifice.

p65[33] have m. on us.

p85[21] have m. on me, O Lord.

p97[13] Master, have m. on us.

p106[38] have m. on me.

p128[20] weightier things, judgment, m. and faith.

Merry. *Happy, joyous.*

p29[21] eat, drink, and be m.

p92[29] that I might make m. with my friends.

Messenger. *Ambassador*

p1[1] I am a messenger of Jesus Christ.

p32[27] I send my m. before my face.

p88[11] I will send you my m.

p107[14] sent a m. after him.

Mete. *Measure.*

p46[3] with what measure ye m.

p58[20] with what measure ye m.

Midnight. *Middle of the night.*

p44[6] have a friend, and go to him at m.

p135[5] at m. there was a cry made.

Midst. *Central part, middle.*

p11[46] Jesus sitting in the m. of the doctors.

p36[30] passing through the m of them.

p67[14] as sheep in the m. of wolves.

p77[9] woman standing alone in the m. of the temple.

p93[20] there am I in the m. of them.

p158[34] Jesus crucified in the m.

Mightier. *Greater, more powerful.*

p14[23] cometh one m. than I.

Mighty. *Strong, great, powerful.*

p4[48] he who is m. hath done great things.

p4^{51} he hath pulled down the m.

p66^{3} such m. works are wrought by his hands?

p66^{7} could do no m. work there.

p69^{15} m. works do show forth themselves.

p94^{22} most of his m. works were done.

p95^{25} if the m. works had been done.

p165^{18} a prophet m. in deed.

Mill. *Place for grinding grain.*

p133^{48} two shall be grinding at the m.

Millstone. *Used for grinding.*

p91^{39} m. were hanged about his neck.

Mind. *Intellect.*

p3^{29} Mary pondered in her m.

p45^{35} neither be ye of doubtful m.

p63^{36} clothed and in his right m.

p125^{28} love the Lord with all thy m.

Minded. *Thought, included.*

p6^{2} m. to put her away privaly.

Mine. *Of me, my.*

p17^{4} m. hour is not yet come.

p47^{17} m. is thine, and thine is m.?

p56^{31} I can of m. own self do nothing.

p72^{38} not to do m. own will.

p75^{16} my doctrine is not m.

p79^{50} seek not m. own glory.

p102^{13} lawful to do with m. own?

p106^{23} not m. to give.

p111^{13} and am known of m. sheep.

p136^{27} received m. own with usury.

p143^{24} the word ye hear is not m.

p146^{15} all things the Father hath are m.

Mingled. *Mixed with.*

p51^{1} whose blood Pilate had m. with their sacrifices.

p160^{29} vinegar m. with gall.

Minister (n). *Cleric, holy man.*

p35^{20} gave it to the m. and sat down.

Minister (v). *Serve, attend, comfort.*

p106^{26} whosoever will be great among you, let him be your m.

p106^{28} Son of Man came to m.

p137^{45} in prison and did not m. unto thee?

Ministration. *Service, work.*

p2^{23} days of his m. were accomplished.

Mint. *Aromatic herb.*

p26^{43} for ye tithe m. and rue.

p128^{20} you pay tithe of m. and anise.

Miracle. *Wonder, phenomenon.*

p90^{37} no man which shall do a m.

p117^{18} they heard he had done this m.

Miserable. *Wretched.*

p122^{43} destroy those m. wicked men.

Mites. *Smallest coin.*

p129^{48} widow cast in two m.

Mixture. *Combination.*

p161^{39} brought a m. of myrrh and aloes.

Mock. *Ridicule.*

p50^{30} unable to finish his work, begin to m. him.

Mocked. *Make fun of, scorn.*

p10^{16} Herod saw that he was m.

p103^{32} Jesus shall be m. and spitefully entreated.

p153^{63} men who held Jesus, m. him.

p155^{11} set him at naught and m. him.

p158^{23} when they had m. him.

Moment. *Instant.*

p96^{45} it shall be done at that very m.

Money. *Currency, exchange.*

p25^{15} poured out the changers of m.

p50^{29} whether he have m. to finish his work?

p94^{26} piece of m. in the fish's mouth.

p118^{17} overthrew the tables of the m. changers.

p124^{18} show me the tribute m.

p129^{47} people cast m. into the treasury.

p135^{18} hid his Lord's m.

p136^{27} put my m. to the exchangers.

p163^{11} gave large m. to the soldiers.

Month. *Four weeks, 30 days.*

p3^{26} sixth m. the angel Gabriel was sent.

p3^{36} sixth m. with her who is called barren.

Moon. *Planet orbiting earth.*

p132^{34} m. shall not give her light.

More. *Additional, extra.*

p13[18] exact no m. than that which is appointed.

p24[10] no m. than our duty to do.

p25[57] of him men will ask the m.

p27[4] after that have no m. that they can do.

p27[7] ye are of m. value than many sparrows.

p32[26] and much m. than a prophet.

p33[1] Jesus baptized m. disciples than John.

p39[3] m. blessed are they who believe on your words.

p41[39] whatsoever is m. than these cometh of evil.

p42[49] what do ye m. than others?

p45[28] life is m. than meat.

p49[8] lest a m. honorable man be bidden.

p55[14] sin no m., lest a worse thing.

p58[20] unto you that continue to receive, shall m. be given.

p68[32] loveth father or mother m. than me.

p74[66] many of his disciples walked no m. with him.

p77[11] go, and sin no m.

p110[10] might have life m. abundantly.

p120[43] loved the praise of men m.

p126[38] love is m. than burnt offerings.

p129[49] widow hath cast in m.

p144[2] that it bring forth m. fruit.

p146[10] because I go to the Father they see me no m.

p150[44] he prayed m. earnestly.

p169[15] lovest me m. than these?

Moreover. *Also.*

p44[17] m., when ye fast.

p93[15] m., if thy brother trespass.

p105[26] m. the dogs licked his sores.

Morning. *Dawn, daybreak.*

p23[31] in the m. Jesus departed into a solitary place.

p77[2] early in the m., he came again to the temple.

p84[2] in the m. the weather is foul.

p97[24] for as the light of the m.

p162[2] women came early in the m.

Most. *Larger amount, majority.*

p1[1] things which are m. surely believed among us.

p54[42] which of them will love him m.?

p94[22] upbraid the cities wherein m. of his mighty works were done.

Mote. *A small particle.*

p46[5] behold the m. in thy brothers eye.

Moth. *Flying insect.*

p23[36] lay not up treasure where m. corrupteth.

p44[19] m. and rust doth corrupt.

Mother. *Female parent.*

p4[59] his m. answered and said, not so.

p11[51] his m. kept these sayings in her heart.

p17[1] m. of Jesus was at the marriage.

p21[27] Simon's wife's m.

p22[40] his m. and brethren stood without.

p22[42] who is my m.? and brethren?

p53[12] the only son of his m.

p68[31] the daughter against her m.

p68[32] who loveth father and m. more.

p69[25] went to her m., what shall I ask?

p73[42] whose father and m. we know?

p83[12] honor they father and thy m.

p99[7] for this cause shall a man leave his father, and m.

p101[28] no man who hath left father, or m.

p105[18] m. of James and John ask Jesus a question.

p159[25] stood by the cross his m.

p160[27] said unto John, behold thy m.!

Mount of Olives. *Hill east of Jerusalem.*

p77[1] Jesus went unto the m. of Olives.

p116[1] Bethphage, on the m. of Olives.

p130[6] Jesus left them and went upon the m. of Olives.

p149[27] they went out into the m. of

Olives.

Mourn. *Weep, lament.*

p20[16] can the children m. as long as the bridegroom is with them?

p39[6] blessed are they that m.

p133[37] then shall the tribes of the earth m.

Mourned. *Mourn.*

p32[32] m. for you and you, have not wept.

p165[18] as the disciples m. and wept.

Mourning. *Mourn.*

p10[18] voice of lamentation and great m.

Mouth (n). *Palate.*

p5[63] his m. was opened.

p84[16] entereth in at the m. goeth into.

p94[26] piece of money in the fish's m.

p160[29] put a hyssop to his m.

Mouth (v). *Say, state.*

p5[69] spake by the m. of his holy prophets.

p15[4] word which prodeedeth forth from the m. of God.

p22[29] abundance of the heart the m. speaketh.

p27[55] seek to catch something out of his m.

p93[16] in the m. of two or three witnesses.

p108[22] out of thine own m. will I judge thee.

p130[13] I will give you a m. and wisdom.

Move. *Lift, transfer.*

p127[3] will not m. one of them with their fingers.

Much. *A large amount.*

p25[57] whomsoever m. is given.

p32[26] m. more than a prophet.

p42[34] to receive as m. again.

p43[7] to be heard for their m. speaking.

p54[47] her sins, are forgiven, for she loved m.

p103[10] faithful in least, is faithful in m.

p129[47] many that were rich cast in m.

p144[5] the same bringeth forth m. fruit.

Multitude. *Large number of people.*

p2[10] m. praying without at the time of incense.

p7[13] m. of heavenly host praising God.

p18[6] a great m. of fishes.

p27[1] an innumerable m. of people.

p39[19] the m. sought to touch him.

p57[9] small ship, because of the m.

p64[24] thou seesth the m. throng thee and asked who touch thee?

p82[37] sent away the m. and took ship.

p117[6] a m. spread their garments.

p122[49] sought to lay hands on him but feared the m.

p138[12] opportunity to betray Jesus in the absence of the m.

Murder. *Kill, slay.*

p156[40] Barabbas, who for m. was cast into prison.

Murders. *Murder.*

p84[18] evil thoughts proceed m.

Murderer. *Murder.*

p79[44] devil a m. from the beginning.

Murderers. *Murder.*

p123[7] destroy those m. and burn up the city.

Murmur. *Muttered complaint.*

p73[43] m. not among yourselves.

Murmured. *Murmur.*

p73[41] the Jews then m. at him.

p74[61] his disciples m. at it.

p76[32] Pharisees heard the people m.

p107[7] m. he was guest with a sinner.

p137[5] disciple m. against Mary.

Murmuring. *Murmur.*

p75[12] there was much m. among the people.

Mused. *Think, ponder.*

p14[22] all men m. in their hearts.

Music. *Song, melody.*

p92[25] eldest brother heard m.

Must (n). *Necessity, duty.*

p11[49] I m. be about my Father's business?

p108[4] I m. work the works of him that

sent me.

Must (v). *Have to, should.*

p29[7] ye m. be born again.

p30[14] m. the Son of Man be lifted up.

p34[26] m. worship in spirit and truth.

p111[16] other sheep I have, them also I m. bring.

p132[25] all I have told you m. come to pass.

p149[37] all that is written m. be accomplished.

p167[43] all things m. be fulfilled.

Mustard. *Herb of the Brassica family.*

p59[30] kingdom of heaven is like a grain of a m. seed.

p89[20] if ye have faith as a grain of a m. seed.

p126[6] if ye have faith as a grain of a m. seed.

Muzzle. *Prevent from eating.*

p45[33] shall not m. the ox.

My. *Mine.*

p16[46] this is m. beloved Son.

p111[27] m. sheep hear m. voice.

p118[19] m. house shall be called the house of prayer?

p126[42] sit thou on m. right hand.

p138[8] wheresoever m. gospel shall be preached.

p149[40] not m. will, but thine be done.

p158[24] for m. vesture they did cast lots.

p160[39] m. God, m. God, why hast thou forsaken me?

Myrrh. *Gum of the rock rose.*

p9[11] gold, frankincense, and m.

p161[39] mixture of m. and aloes.

Myself. *I, me.*

p56[32] I bear witness of m.

p75[17] know of the doctrine, whether I speak of m.

p76[28] I am not come of m.

p78[14] though I bear record of m.

p78[28] I do nothing of m.

p80[54] if I honor m.

p111[18] lay down my life of m.

p142[3] receive you unto m.

p143[21] will manifest m. to him.

p166[38] it is I, m.

Mysteries. *Things known only to the initiated.*

p46[10] m. of the kingdom ye shall keep within yourselves.

p60[9] it is given to know the m. of the kingdom of heaven.

| N

Nails. *Metal fastener.*

p167[25] except I see the print of the n.

Naked. *Unclothed, exposed.*

p136[36] n. and ye clothed me.

p151[57] fled from them n.

p169[7] he was n. and cast himself into the sea.

Name. *Designate.*

p1[12] only to them who believe on his n.

p2[13] thou shalt call his n. John.

p3[31] and shall call his n. Jesus.

p4[48] I will magnify his holy n.

p5[62] his n. is John.

p6[8] and they called his n. Jesus.

p26[23] many believed on his n.

p39[4] be baptized in my n.

p43[10] Hallowed be thy n.

p47[32] prophesied in thy n.

p53[36] cometh in the n. of the Lord.

p57[44] I am come in my Father's n.

p63[6] declare thy n.

p90[36] cast out devils in thy n.

p93[20] gathered together in my n.

p110[3] calleth his sheep by name.

p111[25] works I do in my Father's n.

p130[6] many shall come in my n.

p141[24] believe on my n., for the remission of sins.

p143[13] ye shall ask in my n.

p147[6] I have manifest thy n.

p148[12] I have kept them in thy n.

p167[46] should be preached in his n.

p170[15] in the n. of the Father, the Son, and the Holy Ghost.

p171[31] ye might have life through his n.

Napkin. *Piece of cloth, handkerchief.*

p107[20] pound I have kept in a n.

p114[44] face was bound in a n.

p164[7] n. that was about his head.

Narrow. *Restricted.*

p47[23] strait is the gate and n. is the way.

Nathanael. *The apostle.*

p19[47] in whom is no guile!

Nation. *Country, people.*

p48[5] for he loveth our n.

p85[21] Syrophenecian by n.

p115[48] take away both our place and n.

p115[51] Jesus should die for that n.

p122[45] and given to a n. bringing fruits.

p132[30] for n. shall rise against n.

p154[2] found this man perverting the n.

Nay. *No, not merely.*

p24[9] doth he thank the servant, n.

p41[39] your communication be yea, yea, n., n.

Neck. *Connects head to body.*

p91[39] a millstone hanged about his n.

p92[20] fell upon his n. and kissed him.

Need (n). *Essential, necessary.*

p16[42] I have n. to be baptized of thee.

p45[27] Father will provide whatsoever things ye n. for food.

p91[11] little ones have no n. of repentance.

p153[66] what further n. of witnesses?

Need (v). Require, want.

p19[13] the whole n. not a physician.

p43[8] Father knoweth what ye have n.

p46[14] n. not that any man should teach us.

p116[2] the Lord hath n. of it.

Needed. *Need.*

p10[25] n. not that any man should teach him.

p26[25] n. not that any should testify.

Needful. *Need.*

p116[43] one thing is n.

Needle. *Narrow door, gateway too small for a camel.*

p101[24] easier for a camel to go through the eye of a n.

Needs. *Need.*

p33[6] I must n. go through Samaria.

p96[6] must n. that offences come.

p97[50] n. be that ye have salt in yourselves.

Neighbor. *Friend, fellow citizen.*

p101[19] love thy n. as thyself.

p125[28] to love his n. as himself.

p125[30] who is my n.?

Neither. *Not either.*

p10[25] n. could be taught.

p33[33] came n. eating or drinking.

p34[23] n. in this mountain nor yet in Jerusalem.

p45[29] n. do they reap.

p75[5] n. did his brethren believe in him.

p77[11] n. do I condemn thee.

p105[36] n. will they be persuaded.

p121[25] n. tell I you by what authority.

p127[10] n. go in yourselves.

Net. *Woven fabric, mesh.*

p18[4] let down your n. for a draught.

p18[6] and their n. brake.

p18[19] they left their n. and followed him.

p62[48] kingdom of heaven is like a n.

p169[6] cast the n. on the right side.

p169[8] dragging the n. of fishes.

p169[11] yet was not the n. broken.

Never. *Not ever.*

p34[16] whosoever drinketh shall n. thirst.

p47[33] then will I say ye n. knew me.

p72[35] cometh unto me shall n. hunger.

p77[46] n. man spake like this man.

p79[33] we were n. in bondage to any man.

p79[51] he shall n. see death.

p96[41] into that fire that shall n. be quenched.

New. *Recent, short time.*

p20[21] that which is n., the old is put away.

p20[22] n. cloth on an old garment.

p20[23] n. wine into old bottles.

p20[24] what n. doctrine is this?

p62[53] bring forth that which is n. and old.

p134[39] there shall be n. heavens.

p141[24] my blood of the n. testament.

p142[34] a n. commandment I give.

p162[41] in the garden a n. sepulcher.

p171[17] shall speak with n. tongues.

Next. *After that, subsequently.*

p16[29] the n. day John seeth Jesus.

p16[35] again the n. day after.

p162[64] the n. day that followed the day of preparation.

Nigh. *Near.*

p11[26] the hour of his ministry drew n.

p46[9] kingdom of heaven has come n. unto you.

p95[9] God is come n. unto you.

p133[41] summer is n. at hand.

Night. *Hours of darkness.*

p6[8] keeping watch over their flocks by n.

p8[37] fasting and prayers n. and day.

p9[14] departed into Egypt by n.

p18[5] have toiled all n. and taken nothing.

p24[44] Lord comes as a thief in the n.

p29[22] this n. thy soul shall be required of thee.

p29[2] Nicodemus came to Jesus by n.

p71[50] he came unto them in the fourth watch of the n.

p98[7] avenge his elect who cry day and n. unto him.

p113[10] if a man walk in the n. he stumbleth.

p139[30] Judas went out and it was n.

p162[65] lest his disciples come by n.

p163[12] say ye his disciples came by n. and stole him.

p169[3] that n. they caught nothing.

Ninth. *Hour of daylight, about three pm.*

p160[45] darkness over the earth until the n. hour.

p160[39] at the n. hour Jesus cried with a loud voice.

No. *Not any, in no respect or degree*

p3[33] of his kingdom there is n. end.

p22[34] there shall n. sign be given.

p27[4] have n. more they can do.

p34[19] I have n. husband.

p36[24] n. prophet is accepted in his own country.

p44[24] n. man can serve two masters.

p45[28] take n. thought for your life.

p45[39] take n. thought for the morrow.

p67[17] take ye n. thought what ye shall speak.

p73[44] n. man can come unto me.

p77[11] go, and sin n. more.

p99[62] n. man having put his hand to the plough.

p104[21] you have said in your hearts, there is n. God.

p115[23] n. man knoweth the Son is the Father.

p127[44] n. man was able to answer.

p130[5] take heed that n. man deceive you.

p133[43] day and hour n. one knoweth.

p155[38] I find in him n. fault.

p156[15] we have n. king but Caesar.

p157[9] Jesus gave him n. answer.

Nobleman. *A man of high rank.*

p36[48] n. whose son was sick at Capernaum.

p107[12] a n. went into a far country.

Noised. *Told, let know.*

p5[64] all these sayings were n. abroad.

p37[1] it was n. abroad that he was in the house.

Nothing. *Not anything.*

p3[37] for with God n. can be impossible.

p20[20] receive not your baptism, because it profiteth you n.

p27[2] there is n. covered that shall not be revealed.

p31[28] man can receive n., except it be given him from heaven.

p42[35] lend, hoping for n. again.

p55[19] the Son can do n. of himself.

p58[19] n. hid which shall not be manifest.

p83[15] n. without, shall defile a man.

p89[20] n. shall be impossible to you.

p110[33] if this man were not of God, he could do n.

p115[49] ye know n. at all.

p144[5] without me ye can do n.

p147[24] hitherto have ye ask n. in my name.

p151[20] in secret have I said n.

p157[20] have n. to do with that just man.

p157[26] see that ye do n. unto him.

p159[42] this man hath done n. amiss.

Numbered. *Counted.*

p27[7] hairs of you head are all n.

p158[33] he was n. with the transgressors.

| O

Oath. *Promise, vow.*

p5[72] the o. which he swear to our father Abraham.

p152[72] Peter denied with an o.

Obey. *Follow, comply.*

p20[24] even the unclean spirits do o. him.

p62[25] even the winds and the waters, they o. him.

p126[6] and it should o. you.

Observation. *Watching.*

p97[20] kingdom of God cometh not with o.

Observe. *Watch, heed, keep.*

p26[42] o. to do all things which I have commanded you.

p46[6] they teach but do not o.

p127[2] whatsoever they bid you o., and do.

p141[25] o. to do the things which ye have seen me do.

p170[19] teaching them to o. all things I have commanded you.

Observed. *Gave heed.*

p69[21] John feared God and o. to worship him.

Obtain. *Get, find.*

p39[9] blessed are the merciful; for they shall o. mercy.

Obtained. *Get, acquire.*

p136[29] everyone who hath o. other talents, shall be given.

p138[9] she hath o. a blessing from my Father.

Occupy. *Take care of, magnify.*

p107[13] he said unto them, o. till I come.

Occupieth. *Occupy.*

p108[25] unto everyone who o., shall be given.

Offence. *Stumbling block, sin.*

p86[24] thou art an o. unto me.

Offend. *Hurt, upset, affront.*

p41[32] if thy eye o. thee.

p41[33] if thy right hand o. thee.

p61[43] gather out of his kingdom all things that o.

p74[61] doth this o. you?

p91[39] whosoever shall o. one of these little ones.

p94[26] lest we should o. them.

p96[40] if thy brother o. thee.

Offended. *Offend.*

p32[23] blessed are they who shall not be o. in me.

p61[19] because of the word, he is o.

p66[5] they were o. at him.

p84[11] Pharisees were o.

p127[44] priests and elders were o.

p131[8] then shall many be o.

p139[31] Judas was o. because of his words.

p145[1] these things I have spoke that ye should not be o.

Offer. *Present, give.*

p7[24] to o. a sacrifice according to the law.

p37[39] show thyself to the priests, and o. for thy cleansing.

p40[26] and then come and o. thy gift.

p41[41] better to o. the other cheek.

p47[13] who asks an egg will o. him.

Officer. *Official, police man.*

p40[27] agree with thine adversary

lest the judge deliver thee to the o.

Oft. *Often.*

p93²¹ how o. shall my brother sin against me.

p141²¹ as o. as ye do this ye will remember this hour.

p141²⁴ as o. as ye do this ye will remember me.

Often. *Frequently.*

p53³⁵ how o. would I have gathered.

p129³⁷ how o. would I have gathered your children together.

Ofttimes. *Often times.*

p150² Jesus o. resorted thither with his disciples.

Oil. *Ointment, fuel, symbol useed to increase faith.*

p54⁴⁶ did not anoint my head with o.

p70³¹ anoint with o. many that were sick.

p103⁶ an hundred measures of o.

p125³⁵ bound up his wounds, pouring in o. and wine.

p135³ took no o. for their lamps.

Ointment. *Oil, balm, perfume.*

p54³⁸ Mary anointed Jesus' feet with o.

p137⁴ Mary poured o. on Jesus' head

p137⁵ why was this waste of o. made?

Old. *Age, aged, from the past.*

p10¹⁶ Herod slew the children two years o. and under.

p10⁴² when Jesus was twelve years o.

p20²¹ new is come, the o. is put away.

p20²² piece of new cloth on an o. garment.

p20²³ new wine into o. bottles.

p29⁴ can a man be born when he is o.?

p62⁵³ scribe bringeth forth new and o.

p80⁵⁷ thou art not yet fifty years o.

p134⁴⁰ for the earth is becoming o.

p170¹⁸ when thou shalt be o. thou shalt stretch forth thy hands.

Once. *One time.*

p52²⁵ when o. the Lord is risen up.

One. *Single, individual.*

p11²⁹ voice of o. crying in the wilderness.

p12²⁷ there standeth o. among you.

p14²³ cometh o. mightier than I.

p20²¹ the Holy O. of God.

p44²⁴ hate the o., and love the other.

p48³⁷ taught them as o. having authority.

p68³⁸ give drink unto o. of these little ones.

p74⁷⁰ and o. of you is a devil?

p80⁵ in this place is o. greater than the temple.

p86¹⁵ Jeremais; or o. of the prophets.

p91³⁹ offend o. of these little ones.

p91¹⁰ joy over o. sinner who repenteth.

p99⁷ they two shall be o. flesh.

p105³⁶ neither will they be persuaded, though o. rose from the dead.

p111¹⁶ o. fold and o. shepherd.

p112³⁰ I and my Father are o.

p115⁵⁰ o. man should die for the people.

p120²² I also will ask you o. thing.

p127⁵ o. is your master.

p127⁶ o. is your creator.

p130⁶ shall not leave o. stone upon another.

p134³⁶ what I say unto o., I say unto all.

p137⁴¹ unto o. of the least of these thy brethren.

p139²¹ o. of you shall betray me.

p142³⁴ love o. another.

p148¹¹ that they may be o., as we are.

Only. *None other.*

p1¹² o. to them who believe on his name.

p13³⁶ we o. have power to bring seed unto Abraham.

p15¹⁰ him o. shalt thou serve.

p30¹⁶ for God so loved the world he gave his O. Begotten Son.

p38⁶ who can forgive sins but God o.?

p57⁴⁵ seek not the honor which cometh from God o.?

p90³⁵ receive me, receiveth not me o.

p115^{52} not for that nation o.

p133^{43} no man knoweth but my Father o.

p147^{3} they might know thee the o. true God.

Open (a). *Uncover.*

p19^{51} ye shall see heaven o.

p59^{34} I will o. my mouth in parables.

Open (v). *Unlock.*

p52^{25} Lord, Lord, o. unto us.

Openly. *Exposed.*

p43^{4} shall reward thee o.

p75^{10} Jesus at the feast, not o.

p115^{54} walked no more o. among the Jews.

p151^{20} I spake o. to the world.

Opportunity. *Appropriate time.*

p138^{12} Judas sought o. to betray Jesus.

Ordained. *Appoint, proclaim.*

p23^{13} he o. twelve apostles.

p145^{16} I have chosen you and o. you.

Order (n). *Command.*

p1^{8} in the o. of his priesthood.

Order (v). *Organized.*

p1^{1} to set forth in o. a declaration.

Ordinance. *Authoritative degree.*

p141^{24} as often as ye do this o., ye will remember me.

Other. *Another.*

p10^{25} he spake not as o. men.

p26^{43} and not leave the o. undone.

p41^{41} turn to him the o. cheek.

p44^{24} hate the one, and love the o.

p98^{11} I thank thee, I am not as o. men.

p110^{1} climbeth up some o. way.

p164^{3} Peter went forth with that o. disciple.

p171^{30} many o. signs did Jesus.

Others. *Other.*

p42^{49} what do ye more than o.?

p76^{41} o. said, this is the Christ.

p98^{9} trusted themselves and despised o.

p108^{9} o. said he is like him.

p155^{34} or did o. tell it thee of me?

p159^{45} he saved o.

Otherwise. *Or else.*

p42^{1} o. ye have no reward.

Ought. *Should.*

p26^{43} these o. ye to have done.

p28^{14} in the same hour what ye o. to say.

p56^{35} therefore you o. to receive his testimony.

p98^{1} men o. always to pray.

p140^{26} it o. not be so with you.

p157^{7} by our law he o. to die.

p166^{25} o. not Christ to have suffered.

Outer. *Without.*

p48^{12} cast out into o. darkness.

p123^{13} cast him away into o. darkness.

p136^{31} cast ye the unprofitable servant into o. darkness.

Outrun. *Ran faster.*

p164^{4} the other disciple did o. Peter.

Outside. *Exterior.*

p26^{40} make clean the o. of the cup.

p128^{23} that the o. may be clean also.

Outwardly. *From without.*

p128^{24} which appear beautiful o.

p128^{25} you also appear o. righteous.

Oven. *Furnace, heat.*

p45^{34} and tomorrow is cast into the o.

Over. *Above, beyond.*

p67^{20} ye shall not have gone o. the cities of Israel.

p135^{21} thou hast been faithful o. a few things.

p160^{45} darkness o. the earth.

Over against. *Opposite.*

p129^{47} Jesus sat o. the treasury.

p160^{44} centurion stood o. him.

p162^{63} Mary sitting o. the sepulcher.

Overcome. *Prevail, defeat.*

p131^{11} remaineth steadfast and is not o.

p132^{31} he that is not o. shall be saved.

p147^{33} I have o. the world.

Overshadowed. *Shadow, darken.*

p88^{4} a light cloud o. them.

Owed. *Indebted to.*

p54^{41} the one o. him five hundred

pence.

p93²⁴ him who o. ten thousand talents.

p94²⁸ servant which o. an hundred pence.

Own (n). *To oneself.*

p8³⁵ to the wounding of thine o. soul.

p9¹² they departed into their o. country another way.

p56³¹ I can of mine o. self do nothing.

p72³⁸ not to do mine o. will.

p75¹⁸ speaketh of himself seeketh his o. glory.

p77⁹ convicted by their o. conscience.

p79⁵⁰ I seek not mine o. glory.

p87²⁹ gain the whole world and lose his o. soul?

p147³² scattered every man to his o.

Own (v). *Possess.*

p1¹¹ and his o. received him not.

p102¹³ do what I want with my o.?

p110³ calleth his o. sheep by name.

Ox. *Cow.*

p45³³ shall not muzzle the o.

p49⁵ an o. fall into the pit.

p52¹⁵ loose an o. on the Sabbath.

Oxen. *Cattle.*

p25¹⁴ found in the temple those who sold o. and sheep.

p123⁴ I have prepared my o., and my fatlings.

| P

Pair. *Two.*

p7²⁴ a p. of turtledoves.

Palace. *Residence of a sovereign.*

p138³ assembled together at the p. of the high priest.

p152¹⁵ Jesus went into the p. of the high priest.

Palm. *Flat part of the hand.*

p152²² officer struck Jesus with the p. of his hand.

Palm tree. *Monocotyledonous tree.*

p117⁶ multitude spread branches of

p. trees.

Palsy. *Uncontrollable tremor, paralysis.*

p38⁴ let down a bed wherein the p. lay.

p38²³ healed those that had p.

Parable. *Comparison (see chronology for parables not listed here).*

p59³³ without a p. he spake not unto them.

Paradise. *Place of waiting after death for the righteous.*

p159⁴⁴ today thou shalt be with me in p.

Parcel. *Plot of land.*

p33⁷ p. of ground which Jacob gave to Joseph.

Parents. *Begets offspring.*

p10⁴¹ his p. went to Jerusalem every year.

p67¹⁸ children shall rise up against their p.

p108² who did sin, this man or his p.

p109²³ said his p., he is of age, ask him.

p131¹⁵ ye shall be betrayed both by p.

Part (n). *Portion.*

p87⁴² they shall not have p. in the resurrection.

p90³⁷ he that is not against us is on our p.

p116⁴³ Mary hath chosen that good p.

p140⁸ thou hast no p. with me.

p168⁸ witness unto the uttermost p. of the earth.

Part (v). *Divide.*

p158²³ every soldier a p. of his garment.

Partakers. *Participant.*

p129²⁷ not have been p. in the blood of the prophets.

Parted. *Divided.*

p158²⁴ they p. my raiment among them.

Partners. *Associate.*

p18⁷ beckoned to their p. in the other ship.

p18¹⁰ sons of Zebedee were p. with Peter.

Pass. *Go by, elapse.*

p40²⁰ heaven and earth must p. away.

p105³¹ they who would p. from hence to you.

p106³⁶ blind Bartimaeus hearing the multitude p. by.

p133³⁵ this generation shall not p. away.

p149³⁹ if possible the hour might p. from him.

Passing. *Going.*

p36³⁰ Jesus p. through the midst of them.

Passover. *Jewish feast.*

p25¹³ P. was at hand.

p70⁴ P., was nigh.

p116⁵⁵ P. was nigh at hand.

p116¹ six days before the P.

p137² ye know that after two days is the P.

p138¹³ when the P. must be killed.

p138⁸ go prepare us the P.

p139¹⁵ I have desired to eat this P. with you.

p154²⁸ but that they might eat the P.

p156³⁹ I should release unto you one at the P.

Pasture. *Source of strength.*

p110⁹ if any man enter in, he shall find p.

Patience. *Tolerance.*

p93²⁶ Lord, have p. with me.

p131¹⁸ in your p. possess ye your souls.

Pavement. *Judgment hall.*

p157¹³ in a place called the P.

Pay (n). *Earnings.*

p128²⁰ you p. tithe of mint.

Pay (v). *Recompense, compensate*

p54⁴² when he found they had nothing to p.

p93²⁵ as much as he had nothing to p.

p94²³ doth your master p. tribute?

Payment. *Give back.*

p93²⁵ servant to be sold and p. to be made.

Peace. *Calm, serenity.*

p5⁷⁸ guide our feet into the way of p.

p7¹⁴ on earth, p.; goodwill to men.

p54⁵⁰ thy faith hath saved thee; go in p.

p62²⁴ saith to the sea, p., be still.

p67¹¹ go into a house, let your p. come upon it.

p68³⁰ think not that I am come to send p. on earth.

p97⁵⁰ have p. one with another.

p144²⁷ p. I leave with you, my p.

p147³³ that in me ye might have p.

p153⁶² Jesus held his p.

p166¹⁹ p. be unto you.

Pence. *Denarii.*

p54⁴¹ owed him five hundred p.

p94²⁸ owed him a hundred p.

p137⁵ sold for more than three hundred p.

Penny. *Denarius.*

p102² laborers for a p. a day.

p102¹⁰ received every man a p.

People. *Human beings, citizens, nation, subjects.*

p2¹⁷ make ready a p. for the Lord.

p6⁴ save his p. from their sins.

p7¹⁰ good tidings shall be to all p.

p8³² the glory of thy p. Israel.

p31²⁷ receiveth all p. who come unto him.

p53¹⁶ God hath visited his p.

p64⁴¹ the p. received him.

p76³¹ many of the p. believed on him.

p76⁴³ there was a division among the p.

p115⁵⁰ one man should die for the p.

p127⁴⁴ common p. heard him gladly.

p131¹⁶ great distress upon this p.

p134⁵⁶ wicked to be cut off from among the p.

p138² chief Priests feared the p.

Perceive. *Recognize.*

p34²¹ I p. thou art a prophet.

p60¹³ ye shall see and not p.

p117¹⁹ p. how ye prevail nothing.

Perdition. *Destruction.*

p148¹² none is lost but the son of p.

Perfect. *Complete, faultless.*

p42⁵⁰ be p. even as your Father who is in heaven.

p101²¹ if thou wilt be p.

p148²³ that they may be p. in one.

Perfection. *Completeness, maturity.*

p58⁶ bring no fruit to p.

Perform. *Do, carry out.*

p5⁷¹ to p. the mercy promised to our fathers.

p41³⁷ p. unto the Lord thine oaths.

Perish. *Die, be lost.*

p30¹⁶ believeth on him should not p.

p41³² profitable one of thy member should p.

p51³ except you repent, you shall p.

p53³³ for it cannot be that a prophet p. out of Jerusalem.

p91¹⁴ one of these little ones should p.

p111²⁸ I give unto them eternal life and they shall never p.

p115⁵⁰ the whole nation should p. not.

p151⁵⁰ all they that take the sword shall p. with the sword.

Perplexity. *Confusion, chaos.*

p132²⁵ p. of the sea and waves.

Persecute. *Harass, hunt.*

p27⁵⁰ some they shall slay and p.

p39¹³ blessed are ye when men shall p. you.

p44²⁵ the world will hate you and p. you.

p55¹⁶ the Jews did p. Jesus.

p67²⁰ when they p. you in one city.

Persecuted. *Persecute.*

p39¹² blessed are they that are p. for my name's sake.

p39¹⁴ so p. they the prophets.

p145²⁰ if they have p. me they will persecute you.

Persecution. *Persecute.*

p61¹⁹ when tribulation of p. ariseth because of the word.

Person. *Appearance, individual.*

p124¹⁶ thou regardest not the p. of men.

p157²⁶ I am innocent of this just p.

Persuade. *Influence.*

p163¹³ we will p. the governor.

Persuaded. *Convince.*

p105³⁶ neither will they be p. though one rose from the dead.

Pervert. *Misrepresent, change.*

p104²¹ you p. the right way.

Peter. *The apostle.*

p18⁸ depart from me; O Lord.

p19⁴⁴ Bethsaida, the city of Peter.

p23¹⁴ ordained as one of the twelve apostles.

p65²⁹ no man to follow him, save P., James, and John.

p71²⁵ P. walked on water.

p74⁶⁸ affirms his faith in Jesus.

p86¹⁷ bears testimony of Jesus.

p86²³ began to rebuke the Lord.

p87¹ present at the transfiguration.

p93²¹ asks how often he should forgive his brother?

p138⁸ P. and John sent to prepare the Passover super.

p140⁶ does not want Jesus to wash his feet.

p142³⁷ I will lay down my life for thy sake.

p149³⁸ is present in Gethsemane.

p151¹⁰ cut off the high priest's servants right ear.

p152⁷² denies knowing the Lord.

p153⁶² went out and wept bitterly.

p164⁴ runs to the sepulcher.

p166¹⁹ sees the resurrected Lord.

p169³ goes fishing.

p169¹⁵ Jesus sayeth to him, lovest thou me?

Pharisee. *Jewish clergyman.*

p26³⁸ P. sought Jesus to dine with him.

p54³⁹ Simon the P. spake within himself.

p98¹⁰ parable of the P. and the publican.

Pharisees. *Pharisee.*

p12³³ John calls P. to repentance.

p26[40] Jesus calls P. to repentance.

p32[30] P. rejected the counsel of God.

p40[22] except your righteousness exceed the P.

p52[31] P. warn Jesus of Herod.

p81[7] P. took counsel to destroy Jesus.

p85[7] beware of the leaven of the P.

p120[42] because of the P. they did not confess Jesus.

p126[40] Jesus asks the P. a question.

p127[10] P., hypocrites!

Philip. *The apostle.*

p19[45] findeth Nathanael.

p23[14] chosen to be an apostle.

p70[5] P., whence shall we buy bread?

p118[21] Greeks came to P.

p143[8] Lord, show us the father.

p143[9] hast thou not known me, P.?

Physician. *Doctor.*

p19[13] the whole need not a p.

p36[23] p., heal thyself.

Piece. *Part, portion.*

p20[22] a p. of new cloth on an old garment.

p91[9] found the p. which was lost.

p94[26] p. of money in the fishes mouth.

p167[41] gave Jesus a p. of broiled fish

Pierce. *Stab, puncture.*

p8[35] a spear shall p. through him.

Pierced. *Pierce.*

p161[34] soldier with a spear p. his side.

p161[37] look upon him whom they p.

Pilate. *Full name Pontius Pilate.*

p11[1] P. governor of Judea.

p51[1] mingled the blood of the Galileans with their sacrifices.

p154[28] Jesus is brought before P. to be judged the first time.

p156[13] Jesus is brought before P. a second time.

p157[12] wanted to release Jesus.

p157[26] washed his hands before the multitude.

p159[19] wrote a title, and put it upon the cross.

p162[64] Jews asked P. for a watch to guard the sepulcher.

Pillow. *Cushion.*

p62[23] Jesus asleep on a p. in the ship.

Pineth. *Lose vigor, health.*

p89[15] gnasheth his teeth, and p. away.

Pinnacle. *Summit, peak.*

p15[5] Spirit setteth Jesus on the p. of the temple.

Piped. *Played music.*

p32[32] have p. for you and ye have not danced.

Pit. *Well, hole.*

p49[5] have an ox fall into a p.

p81[9] a sheep fall into a p.

Pitcher. *Container.*

p138[10] meet a man bearing a p. of water.

Pity. *Compassion, sympathy.*

p94[32] thy fellow servant, even as I had p. on thee?

Place (n). *Location, rank, status.*

p9[4] where is the p. that Christ should be born?

p12[28] whose p. I am not able to fill.

p19[10] sitting at the p. where they receive tribute.

p23[31] departed into a solitary p.

p35[17] he found the p. where it was written.

p80[5] in this p. is one greater than the temple.

p89[20] say to this mountain, remove to yonder p.

p115[48] Romans shall come and take away our p.

p131[12] stand ye in the holy p.

p142[2] I go and prepare a p. for you.

Place (v). *Acceptance, Identify.*

p79[37] my word hath no p. in you.

Plague. *Disease.*

p64[26] go in peace and be whole of thy p.

Plainly. *Understandably, clearly.*

p111[24] if thou be the Christ, tell us p.

p113^{14} Jesus said p., Lazarus is dead.

p147^{25} shall show you p. of the Father.

p147^{29} Lo, now speakest thou p.

Plant. *Vine, weed.*

p84^{12} every p. which my Father hath not planted.

Platter. *Plate.*

p26^{40} clean the outside of the p.

p128^{22} make clean the outside of the p.

Please. *Delight, make happy.*

p78^{29} do those things that p. the Father.

Pleasure. *Happiness, satisfaction.*

p45^{35} your Father's p. to give you the kingdom.

Plenteous. *Abundant, plentiful.*

p66^{43} the harvest truly is p.

Plough. *Tilling the earth.*

p99^{62} having put his hand to the p. and looking back.

Plowing. *Plow.*

p23^{7} having a servant p., or feeding cattle.

Pluck. *Pull, snatch, remove.*

p41^{32} eye offend thee, p. it out.

p96^{46} transgressor offend thee, p. him out.

p111^{28} neither shall any man p. them out of my hand.

p112^{29} no man is able to p. them out of my Father's hand.

Pondered. *Consider, weigh.*

p3^{29} Mary p. in her mind.

p7^{19} Mary p. them in her heart.

Poor. *Needy, humble.*

p32^{22} to the p. the gospel is preached.

p39^{5} blessed are the p. in spirit.

p49^{13} thou makest a feast, call the p.

p101^{21} sell that thou hast and give to the p.

p107^{8} the half of my goods I give to the p.

p129^{48} came a certain p. widow.

p137^{5} might have been sold and given to the p.

Porch. *Covered entrance, vestibule.*

p111^{23} Jesus walked in Solomon's p.

p152^{59} Peter went out into the p.

Portion. *Part, share.*

p13^{19} appointed every man his p.

p24^{51} servant who watcheth to impart his p. of meat in due season.

p25^{55} will appoint his p. with the unbelievers.

p91^{12} give me the p. of goods which falleth to me.

p134^{55} appoint his p. with the hypocrites.

Possess. *Acquire.*

p131^{18} in your patience p. your souls.

Possessed. *Having hold on.*

p21^{29} brought unto Jesus those p. with devils.

p63^{29} there met him a man p. with devils.

p65^{38} a dumb man p. with a devil.

Possible. *Able, feasible.*

p89^{20} this is p. to him that believeth.

p101^{26} with God all things are p.

p132^{23} if p., shall deceive the very elect.

p149^{39} if p. the hour might pass from him.

p149^{40} Father, all things are p. unto thee.

Potters. *Maker of clay pots.*

p154^{8} bought with them the p. field.

Pound. *Sum of money, unit of measurement.*

p107^{16} thy p. hath gained ten pounds

p107^{20} thy p. which I have kept in a napkin.

p161^{39} myrrh and aloes, about an hundred p. weight.

Powder. *Dust.*

p122^{46} stone shall fall, it will grind him to p.

Power. *Might, strength, ability, authority.*

p1^{12} gave he p. to become the sons of

God.

p2^{17} in the spirit and p. of Elias.

p14^{10} for it is a day of p.

p17^{13} returned in the p. of the spirit.

p21^{23} unto them is given p. over devils.

p23^{13} to have p. to heal sicknesses.

p27^{5} who hath p. to cast into hell.

p38^{23} does it require more p. to forgive sins?

p38^{9} we never saw the p. of God after this manner.

p43^{15} thine is the kingdom and the p.

p66^{1} p. over unclean spirits.

p115^{20} give you p. over serpents.

p124^{28} they did not understand the p. of God.

p144^{30} prince of darkness hath no p. over me.

p153^{65} sitting on the right hand of p.

p157^{10} I have p. to crucify thee.

p168^{8} ye shall receive p., after the Holy Ghost is come upon you.

p170^{17} all p. is given unto me in heaven.

Praise. *Give thanks, glorify.*

p106^{43} disciples gave p. unto God.

p109^{24} give God the p.

p118^{14} out of the mouths of babes thou hast perfected p.?

p120^{43} love the p. of men more than the p. of God.

Pray. *Call upon, ask God.*

p42^{46} p. for them which despitefully use you.

p43^{5} love to p. standing in the synagogues.

p43^{6} p. to thy Father in secret.

p66^{44} p. ye the Lord of the harvest.

p71^{48} Jesus departed into a mountain to p.

p86^{18} he went alone with his disciples to p.

p98^{1} men ought always to p.

p98^{10} two men went to the temple to p.

p126^{26} when ye p., believe that ye

receive.

p131^{17} p. that your flight not be in winter.

p134^{36} p. always.

p147^{26} I will p. the Father for you.

p148^{9} I p. not for the world.

p149^{37} sit ye here while I p.

p150^{42} p. lest ye enter into temptation.

p151^{51} thinkest I cannot now p. to my Father and he shall give me.

Prayer. *Pray.*

p43^{10} Lord's p.

p89^{21} goeth not out but by p. and fasting.

p118^{19} my house shall be called the house of p.?

Preach. *Proclaim.*

p23^{13} apostles sent forth to p.

p35^{18} anointed me to p. the gospel.

p35^{18} p. deliverance to the captives.

p35^{19} p. the acceptable year of the Lord.

p36^{16} Jesus began to p.

p67^{6} p., saying the kingdom of heaven is at hand.

p68^{24} tell you in darkness, p. ye in the light.

p99^{60} go and p. the kingdom of God.

p170^{14} p. the gospel to every creature.

Preaching. *Preach.*

p11^{27} John p. in the wilderness.

p13^{34} ye receive not the p. of John.

p13^{6} make possible the p. unto the Gentiles.

p22^{35} repented at the p. of Jonas.

p38^{22} Jesus went about p. the gospel

p121^{34} the p. of John shall condemn you.

Precept. *Rule, law.*

p99^{5} for the hardness of your hearts Moses wrote you this p.

Precious. *Rare, costly.*

p137^{4} box of spikenard, very p.

Preferred. *Give precedence.*

p12^{28} who coming after me is p. before me.

p16[30] cometh a man who is p. before me.

Preferring. *Preferred.*

p33[4] for an example, p. one another.

Prepare. *Make ready.*

p11[29] p. ye the way of the Lord.

p32[27] my messenger who shall p. thy way before thee.

p88[13] Elias, whom I sent to p. the way before me.

p138[8] go and p. the Passover.

p142[2] I go and p. a place for you.

Prepared. *Prepare.*

p2[17] make ready a people p. for the Lord.

p106[23] for whom it is p. of my Father.

p123[4] I have p. my oxen.

p136[35] inherit the kingdom p. from the foundation of the world.

p137[42] p. for the devil and his angels.

p162[57] they p. spices and ointments.

Presence. *Being there, in sight of.*

p2[19] I am Gabriel, who stand in the p. of God.

p52[26] have we not drunk in thy p.

p91[10] joy in the p. of the angels.

p171[30] other signs did Jesus in the p. of his disciples.

Present (a). *In attendance.*

p51[1] there were p. some who spake of the Galileans.

p143[25] things I have spoken unto you being yet p. with you.

Present (v). *Give.*

p7[22] brought Jesus to Jerusalem to p. him to the Lord.

Presently. *Immediately.*

p151[51] he shall p. give me twelve legions of angels.

Press. *Multitude, crowd.*

p38[4] could not come unto him for the p.

p64[21] she came in the p. behind.

p106[3] Zacchaeus could not see Jesus for the p.

Prevail. *Triumph, overcome.*

p86[19] gates of hell shall not p.

p117[19] perceive how ye p. nothing?

p157[26] Pilate saw that he could p. nothing.

Price. *Cost, value, worth.*

p62[47] one pearl of great p.

p154[7] because it is the p. of blood.

p154[9] the p. of him that was valued.

Priest. *Officer in the priesthood.*

p1[5] a p. named Zacharias.

p115[49] Caiaphas, being the high p.

p125[32] there came down a p. that way.

p138[3] assembled to the palace of the high p.

p151[50] healed the servant of the high p.

p151[19] high p. asked Jesus of his disciples.

p152[56] led Jesus away to the high p.

p152[15] disciple was known unto the high p.

p153[66] the high p. rent his clothes.

Prince. *Monarch.*

p9[6] in Bethlehem shall be born a p.

p21[20] Beelzebub p. of the devils.

p119[31] p. of this world shall be cast out.

p144[30] p. of darkness cometh.

p146[11] p. of this world is judged.

Print. *Mark, wound.*

p167[25] except I see the p. of the nails.

Prison. *Jail.*

p31[27] John was cast into p.

p137[37] in prison, and ye came unto me.

Privately. *Alone, confidentially.*

p70[33] they departed by ship p.

p89[25] his disciples asked him p.

p115[24] turned to his disciples and said p.

p130[7] disciples came to him p.

Proceed. *Ensue, advance.*

p84[17] those things which p. out of the mouth.

p84[18] out of the heart p. evil thoughts.

Proclaimed. *Make known.*

p27[3] shall be p. upon the house tops.

Profane. *Make common.*

p80[4] priests p. the Sabbath.

Profitable. *Gain or profit.*

p41³² p. one of thy members should perish.

Profited. *Profitable.*

p83¹³ by whatsoever thou mightest be p. by me.

p87²⁹ for what is a man p., if he gain.

Profiteth. *Profitable.*

p20²⁰ your baptism p. you nothing.

p74⁶³ the flesh p. nothing.

Promise. *Oath, assurance.*

p168⁴ wait for the p. of the Father.

p168⁴⁸ I send you the p. of my Father.

Promised. *Promise.*

p5⁷¹ perform the mercy p. to our fathers.

p34²⁶ unto such God p. his Spirit.

p76³⁹ the Holy Ghost was p. to them.

Prophecy. *Foretell, prediction.*

p60¹³ in them is fulfilled the p. of Esaias.

p134⁵⁶ end of the wicked according to the p. of Moses.

Prophesied. *Prophecy.*

p5⁶⁶ Zacharias p. of John's mission.

p32¹³ p. the violent shall have no power.

p32¹⁴ as many as have p. have foretold of these days.

p47³² have we not p. in thy name.

p83⁷ well hath Isaiah p. of you hypocrites.

p115⁵¹ Caiaphas, being high priest p.

Prophesy. *Prophecy.*

p153⁷¹ p., who smote thee?

Prophet. *Seer, revelator.*

p5⁷⁵ John to be called the p. of the highest.

p12²² art thou that p.?

p32²⁶ what came ye out to see, a p.?

p32²⁸ not a greater p. than John.

p34²¹ I perceive that thou art a p.

p36²⁴ no p. is accepted in his own country.

p53³³ cannot be that a p. perish out of Jerusalem.

p53¹⁶ a great p. is risen among us.

p54³⁹ if he were a p. he would have known.

p68³⁶ receive a p., in the name of a p.

p71¹⁴ this is of a truth that p.

p77⁵² out of Galilee ariseth no p.

p109¹⁷ he said, he is a p.

p117⁹ Jesus of Nazareth, the p. of Galilee.

p122⁴⁹ learned the multitude took Jesus as a p.

p165¹⁸ Jesus who was a p. mighty in deed.

Prophetess. *Female prophet.*

p8³⁶ Anna, a p.

Proselyte. *Convert, believer.*

p128¹² compass land and sea to make one p.

Proud. *Exultant, haughty.*

p4⁵⁰ he hath scattered the p.

Prove. *Show.*

p70⁶ this he said to p. him.

Proverb. *Saying, adage.*

p147²⁹ now speakest thou no p.

Provide. *Supply.*

p23³⁶ p. not for yourselves.

p45²⁷ your heavenly Father will p.

p45³⁴ how much more will he not p. for you.

p67⁸ p. neither gold nor silver.

p70⁹ we can p. no more food.

Provoke. *Incite.*

p27⁵⁴ endeavoring to p. Jesus.

Prudent. *Wise, practical.*

p95²⁷ hid things from the wise and p.

Psalms. *Songs of praise.*

p126⁴² David saith in the book of P.

p167⁴³ prophets and the P. concerning me.

Publican. *Tax collector.*

p66² Matthew the p.

p93¹⁷ be unto you as a heathen and a p.

p98¹⁰ Pharisee and the p.

Public. *Community.*

p6² not willing to make a p. example

Publish. *Tell abroad.*
p37^{40} he went out and began to p. it much.
p64^{17} he went out and began to p. in Decapolis.

Pull. *Take down, take out.*
p29^{20} I will p. down my barns.
p46^{5} let me p. out the mote.
p49^{5} p. an ox out on the Sabbath.

Punishment. *Penalty.*
p127^{11} ye shall receive the greater p.
p137^{47} these shall go into everlasting p.

Pure. *Clean, refined.*
p39^{10} the p. in heart shall see God.

Purge. *Cleanse, purify.*
p14^{24} he will thoroughly p. his floor.

Purgeth. *Purge.*
p144^{2} every branch which beareth fruit, he p. it.

Purify. *Cleanse.*
p116^{55} before the Passover, to p. themselves.

Purifying. *Curing.*
p17^{6} after the manner of the p. of the Jews.

Purple. *Color to distinguish wealth or royalty.*
p104^{24} a certain rich man clothed in p.
p156^{20} they clothed Jesus in p.
p156^{5} wearing a p. robe.
p158^{23} they took off the p. from him.

Purse. *Used to carry money.*
p95^{4} neither carry p. nor scrip.
p149^{35} I sent you without p. and scrip.
p149^{36} he who hath a p. let him take it.

| Q

Quake. *Shake.*
p160^{55} the earth did q.

Quarrel. *Contention argument.*
p69^{20} Herodias had a q. against John.

Quarter. *Border, land.*
p37^{40} they came to him from every q.

Queen. *Princess, female monarch.*

p22^{36} the q. of the south shall rise up in the day of judgment.

Quench. *Extinguish, subdue.*
p57^{16} smoking flax shall he not q.

Quenched. *Quench.*
p96^{41} into the fire that shall never be q.
p96^{48} where the fire is not q.

Question. *Ask, examine.*
p126^{40} durst not ask him any q. at all.

Questioned (n). *Inquiry.*
p20^{24} insomuch they q. among themselves.

Questioned (v). *Question.*
p89^{14} what q. ye them?
p155^{9} then he q. him in many words.

Questioning (n). *Inquiry.*
p88^{8} q. one with another what the rising of the dead should mean.

Questioning (v). *Ask, examine.*
p88^{12} scribes q. the disciples.

Questions (n). *Questioned.*
p11^{46} doctors asking Jesus q.
p127^{44} durst any man ask him any more q.
p155^{15} he answered him not to his q.

Quickeneth. *Resurrect.*
p56^{21} the Son q. whom he will.
p74^{63} the spirit q. the flesh.

Quickly. *Swiftly.*
p40^{27} agree with thine adversary q.
p103^{6} sit down q. and write.
p114^{29} Mary arose q. and came to him.
p139^{27} what thou doest, do q.
p163^{6} they departed q. from the sepulcher.

| R

Rabbi. *Teacher, master.*
p17^{38} R., where dwellest thou?
p19^{49} R., thou art the Son of God.
p29^{2} R., we know thou art a teacher come from God.
p127^{4} to be called of men R.,R.
p127^{5} be not ye called R.

Raca. *Devoid of intelligence.*

p40²⁴ shall say to his brother, r.

Railed. *Revile, abusive language.*

p159⁴⁰ one of the malefactors r. on him.

Raiment. *Clothing.*

p32²⁴ a man clothed in soft r.?

p45²⁷ your heavenly Father will provide r.

p44²⁸ body more than r.?

p45³² why take ye thought for r.?

p87¹ his r. white as light.

p158²⁴ they parted my r. among them.

p163³ their r. white as snow.

Rain. *Water drops.*

p42⁴⁷ sendeth r. on the just and on the unjust.

Raise. *Bring up, cause.*

p13³⁶ God is able of these stones to r. up children.

p25¹⁹ in three days I will r. it up.

p67⁷ cleanse the lepers, r. the dead.

p73⁴⁰ I will r. him up in the resurrection of the just.

Ransom. *Deliver, free.*

p106²⁸ gave his life a r. for many.

p141²¹ my body which I give a r.

Rather. *Instead, sooner.*

p26⁴² ye would r. give alms of such things as ye have.

p30¹⁹ love darkness r. than light.

p67⁵ but r. go to the lost sheep.

p68²⁵ r. fear him who is able to destroy.

Ravening. *Greedy, predatory.*

p26⁴⁰ Pharisees full of r.

p47²⁴ false prophets who are r. wolves.

Read. *Verbalize written words.*

p35¹⁶ Jesus stood up to r.

p80⁴ have ye not r. in the law.

p118¹⁴ have ye never r. the scriptures.

p124³⁰ have ye not r. that which was spoken of by God.

p159²⁰ this title r. many of the Jews.

Ready. *Prepare, willing.*

p2¹⁷ to make r. a people prepared for the Lord.

p75⁶ your time is always r.

p134⁵¹ be ye also r.

p142³³ I am r. to go to prison and to die.

Reap. *Gather.*

p35⁴⁰ I sent you to r.

p45²⁹ fowls do not sow neither do they r.

p136²⁶ thou knewest that I r. where I sowed not.

Reaping. *Reap.*

p108²² r. that I did not sow.

p136²⁴ r. where thou hast not sown.

Rear. *Cause to rise.*

p26²⁰ wilt thou r. up the temple in three days?

Reason (n). *Cause, rationale.*

p116¹¹ by r. of him many of the Jews went away.

Reason (v). *Analyze, deduce.*

p38⁷ why r. ye these things in your hearts?

p85⁹ why r. ye these things among yourselves.

Reasoned. *Reason.*

p28¹¹ they r. he knoweth our hearts.

p121²⁴ they r. if we say from heaven.

p165¹⁴ communed together, and r.

Rebuke (n). *Censure, reprimand.*

p118³⁸ Master, r. thy disciples.

Rebuke (v). *Reprove, admonish.*

p86²³ Peter began to r. Jesus.

p93¹⁵ if thy brother trespass against thee, r. him.

Rebuked. *Rebuke.*

p20²² Jesus r. the unclean spirit.

p62²⁴ Jesus r. the wind.

p89²² Jesus r. the foul spirit.

p94²⁴ Jesus r. Peter.

p99⁵⁵ Jesus r. James and John.

p100¹¹ disciples r. those that brought the little children.

p149³⁸ Jesus r. Peter, James, and John.

p159⁴¹ one of the malefactors r. the other.

Receive. *Accept, obtain.*

p13³⁴ ye r. not the preaching.

p20[18] why will ye not r. us with our baptism.

p30[11] and ye r. not our witness.

p31[28] a man can r. nothing, except it be given him from heaven.

p31[32] few men r. his testimony.

p31[36] he who believeth on the Son, shall r. of his fullness.

p32[15] if ye will r. it, this was Elias.

p39[4] r. a remission of their sins.

p42[34] lend to them to whom ye hope to r.

p46[11] world cannot r. what ye are not able to bear.

p57[42] I r. not honor from men.

p57[44] I came down in my Father's name, and ye r. me not.

p58[20] continue to r., more shall be given.

p68[36] shall r. a prophet's reward.

p90[35] r. me, receiveth the Father.

p95[7] into whatsoever house they r. you.

p96[45] believing that ye shall r.

p100[11] all cannot r. this saying.

p100[13] shall not r. the kingdom of God as a little child, shall not enter in.

p142[3] and r. you unto myself.

p147[24] ask, and ye shall r.

p167[22] r. ye the Holy Ghost.

Received. *Receive.*

p1[11] and his own r. him not.

p1[12] as many as r. him, gave he power.

p20[19] if ye had kept the law ye would have r. me.

p67[7] freely ye have r., freely give.

p111[18] this commandment I have r. of my Father.

p168[50] a cloud r. him out of their sight.

Receiving. *Receive.*

p13[19] the custom of their law in r. money.

Recompense (n). *Reward.*

p53[36] a just r. for all your sins.

Recompense (v). *Compensate, repay.*

p49[12] lest they bid thee and a r. be made.

p50[14] thou shalt be blessed for they cannot r. thee.

Reconciled. *Put right, resolve.*

p40[26] first be r. to thy brother, then offer thy gift.

Record. *Testimony, witness.*

p12[20] this is the r. of John.

p16[30] John bear r. of him unto the people.

p73[44] the Father beareth r. of him.

p78[13] thou bearest r. of thyself.

p117[17] people beareth r. Lazarus was raised from the dead.

p141[25] I give a commandment that ye shall bear r. of me.

p161[35] John the apostle bear r.

Recover. *Get well.*

p171[19] lay hands on the sick and they shall r.

Red. *color.*

p84[2] the sky is r. and lowering.

Redeemed. *Purchase, free, loose.*

p5[67] he hath r. his people.

p104[20] Father sent me that ye might all be r.?

p165[20] trusted it had been he who should have r. Israel.

Redemption. *Redeemed.*

p8[38] to all those who looked for r. in Jerusalem.

Reed. *Various tall grass, stalk.*

p32[24] a r. shaken in the wind.

p57[16] a bruised r. shall he not break.

p156[22] they smote him on the head with a r.

Regard. *Look upon, respect.*

p98[4] fear not God nor r. man.

Region. *Place, area.*

p36[15] unto them that sat in the r. and shadow of death.

p53[17] rumor spread through the r. round about.

Reign. *Be king, rule.*

p3[33] Jesus to r. over the house of Jacob

forever.

p11[1] fifteenth year of the r. of Caesar.

p107[14] we will not have this man to r. over us.

p123[56] Lord should descend out of heaven to r. in his vineyard.

Reject. *Refuse.*

p69[27] Herod would not r. her.

p83[9] altogether ye r. the commandment of God.

p122[51] those wicked ones r. me.

Rejoice. *Joy, be glad.*

p2[14] many shall r. at his birth.

p35[38] he who reapeth and he who soweth may r. together.

p56[36] ye were willing to r. for a season.

p115[21] r. not that the spirits are subject unto you.

p144[28] if ye loved me ye would r.

p146[20] ye shall lament but the world shall r.

p147[22] I shall see you again and your heart shall r.

Rejoiceth. *Rejoice.*

p4[46] my spirit r. in God my Savior.

p31[30] friend of the bridegroom r. greatly.

p91[13] r. more over that which was lost.

Rejoicing. *Rejoice.*

p91[5] layeth the sheep on his shoulders, r.

Release. *Let go, free.*

p156[16] chastise him, and r. him.

p156[39] a custom to r. one at Passover.

p157[10] and have power to r. thee?

p157[12] Pilate sought to r. him.

Remain. *Are left, stay.*

p71[12] gather up the fragments that r.

p95[7] whatsoever house they receive you, r. eating and drinking.

p144[11] that my joy might r. in you.

p145[16] that your fruit should r.

p161[31] that the bodies should not r. upon the cross.

Remember. *Recall, take into account.*

p5[71] and to r. his holy covenant.

p40[25] r. that thy brother hath aught against thee.

p68[21] r. the disciple is not above his master.

p141[21] ye will r. this hour that I was with you.

p145[20] r. the servant is not greater than his lord.

p145[4] ye may r. that I told you of them.

p159[43] r. me when thou comest into thy kingdom.

p162[64] we r. that that deceiver said.

p163[5] r. how he spake unto you when he was in Galilee.

Remembered. *Remember.*

p25[17] disciples r. that it was written.

p103[34] neither r. they the things which were spoken.

p117[16] r. that these things were written of him.

p153[61] Peter r. the word of the Lord.

p163[7] and they r. his words.

Remembrance. *Remember.*

p4[53] helped his servant Israel in r. of mercy.

p126[23] Peter calling to r. the fig tree.

p138[8] Mary has done, shall be in r.

p141[21] do in r. of my body.

p141[24] do in r. of my blood.

p143[26] Holy Ghost shall bring all things to your r.

Remission. *Release from penalty and guilt.*

p5[76] baptism for the r. of their sins.

p39[4] visited by the Holy Ghost for a r. of their sins.

p141[24] believe on my name for a r. of their sins.

p167[46] repentance and r. of sins should be preached.

Remit. *Remission.*

p167[23] whosoever sins ye r.

Remove. *Relocate.*

p89[20] say to this mountain, r. to yonder place.

Rend. *Split, rip.*

p46[11] lest they turn again and r. you.

p158[24] let us not r. it, but cast lots for it.

Rent. *Tear, split, rip, rendered.*

p20[22] new cloth, the r. is made worse.

p89[23] the deaf spirit r. him sore.

p153[66] the high priest r. his clothes.

p160[55] the veil of the temple was r. in twain.

p162[2] earth quake and the rocks r.

Repay. *Settle up.*

p125[36] when I come again I will r. thee.

Repent. *Turn from sin.*

p11[28] r. ye; for the kingdom of heaven is at hand.

p46[9] r., for the kingdom is nigh unto you.

p47[22] r., and enter in at the strait gate.

p51[3] except ye r., ye shall likewise perish.

p93[15] rebuke him; and if he r., forgive him.

p93[4] r. seven times in a day, you shall forgive him.

p105[35] if one went from the dead, they will r.

p121[33] cannot believe me, except he first r.

Repentance. *Repent.*

p13[35] bring forth fruits meet for r.

p19[14] I am come to call sinners to r.

p91[11] little ones have no need of r.

p167[46] r. should be preached.

Repetitions. *Repeat.*

p43[7] use not vain r., as the hypocrites do.

Report. *Account, testimony.*

p119[38] who hath believed our r.?

Reproach. *Shame, insult.*

p3[25] take away my r. among men.

Reproachest. *Blame, chide, revile.*

p26[46] Master, thus saying, r. us also.

Reprove. *Accuse, rebuke.*

p146[8] he will r. the world of sin.

Reproved. *Reprove.*

p30[20] neither cometh to the light, lest

his deeds should be r.

p31[26] Herod, being r. of John.

Require. *Need, call for.*

p38[23] does it r. more power to forgive sins.

Required. *Require.*

p25[57] to whom much is given, much is r.

p27[52] shall be r. of this generation.

p29[22] this night thy soul shall be r.

Resist. *Fight back, defend.*

p41[41] I say unto you, r. not evil.

p130[13] your adversaries shall not be able to gainsay nor r.

Rest (n). *Repose, cease.*

p80[26] Sabbath was given as a day of r.

p95[29] come unto me and I will give you r.

p95[6] your peace shall r. upon it.

Rest (v). *relax, set down, sleep.*

p70[32] come to a solitary place, and r.

p150[46] take r.; it is enough.

Restore. *Re-establish, bring back.*

p12[22] I am not that Elias who was come to r. all things.

p88[10] Elias shall come, and r. all things.

p88[14] another who should come and r. all things.

p107[8] if I have taken by unjust means, I r. fourfold.

p168[6] wilt thou r. again the kingdom to Israel?

Resurrection. *Reuniting sprit and body.*

p13[7] to bring to pass the r. of the dead.

p50[14] thou shalt be resurrected at the r. of the just.

p56[29] they who have done evil in the r. of the unjust.

p73[40] everyone believeth on the Son, I will raise him up in the r. of the just.

p73[44] doeth the will, I will raise up in the r. of the just.

p73[54] eateth my flesh, I will raise up in the r. of the just.

p87[42] whosoever is ashamed of me,

shall have no part in that r.

p87[31] Moses and John spake of Jesus' death, and r.

p101[28] apostles in the r., shall sit upon twelve thrones.

p113[25] I am the r., and the life.

p124[23] Sadducees say that there is no r.

p124[29] in the r., they neither marry nor are given in marriage.

p163[57] after his r., went to the holy city.

Retain. *Keep, maintain.*

p167[23] whosoever sins ye r., they are retained.

Return. *Go back.*

p9[12] warned in a dream they should not r. to Herod.

p64[40] r. to thine own house and show what great things God hath done.

p67[11] let your peace r. to you.

p131[14] he who is on the housetop, flee, and not r.

Returned. *Return.*

p17[13] Jesus r. in the power of the spirit.

p63[38] Gadarenes besought Jesus to depart; and he r. back again.

p64[41] when Jesus r., the people received him.

p97[18] that r. save this stranger.

p115[18] seventy r. again with joy.

p160[49] smote their breasts and r.

p166[32] that same hour and r. to Jerusalem.

p168[51] they worshipped him and r. to Jerusalem.

Reveal. *Make known.*

p95[28] to whom the Son will r. himself.

p115[23] no man knoweth the Son is the Father, but to whom the Son will r. it.

Reverence. *Respect, worship.*

p121[39] they will r. my son.

Revile. *Insult, scorn, despise.*

p39[13] when men shall r. you.

p41[41] better to offer the other cheek than to r. again.

Reviled. *Revile.*

p104[22] Pharisees r. Jesus.

p109[28] Pharisees r. the blind man.

p159[44] r. Jesus while he hung on the cross.

Reward. *Recompense.*

p39[14] great shall be your r. in heaven

p42[34] whom ye hope to receive, what r. have you?

p42[48] which love you, what r. have you?

p42[1] do alms before men, ye have no r.

p43[6] who seeth in secret shall r. thee openly.

p68[36] receiveth a prophet, shall receive a prophet's r.

p87[41] r. every man according to his works.

p90[38] he shall not loose his r.

p159[42] we receive the r. of our deeds.

Rewarded. *Reward.*

p121[34] I speak in parables that your unrighteousness may be r. unto you.

Rich. *Wealthy.*

p4[52] the r. he hath sent away empty.

p29[23] who is not r. towards God.

p101[24] than for a r. man to enter the kingdom of God.

p104[23] parable of the r. man.

p106[2] Zacchaeus was r.

p129[47] the r. cast in much.

p130[50] the r. cast in of their abundance.

p161[51] a r. man named Joseph.

Riches. *Rich.*

p101[22] how hardly shall they that have r. enter the kingdom.

p101[23] hard for them who trust in r.

p104[11] who will commit to your trust the true r.?

Right (a). *Correct, well.*

p63[36] clothed, and in his r. mind.

p102[4] whatsoever is r., I will give you.

p104[21] you pervert the r. way.

p125[29] thou hast answered r.

Right (n). *Opposite of left.*

p13[7] Jesus to dwell on the r. hand of the

Father.

p41[32] if thy r. eye offend thee.

p41[41] shall smite thee on thy r. cheek.

p43[3] not knowing what thy r. hand
doeth.

p87[43] on the r. hand of the Son of Man.

p126[42] sit thou on my r. hand.

p129[41] after Jesus was crowned on
the r. hand of God.

p136[33] the sheep on his r. hand.

p151[10] cut off the servant's r. ear.

p153[65] Son of Man sitting on the r.
hand of power.

p169[6] cast the net on the r. side.

p171[20] Jesus sat on the r. hand of God.

Righteous. *Moral, good, blameless.*

p19[14] not come to call the r., but
sinners to repentance.

p46[2] but judge r. judgment.

p46[14] we ourselves are r.

p62[45] then shall the r. shine forth.

p68[37] in the name of a r. man.

p98[9] they were r. and despised others.

p128[25] you outwardly appear r.

p129[32] upon you may come all the r.
blood shed upon the earth.

p137[38] then shall the r. answer him.

p137[47] the r. into life eternal.

Righteousness. *Righteousness.*

p5[74] that we might serve him in r.

p16[43] it becometh us to fulfill all r.

p39[8] blessed are they who hunger and
thirst after r.

p45[38] seek ye first to establish his r.

p134[39] a new earth, wherein dwelleth r.

p146[8] he will reprove the world of r.

Rightly. *Correctly.*

p54[43] thou hast r. judged.

Riotous. *Rebellious, extravagant.*

p91[13] wasted his substance with r.
living.

Rise. *Come forth, arise.*

p22[35] men of Ninevah shall r. up in
judgment.

p22[36] queen of the south shall r. up

in judgment.

p42[47] he maketh the sun to r. on the
evil and the good.

p55[8] r., take up thy bed and walk.

p67[18] children shall r. up against their
parents.

p103[33] the third day he shall r. again.

p105[36] though one should r. from the
dead.

p113[23] thy brother shall r. again.

p131[9] false prophets shall r.

p162[64] after three days I shall r. again.

p164[9] as yet they knew not the scripture, he must r. again.

p167[45] thus it is written, Christ must r.
from the dead.

Rising. *Rise.*

p8[34] this child is set for the fall and r.
again of many.

p23[31] Jesus r. up a great while before day.

p88[8] apostles questioned what the r. of
the dead should mean.

p162[2] came to the sepulcher at the r. of
the sun.

Rivers. *Continuous supply.*

p76[38] out of his belly shall flow r. of
living water.

Roaring. *Loud noise.*

p132[25] the sea and the waves r.

Robber. *Thief.*

p110[1] the same is a thief and a r.

Robe. *Mantle, garment.*

p92[22] bring forth the best r. and put it
on him.

p155[11] Jesus was arrayed in a gorgeous r.

p156[5] wearing the crown of thorns and
the purple r.

Rock. *Foundation, revelation.*

p47[34] built his house upon a r.

p86[19] upon this r. I will build my
church.

Roll. *Move.*

p162[2] who shall r. us away the stone
from the door of the sepulcher?

Roof. *Top, covering.*

p38[4] uncovered the r. and let down the bed.

p48[6] not worthy thou should enter under my r.

Room. *Place, space.*

p6[7] none to give r. for them in the inns.

p49[8] sit not down in the highest r.

p58[37] candle doth give light in all the r.

p139[12] he shall show you a large upper r. furnished.

Root. *Basis, origin, source.*

p13[37] the ax is laid unto the r.

p58[5] because it had no r., it withered away.

p59[28] ye r. up also the wheat with them.

p61[19] yet he hath not r. in himself.

Rue. *Herb of the Rutacaea family.*

p26[43] ye tithe mint, and r.

Ruler. *Sovereign, leader, steward.*

p25[53] make him r. over all he hath.

p51[14] r. of the synagogue was filled with indignation.

p134[52] a wise servant whom the Lord hath made r.

p135[21] I will make thee r. over many things.

Rulers. *Ruler.*

p24[49] I speak unto the r. of his household.

p75[26] do the r. know indeed that this is the Christ?

p77[48] have any r. of the Pharisees believed on him?

p120[42] among the chief r. many believed on him.

p130[11] brought before kings and r. for my name's sake.

p156[13] Pilate called together the r., and the people.

p165[19] chief priests and r. delivered him to be condemned.

Rumor. *Report, gossip.*

p53[17] r. went forth throughout all Judea.

Rumors. *Rumor.*

p132[25] wars, and r. of wars.

Run. *Hurry, sprint.*

p163[6] and did r. to bring his disciples word.

S

Sabachthani. *Thou hast forsaken me.*

p160[39] Eloi, Eloi, lama s.?

Sabbath. *Day of rest. Seventh day of the week under the old covenant.*

p49[3] is it lawful to heal on the S. day?

p51[14] because Jesus healed on the S. day.

p55[16] Jews persecuted Jesus because of things he did on the S. day.

p80[1] on the S. day he went through a corn field.

p80[4] priests in the temple profane S.

p80[26] S. was given unto man.

p81[6] Son of Man is Lord of the S.

p81[9] if a sheep fall into a pit on the S.

p109[16] this man is not of God because he keepeth not the S. day.

p131[17] that your flight not be on the S. day.

p161[31] should not remain upon the cross on the S. day.

p162[57] they rested the S. day.

Sackcloth. *Made of goats hair.*

p94[23] would have repented in s. and ashes.

Sacrifice (n). *Slaughtered offering.*

p7[24] to offer a s. according to the law.

Sacrifice (v). *Give up, surrender.*

p19[14] I will have mercy and not s.

p96[49] every s. shall be salted with salt.

Sake. *Purpose, benefit.*

p39[12] blessed are they who are persecuted for my name's s.

p50[26] lay down their life for my s.

p87[28] lose his life for my s.

p100[12] made themselves eunuchs for the kingdom of heaven's s.

p101[26] leave all for my s.

p116[9] came not for Jesus' s. only.

p130[11] brought before kings and

rulers for my name's s.

p131[16] hated of all the world for my name's s.

p132[29] I speak for mine elect's s.

p143[11] believe me for the works' s.

Salt. *Sodium chloride.*

p39[15] chosen you to be the s. of the earth.

p50[36] liken it unto s. which is good.

p96[49] every sacrifice shall be salted with s.

Saltiness. *Salt.*

p97[50] if the salt have lost his s.

Salute. *Greet, embrace.*

p42[49] if ye s. your brethren only.

p67[11] come into a house, s. it.

p95[4] nor s. any man by the way.

p156[21] began to s. him, saying, Hail.

Saluted. *Salute.*

p3[40] Mary s. Elizabeth.

p88[13] people running to him, s. him.

Salvation. *Saved from death.*

p5[68] raised an horn of s.

p8[30] mine eyes have seen thy s.

p13[5] bring s. unto the heathen.

p14[11] all flesh shall see the s. of God.

p34[24] s. is of the Jews.

p46[15] we have the law for our s.

p107[9] s. is come unto this house.

Sanctify. *To make holy.*

p148[19] for their sakes I s. myself.

Sand. *Loose granular material.*

p48[35] who built his house upon the s.

Save. *Rescue, keep, except.*

p6[4] he shall s. his people from their sins.

p71[25] Lord, s. me.

p81[9] to s. life, or to destroy?

p87[37] whosoever will s. his life shall lose it.

p87[29] forsake the world and s. your souls.

p91[11] came to s. that which is lost.

p97[18] not found, s. this stranger.

p99[56] not come to destroy men's

lives, but to s. them.

p119[27] Father, s. me from this hour.

p120[47] I came not to judge the world but to s. the world.

p159[44] s. thyself. If thou be the Son of God.

p159[40] if thou be the Christ, s. thyself.

p160[53] if Elias will come to s. him.

Saved. *Save.*

p30[17] the world through him might be s.

p40[21] he shall in no wise be s. in the kingdom of heaven.

p52[23] are there few only that be s.?

p54[50] thy faith hath s. thee.

p56[35] these things I say that ye might be s.

p67[19] he that endureth to the end shall be s.

p100[11] little children shall be s.

p101[25] who then can be s.?

p110[9] if any man entering in, he shall be s.

p131[11] he that is not overcome, shall be s.

p131[19] except those days should be shortened, there should none be s.

p159[45] he s. others, himself he cannot save.

p170[15] he that believeth and is baptized shall be s.

Savior. *One who saves.*

p4[46] rejoiceth in God my S.

p7[11] born this day a S. who is Christ the Lord.

p35[44] this is the Christ, the S. of the world.

Savor. *Taste.*

p39[15] if the salt shall lose it s.

p51[37] if the salt has lost its s.

Savorest. *Appreciate, enjoy.*

p86[24] thou s. not the things of God.

Saying. *Maxim, aphorism, adage.*

p7[17] made known abroad the s. concerning the child.

p26[46] thus s., thou reproachest us also.

p80[52] if a man keep my s., he shall never

taste of death.

p84[11] Pharisees were offended after they heard this s.?

p88[8] they kept that s. with themselves.

p100[11] all cannot receive this s.

p145[20] if they have kept my s.

p150[9] that the s. might be fulfilled.

p164[14] this s. is commonly reported.

p170[23] then went this s. abroad.

Scattered. *Disperse, spread.*

p4[50] he hath s. the proud.

p115[52] he should gather all that were s. abroad.

p136[24] gathered were thou hast not s.

p147[32] the hour is come that ye shall be s.

Scorched. *Whithered.*

p58[5] when the sun was up, it s.

Scorpion. *Scorpionida of arachnids.*

p47[13] will he offer him a s.?

Scorpions. *Scorpion.*

p115[20] power over serpents and s.

Scourge (n). *Whip.*

p25[15] he made a s. of small cords.

Scourge (v). *To whip.*

p103[33] they shall s. and put him to death.

p129[31] prophets, you shall s. in your synagogues.

Scourged. *Whipped.*

p158[18] when he had s. him, to be crucified.

Scribe. *Writer and teacher of the law.*

p62[53] every s. well instructed.

p99[57] a certain s. said unto him.

p126[37] s. said unto him, well, Master.

Scribes. *Scribe.*

p9[4] Herod demanded of the s.

p20[20] taught them with authority, and not as the s.

p27[54] s. began to be angry.

p46[6] s. and Pharisees do not observe the law.

p88[9] why then say the s. Elias must first come?

p88[12] s. questioning with the disciples.

p118[20] s. sought how they might destroy Jesus.

p127[1] S. sit in Moses' seat.

p127[10] woe unto you, S. and Pharisees.

p129[31] I send unto you prophets, wise men, and s.

p138[2] chief Priests and S. sought how they might kill Jesus.

p155[10] chief Priests and S. accused him.

p159[45] chief Priests and S. mocking.

Scrip. *Knapsack, bag.*

p67[9] nor s. for your journey.

p95[4] carry neither purse not s.

p149[35] I sent you without purse and s.

Scripture. *Sacred writings.*

p35[21] this day is s. fulfilled in your ears.

p76[38] as the s. hath said, out of his belly.

p76[42] Christ cometh of the seed of David, as the s. said.

p112[35] ye are gods and the s. cannot be broken.

p141[18] the S., he that eateth bread with me hath lifted up.

p148[12] none is lost but the son of perdition; that the s. might be fulfilled.

p158[33] s. which said he was numbered among the transgressors.

p158[24] s. said they parted my raiment.

p160[28] s. fulfilled, saith I thirst.

p161[36] s., a bone in him shall not be broken.

p161[37] s. saith, they look upon him whom they pierced.

p164[9] knew not the s. that he must rise again from the dead.

Sea. *Large body of water.*

p62[48] kingdom like a net that was cast into the s.

p62[24] Jesus calms the s.

p71[50] Jesus walks upon the s.

p91[39] a millstone were hanged about his neck, and he were cast into the s.

p126[6] sycamore tree be planted in the s.

p128[12] ye compass s. and land to make one proselyte.

p132[25] distress like the s. and the waves.

Seal. *Conformation.*

p31[33] hath set his s. that God is true.

Sealed (n). *Assured, guarantee.*

p72[27] for him hath God the Father s.

Sealed (v). *Close, finalize.*

p14[8] law and the testimony shall be s.

Sealing. *Close up, fasten.*

p162[67] sepulcher sure, s. the stone.

Seam. *Joining of two pieces.*

p158[23] Jesus' coat was without s.

Search. *Look for, seek.*

p9[8] s. diligently for the young child.

p57[40] s. the scriptures, for in them ye think ye have eternal life.

p77[52] s., and look; for out of Galilee ariseth no prophet.

Season (n). *Period of time, time of year.*

p16[12] departed from him for a s.

p24[51] give his portion of meat in due s.

p55[4] an angel went down at a certain s. into the pool.

p56[36] were willing for a s. to rejoice.

p121[36] the s. of the harvest drew near.

Season (v). *Flavor.*

p97[50] for if the salt has lost his saltiness, wherewith will ye s. it?

Seasons. *Season.*

p122[43] render him the fruits in their s.

p168[7] not given you to know the times or the s.

Seat. *Place of judgment.*

p127[1] Pharisees sit in Moses' s.

p157[20] Pilate set in the judgment s.

p157[13] judgment s. in the place called the pavement.

Second. *After first.*

p29[4] can he enter a s. time into his mother's womb.

p37[56] this being the s. miracle.

Secret. *Private, hidden, mystery.*

p42[30] your Father who seeth in s.

p43[4] thine alms may be in s.

p43[6] pray in s.

p44[18] fast in s.

p58[19] neither was anything kept s.

p59[34] have been kept s. from the foundation of the world.

p74[4] no man that doeth anything in s.

p75[10] Jesus went to the feast in s.

p132[26] behold he is in s. chambers.

p151[20] in s. have I said nothing.

Secretly. *Privately.*

p113[28] called Mary s.

p161[51] Joseph, s. a disciple of Jesus.

Secure. *Protect, appease.*

p163[13] we will persuade him and s. you.

Sedition. *Uprising, incitement.*

p156[40] Barabbas, who for a certain s.

See. *Behold, look, discern.*

p7[15] let us now go, and s. this thing.

p14[11] all flesh shall s. the salvation of God.

p16[32] thou shalt s. the Spirit descending.

p17[39] Jesus said to them; come and s.

p19[51] ye shall s. heaven open.

p32[22] the blind s., the lame walk.

p37[50] except ye s. signs and wonders, ye will not believe.

p39[10] blessed are the pure in heart; for they shall s. God.

p40[18] that they may s. your good works.

p60[12] seeing, they s. not.

p60[16] prophets have desired to s.

p85[25] I s. men as trees walking.

p95[28] they shall s. the Father also.

p107[4] climbed up a sycamore tree to s. him.

p110[39] they which s. might be made blind.

p110[41] you say, we s.; therefore your sin remaineth.

p115[24] blessed are the eyes which s.

p119[40] they should not s. with their eyes.

p132[25] s. that ye be not troubled.

p133^{38} they shall s. the Son of Man coming.

p143^{19} a little while, and ye shall s. me.

p153^{65} ye shall s. the Son of Man.

p163^{5} s. the place where the Lord lay.

Seed. *Posterity, grains of ripened ovules.*

p4^{54} spake to Abraham, and his s. forever.

p13^{36} we only have power to bring s. unto Abraham.

p58^{7} other s. fell on good ground.

p59^{22} a man who sowed good s.

p59^{30} heaven is like unto a mustard s.

p60^{21} kingdom of God; is as if a man should cast s. into the ground.

p61^{36} he that soweth good s. is the Son of Man.

p76^{42} Christ cometh of the s. of David.

p89^{20} if you have faith as a grain of mustard s.

p124^{23} rise up s. unto his brother.

Seeing. *See.*

p60^{12} they s., see not.

p159^{41} s. thou art in the same condemnation.

Seek. *Look for, try to.*

p44^{10} s., and ye shall find.

p45^{38} s. ye first to build up the kingdom of God.

p52^{24} many shall s. to enter in.

p56^{31} I s. not mine own will.

p57^{45} who s. honor one of another.

p79^{50} I s. not mine own glory.

p107^{10} Son of man is come to s. and to save.

p150^{4} whom s. ye?

p163^{4} why s. ye the living among the dead?

Seemed. *Appeared.*

p95^{27} Father, it s. good in thy sight.

p164^{10} their words s. as idle tales.

Self. *Person, own self.*

p56^{31} I can of mine own s. do nothing.

p147^{5} Father, glorify me with thine own s.

Sell. *Put up for sale, dispose of.*

p23^{36} s. that ye have and give alms.

p101^{21} if thou wilt be perfect, s. that thou hast and give to the poor.

p135^{8} go to them that s. and buy for yourselves.

p149^{36} let him s. his garment and buy a sword.

Send. *Cause to go, dispatch.*

p23^{13} Jesus to s. the twelve forth to preach.

p25^{58} I am come to s. fire on the earth.

p27^{50} I will s. them prophets, and apostles.

p32^{27} I s. my messenger before my face.

p57^{16} s. forth judgment unto victory.

p61^{42} he will s. forth his angels and his messengers.

p67^{3} began to s. them forth by two.

p68^{30} I am not come to s. peace.

p82^{30} I will not s. them away fasting.

p85^{22} s. her away.

p88^{11} I will s. you my messenger.

p95^{2} Lord of the harvest will s. forth laborers.

p95^{3} I s. you forth as lambs.

p148^{8} they believe thou didst s. me.

p168^{48} I s. the promise of my Father.

Separate. *Divide.*

p136^{33} all nations shall be gathered and he shall s. them.

Sepulcher. *Place of burial.*

p162^{41} in the garden a new s.

p162^{56} women beheld the s., and how his body was laid.

p162^{62} stone to the door of the s.

p162^{63} Mary sitting against the s.

p162^{65} command therefore, that the s. be made sure.

Serpent. *Snake, creeping thing.*

p30^{14} Moses lifted up the s.

p47^{19} ask a fish, will give him a s.?

Serpents. *Serpent.*

p115^{20} I give you power over s.

p129^{30} you s., and generation of

vipers!

Servant. *One who serves, performs duties.*

p8²⁹ let thy s. depart in peace.

p24⁹ doth he thank the s.

p25⁵⁶ the s. who knew his Lord's will.

p48² centurion's s.

p57¹⁴ behold my s., whom I have chosen.

p79³⁴ committeth sin is the s. of sin.

p79³⁵ s. abideth not in the house forever.

p90³² if any man desire to be first, he shall be s. of all.

p104¹³ no s. can serve two masters.

p106²⁷ whosoever will be chief among you, let him be your s.

p134⁵² who then is a faithful and a wise s.

p135²¹ well done, good and faithful s.

p136³¹ cast ye the unprofitable s. into outer darkness.

p141¹⁶ the s. is not greater than his Lord.

Servants. *Servant.*

p24⁴⁰ blessed are those s. whom the Lord shall find watching.

p67¹⁴ be ye therefore wise s.

p92¹⁹ make me as one of thy hired s.

p93²³ king who took account of his s.

p123³ when the marriage was ready he sent forth his s.

p145¹⁵ henceforth I call you not s.

p155³⁶ if my kingdom were of this world, then would my s. fight.

Serve. *Assist, wait on, attend.*

p15¹⁰ God, only shalt thou s.

p44²⁴ no man can s. two masters.

p116⁴¹ my sister hath left me to s.

p119²⁶ if any man s. me.

p121²⁸ I will s.; and went not.

Service. *Benefit, good turn.*

p145² killeth you will think he doeth God s.

Set. *Put, establish, placed.*

p1¹ taken in hand to s. forth a declaration.

p8³⁴ child is s. for the fall and rising.

p35¹⁸ to s. at liberty them that are bruised.

p40¹⁶ a city that is s. on a hill.

p48⁸ I am a man s. under authority.

p68³¹ I am come to s. a man at variance.

Setting. *Set.*

p162⁶⁷ sealing the stone and s. a watch.

Settle. *Resolve, reconcile.*

p50²⁸ s. this in your hearts.

p130¹² s. this therefore in your hearts, not to meditate.

Seven. *Number after six.*

p8³⁶ lived with a husband only s. years.

p28³⁹ s. other spirits more wicked than himself.

p82³² s. loaves and a few little fishes.

p82² out of whom went s. devils.

p93²¹ forgive till s. times?

p124²⁴ there was with us s. brethren.

Seventy. *Number 70, office in the priesthood.*

p93²² forgive s. times seven.

p95¹ Lord appointed other s.

p115¹⁸ the s. returned.

Several. *Separate.*

p135¹⁵ every man according to his s. ability.

Shadow. *Gloom.*

p5⁷⁸ who sit in darkness and the s. of death.

p36¹⁵ that sat in the region and s. of death.

Shake. *Remove, tremble.*

p67¹² s. off the dust of your feet.

p163³ keepers did s. and became as though they were dead.

Shame. *Embarrassment.*

p49⁹ begin with s. to take the lowest room.

Shape. *Form.*

p56³⁸ hath never heard the Father

nor seen his s.

Shed. *Get rid of, discard, given up.*

p27⁵¹ blood of the prophets which was s.

p129³² upon you may come all the righteous blood s.

p141²⁴ my blood which is s. for as many as believe.

Sheep. *Ruminant mammal.*

p54² by the s. market, a pool called Bethesda.

p67⁵ go to the lost s. of the house of Israel.

p67¹⁴ I send you forth as s. in the midst of wolves.

p81¹⁰ is a man better than a s.?

p85²³ I am not sent but to the lost s. of the house of Israel.

p91¹² if a man have an hundred s.

p110⁴ the s. know his voice.

p111¹⁶ other s. I have which are not of this fold.

p111²⁷ my s. hear my voice.

p136³³ divideth the s. from the goats.

p170¹⁶ feed my s.

Sheepfold. *Enclosure, cote.*

p13⁵ who are of the s. of Israel.

p110¹ entereth not by the door of the s.

p110⁷ I am the door of the s.

Shepherd. *Who tends sheep.*

p66⁴² as sheep having no s.

p110² he that entereth the door is the s.

p111¹¹ I am the good s.

p111¹³ I am the good shepherd and know my s.

p111¹⁶ there shall be one fold and one s.

Shewbread. *Unleavened bread.*

p80⁴ David took and ate the s.

Shine. *Stand out, glow.*

p40¹⁸ let your light so s.

p62⁴⁵ the righteous to s. as the sun.

p87¹ his face did s. as the sun.

Shining. *Glow, light.*

p56³⁶ John was a s. light.

p58³⁷ as the light of a s. candle.

Ship. *Boat.*

p18³ Jesus taught out of the s.

p57⁹ a small s. should wait on him.

p61²⁹ took him as he was in the s.

p62²³ was, in the s. asleep.

p70³³ departed to a solitary place by s.

p71⁴⁷ his disciples to get into the s.

p169⁶ cast your net on the right side of the s.

Shoes. *Footwear.*

p14²³ whose s. I am not worthy to unloose.

p95⁴ carry neither purse, nor scrip, nor s.

p149³⁵ I sent you without purse, and scrip, or s.

Shore. *Edge, beach.*

p169⁴ Jesus stood on the s.

Shortened. *Made short.*

p131¹⁹ except those days should be s.

Show. *Demonstrate, present, reveal.*

p37³⁹ s. thyself to the priests.

p64⁴⁰ s. how great things God hath done.

p74⁴ s. thyself to the world.

p86²² Jesus began to s. his disciples.

p97¹⁴ go s. yourselves to the priests.

p124¹⁸ s. me the tribute money.

p143⁸ Lord, s. us the Father.

p146¹³ he will s. you things to come.

Shut. *Close, lock.*

p31²⁷ Herod s. John up in prison.

p36²⁵ heaven was s. up three years and six months.

p52²⁵ he hath s. the door of the kingdom.

p127¹⁰ ye s. the kingdom of heaven against men.

p166¹⁹ doors were s. and the disciples were assembled.

Sick. *Ill, unwell.*

p19¹³ the whole need not a physician, but they that are s.

p21³⁰ he healed many that were s. of diverse diseases.

p66⁷ laid his hands upon a few s. folks.

p67^7 healed the s. and cleansed the lepers.

p81^{58} laid the s. in the streets.

p112^1 Lazarus was s.

p137^{37} I was s. and ye visited me.

p171^{19} lay hands on the s. and they shall recover.

Sickle. *Reaping tool.*

p60^{23} putteth in the s. because the harvest is come.

Sickness. *Sick.*

p38^{22} healing all manner of s.

p66^{41} healing every s. and disease.

p112^4 this s. is not unto death.

Sicknesses. *Sick.*

p21^{17} himself bear our s.

p23^{13} disciples given power to heal s.

Side. *Right or left of center, region.*

p161^{34} soldier with a spear pierced his s.

p167^{20} showed them his hands and his s.

p167^{25} will not believe until I thrust my hand into his s.

Sighed. *Deep audible breath, groan*

p84^{11} Jesus s. deeply in his spirit.

p90^{33} looking up to heaven, he s.

Sight (a). *Based on recognition or comprehension.*

p2^{15} he shall be great in the s. of the Lord.

p95^{27} so it seemed good in thy s.!

p104^{15} abomination in the s. of God.

p115^{22} Father; it seemed good in thy s.

Sight (n). *Vision, eyesight.*

p32^{21} unto many blind he gave s.

p106^{41} that I may receive my s.

p108^{11} washed, and I received s.

Sight (v). *Notice, observe, view.*

p160^{49} people came together to that s.

p166^{30} Jesus was taken up out of their s.

Sign. *Remarkable event, signal.*

p22^{33} Master, we would see a s.

p22^{34} adulterous generation seeketh after a s.

p25^{18} what s. showest thou unto us.

p72^{30} what s. showest thou then.

p84^1 tempting Jesus to show them a s.

p84^{11} why doth this generation seek after a s.?

p84^4 but the s. of the prophet Jonas.

p130^9 what is the s. of thy coming.

p133^{37} then shall appear the s. of the Son of Man.

p150^{45} he that betrayed him gave them a s.

Signifying. *Mean, indicate, show.*

p50^{31} s. there should not any man.

p51^{38} s. that which is written.

p53^{34} this he spake, s. of his death.

p119^{33} s. what death he should die.

p134^{38} s. the gathering of his saints.

p154^{32} s. what death he should die.

p158^{32} s. the scattering of Israel.

p170^{19} s. by what death Peter should glorify God.

Silence. *Make quiet.*

p125^{33} heard he had put the Sadducees to s.

Silver. *Valuable metal, money.*

p67^8 provide neither gold, nor s.

p91^8 woman having ten pieces of s.

p138^{11} covenanted for thirty pieces of s.

p153^3 brought again the thirty pieces of s.

p154^8 bought the potter's field with the thirty pieces of s.

Simeon. *Prophesies at the temple.*

p8^{25} prophesies and blesses Joseph, Mary, and Jesus.

Simon. *Also see Peter.*

p18^{41} he findeth his own brother S.

p18^4 he said unto S., let down your net.

p18^{10} James and John, were partners with S.

p21^{26} entered the house of S.

p23^{14} chosen to be an apostle.

p53^{36} Jesus eats with S. the Pharisee.

p66^4 S., brother of Jesus.

p86^{18} blessed art thou, S. Barjona.

p94^{25} what thinkest thou, S.?

p137^4 Jesus anointed in the home of S.

the leper.

p139²⁴ S. beckoned to John.

p142³¹ S.,S., Satan hath desired to have you.

p158²⁴ compelled S., a Cyrenian, to bear his cross.

p170¹⁶ S., son of Jonas, lovest thou me?

Simon. *The Canaanite.*

p23¹⁴ chosen to be an apostle.

Sin. *Willful disobedience.*

p16²⁹ Lamb of God, who taketh away the s. of the world!

p28³⁷ s. against the Holy Ghost shall not be forgiven.

p38⁶ go thy way and s. no more.

p46⁶ all are under s.

p55¹⁴ thou art made whole; s. no more.

p77⁷ he that is without s among you.

p77¹¹ neither do I condemn thee, s. no more.

p79³⁴ committeth s. is the servant of s.

p108² who did s., this man or his parents.

p110⁴¹ if ye were blind ye should have no s.

p128²¹ would not commit the least s.

p134⁴⁰ earth to be cleansed from all s.

p145²² if I had not spoken unto them, they had not had s.

p146⁸ Jesus to reprove the world of s.

p157¹¹ he that delivered me unto thee hath the greater s.

Single. *Specific, only.*

p44²² eye be s. to the glory of God.

p58³⁵ when thine eye is s., thy whole body is full of light.

Sink. *Go down, under the surface.*

p18⁷ both ships began to s.

p71²⁵ Peter beginning to s.

Sinner. *One who sins.*

p53³⁷ a woman in the city, who was a s.

p91¹⁰ joy over one s. who repenteth.

p98¹³ God, be merciful to me a s.

p107⁷ Jesus was guest with a man who was a s.

p109¹⁶ How can a s. do such miracles?

p109²⁴ we know this man is a s.

Sister. *Female sibling.*

p22⁴⁴ the same is my brother and s.

p112² Mary was Lazarus' s.

p112² Mary, s. of Martha.

p113²⁸ Martha called Mary her s.

p116⁴¹ my s. hath left me to serve.

p159²⁵ Jesus' mother's s. Mary.

Sit. *Seated, situated.*

p5⁷⁸ give light to them who s. in darkness.

p24⁴⁰ make his servants to s. and serve them.

p49⁸ s. not down in the highest room.

p70⁴¹ make all s. down by companies.

p82³³ commanded the multitude to s. down on the ground.

p101²⁸ ye shall s. upon twelve thrones.

p105²⁰ grant these my sons may s.

p127¹ Pharisees s. in Moses' seat.

p136³² Son of Man shall s. upon the throne of his glory.

p149³⁷ s. ye here while I pray.

Sitting. *Sit.*

p11⁴⁶ Jesus s. in the midst of the doctors.

p32³² like unto children s. in the market place.

p63³⁶ man s. at the feet of Jesus.

p101²⁸ Son of Man shall come s. on his throne of glory.

p153⁶⁵ Son of Man s. on the right hand of power.

p159³⁸ s. down they watched him.

p162⁶³ Mary s. over against the sepulcher.

p164¹² two angels in white s.

Six. *Number after five.*

p17⁶ there were s. water pots.

p51¹⁴ there are s. days in which men ought to work.

p116¹ Jesus s. days before Passover

Sixth. *Six.*

p3²⁶ s. month Gabriel was sent.

p3³⁶ Elizabeth in her s. month.

p102⁵ he went out about the s. hour.

p160⁴⁵ about the s. hour there was darkness.

Sixty. *Ten times six.*

p58⁷ some thirty fold, some s.

Sky. *Atmosphere, firmament.*

p84² the s. is red and lowering.

p84³ ye can discern the face of the s.

Slay. *Kill, murder.*

p27⁵⁰ s. prophets, and apostles.

p55¹⁶ Jews sought to s. Jesus.

Sleep. *Natural periodic suspension of consciousness.*

p88³² they were heavy with s.

p113¹¹ awake Lazarus out of s.

p150⁴⁶ s. on now and take rest.

Slow. *Sluggish, unhurried.*

p166²⁴ O fools, and s. of heart.

Small. *Little, tiny, lesser.*

p25¹⁵ made a scourge of s. cords.

p57⁹ a s. ship should wait on him.

p70⁹ barley loaves and two s. fishes.

Smite. *To strike heavily, inflict injury.*

p41⁴¹ shall s. thee on thy right cheek.

p134⁵⁵ began to s. his fellow servants.

p151⁴⁹ shall we s. with a sword?

Smooth. *Flat, even.*

p14¹⁰ rough ways made s.

Snow. *Water crystals.*

p163³ countenance was white as s.

Soft. *Silky, velvety.*

p32²⁴ a man clothed in s. raiment.

Soldier. *Warrior, fighter.*

p158²³ to every s. a part.

Soldiers. *Soldier.*

p13²¹ s. demanded of John.

p48⁸ having under me s.

p156¹⁹ s. led Jesus away.

p158²³ s. crucified Jesus.

p159³⁵ Father, forgive the s.

p161³⁴ one of the s. pierced his side.

p163¹¹ they gave large money to the s.

Solitary. *Separate, out of the way.*

p23³¹ departed into a s. place.

p37⁴⁰ but was without in s. places.

p70³² come ye into a s. place.

p70³⁶ this is a s. place and the time for departure.

Something. *Undetermined, unspecific.*

p27⁵⁵ seeking to catch s. out of his mouth.

p65³⁵ s. given her to eat.

p139²⁹ Judas should give s. to the poor.

Somewhat. *Important, noteworthy.*

p54⁴⁰ Simon, I have s. to say unto thee.

Son. *Male child.*

p1¹ S. was with God and of God.

p2¹³ Elizabeth shall bear thee a s.

p3³¹ Mary shall bring forth a s.

p3³² called S. of the Highest.

p6⁶ virgin shall bring forth a s.

p6⁷ she brought forth her first born s.

p10¹⁵ out of Egypt have I called my s

p30¹⁶ he gave his Only Begotten S.

p31³⁶ the S. hath everlasting life.

p53¹² the only s. of his mother.

p55¹⁹ the S. can do nothing of himself.

p56²¹ the S. quickeneth whom he will.

p56²² committed all judgment to the S.

p56²³ all men should honor the S.

p65³³ Jesus, thou S. of David.

p74⁶⁹ thou art the S. of the living God.

p79³⁵ the S. abideth ever.

p88⁴ this is my beloved S.

p95⁶ if the s. of peace be there.

p115²³ no man knoweth the S.

p127⁴³ if David called him Lord, how is he his s.?

p143¹³ Father may be glorified in the S.

p160²⁶ Woman, behold thy s.!

p170¹⁵ is baptized in the name of the S.

Son of God. *Jesus is the only begotten son of his Father.*

p3³⁵ the holy child shall be called the S.

p15³ If thou be the S.

p19⁴⁹ Rabbi, thou art the S.

p30¹⁸ hath not believed on the name of the S.

p57¹⁰ Thou art the S.

p71[28] Of a truth thou art the S.

p112[36] because I said, I am the S.?

p112[4] that the S. might be glorified.

p157[7] he made himself the S.

p159[44] If thou be the S.

p160[44] Truly, this is the S.

p171[31] Jesus is the Christ, the S.

Sop. *Piece of food dipped.*

p139[26] to whom I shall give a s.

p139[30] then having received the s.

Sore. *Painful, angry, greatly.*

p89[23] spirit cried and rent him s.

p118[13] priests and Scribes were s. displease.

p149[36] disciples began to be s. amazed.

Sorrow. *Grief, sadness.*

p146[6] s. hath filled your heart.

p146[20] s. shall be turned to joy.

p146[21] woman when she is in travail hath s.

Sorrowful. *Sorrow.*

p146[20] world shall rejoice; but ye shall be s.

p149[38] my soul is exceeding s.

Sorrowing. *Distress.*

p11[48] father and I have sought thee s.

Sorry. *Remorseful.*

p69[27] Herod was exceeding s.

p94[31] fellow servants were very s.

Soul. *Person, spirit and body.*

p4[45] my s. doth magnify the Lord.

p8[35] wounding of thine own s. also.

p29[22] this night thy s. shall be required of thee.

p57[14] in whom my s. is well pleased.

p68[25] but are not able to kill the s.

p87[29] gain the world and lose his own s.?

p119[27] now is my s. troubled.

p125[28] love God with all thy s.

p149[38] my s. is exceeding sorrowful.

Sound. *Audible noise.*

p30[8] wind bloweth and thou hearest the s.

p43[2] doest alms, do not s. a trumpet.

p133[40] send his angels before him with a great s.

South. *Opposite of north.*

p22[36] queen of the s.

p52[29] they shall come from the north and the s.

Sow. *Plant.*

p45[29] fowls of the air s. not.

p59[25] didst not thou s. good seed.

p108[21] reapest that which thou didst not s.

Sower. *Someone who plants.*

p58[3] there went out a s. to sow.

p60[17] hear ye the parable of the s.

Space. *Period, time.*

p152[59] Peter on the porch about the s. of one hour.

Sparrows. *Small common bird.*

p68[26] two s. sold for a farthing?

p68[27] are of more value than many s.

Speak. *Talk.*

p2[20] thou shalt be dumb and not able to s.

p21[30] suffered not the devils to s.

p22[29] how can ye, being evil s. good things?

p22[31] every idle word that men shall s.

p22[40] mother and brethren desired to s. with Jesus.

p27[54] endeavoring to provoke him to s. many things.

p28[12] whosoever shall s. a word against the Son of Man.

p29[15] Master, s. to my brother.

p30[11] we s. that we do know.

p34[28] I who s. unto thee am the Messias.

p67[17] take no thought what ye shall s.

p75[17] if it be of God or whether I s. of myself.

p79[38] I s. that which I have seen with my Father.

p82[29] when they saw the dumb to s.

p120[49] Father gave me commandment, what I should s.

p121³⁴ you that believe not, I s. in parables.

p132²⁴ I s. these things unto you for the elect's sake.

p146¹³ spirit of truth, shall not s. of himself.

p171¹⁷ they shall s. with new tongues.

Speaking. *Speak.*

p43⁷ think that they shall be heard for their much s.

Spear. *Lance, javelin.*

p8³⁵ a s. shall pierce him to the wounding of thine own soul.

p161³⁴ one of the soldiers with a s. pierced his side.

Speech. *Words, speaking, dialect.*

p79⁴³ why do ye not understand my s.

p90³¹ who had an impediment in his.

p152⁵⁹ for thy s. betrayeth thee.

Speechless. *Dumb, wordless.*

p2²² Zacharias remained s.

p123¹² not having a wedding garment? And he was s.

Spices. *Aromatic plant products.*

p162⁴⁰ in linen clothes with the s.

p162⁵⁷ they prepared s. and ointments.

p162¹ brought sweet s. that they might anoint him.

Spikenard. *Highly perfumed ointment.*

p137⁴ an alabaster box of s.

Spirit. *Character, inner self.*

p2¹⁷ in the s. and power of Elias.

p4⁴⁶ my s. rejoiceth in God.

p15¹ Jesus led of the S., into the wilderness.

p16⁴⁵ s. of God like a dove.

p17¹³ returned in power of the S.

p20²¹ man with an unclean s.

p21²³ cast out devils by the S. of God.

p29⁵ except a man be born of water, and the S.

p31³⁴ giveth him not the S. by measure.

p34²⁵ worship the Father in s.

p35¹⁸ the S. of the Lord is upon me.

p39⁵ blessed are the poor in s.

p51¹¹ woman who had a s. of infirmity.

p67¹⁷ S. which speaketh in you.

p71⁵¹ they supposed it had been a s.

p74⁶³ the s. quickeneth; the flesh.

p84¹¹ Jesus sighed deeply in his s.

p89¹⁷ torn by the s.

p99⁵⁵ what manner of s. ye are of.

p114³³ Jesus groaned in the s.

p115²² Jesus rejoiced in s.

p139²¹ Jesus was troubled in s.

p143¹⁷ even the s. of truth.

p150⁴³ s. is ready, but the flesh is weak.

p160⁵⁴ into thy hands I commend my s.

p166³⁸ a s. hath not flesh and bones.

Spit. *Eject saliva from mouth.*

p85²⁴ when he had s. upon his eyes.

p90³² he s. and touched his tongue.

p153⁷¹ some began to s. on him.

p156²² smote him an s. upon him.

Spitefully. *Maliciously, shamefully.*

p103³² shall be mocked, and s. entreat.

p123⁶ entreated them s., and slew them.

Spoil. *Take, plunder.*

p21²⁴ enter the strong man's house and s. his goods.

p122⁴⁸ think that he alone can s. this great kingdom?

Spoken. *Speak.*

p6⁵ be fulfilled, which were s. of the Lord.

p8³³ which were s. of the child.

p11²⁹ I am he who was s. of by the prophet.

p27³ whatsoever ye have s. in darkness.

p28¹⁰ because they had s. evil against him.

p59³⁴ that which was s. by the prophets.

p103³⁴ neither remembered the things which were s.

p120⁴⁸ the word I have s., shall judge him.

p120⁴⁹ I have not s. of myself.

p144³ clean through the word which I have s. unto you.

p145²² if I had not come and s. unto

them.

p147²⁵ I have s. unto you in proverbs.

p147³³ s. unto you that you might have peace.

p152²³ if I have s. evil.

p153⁶⁶ he hath s. blasphemy.

p167³⁹ when he had s., he showed them his hands.

Sponge. *Material able to absorb liquid.*

p160²⁹ a s. was put upon hyssop, and put to Jesus' mouth.

Spring. *Source, supply, sprout.*

p5⁷⁷ the day s. from on high.

p60²¹ seed should s. and grow up.

Stand. *In a position of, remain, being erect.*

p21²¹ house divided against itself, shall not s.

p52²⁵ ye shall s. without, and knock.

p81⁸ said to the man to s. forth.

p96⁴⁴ let every man s. or fall, by himself.

p114⁴² the people which s. by I said it.

p134³⁶ s. before the Son of Man.

p168¹¹ why s. ye gazing up into heaven?

Star. *Luminous body in the sky.*

p8² we have see his s. in the east.

p9⁷ inquired what time the s. appeared.

p9¹⁰ when they saw the s., they rejoiced.

Staves. *Walking stick, pole.*

p150⁴⁴ a multitude with swords and s.

p151⁵³ are you come out with swords and s., to take me?

Steal. *Rob, take.*

p44¹⁹ thieves break through and s.

p101¹⁸ thou shalt not s.

p110¹⁰ the thief cometh to s.

p162⁶⁵ lest his disciples come and s. him away.

Steadfast. *Unwavering, steady.*

p131¹¹ he that remaineth s., shall be saved.

Steep. *Rapid decline.*

p63³⁴ swine ran down a s. place.

Steward. *Head of or chief over.*

p82³ wife of Chuza, Herod's s.

p103¹ parable of the unjust s.

Still. *Motionless.*

p53¹⁴ the bier stood s.

p62²⁴ Peace, be s. And the wind ceased.

Stinketh. *Bad smell.*

p114³⁹ Lord, by this time he s.

Stone. *Rock, building block, paver.*

p15⁶ thou dash thy foot against a s.

p17⁶ were set six water pots of s.

p47¹⁸ ask bread, will give him a s.?

p77⁷ let him cast the first s.

p112³¹ took up stones to s. him.

p112⁸ Jews sought to s. thee.

p114³⁸ was a cave, and a s. lay upon it.

p122⁴⁴ the s. which the builders rejected.

p122⁴⁶ whosoever shall fall on this s.

p130⁶ there shall not leave one s. upon another.

p162⁶² rolled a great s. to the door of the sepulcher.

p162⁶⁷ sealing the s. and setting a watch.

p162² who shall roll away the s.

Stony. *Rocky.*

p58⁵ some fell on s. ground.

p61¹⁹ received seed into s. places.

Stooped. *Bent over, crouched down.*

p77⁶ Jesus s. down and wrote on the ground.

p164¹¹ Mary s. down, and looked into the sepulcher.

Storm. *Tempest, squall.*

p62²³ there came a s. on the lake.

Straight. *Direct, plain, even, whole.*

p11²⁹ make his paths s.

p12²⁴ make s. the way of the Lord.

p14¹⁰ crooked shall be made s.

p51¹³ woman was made s.

Straighten. *Stand erect.*

p51¹¹ woman could not s. up.

Strain. *Struggle, take exception.*

p128²¹ s. at a gnat, and swallow a camel.

Strait. *Restrictive, passage.*

p47^{22} enter in at the s. gate.

p47^{23} s. is the gate.

Straitly. *Strictly.*

p37^{39} Jesus s. charged a leper.

p65^{35} s. charged the damsel's parents.

Stranger. *Foreigner, sojourner, imposter.*

p97^{18} not return save this s.

p110^{5} a s. they will not follow.

p136^{36} I was a s., and ye took me in.

p165^{17} art thou a s. in Jerusalem.

Streets. *Roads.*

p43^{2} do not sound a trumpet in the s.

p43^{5} pray standing in the s.

p52^{26} thou hast taught in our s.

p81^{58} laid the sick in the s.

Strength. *Power, might.*

p4^{50} hath shown s. with his arm.

p125^{28} love God with all thy s.

Strengthen. *Reinforce, bolster.*

p142^{32} when thou art converted s. thy brethren.

Stretch. *Extend.*

p81^{5} s. forth thy hand.

p170^{18} when thou art old thou shalt s. forth thy hands.

Strife. *Contention.*

p140^{24} there was a s. among them.

String. *Cord (symbolic).*

p90^{34} the s. of his tongue was loosed

Stripes. *Blow, beating, whipped.*

p25^{56} shall be beaten with many s.

Stripped. *Removed clothing.*

p125^{31} s. him of his raiment.

Strive. *Endeavor, contend.*

p52^{24} s. to enter the strait gate.

p52^{24} Lord will not always s. with man.

p57^{15} he shall not s., nor cry.

Strong. *Powerful, alcohol.*

p2^{15} neither wine nor s. drink.

p5^{79} child waxed s. in spirit.

p10^{24} Jesus grew up and waxed s.

p21^{24} enter a s. man's house.

Stumbleth. *Stumble, trip.*

p113^{9} walk in the day, he s. not.

Subject. *Accountable, under authority.*

p11^{51} Jesus was s. to them.

p115^{18} devils are s. to us.

p115^{21} rejoice not that the spirits are s. unto you.

Substance. *Possessions, money.*

p82^{3} gave Jesus of their s.

p91^{13} wasted his s. with riotous living.

Subtlety. *Deceit, guile.*

p138^{3} might take Jesus by s.

Suck. *Suckle, nurse.*

p131^{16} woe unto them that give s. in those days.

p158^{29} blessed are the paps which never gave s.

Sue. *Legal action.*

p42^{42} if any man will s. thee.

Suffer. *Undergo, endure.*

p43^{14} s. us not to be led into temptation.

p86^{22} Jesus began to show how he must s. many things.

p97^{25} first he must s. many things.

p167^{45} behooved Christ to s.

Sufficient. *Enough, adequate.*

p45^{39} s. unto the day shall be the evil thereof.

p46^{15} we have the law, that is s. for us.

Sun. *Luminous celestial body.*

p42^{47} maketh the s. to rise on the evil

p62^{45} righteous shall shine forth as the s.

p87^{1} raiment did shine as the s.

p132^{34} s. shall be darkened.

p162^{2} came to the sepulcher at the rising of the s.

Sung. *Sang.*

p149^{27} when they had s. an hymn.

Superscription. *Engraved or molded.*

p124^{20} whose image is this, and s.?

Supper. *Evening meal.*

p49^{12} makest a s., call not thy friends.

p69^{22} Herod made a s. for his lords.

p116² made him a s., and Martha served.

p140² s. being ended, the devil.

p170²⁰ leaned on his breast at s.

Suppose. *Think, assume.*

p51² s. ye these Galileans were sinners.

p54⁴³ I s. he who forgave most.

Sure. *Certain.*

p74⁶⁹ we are s. thou art that Christ.

p147³⁰ now are we s. thou knowest all things.

p162⁶⁵ make the sepulcher s.

Surely. *Sure.*

p1¹ most s. believed among us.

p36²³ s. say unto me this proverb.

p148⁸ have known s. that I came out from thee.

Surname. *Last name.*

p66² whose s. was Thaddeus.

Swaddling. *Narrow strips of cloth.*

p6⁷ wrapped him in s. clothes.

p7¹² he is wrapped in s. clothes.

Swallow. *Ingest (symbolic).*

p128²¹ s. a camel.

Swear. *Vow, claim, curse.*

p41³⁸ s. not at all.

p152⁶⁰ Peter began to s.

Sweat. *Perspire, excrete.*

p150⁴⁴ he began to s. great drops of blood.

Sweep. *Clean, remove.*

p91⁸ s. the house and seek diligently.

Sweet. *Pleasant, pleasing.*

p162¹ women brought s. spices.

Swept. *Sweep.*

p28³⁸ spirit findeth him s. and garnished.

Swine. *Omnivorous mammal.*

p46¹⁰ neither cast your pearls unto s.

p63³¹ a herd of many s. feeding.

p63³⁴ devils entered into the s.

p92¹⁵ sent to the fields to feed s.

Sword. *Weapon.*

p68³⁰ not send peace but a s.

p131²³ they shall fall by the edge of the s.

p149³⁶ hath no s., let him sell his garment.

p151⁴⁹ shall we smite with a s.?

p151⁵⁰ he that taketh the s. shall perish by the s.

Sycamore. *Similar but inferior to the common fig tree.*

p126⁶ say to this s. tree.

Synagogue. *Jewish house of worship.*

p20¹⁹ he entered the s. and taught.

p26⁴⁴ uppermost seats in the s.

p35²¹ eyes of all those who were in the s.

p48⁵ centurion hath built us a s.

p51¹⁴ ruler of the s. was filled with indignation.

p64⁴² Jairus, a ruler of the s.

p66² he began to teach in the s.

p109²² any man confess he was the Christ, he should be put out of the s.

p151²⁰ I ever taught in the s.

| T

Tabernacles. *Temporary shelter.*

p88³ let us make here three t.

Table. *Desk, counter, tablet.*

p86²⁶ dogs eat the crumbs that fall from the master's t.

p105²⁶ crumbs from the rich man's t.

p116² Lazarus sat at the t. with him.

p139²⁸ no man at the t. knew.

p142³⁰ eat at my t. in my kingdom.

Take. *Procure, give (antonym).*

p28¹³ t. no thought what ye shall answer.

p38⁸ t. up thy bed.

p45²⁸ t. no thought for your life.

p45³⁹ t. no thought for the morrow.

p67¹⁷ t. no thought of what ye shall speak.

p95³⁰ t. my yoke upon you.

p101²¹ t. up the cross, and follow me.

p111¹⁷ I lay down my life, that I might t. it again.

p124[26] they could not t. hold of his words.

p141[20] t. it, and eat.

p149[40] t. away this cup from me.

Talent. *Weight of a sum of money.*

p136[25] I was afraid, and hid thy t.

p136[28] I will take the t. from you.

Talitha. *Maiden, damsel.*

p65[33] said unto her, T. cumi.

Talk. *Speech, converse.*

p123[15] how they might entangle him in t.

p144[30] hereafter I will not t. much with you.

Tame. *Discipline, subdue, reclaim.*

p63[3] neither could any man t. him.

Tares. *Darnel grass, poisonous weed.*

p59[24] then appeared the t. also.

p59[29] t. to be burned.

p61[35] declare unto us the parable of the t.

Tarry. *Stay, delay, abide.*

p35[42] Samaritans besought him to t. with them.

p149[38] t. ye here and watch.

p166[28] Jesus went in to t. with them.

p170[23] that John t. till I come.

Tarried. *Past tense of tarry.*

p2[21] Zacharias t. so long in the temple.

p11[43] Jesus t. behind in Jerusalem.

p112[6] t. two days after he heard Lazarus was sick.

p135[4] bridegroom t., they all slumbered.

Taste. *Experience.*

p80[52] he shall never t. of death.

p87[44] some which shall not t. of death.

Taxed. *Levy, register.*

p6[1] that his empire should be t.

p6[3] all went to be t.

p6[5] Joseph went to be t. with Mary.

Teach. *Instruct, educate.*

p10[25] needed not that any man should t. him.

p40[21] and t. men so to do.

p46[6] they t., but do not observe.

p46[14] need not that any man should t. us.

p50[28] do the things which I shall t.

p99[1] as he was accustomed to t.

p104[20] why t. the law and deny.

p143[26] the Holy Ghost shall t. you all things.

p170[14] go ye into all the world and t. all nations.

Teacher. *One who teaches.*

p29[2] we know thou art a t. come from God.

Teaching. *Teach.*

p38[22] went about all Galilee t.

p45[26] go from house to house, t.

p66[41] all the cities and villages, t.

p83[7] t. doctrines and commandments of men.

p120[21] elders came to him while he was t.

p151[53] daily with you in the temple, t.

p170[19] t. them to observe all things.

Tears. *Fluid from the lachrymal gland (eye).*

p54[38] washed his feet with her t.

p89[21] father said, with t.

Tell. *Inform, let know.*

p30[12] if I t. you heavenly things?

p32[22] t. John what things.

p34[27] when he is come, he will t. us all things.

p52[32] go ye and t. Herod.

p68[24] what I t. you in darkness.

p79[45] I t. you the truth.

p86[21] t. no man that he was the Christ.

p111[24] if thou be the Christ, t. us.

p121[25] neither t. I you by what authority.

p142[34] I t. you, Peter.

p153[64] t. us whether thou be the Christ.

p155[34] or did others t. it of me?

p163[5] go your way, t. his disciples.

p164[15] t. me where thou hast laid him.

Temple. *House of God.*

p11[46] after three days, found him in the t.

p15[5] setteth him on the pinnacle of the t.

p25[15] he drove them out of the t.

p25[19] destroy this t., and in three days.

p27[51] Zacharias perished between the alter and the t.

p55[14] Jesus findeth him in the t.

p75[14] Jesus went into the t., and taught.

p77[9] (the woman taken in adultery) standing in the midst of the t.

p80[5] is one greater than the t.

p98[10] two men went to the t. to pray.

p118[17] Jesus went into the t., and began to cast them out.

p128[13] shall swear by the t.

p130[5] not be left here upon this t., one stone upon another.

p151[53] I sat daily with you in the t.

p154[6] Judas cast down the pieces of silver in the t.

p159[44] Thou that destroyest the t.

p160[55] the veil of the t. was rent.

p168[52] continually in the t., praising and blessing God.

Tempt. *Test, prove.*

p15[7] Thou shalt not t. the Lord.

p99[2] this they said, to t. him.

p124[18] Why t. ye me?

Temptation. *Trial.*

p16[12] devil had ended all the t.

p43[14] suffer us not to be led into t.

p150[42] pray, lest ye enter into t.

Tempter. *Lucifer, Satan.*

p15[3] and when the t. came to him.

Ten. *Number after nine.*

p91[8] woman having t. pieces of silver.

p93[24] who owed t. thousand talents.

p97[12] t. men who were lepers.

p106[24] t. disciples moved with indignation.

p107[13] called his t. servants.

p107[17] have authority over t. cities.

p134[1] likened unto t. virgins.

Tender. *Sensitive, new growth.*

p5[77] through the t. mercy of our God.

p133[41] fig tree branches are yet t.

Testament. *Covenant.*

p141[24] in remembrance of my blood of the new t.

Testify. *Bear witness.*

p26[25] need not that any man should t. of man.

p30[11] and t. that we have seen.

p39[3] blessed are those who believe when ye t.

p57[40] scriptures t. of me.

p104[17] the law and the prophets t. of me.

p145[26] the Father will t. of me.

Testimony. *Witness.*

p14[8] the law and the t. shall be sealed.

p31[32] few men receive his t.

p56[33] the t. he giveth is true.

p56[35] he received not his t. of man.

p56[37] I have a greater witness than the t. of John.

p67[12] dust off your feet for a t. against them.

p73[44] he who receiveth the t.

p78[17] the t. of two men is true.

p129[34] ye bear t. against your fathers.

p131[14] it shall turn to you for a t.

p171[24] and we know that this t. is true.

Tetrarch. *Governor, ruler over a portion.*

p11[1] Herod being t. of Galilee.

p11[1] Phillip t. of Iturea.

p11[1] Lysanias the t. of Abilene.

p31[26] Herod, the t. being reproved.

Thank. *Express gratitude.*

p24[9] doth he t. the servant.

p95[27] I t. thee, O Father.

p98[11] I t. thee, I am not as other men.

p114[41] Father, I t. thee that thou hast

heard me.

p115²² I t. thee, O Father.

Thief. *Robber.*

p23³⁶ where no t. approacheth.

p24⁴⁴ coming of the Lord is as a t. in the night.

p24⁴⁶ had known what hour the t. would come.

p110¹ the same is a t. and a robber.

p151⁵³ ye are come out against me as a t.

Things. *Word, matter, object.*

p1³ all t. were made by him.

p19⁵⁰ thou shalt see greater t. than these.

p26²⁴ Jesus knew all t.

p43⁸ Father knoweth what t. ye have need of.

p45³⁸ and all these t. shall be added.

p88¹⁴ who should come and restore all t.

p95²⁸ all t. are delivered unto me of my Father.

p101²⁶ for with such, all t. are possible.

p124²¹ render unto God the t. which are God's.

p141²⁵ do the t. which ye have seen me do.

p146¹⁵ all t. which the Father hath are mine.

p149⁴⁰ Father, all t. are possible unto thee.

p167⁴³ all t. must be fulfilled.

Think. *Reason.*

p57⁴⁰ search the scriptures for in them ye t. ye have eternal life.

p126⁴⁰ What t. ye of Christ?

Third. *After second.*

p52³² the t. day I shall be perfected.

p86²² be raised again the t. day.

p103³³ the t. day he shall rise again.

p150⁴⁶ cometh to them the t. time.

p158²⁸ it was the t. hour, when he was crucified.

p167⁴⁵ to rise from the dead the t. day.

p169¹⁴ t. time that Jesus had shown himself to his disciples.

p170¹⁷ saith unto Simon the t. time.

Thirst. *Desire, hunger, need for liquids.*

p33¹⁵ drink of this well, shall t.

p34¹⁶ water which I give he shall never t.

p39⁸ blessed are they who hunger and t.

p72³⁵ he that believeth on me shall never t.

p76³⁷ if any man t., let him come unto me.

p160²⁸ I t.

Thirsty. *Need for liquids.*

p136³⁶ I was t., and ye gave me drink.

Thirty. *Three times ten.*

p14³⁰ Jesus began to be about t. years of age.

p58⁷ some t. fold, some sixty, some an hundred.

p138¹¹ covenanted with him for t. pieces of silver.

p153³ brought the t. pieces again to the chief priests.

p154⁹ t. pieces of silver, the price of him that was valued.

Thomas. *The apostle.*

p23¹⁴ chosen to be an apostle.

p113¹⁶ let us go, that we may die with him.

p142⁵ Lord, we know not whither thou goest.

p167²⁵ except I see the prints of the nails.

p167²⁷ reach hither thy finger.

p169² Jesus appears to T. and the apostles in Galilee.

Thorns. *Prickle, barb.*

p58⁶ seed fell among the t.

p61²⁰ he who received seed among the t.

p156²⁰ a crown of t. about his head.

p156⁵ wearing a crown of t.

Thought. *Consideration, contemplation, deliberation.*

p28¹³ take no t. what ye shall answer.

p45²⁸ take no t. for your life.

p45³¹ by taking t. can add one cubit.

p45³² take no t. for raiment?

p45³⁵ take no t. what shall we eat?

p45³⁹ take no t. for the morrow.

p48⁷ neither t. myself worthy.

p67¹⁷ take no t. what ye shall speak.

Three. *Number after two.*

p4⁵⁵ Mary abode with Elizabeth about t. months.

p11⁴⁶ after t. days they found him in the temple.

p22³⁴ Jonas was t. days and t. nights.

p25¹⁹ destroy this temple and in t. days I will raise it up.

p59³² leaven hid in t. measures of meal.

p82³⁰ multitude continue with me t. days.

p88³ let us make t. tabernacles.

p93¹⁶ in the mouth of two or t. witnesses.

p93²⁰ where two or t. are gathered.

p153⁶⁰ build temple in t. days.

p162⁶⁴ after t. days I will rise again.

Thrice. *Three.*

p153⁶¹ thou shalt deny me t.

Throne. *Seat for a king.*

p3³² Jesus given t. of David.

p41³⁸ swear not by God's t.

p101²⁸ Son of Man come sitting on the t. of his glory.

p136³⁴ he shall sit upon his t.

Though. *Although, however.*

p33³ t. he himself baptized not so many.

p78¹⁴ t. I bear record of myself.

p98⁴ t. I fear not God.

p105³⁶ t. one should rise from the dead.

p113²⁵ he that believeth in me, t. he were dead.

Thrust. *Push, shove, force.*

p18³ t. out a little from land.

p36²⁹ t. him out of the city.

p52²⁸ t. out of the kingdom of God.

p167²⁵ t. my hand into his side.

p167²⁷ t. thy hand into my side.

Thunder. *Noise, rumble.*

p23¹⁴ James and John, the sons of t.

Tidings. *News, report, word.*

p2¹⁹ to show you these glad t.

p7¹⁰ I bring you good t. of great joy.

p82¹ preaching and showing the glad t. of the kingdom.

Time. *Moment, occasion, point.*

p9⁷ Herod inquired what t. the star appeared.

p10²⁴ Jesus waited for the t. of his ministry to come.

p14⁸ Until the fullness of t.

p29⁴ enter his mother's womb a second t.

p59²⁹ grow together until the t. of harvest.

p63³⁰ come to torment us before the t?

p74⁶⁶ from that t. many of his disciples went back.

p75⁶ my t. is not yet come.

p118⁴³ knowest not the t. of thy visitation.

p143⁹ have I been so long t. with you.

p169¹⁴ the third t. Jesus showed himself to his disciples.

p170¹⁷ saith unto Peter the third t.

Tithe. *Tenth part given to the Lord.*

p128²⁰ you pay t. of mint and anise.

Title. *Recognized claim, inscription.*

p159¹⁹ Pilate wrote a t., and put it on the cross.

Tittle. *Accent mark in the Hebrew alphabet.*

p40²⁰ one jot or t. shall not pass.

p104¹⁹ earth to pass, than for one t.

Together. *Jointly, as one.*

p5¹ before they came t.

p93²⁰ where two or three are gathered t.

p99⁷ what God hath joined t.

p115⁵² he should gather t. the children of God.

p166³² eleven were gathered t.

Toil. *Labor.*

p45³² lilies t. not, neither do they spin.

Tolerable. *Acceptable, reasonable.*

p67[13] more t. for Sodom and Gomorrah.

p94[24] more t. for Tyre and Sidon.

Tomb. *Burial place.*

p69[30] took John's body and laid it in a t.

Tongue. *Mouth, language.*

p5[63] Zacharias spake with his t.

p54[2] called in the Hebrew t., Bethesda.

p90[32] he spit and touched his t.

p105[29] his finger in water, to cool my t.

Tooth. *Hard appendages in mouth.*

p41[40] eye for an eye, and a t. for a t.

Top. *Highest part.*

p158[23] woven from the t. throughout.

p160[55] veil of the temple was rent from the t. to the bottom.

Torment. *Anguish, suffering.*

p63[30] art thou come hither to t. us before the time.

p105[33] lest they also come to this place of t.

Tormentors. *Those who inflict suffering.*

p94[33] deliver him to the t.

Touch. *Feel, handle, lay hands on.*

p26[47] ye t. not the burdens with one of your fingers.

p39[19] the multitude sought to t. him.

p64[21] if I may t. but his clothes.

p81[58] they might t. the border of his garments.

p85[23] blind man asked Jesus to t. him.

p100[11] brought children for Jesus to t. them.

Touched. *Touch.*

p53[14] he came and t. the bier.

p64[23] Who t. my clothes?

p65[35] then t. he their eyes.

p81[58] many as t. him were made whole.

p90[32] put his finger in his ears and t. his tongue.

Touching. *Concerning.*

p93[19] t. anything they shall ask.

p124[30] as t. the resurrection.

p156[14] t. those things ye accuse him.

Toward. *In the direction, regarding.*

p29[23] is not rich t. God.

p53[22] journeying t. Jerusalem.

p166[28] abide with us for it is t. evening.

p168[10] they look steadfastly t. heaven.

Towel. *Linen, cloth.*

p140[4] took a t. and girded himself.

Tower. *High structure, overlook.*

p50[29] which of you intending to build a t.

p51[4] eighteen on whom the t. fell.

p121[35] digged a winepress and built a t.

Town. *Village, settlement.*

p67[10] into whatsoever t. ye enter.

p76[42] out of the t. of Bethlehem.

p112[1] Lazarus was of the t. of Bethany.

Tradition. *Custom, practice, belief.*

p83[8] laying aside the commandment of God, ye hold the t. of men.

p83[13] making the word of God of none effect through your t.

Traditions. *Tradition.*

p75[24] judge not according to your t.

p83[6] according to the t. of the elders.

p83[9] ye may keep your own t.

Trample. *Walk on.*

p46[10] lest they t. them under their feet.

Transfigured. *Changed in appearance.*

p87[1] Jesus was t. before them.

Transgress. *Disobey, violate.*

p128[21] you t. the whole law.

Transgressor. *One who transgresses.*

p83[12] let him die the death of the t.

p96[42] if he become a t. he shall be cut off.

p96[46] become a t. and offend thee.

Travail. *Labor.*

p146[21] when a woman is in t.

Treasure. *Riches, wealth.*

p22[30] a good man out of the t. of his heart.

p23[37] where your t. is, there will your heart be also.

p44[20] lay up for yourselves t. in heaven.

p62[46] t. hid in a field.

p62⁵³ every scribe bringeth forth out of his t. both new and old.

p101²¹ thou shalt have t. in heaven.

Treasury. *Place were money is kept.*

p13¹⁹ according to the custom of receiving money into the t.

p78²⁰ these words Jesus spake in the t.

p129⁴⁷ Jesus sat over against the t.

p129⁴⁹ poor widow cast more into the t.

p154⁷ not lawful to put the thirty pieces of silver into the t.

Tree. *Woody perennial plant.*

p13³⁷ every t. which bringeth forth not good fruit.

p19⁴⁸ Phillip called you when you were under the fig t.

p22²⁸ the t. is known by the fruit.

p47²⁷ a good t. cannot bring forth evil fruit.

p59³¹ mustard seed becometh a t.

p107⁴ Zacchaeus climbed a sycamore t.

p126²³ a fig t. Jesus cursed is dried up.

p126⁶ say to this sycamore t. be planted in the sea.

p133⁴¹ parable of the fig t.

p154⁶ Judas hanged himself on a t.

p158³¹ if these things are done in the green t.

Trespass. *Violation of moral or social ethics.*

p93¹⁵ if thy brother shall t. against thee.

p93⁴ and if he t. against you seven times.

Trespasses. *Trespass.*

p43¹³ forgive us our t.

p94³⁴ forgive every brother their t.

p126²⁷ that your Father may forgive your t.

Tribe. *People, clan, social group.*

p8³⁶ Phanuel of the t. of Asher.

Tribes. *Tribe.*

p133³⁷ shall all the tribes of the earth mourn.

p142³⁰ judging the twelve t. of Israel.

Tribulation. *Distress, affliction.*

p61¹⁹ when t. ariseth he is offended.

p132³⁴ after the t. of those days.

p147³³ in the world ye shall have t.

Tribute. *Levy, tax.*

p94²³ doth your master pay t.?

p94²⁵ of whom do kings take t.?

p124¹⁷ Is it lawful to give t. unto Caesar.

p154² forbidding to give t. to Caesar.

Trouble. *Concern, problem, worry.*

p48⁶ Lord, t. not thyself.

p137⁶ why t. ye her?

Troubled. *Trouble.*

p71⁵² they all saw him, and were t.

p114³³ Jesus groaned in the spirit, and was t.

p116⁴² Martha, thou art t. about many things.

p119²⁷ now is my soul t.

p132²⁵ see that ye be not t.

p132²⁵ the earth also shall be t.

p139²¹Jesus was t. in spirit.

p144²⁷ let not your heart be t.

p166³⁷ Why are you t.

True. *Actual, genuine, correct.*

p31³³ hath set his seal that God is t.

p56³² witness of myself, yet my witness is t.

p75¹⁸ he that seek the glory of him that sent him is t.

p78¹⁷ testimony of two men is t.

p104¹¹ who will commit to you the t. riches?

p112⁴¹ all the things that John spake were t.

p124¹⁶ we know that thou art t.

p144¹ I am the t. vine.

p147³ that they might know thee the only t. God.

p161³⁵ and his record is t.

p171²⁴ we know that his testimony is t.

Truly. *True.*

p34²⁰ in that saidest thou t.

p160⁴⁴ T.; this is the Son of God.

Trumpet. *Metal horn, instrument.*
p43² doest alms, do not sound a t.
p133⁴⁰ send the angels before him with the sound of a t.

Trust. *Confidence, belief, reliance.*
p57¹⁷ in his name shall the Gentiles t.
p101²³ how hard is it for them that t. in riches.
p101²⁶ possible with men who t. in God.
p104¹¹ who will commit to your t. the true riches?

Truth. *Certainty, honesty, veracity, fact.*
p30²¹ loveth the t., cometh to the light.
p34²⁵ worship the Father in t.
p56³⁴ John bear witness unto the t.
p71¹⁴ This is of a t. that prophet.
p71²⁸ Of a t. thou art the Son of God.
p79³² the t. shall make you free.
p79⁴⁴ there is no t. in the devil.
p79⁴⁵ I tell you the t., ye believe me not.
p104¹⁸ every man who seeketh t.
p142⁶ I am the way, the t., and the life.
p143¹⁷ spirit of t. whom the world cannot receive.
p148¹⁷ sanctify them through thy t.
p155³⁷ every one that is of the t. heareth my voice.
p155³⁸ What is t.?

Turn. *Change, alter, convert.*
p2¹⁶ Israel shall he t. to the Lord.
p2¹⁷ t. the hearts of the fathers.
p41⁴¹ t. to him thine other cheek.
p46¹¹ t. again and rend you.
p131¹⁴ t. to you for a testimony.

Twelve. *Number after eleven.*
p10⁴² when Jesus was t. years old.
p23¹³ he ordained t. apostles.
p65³⁴ daughter was t. years old.
p71¹³ gathered and filled t. baskets.
p101²⁸ judging the t. tribes of Israel.
p113⁹ t. hours in a day?
p151⁵¹ give me t. legions of angels?

Twice. *Two times.*
p98¹² I fast t. in the week.

Two. *Number after one.*

p18⁴⁰ the t. who heard John.
p31¹⁹ John calling t. of his disciples.
p35⁴² Jesus abode with the Samaritans t. days.
p44²⁴ no man can serve t. masters.
p54⁴¹ creditor who had t. debtors.
p65³³ t. blind men followed him.
p67³ sent forth the apostles t. and t.
p68²⁶ t. sparrows sold for a farthing.
p70⁹ five loaves, and t. small fishes.
p78¹⁷ testimony of t. men is true.
p91¹¹ a man had t. sons.
p93¹⁶ in the mouth of t. or more witnesses.
p93²⁰ where t. or three are gathered.
p98¹⁰ t. men went to the temple to pray.
p99⁷ they t. shall be one flesh.
p121²⁶ a man had t. sons.
p125³⁹ on these t. commandments.
p129⁴⁸ poor widow, cast in t. mites.
p133⁴⁷ t. shall be in the field.

| U

Unbelief. *Skepticism, lack of faith.*
p66⁸ he marveled because of their u.
p89²¹ help thou mine u.
p89²⁰ apostles could not cast out because of their u.
p167¹³ upbraided them because of their u.

Unclean. *Disobedient, defiled.*
p20²⁴ commandeth the u. spirits.
p28³⁸ when the u. spirit is gone out.
p57¹⁰ as many as had u. spirits.
p66¹ he gave them power over u. spirits.
p134⁴⁰ no u. thing remain upon the earth.

Uncovered. *Took apart.*
p38⁴ u. the roof where he was.

Understand. *Comprehend, recognize.*
p60¹³ hearing, shall not u.
p79⁴³ why do ye not u. my speech?
p113¹⁶ as yet they did not u. the power of God.
p119⁴⁰ not see with their eyes nor u. with their heart.

p124[28] u. not the scriptures.

p131[12] whoso readeth let him u.

Understanding. *Understand.*

p11[47] were astonished at his u.

p126[38] love God with all the u.

p167[44] opened their u., that they might understand.

Unfruitful. *Not bearing fruit.*

p61[20] riches choke the word, and he become u.

Unjust. *Unrighteous.*

p42[47] sendeth rain on the just and on the u.

p56[29] in the resurrection of the u.

p98[6] hear what the u. judge saith.

p103[8] lord commended the u. steward.

p103[10] he who is u. in the least.

Unleavened. *Without leaven (yeast).*

p138[13] the feast of u. bread.

Unloose. *Loose, untie.*

p12[28] whose shoe's latchet I am not worthy to u.

p14[23] whose shoes I am not worthy to u.

Unprofitable. *Not profitable.*

p24[10] say we are u. servants.

p136[31] cast ye the u. servant into outer darkness.

Unquenchable. *Unending.*

p14[24] the chaff he will burn with fire u.

Unrighteous. *Worldly wealth.*

p104[11] if ye have not been faithful in u. mammon.

Unrighteousness. *Iniquity, evil.*

p75[18] no u. is in him.

p103[9] make friends of the mammon of u.

p121[34] that your u. may be rewarded unto you.

Unthankful. *Ungrateful.*

p42[35] he is kind to the u. and the evil.

Unwashen. *Unwashed.*

p83[2] disciples eat bread with u. hands.

p84[19] to eat bread with u. hands defileth not a man.

Upbraid. *Rebuke, censure.*

p94[22] Jesus began to u. the cities.

Upbraided. *Upbraid.*

p167[13] he u. the apostles for their unbelief.

Upper. *Above, higher than something.*

p139[12] he shall show you a large u. room.

Uppermost. *Most important, highest.*

p26[44] Pharisees love the u. seats.

p127[4] scribes and Pharisees love the u. rooms.

Uproar. *Tumult, riot.*

p138[4] not on the feast day, lest there be an u.

Urge. *Provoke.*

p27[54] Pharisees began to u. Jesus vehemently.

Use. *Treatment, practice, habit.*

p42[46] pray for them which despitefully u. you.

p43[7] when ye pray, u. not vain repetitions.

Usury. *Interest.*

p136[27] I should have received my own with u.

Utter. *Speak.*

p59[34] I will u. things which have been kept secret.

Uttermost. *Farthest, utmost.*

p13[7] bring light to the u. parts of the earth.

p40[28] thou hast paid the u. farthing.

p168[8] ye shall be witnesses to the u. part of the earth.

| V

Vain. *Useless, futile.*

p43[7] when ye pray use not v. repetitions.

p83[7] in v. do they worship me.

Value. *Worth.*

p27[7] ye are of more v. than many sparrows.

p154[9] the price of him the children of Israel did v.

Vehemently. *Strongly, loud.*

p27[54] Pharisees urged Jesus v.

p155[10] priests and scribes v. accused him.

Veil. *Curtain.*

p160[55] the v. of the temple was rent.

Vessel. *Container, jug.*

p118[18] any man should carry a v.

p160[29] there was a v. full of vinegar mingled with gall.

Vexed. *Troubled, possessed.*

p85[21] my daughter is grievously v. with a devil.

Victory. *Triumph.*

p57[16] till he send forth judgment unto v.

Vine. *Plant whose branches get pruned.*

p141[26] not drink of this fruit of the v.

p144[1] I am the true v.

Vinegar. *Fermentation of diluted alcoholic liquid.*

p160[29] vessel of v. mingled with gall.

p160[29] when he had tasted the v., he would not drink.

Vineyard. *Where grapes are grown.*

p51[6] fig tree planted in a v.

p102[1] an householder, hire laborers in his v.

p121[26] Son, go work this day in my v.

p121[35] householder, who planted a v.

Violence. *Aggression, force.*

p13[21] do v. to no man.

p32[12] kingdom of heaven suffereth v.

p104[21] in your v. you seek to destroy the kingdom.

Violently. *Violence.*

p63[34] swine ran v. down a steep place.

Vipers. *Venomous snake.*

p12[33] generation of v. who hath warned thee.

p22[29] how can ye v. speak good things.

p129[30] v.! How can ye escape the damnation of hell.

Virgin(s). *Morally chaste, has not had sexual intercourse.*

p3[27] the v. name was Mary.

p3[28] Hail, thou v. who art highly

favored of the Lord.

p6[6] Behold, a v. shall be with child.

Virtue. *Strength, power.*

p39[19] there went v. out of him.

p64[23] knowing that v. had gone out of him.

Vision. *Seeing something.*

p2[22] Zacharias' v. in the temple.

p6[3] Lord appeared unto Joseph in a v.

p9[13] Lord appeared unto Joseph in a v.

p88[8] tell the v. to no man.

p157[20] Pilate's wife had a v.

p166[22] they had seen a v. of angels.

Visited. *Come to see, call on, stay.*

p5[67] the Lord hath v. his people.

p39[4] shall be v. with fire and the Holy Ghost.

p53[16] God hath v. his people.

p137[37] I was sick and ye v. me.

Voice. *Speech, articulate, sound.*

p4[43] as soon as the v. of thy salutation.

p10[18] in Ramah there was a v. heard.

p11[29] the v. of one crying in the wilderness.

p16[46] he heard a v. from heaven.

p31[30] rejoiceth greatly because of the bridgroom's v.

p56[25] dead shall hear the v. of the Son of God.

p56[28] those who are in their graves shall hear his v.

p88[4] behold a v. out of the cloud.

p95[27] there came a v. out of heaven.

p111[27] my sheep hear my v.

p119[28] there came a v. from heaven.

p155[37] everyone that is of the truth heareth my v.

p160[39] Jesus cried with a loud v.

W

Wages. *Pay, salary.*

p13[21] be content with your w.

p35[38] he who reapeth, receiveth w.

Wailing. *Howl, mournful cry.*

p61[43] there shall be w. and gnashing

of teeth.

Wait (n). *Watchfulness, expectancy.*

p24³⁹ ye yourselves like unto men who w. for their Lord.

p27⁵⁵ Pharisees laying w. for Jesus.

Wait (v). *Stay in a place, remain.*

p57⁹ a small ship should w. on him.

p168⁴ w. in Jerusalem for the promise of the Father.

Walk (n). *Act.*

p119³⁵ W. while ye have light.

Walk (v). *Move on foot.*

p26⁴⁵ as graves which men w. over.

p32²² the blind see, the lame w.

p55⁸ take up thy bed and w.

p74¹ he would not w. in Jewry.

p78¹² he that followeth me shall not w. in darkness.

p113⁹ if any man w. in the day.

Walked. *Walk.*

p17³⁶ John and his disciples looked upon Jesus as he w.

p74⁶⁶ many of his disciples w. no more with him.

p115⁵⁴ Jesus w. no more openly among the Jews.

Walking. *Walk.*

p71⁵⁰ Jesus came to his disciples w. upon the sea.

p85²⁵ I see men as trees w.

Want. *Need.*

p92¹⁴ prodigal son began to be in w.

p130⁵⁰ notwithstanding her w., did cast in all her living.

War. *Combat, battle.*

p50³² what king going to make w.

p155¹¹ Herod with his men of w. set him at naught.

Warmed. *Get warm.*

p152¹⁸ Peter and the servants w. themselves.

Warned. *Informed, alerted.*

p9¹² wise men w. in a dream.

p10²² Joseph being w. in a vision.

p12³³ who hath w. you of the wrath

to come.

Wars. *War.*

p132²⁵ hear of w. and rumors of w.

Wash. *Clean, bathe.*

p44¹⁸ when thou fast, w. thy face.

p54³⁸ began to w. his feet with tears.

p83³ except they w. their hands oft.

p108⁷ go, w. in the pool of Siloam.

p140⁵ Jesus began to w. the disciples' feet.

p140¹⁴ so ye ought to w. one another's feet.

Washed. *Wash.*

p26³⁹ marveled that he had not w. before dinner.

p54⁴⁴ she w. my feet with her tears.

p108⁷ he w. and came seeing.

p140¹⁰ he that hath w. his hands and his feet.

p157²⁶ Pilate w. his hands before the multitude.

Washing. *Wash.*

p83⁵ tradition of men as the w. of pots and cups.

Watch (n). *Sentry, guard.*

p24⁴¹ he cometh in the first w.

p162⁶⁶ ye have a w.; go your way.

p163¹⁰ some of the w. came into the city.

Watch (v). *Observe, look after.*

p6⁸ shepherds keeping w. over their flocks.

p134³⁶ w., and pray always.

p135¹² w.; for you know neither the day nor the hour.

p149³⁸ tarry ye here and w.

Watched. *Watch.*

p81⁷ w. whether he would heal on the Sabbath day.

p159³⁸ sitting down they w. him.

Watching. *Watch.*

p24⁴⁰ blessed are the servants, when he come shall find w.

p160⁴⁴ centurion w. Jesus.

Water. *Liquid that comes from clouds.*

p12[28] shall baptize not only with w.

p16[44] John went down into the w. and baptized him.

p17[9] w. which was made wine.

p29[5] except a man be born of w. and the spirit.

p30[24] in Enon, because there was much w. there.

p33[9] woman of Samaria came to draw w.

p34[16] he that drinketh of the w. I shall give him shall never thirst.

p54[44] thou gavest me no w. for my feet.

p55[4] an angel troubled the w.

p71[25] Peter walked on the w.

p76[38] out of his belly shall flow rivers of w.

p89[19] it cast him into the w., to destroy him.

p90[38] whosoever shall give you a cup of w. in my name.

p105[29] dip the tip of his finger in w.

p138[10] a man bearing a pitcher of w.

p157[26] Pilate took w., and washed his hands.

p161[34] there came out blood and w.

Waves. *Surf, swell.*

p132[25] sea and the w. roaring.

Wax. *Become, grow.*

p23[36] provide not bags which w. old.

p131[10] the love of many shall w. cold.

Waxed. *Wax.*

p5[79] the child grew, and w. strong.

p10[24] Jesus grew up with his brethren, and w. strong.

p60[14] the people's heart is w. gross.

p134[40] as a garment having w. in corruption.

Way. *Path, route, means, manner.*

p5[78] guide our feet into the w. of peace.

p9[12] departed into their own country another w.

p11[29] prepare ye the w. of the Lord.

p22[44] I go my w. for my Father hath sent me.

p32[27] my messenger who shall prepare thy w. before thee.

p38[5] go thy w. and sin no more.

p40[27] agree with thine adversary while thou art in the w.

p46[6] all have gone out of the w.

p47[22] broad is the w. that leadeth to sin.

p47[23] narrow is the w. unto life.

p63[29] no man could pass by that w.

p78[21] I go my w. and ye shall seek me.

p88[11] Elias shall prepare the w. before me.

p90[30] that ye disputed by the w.?

p97[19] go thy w.; thy faith hath made thee whole.

p104[21] you pervert the right w.

p110[1] he climbeth up some other w.

p142[6] I am the w., the truth, and the life.

Weak. *Tired, feeble.*

p150[43] the spirit is ready, but the flesh is w.

Wear. *Attire, dress in.*

p45[27] your Father will provide what ye shall w.

Weather. *climate, conditions.*

p84[2] The w. is fair.

Wedding. *Marriage ceremony.*

p24[39] wait for their Lord when he return from the w.

p49[7] those who were bidden to a w.

p123[3] call his servants who were bidden to the w.

p123[11] man who had not a w. garment.

Week. *Seven day cycle.*

p17[1] marriage on the third day of the w.

p98[12] I fast twice in the w.

p162[2] early in the morning, the first day of the w.

p166[19] being the first day of the w.

Weep. *Cry.*

p53[34] Jesus began to w. over Jerusalem.

p129[36] Jesus began to w. over Jerusalem.

p146[20] ye shall w. and lament.

p158[28] Jerusalem, w. not for me.

West. *Opposite of east.*

p48[11] come from the east and the w.

p132[27] shineth even unto the w.

Whale's. *Large aquatic mammal, fish.*

p22[34] Jonas was three days in the w. belly.

Wheat. *Grain.*

p14[24] gather the w. into his garner.

p59[23] sowed tares among the w.

p103[7] a hundred measures of w.

p119[24] except a corn of w. fall to the ground.

p142[31] sift the children of the kingdom as w.

Where. *At, in, or what place.*

p8[2] w. is the child that is born.

p9[9] star stood over w. the child was.

p17[38] Master, W. dwellest thou?

p23[37] w. your treasure is.

p62[25] W. is your faith?

p77[10] Woman, w. are thine accusers?

p78[19] W. is thy Father?

p93[20] w. two or three are gathered.

p99[58] hath not w. to lay his head.

p116[57] if any man knew w. Jesus was.

p119[26] w. I am, shall also my servants be.

p142[3] w. I am, ye may be also.

p164[15] tell me w. thou hast laid him.

Whether. *Alternative conditions, either.*

p14[22] w. John was the Christ or not.

p75[17] w. the doctrine be of God.

p109[25] w. he be a sinner or no.

p121[29] w. of the twain did the will of their father.

p153[64] tell us w. thou be the Christ.

p160[53] let us see w. Elias will come.

White. *Light, opposite of black.*

p35[37] fields; are w. already to harvest.

p41[38] canst not make one hair w. or black.

p87[1] his raiment was w. as the light.

p163[2] two angels clothed in w. garments.

p164[12] seeth two angels in w.

Who. *What or which one.*

p12[20] W. art thou?

p16[30] w. is preferred before me.

p20[19] I am he w. gave the law.

p22[42] W. is my mother?

p43[10] Our Father w. art in heaven.

p51[38] He w. hath ears to hear, let him hear.

p53[36] blessed is he w. cometh in the name of the Lord.

p64[23] W. touched my clothes?

p67[10] inquire w. in it is worthy.

p68[35] He w. receiveth you.

p74[64] Jesus knew from the beginning w. should betray him.

p78[25] W. art thou?

p88[13] W. is Elias?

p90[31] disputed w. was greatest among them.

p101[25] W. then can be saved?

p108[25] unto everyone w. occupieth, shall be given.

p108[2] w. did sin, this man, or his parents.

p110[36] W. is he, Lord, that I might believe on him?

p117[8] all the city was moved, saying, W. is this?

p119[34] w. is this Son of Man?

p119[38] w. hath believed our report?

p120[21] w. gave thee this authority?

p125[30] w. is my neighbor?

p134[52] W. then is a wise servant.

p139[25] Lord, w. is it?

p140[24] w. should be the greatest.

p153[71] w. is it that smote thee?

p169[12] disciples durst not ask him, W. art thou?

Whole. *Entire, complete, well.*

p19[13] the w. need not a physician.

p20[18] seeing we keep the w. law?

p41[32] not that thy w. body be cast into hell.

p44[22] thy w. body shall be full of light.

p55[6] Wilt thou be made w.?

p64[26] thy faith hath made thee w.

p81[58] as many as touched him were made w.

p87[29] if a man gain the w. world.

p97[19] thy faith hath made thee w.

p115[50] that the w. nation perish not.

p126[38] worth more than w. burnt offerings.

p138[9] the gospel is preached throughout the w. world.

Whose. *Of whom.*

p12[28] w. shoe's latchet I am not worthy.

p29[22] then w. shall those things be.

p51[1] w. blood Pilate mingled with their sacrifices.

p124[20] W. image is this.

p124[27] w. wife shall she be.

p126[40] W. son is he?

Wicked. *Evil.*

p28[39] seven other spirits more w. than himself.

p42[30] bring that w. one to judgment.

p48[12] children of the w. one shall be cast out.

p61[39] the destruction of the w.

p84[4] a w. generation seeketh after a sign.

p94[32] thou w. servant!

p122[43] he will destroy those w. men.

p122[51] those w. ones reject me.

p134[56] then cometh the end of the w.

Wickedness. *Wicked.*

p124[18] Jesus perceived their w.

p129[28] you are witnesses of your own w.

p129[34] you are partakers of the same w.

Wide. *Large, broad.*

p47[22] w. is the gate.

Widow. *Bereft of husband.*

p8[37] Anna had lived a w.

p36[26] Serepta, who was a w.

p53[12] the w. of an only son.

p98[5] this w. troubleth me.

p129[48] a certain poor w.

Wife. *Female spouse.*

p2[13] thy w. Elisabeth shall bear thee a son.

p6[3] fear not to take unto thee Mary thy w.

p31[26] Herodias, his brother Philip's w.

p41[36] whosoever shall put away his w.

p50[26] if any man shall come unto me and hate not his w.

p82[3] Joanna the w. of Chuza.

p99[2] put away his w. for every cause?

p99[7] a man shall cleave unto his w.

p100[10] if the case of a man be so with a w.

p101[28] a man who hath left his w.; shall receive a hundred fold now.

p104[23] Whoso putteh away his w. and marrieth another.

p124[27] whose w. shall she be of the seven?

p157[20] Pilate's w. has a vision.

p159[25] Mary the w. of Cleophas.

Wild. *Natural, undomesticated.*

p12[30] John ate locusts and w. honey.

Wilderness. *Desolate place, desert.*

p11[2] the word of God came unto John, in the w.

p11[29] the voice of one crying in the w.

p15[1] Jesus was led of the spirit, into the w.

p30[14] as Moses lifted up the serpent in the w.

p32[24] What went ye out into the w. to see?

p73[50] your fathers did eat manna in the w.

p91[12] leave the ninety and nine and go into the w.

p115[54] walked no more openly but went into the w.

Will. *Desire, command, accept.*

p1[13] Jesus was born not of the w. of man.

p25[56] the servant who knew his Lord's w.

p32[13] the day w. come, when the violent shall have no power.

p32[15] if ye w. receive it, he was Elias.

p43[11] Thy w. be done.

p47[30] he that doeth the w. of my Father.

p50[28] that ye w. do the things which I shall teach.

p56[31] I seek not my own w., but the w. of the Father.

p73[39] this is the Father's w.

p74[67] W. ye also go away?

p75[17] if any man will do his w.

p87[37] whosoever w. save his life.

p91[14] it is not the w. of your Father.

p121[29] Whether of the twain did the w. of their father?

p126[28] neither w. your Father who is in heaven.

p133[36] the days w. come.

p149[40] not my w., but thine be done.

p160[54] it is finished, thy w. is done.

Willing. *Wanting.*

p6[2] not w. to make her a public example.

p56[36] ye were w. for a season to rejoice.

p87[37] shall be w. to lay down his life.

p125[30] but he, w. to justify himself.

p156[20] Pilate, w. to release Jesus.

p158[18] Pilate, w. to content the people.

Wind. *Current of air, breeze.*

p30[8] the w. bloweth where it listeth.

p32[24] a reed shaken in the w.?

p62[24] Jesus rebuked the w.

p71[49] the w. was contrary to them.

p71[27] when they came into the ship, the w. ceased.

Wine. *See dictionary – wine.*

p2[15] neither w. nor strong drink.

p17[9] water which was made w.

p20[23] do men put new w. into old bottles.

p33[33] John came neither drinking w.

p33[34] the Son of Man, a w. bibber.

p36[48] Cana where he made the water w.

p125[35] pouring in oil and w.

Winepress. *Used to make wine.*

p121[35] planted a vineyard and digged

a w.

Wings. *Paired appendage used to fly.*

p129[37] a hen gathers her chicks under her w.

Winter. *Coldest season of the year.*

p111[22] feast of dedication, was in w.

p131[17] pray your flight be not in the w.

Wipe. *Clean, dry.*

p54[38] did w. his feet with her hair.

p96[11] w. the dust of your city off against you.

p140[5] w. the apostles feet with a towel.

Wisdom. *Understanding, prudence.*

p2[17] turn the disobedient to the w. of the just.

p11[52] Jesus increased in w. and stature.

p22[36] to hear the w. of Solomon.

p27[50] therefore also said the w. of God.

p33[35] w. is justified of all her children.

p66[3] what w. is this that is given unto him.

p130[13] I will give you a mouth and w.

Wise. *Knowing, astute.*

p8[1] there came w. men from the east.

p24[50] he that is faithful and a w. servant?

p40[20] jot or tittle shall in no w. pass from the law.

p47[34] I will liken him unto a w. man.

p67[14] w. servants and harmless as doves.

p95[27] hid these things from the w. and prudent.

p129[31] I send you prophets and w. men.

p135[2] five of the virgins were w.

Wisely. *Wise.*

p103[8] commended the unjust steward, because he had done w.

Wiser. *Acumen, keenness, discernment.*

p103[8] the children of this world are w. in their generation.

Withered. *Shrivel, shrink.*

p58[5] because it had no root it w. away.

p81[6] a man whose right hand was w.

p126[23] the fig tree is w. away.

p144[6] if a man abide not in me he is

cast forth as a branch, is w.

Within. *Inside, among.*

p26[41] make that which is w. also?

p38[7] scribes reasoned w. themselves.

p46[10] mysteries ye shall keep w. yourselves.

p54[39] Pharisee reasoned w. himself.

p128[22] w. ye are full of extortion and excess.

p128[23] first cleanse the cup and the platter w.

p166[31] did not our hearts burn w. us.

p167[26] after eight days his disciples were w.

Without. *Outside, apart from.*

p1[3] w. him was not anything made.

p5[73] might serve him w. fear.

p22[40] mother and brethren stood w.

p26[41]he who made that which is w., make that which is within.

p52[25] then ye will stand w. and knock at the door.

p59[33] w. a parable spake he not.

p66[6] a prophet is not w. honor.

p77[7] he that is w. sin among you.

p83[15] nothing w. entering into a man.

p84[15] are ye also w. understanding?

p144[5] w. me ye can do nothing.

p145[25] hated me w. a cause.

p149[35] w. purse and scrip.

p158[23] coat was w. seam.

p164[11] Mary stood w. at the sepulcher.

Witness (n). *See, observe, one who testifies.*

p30[11] ye receive not our w.

p35[22] and all bear him w.

p56[32] yet my w. is true.

p101[18] thou shalt not bear false w.

p111[25] the works I do bear w. of me.

p132[32] this gospel preached for a w. unto all nations.

p145[27] ye shall bear w. because ye have been with me.

p153[58] chief priests sought false w.

p155[37] to this end was I born that I should bear w. unto the truth.

Witness (v). *Testify, show, prove.*

p56[33] there is another who beareth w. of me.

p56[37] I have a greater w. than the testimony of John.

p56[38] the Father hath borne w. of me.

p78[18] I bear w. of myself.

Witnesses. *More than one witness.*

p93[16] in the mouth of two or three w.

p129[28] w. unto yourselves of your own wickedness.

p153[59] though many false w. came.

p153[66] what further need have we of w.?

p168[8] after the Holy Ghost comes ye shall be w. unto me.

p171[47] ye are w. of these things.

Woe. *Misery, grief.*

p26[43] W. unto you Pharisees!

p26[47] W. unto you lawyers, also!

p94[23] W. unto thee, Chorazin!

p96[6] W. unto the world because of offences!

p104[21] W. unto ye adulterers!

p127[11] W. unto you, scribes and Pharisees!

p131[16] w. unto them that are with child.

Wolf. *Dog like carnivorous mammal.*

p111[12] as a hireling, who seeth the w. coming and leaveth the sheep.

Woman. *Adult female.*

p17[4] W. what wilt thou have me do.

p33[9] a w. of Samaria who came to draw water.

p41[30] looketh on a w. to lust after her.

p51[11] w. who had a spirit of infirmity.

p54[39] if he were a prophet, would have known what manner of w.

p54[50] Jesus said to the w., Thy faith hath saved thee.

p64[21] a w., which had an issue of blood.

p77[3] a w. taken in adultery.

p85[21] a w. of Cannan.

p100[10] if a w. shall put away her husband.

p124[26] last of all the w. died also.

p146[21] a w. when she is in travail.

p152[57] W., I know him not.

p160[26] W., behold thy son!

p164[15] W., why weepest thou?

Womb. *Uterus, belly.*

p2[15] filled with the Holy Ghost from his mother's w.

p3[41] babe leaped within her w.

p4[42] blessed is the fruit of thy w.

p7[23] every male which openeth the w. shall be called holy.

p28[28] blessed is the w. which bear thee.

p29[4] can he enter a second time into his mother's w.

Wondered. *Amazed, astonished.*

p7[18] All who heard it, w.

p35[22] All bear him witness, and w.

p62[25] they being afraid, w.

p82[29] the multitude w.

p167[40] apostles w. and believed not for joy.

Word (n). *Name of Jesus Christ.*

p1[14] the W. was made flesh.

Word (v). *Saying, speech.*

p1[1] the gospel was the w.

p3[38] let it be according to thy w.

p9[6] the w. of the Lord came unto us.

p9[8] when thou hast found the child, bring me w.

p11[2] in that same year, the w. of God came unto John.

p15[4] by every w. that proceedeth out of the mouth of God.

p22[31] every idle w. that men shall speak.

p26[22] they remembered the w. which Jesus had said unto them.

p28[12] speak a w. against the Son of Man.

p48[7] say the w., and my servant shall be healed.

p57[39] you have not his w. abiding in you.

p78[31] if ye continue in my w.

p83[13] making the w. of God of none effect.

p85[22] he answered her not a w.

p93[16] in the mouth of two or three witnesses every w.

p120[48] the w. I have spoken, shall judge him.

p127[44] no man was able to answer him a w.

p133[36] my w. shall not pass away.

p144[3] ye are clean through the w.

p147[6] and they have kept thy w.

p148[17] thy w. is truth.

p153[61] Peter remembered the w. of the Lord.

p165[18] a prophet mighty in deed and w.

p171[21] confirming the w. with signs.

Work. *Labor, toil.*

p35[36] do his will and finish his w.

p50[29] whether he have money to finish his w.?

p51[14] there are six days in which men ought to w.

p55[17] my Father worketh hitherto, and I w.

p66[7] he could do no mighty w. there.

p72[28] that we might w. the works of God?

p75[21] I have done one w. and ye marvel.

p108[4] I must w. the works of him that sent me.

p121[26] go w. today in my vineyard.

p137[6] she hath wrought a good w. on me.

p147[4] I have finished the w. thou gavest me to do.

Workman. *Worker.*

p67[9] the w. is worthy of his meat.

World. *Earth, all mankind.*

p1[5] the light shineth in the w.

p15[8] showed him all the kingdoms of the w.

p16[29] Lamb of God, who taketh away the sin of the w.!

p30[16] God so loved the w.

p40[18] Therefore, let your light shine before this w.

p46[9] Go ye into the w.

p46[11] w. cannot receive that which ye are not able to bear.

p87[29] what is a man profited, if he gain the whole w.

p101[29] and in the w. to come eternal life.

p103[8] children of this w. are wiser.

p108[5] I am the light of the w.

p120[47] I came to save the w.

p130[9] what is the sign of the end of the w.

p132[32] this gospel shall be preached in all the w.

p147[33] I have overcome the w.

p155[36] my kingdom is not of this w.

p170[14] go ye into all the w.

Worm. *Suffering, anguish (symbolic of the decay of the body).*

p96[41] where their w. dieth not.

Worse. *Inferior, bad, poor quality.*

p20[22] the rent is made w.

p28[39] end of the man is w. than the first.

p55[14] lest a w. thing come unto thee.

p162[65] this last imposture be w. than the first.

Worship. *Adoration, love, reverence, respect.*

p8[2] we have seen his star and have come to w. him.

p9[8] bring me word that I may w. him also.

p15[9] if thou wilt fall down and w. me.

p34[24] ye w. ye know not.

p34[26] must w. him in spirit and truth.

p83[7] in vain do they w. me.

p118[20] Greeks came to w. at the feast.

Worshipers. *Worship.*

p34[25] true w. shall worship the Father.

Worthy. *Having worth, honorable.*

p12[28] whose shoe's latchet I am not w. to unloose.

p48[4] he was w. for whom he should do this.

p67[10] inquire who is w. and there abide.

p68[33] he who will not take his cross is not w. of me.

p92[19] no more w. to be called thy son.

p95[7] laborer is w. of his hire.

p134[36] keep my commandments that ye may be counted w.

p153[67] he is w. of death.

p156[15] lo, nothing w. of death.

Wound. *Wrap, bind.*

p162[40] took the body and w. it in linen clothes.

Wrath. *Anger, fury.*

p12[33] who hath warned you to flee from the w. to come.

p31[36] for the w. of God is upon him.

p36[28] they in the synagogue, were filled with w.

p131[16] distress and w. upon this people.

Write. *Inscribe, record.*

p19[45] of whom Moses and the prophets, did w.

p99[4] Moses suffered to w. a bill of divorcement.

p159[21] chief priest asked Pilate not to w.

Writing. *Write.*

p41[35] give her a w. of divorcement.

p159[19] the w. was, Jesus of Nazareth.

Written. *Past tense of write.*

p9[4] Where is the place that is w. of by the prophets.

p13[5] he shall come, as is w. in the book of the prophets.

p15[4] it is w., man shall not live by bread alone.

p15[6] it is w., he shall give his angels charge.

p18[18] I am he of whom it is w. by the prophets.

p24[42] he hath come, as is w. of him.

p31[20] Art thou he of whom it is w.

p32[27] it is w., I send my messenger before my face.

p35[17] he found the place it was w.

p50[36] for this intent they were w.

p51[38] that which is w., must all be fulfilled.

p104[20] why teach ye the law, and deny that which is w.

p115[21] your names are w. in heaven.

p125[27] What is w. in the law?

p159[20] w. in Hebrew, Greek, and Latin.

p159[22] what I have w. I have w.

p167[45] it is w., behooved Christ to suffer, and rise the third day.

p171[31] these are w., that ye might believe.

Wrong. *Harm, amiss, illegal.*

p102[12] Friend, I do thee no w.

Wroth. *Highly incensed.*

p10[16] Herod was exceeding w.

p94[33] his lord was w., and delivered him to the tormentors.

p123[7] his servants were dead, the king was w.

| Y

Yea. *Yes, indeed, truly.*

p41[39] let your communication be y., y.

p169[15] Y. Lord, thou knowest I love thee.

Year. *Twelve month cycle.*

p10[41] his parents went to Jerusalem every y.

p11[2] this same y. came the word of the Lord unto John.

p35[19] the acceptable y. of the Lord.

p51[8] let it alone this y. also.

p115[49] Caiaphas, being the high priest that same y.

p151[13] Caiaphas, which was the high priest that same y.

Yesterday. *Day prior.*

p37[54] he began to mend y. at the seventh hour.

Yet. *Until now, so far, however.*

p17[4] mine hour is not y. come.

p75[6] my time is not y. come.

p76[33] Y. a little while I am with you.

p78[14] y. my record is true.

p101[20] what lack I y.?

p113[25] though he were dead, y. shall he live.

p133[36] y. my word shall not pass away.

p134[56] the end is not y.

p143[9] and y. hast thou not known me.

p162[64] we remember while he was y. alive.

p164[9] as y. they knew not the scripture.

p165[17] I am not y. ascended to my Father.

Yield. *Produce, bear.*

p58[7] seed fell on good ground, and did y. fruit.

Yoke. *Joined in work, servitude.*

p95[30] take my y. upon you.

Yonder. *Farther removed, distant.*

p89[20] say to this mountain, remove to y. place.

Young. *Youthful.*

p9[8] search diligently for the y. child.

p9[13] take the y. child and his mother.

p53[14] Y. man, I say unto thee, Arise.

p100[11] they brought y. children unto him.

p151[57] there followed him a certain y. man.

p170[18] when thou wast y., thou girdedst thyself.

Younger. *Not as old.*

p91[12] the y. of them said to his father.

p140[26] he who is greatest, let him be as the y.

Your. *Belonging to you.*

p23[37] where y. treasure is.

p39[14] great shall be y. reward in heaven.

p40[18] let y. light so shine.

p41[31] take up y. cross.

p115[21] y. names are written in heaven.

p131[18] in y. patience possess ye y. souls.

p142[1] let not y. heart be troubled.

p146[20] y. sorrow shall be turned to joy.

p156[5] Behold y. King!

Yours. *Your.*

p145[20] having kept my saying they will keep y. also.

Yourselves. *Your.*

p73[43] murmur not among y.

p128[12] more the child of hell, like unto y.

p135[8] go, and buy for y.

Youth. *Young adult, child.*

p8[36] whom she married in her y.

p101[20] all these things have I kept from my y. up.

| Z

Zacharias. *Father of John the Baptist.*

p1[5] of the course of Abia.

p2[9] his lot was to burn incense.

p2[11] appeared unto him an angel.

p2[20] was struck dumb by the angel.

p5[62] asks for a writing table.

p5[63] praised God.

p5[66] prophesies of John's mission.

Zacharias. *O.T. prophet.*

p129[32] the blood of Z. son of Barachias.

Zeal. *Ardent interest, eagerness.*

p25[17] the z. of thine house hath eaten me up.

Zion. *The pure in heart.*

p117[4] tell ye the daughter of z.

SOURCES

1. *A Plainer Translation*, Robert J. Matthews

2. *Greek/English lexicon*, biblestudytools.com

3. *Biblical Pilgrimage Festivals and Major Feast Days of Ancient Israel and Modern Judaism*, Felix Just, S.J.

4. *History of the Church*, B. H. Roberts

5. *Jesus Christ and the World of the New Testament*, Richard N. Holzapfel, Eric D. Huntsman, and Thomas A. Wayment

6. *Joseph Smith's New Translation Of The Bible; Original Manuscripts*, Scott H. Faulring, Kent P. Jackson, and Robert J. Matthews

7. *Judaism 101*, Tracey R. Rich

8. *Smiths's Bible Dictionary*, Published by A.J. Holman Company

9. *Skype: digiwisdom*, David Broad

10. *Teachings of the Prophet Joseph Smith*, The Church of Jesus Christ of Latter-day Saints

11. *The Book of Mormon*, The Church of Jesus Christ of Latter-day Saints

12. *The Chronology of New Testament Times*, Ernest L. Martin

13. *The Doctrine and Covenants*, The Church of Jesus Christ of Latter-day Saints

14. *The Holy Bible*, The Church of Jesus Christ of Latter-day Saints

15. *The Holy Scriptures 1867*, The Church of Jesus Christ of Latter-day Saints.

16. *The One Volume Bible Commentary*, J.R. Dummelow.

17. *The Scrolls and the Scribes of the New Testament*, Joseph H. Dampier.

18. *True to the Faith*, The Church of Jesus Christ of Latter-day Saints.

19. *Webster's Seventh New Collegiate Dictionary*, A. Merriam Webster.

20. *Wikipedia*.